3

STUDYING FAMILY AND COMMUNITY HISTORY
19th and 20th Centuries

SOURCES AND METHODS FOR FAMILY AND COMMUNITY HISTORIANS:
A HANDBOOK

This accessible and innovative series will stimulate and develop personal research in family and community history, and set it within a wider framework. You will find practical suggestions for research projects, activities to enhance relevant skills and understanding, and ideas about how to exploit appropriate written, oral and visual sources. The series also brings together specialist contributors who use current developments in demography, social and economic history, sociology, historical geography and anthropology to suggest new insights and lines of enquiry. With its aim of placing individual and localized cases in their social and historical context, the series will interest anyone concerned with family and community.

This volume supports the series as a whole. It serves as an invaluable tool for any research project on family or community history by offering guidance on: how to find, assess and use sources of all kinds; research strategies; quantitative techniques; oral history; computing opportunities; major reference works and local societies; the relevant libraries and archives in England, Wales, Scotland and Ireland; and how to present findings in written, audio or video form.

STUDYING FAMILY AND COMMUNITY HISTORY: 19TH AND 20TH CENTURIES

Series editor: Ruth Finnegan

All four titles in the series are published by Cambridge University Press in association with The Open University.

This book forms part of the third-level Open University course DA301 *Studying family and community history: 19th and 20th centuries.* Other materials associated with the course are:

Drake, M. (ed.) (1994) *Time, family and community: perspectives on family and community history,* Oxford, Blackwell in association with The Open University (Course Reader).

Braham, P. (ed.) (1993) *Using the past: audio-cassettes on sources and methods for family and community historians,* a series of six audio-cassettes with accompanying notes, Milton Keynes, The Open University.

Calder, A. and Lockwood, V. (1993) *Shooting video history,* a video workshop on video recording for family and community historians, with accompanying notes, Milton Keynes, The Open University.

For availability of the video- and audio-cassette materials, contact Open University Educational Enterprises Ltd (OUEE), 12 Cofferidge Close, Stony Stratford, Milton Keynes, MK11 1BY.

Comments on errors or omissions in this material are welcome and should be sent to the DA301 Course Manager, Gardiner Building, Faculty of Social Sciences, The Open University, Milton Keynes, MK7 6AA.

If you wish to study this or any other Open University course, details can be obtained from the Central Enquiry Service, PO Box 200, The Open University, Milton Keynes, MK7 6YZ.

SOURCES AND METHODS FOR FAMILY AND COMMUNITY HISTORIANS:

A HANDBOOK

Edited by Michael Drake and Ruth Finnegan

with Jacqueline Eustace

Published by the Press Syndicate of the University of Cambridge in association with The Open University
The Pitt Building, Trumpington Street, Cambridge CB2 1RP
40 West 20th Street, New York, NY 10011-4211, USA
10 Stamford Road, Oakleigh, Melbourne 3166, Australia

First published 1994

Edited, designed and typeset by The Open University

Printed in Great Britain by Butler and Tanner Ltd, Frome

A catalogue record for this book is available from the British Library

Library of Congress cataloguing in publication data applied for

ISBN 0 521 46004 2   hardback

ISBN 0 521 46580 X   paperback

CONTENTS

PART IV: PRESENTATION, DISSEMINATION AND PUBLICATION

PART V: LOCATING SOURCES AND REFERENCES

LIST OF PLATES, FIGURES AND TABLES

Plates

Figures

Tables

CONTRIBUTORS

Joanna Bornat, Lecturer, School of Health, Welfare and Community Education, Open University

Peter Braham, Lecturer in Sociology, Faculty of Social Sciences, Open University

Angus Calder, Senior Lecturer and Staff Tutor in History, Faculty of Arts and the Open University in Scotland

Brenda Collins, Social and economic historian, Tutor-Counsellor, the Open University in Northern Ireland

Jane Cox, Historian and genealogist, former Principal Assistant Keeper of Public Records, PRO

Ian Donnachie, Senior Lecturer and Staff Tutor in History, Faculty of Arts and the Open University in Scotland

Michael Drake, Emeritus Professor and first Dean of Faculty of Social Sciences, Open University; Visiting Professor of History, University of Tromsø

David Englander, Senior Lecturer, European Studies, Faculty of Arts, Open University

Jacqueline Eustace, Course Manager, Faculty of Social Sciences, Open University

Ruth Finnegan, Professor in Comparative Social Institutions, Faculty of Social Sciences, Open University

John Golby, Senior Lecturer and Staff Tutor in History, Faculty of Arts and the Open University, South

John Hunt, Project Officer, Faculty of Social Sciences, Open University

Magnus John, Information Services Manager, International Centre for Distance Learning, Institute of Educational Technology, Open University

Gill Kirkup, Senior Lecturer in Educational Technology, Institute of Educational Technology, Open University

Roy Lewis, Senior Lecturer in Geography, University of Wales, Aberystwyth

Deirdre Mageean, Assistant Professor, Public Administration, University of Maine, USA

Arthur Marwick, Professor of History, Faculty of Arts, Open University

Dennis Mills, Historical geographer, previously Senior Lecturer and Staff Tutor in Human Geography, Faculty of Social Sciences and the Open University, South

W.T.R. Pryce, Senior Lecturer and Staff Tutor in Human Geography, Faculty of Social Sciences and the Open University in Wales

Kevin Schürer, Senior Research Associate, Cambridge Group for the History of Population and Social Structure, and Assistant Director ESRC Data Archive

Paul Smith, Assistant Librarian, Open University

David Wilson, Editor, Book Trade, Publishing Services, Open University

PREFACE

Many thousands of people are currently exploring their family trees or investigating the history of their localities. It is an absorbing hobby – and more than just a hobby. It combines the excitement of the chase and the exercise of demanding investigative skills. It also leads to personal rewards, among them perhaps an enhanced awareness of identity, achieved through the process of searching out your roots within the unending cycle of the past, and something to hold on to in the confusions of the present.

At the same time scholars within a series of social science and historical disciplines are increasingly realizing the value of small-scale case studies, extending and questioning accepted theories through a greater understanding of local and personal diversities. Sociologists now look to individual life histories as well as generalized social structure; geographers emphasize the local as well as the global; demographers explore regional divergences, not just national aggregates; historians extend their research from the doings of the famous to how 'ordinary people' pursued their lives at a local level.

This volume and the series of which it is a part have as their central purpose the encouragement of active personal research in family and community history – but research that is also linked to more general findings and insights. The series thus seeks to combine the strengths of two traditions: that of the independent personal researcher into family tree or local history, and that of established academic disciplines in history and the social sciences.

Now is a particularly appropriate moment to bring these two sides together. The networks of family and local historians up and down the country have in the past had scant recognition from within mainstream university circles, which (in contrast to the active involvement of further education and extra-mural departments) have sometimes given the impression of despising the offerings of 'amateur researchers'. Explicitly academic publications, for their part, have been little read by independent investigators – understandably, perhaps, for, with a few honourable exceptions, such publications have been predominantly directed to specialist colleagues. But there are signs that this situation may be changing. Not only is there an increasing awareness of the research value of micro studies, but higher education as a whole is opening up more flexible ways of learning and is recognizing achievements undertaken outside traditional 'university walls'. Our hope is to further this trend of mutual understanding, to the benefit of each.

There are thus two main aims in these volumes, overlapping and complementary. The first is to present an interdisciplinary overview of recent scholarly work in family and community history, drawing on the approaches and findings of such subjects as anthropology, social and economic history, sociology, demography, and historical geography. This should be illuminating not only for those seeking an up-to-date review of such work, but also for anyone interested in the functioning of families and communities today – the essential historical background to present-day concerns. The second, equally important aim is to help readers develop their own research interests. The framework here is rather different from traditional genealogy or local history courses (where excellent DIY guides already exist) since our emphasis is on completing a project and relating it to other research findings and theories, rather than on an unending personal quest for yet more and more details. It differs too from most conventional academic publications, in that the focus is on *doing* research, rather than absorbing or reporting the research of others. These volumes are therefore full of practical advice on sources and methods, as well as illustrations of the kinds of projects that can be followed up by the individual researcher.

Given the infinite scope of the subject and the need to provide practical advice, we have put some limits on the coverage. The timescale is the nineteenth and twentieth centuries, a period for which the sources are plentiful and – for the recent period at least – oral investigation feasible. (The critical assessment and exploitation of primary sources within this timescale will, of course, develop skills which can be extended to earlier periods.) There is no attempt to give a detailed historical narrative of nineteenth- and twentieth-century history. Rather we present a blend of specific case studies, findings and theoretical ideas, selected with a view to giving both some taste of recent work, and a context and stimulus for further investigation.

In terms of area, the focus is on the United Kingdom and Ireland, or, to put it differently, on the countries of the British Isles (these and similar terms have both changing historical applications and inescapable political connotations, so since we wish to write without prejudice we have deliberately alternated between them). This focus is applied flexibly, and there is some reference to emigration abroad; but we have not tried to describe sources and experiences overseas. Thus while much of the general theoretical background and even specific ideas for research may relate to many areas of the world, the detailed practical information about sources or record repositories concentrates on those available to students working in England, Ireland (north and south), Scotland and Wales.

The emphasis is also on encouraging small-scale projects. This does not mean that larger patterns are neglected: indeed, like other more generalized findings and theories, they form the background against which smaller studies can be set and compared. But small, manageable projects of the kinds focused on in this volume have two essential merits. First, they link with the emerging appreciation of the value of research into diversities as well as into generalizations: many gaps in our knowledge about particular localities or particular family experiences remain to be filled. Second, they represent a form of research that can be pursued seriously within the resources of independent and part-time researchers.

This volume supports the series as a whole by offering practical and systematic guidance on how to plan, execute and communicate research: it explains the various sources and methods on offer, and how to exploit them effectively. The companion volumes (listed on p.ii) turn the spotlight on to individual families and the broader patterns of family history revealed by recent research (Volume 1); migration and community (Volume 2); and, in Volume 3, on to family- or community-based activities that can be studied at a local level such as work, social mobility, local politics, religion, or leisure.

This book forms one part of the Open University course DA301 *Studying family and community history: 19th and 20th centuries* (the other components are listed on p.ii). DA301 is an honours-level undergraduate course for part-time adult learners studying at a distance, and it is designed to develop the skills, methods and understanding to complete a guided project in family or community history within the time constraints of a one-year course – comparable, therefore, to the dissertation sometimes carried out in the final year of a conventional honours degree. It also looks forward to ways in which such a project could be extended and communicated at a later stage. However, these volumes are also designed to be used, either singly or as a series, by anyone interested in family or community history. The introduction to recent research, together with the practical exercises, advice on the critical exploitation of primary sources, and suggestions for research projects, should be of wide interest and application. Collectively the results of such research should not only develop individuals' investigations but also enhance our more general understanding of family and community history. Much remains to be discovered by the army of amateur and professional researchers throughout the British Isles.

Since a series of this kind obviously depends on the efforts of many people, there are many thanks to express. As in other Open University courses, the material was developed collaboratively. So while authors are responsible for what they have written, they have also been both influenced and supported by other members of the course team: not just its academic contributors, but also those from the editorial, design, and production areas of the university. There was also the highly skilled group who prepared the manuscript for electronic publishing, among them Molly Freeman, Maggie Tebbs, Pauline Turner, Betty Atkinson, Maureen Adams, and above all Dianne Cook, our calm and efficient course secretary throughout most of the production period. For advice and help on references in various chapters in this volume we would especially like to thank Jane Cox, Ian Donnachie, John Golby, David Smith of the Gloucestershire County Record Office, Paul Smith, and Monica Shelley. For the series generally we are greatly indebted to four external critical readers who provided wonderfully detailed comments on successive drafts of the whole text: Brenda Collins, particularly for her informed advice on Ireland; Janet Few, both in her own right and as Education Officer of the Federation of Family History Societies; Dennis Mills, with his unparalleled command not only of the subject matter but of the needs of distance students; and Colin Rogers of the Metropolitan University, Manchester, for sharing the fruits of his long experience in teaching and furthering the study of family history. Finally, particular thanks go to our external assessor, Professor Paul Hair, for his constant challenges, queries and suggestions. Our advisors should not be held responsible for the shortcomings that remain, but without their help these volumes would certainly have been both less accurate and less intelligible.

Our list of thanks is a long one and even so does not cover everyone. In our case its scope arises from the particular Open University form of production. But this extensive cooperation also, we think, represents the fruitful blend of individual interest and collaborative effort that is typical in the field of studying family and community history: a form of collaboration in which we hope we can now engage with you, our readers.

USING THIS BOOK

Activities
Many chapters in this volume are designed not just as a texts for reading or reference but also for active study. They are therefore punctuated by a series of activities, signalled by different formats. These include:

(a) *Short questions*: these provide the opportunity to stop and consider for a moment before reading on. They are separated from the surrounding text merely by being printed in a different colour.

(b) *Exercises*: these are activities to be carried out as part of working through the text. Follow-up discussion comes either immediately after in the main text or (when so indicated in the exercise) in the separate comments and answers at the end of the book.

Schemas
These are lists of questions, factors or key stages in research

References
While this book is free-standing, there are cross-references to other volumes in the series which appear, for example, in the form 'see Volume 3, Chapter 6'. This is to aid readers using all the books.

The lists of books or articles at the end of chapters or sections follow the scholarly convention of giving details of all works cited; they are not intended as obligatory further reading.

Abbreviations
Commonly used abbreviations – such as CEBs (census enumerators' books), FFHS (Federation of Family History Societies) or PRO (Public Record Office) – are explained on their first main appearance in the text. In cases of difficulty, the index should supply the necessary reference or information.

RUTH FINNEGAN

INTRODUCTION

by Michael Drake and Ruth Finnegan

This is a volume for people who are, or want to be, *active* researchers in family and community history. Its emphasis, therefore, is on *doing* things: how to find sources and how to use them; how to acquire techniques and how to apply them; how to make discoveries and how to present them in a manner most suited to the intended audience.

You will find plenty of useful information here too, of course: how to use record offices and bibliographies, for example, or where to find out more about particular topics. But the focus is always on the effective *doing* of research. We take you through the practical stages: how to assess your own resources, plan your research strategy, use the relevant sources critically and analytically (the essential step in all high-level research), learn how to apply particular methods – from oral recording to computing – and, finally, how to present and publish your research to a wider audience.

With that emphasis in mind, we have not attempted a spurious comprehensiveness – spurious in the sense that, with the space available, we could only have covered 'everything' so superficially as to be long on promise and short on performance. We have, then, in the main adopted an in-depth, indicative approach. Thus, you will find that we have examined in some depth a Medical Officer of Health report and shown how it can be used, with a view to indicating the riches available in local authority records generally. Again, our treatment of quantitative techniques has been aimed at the novice, hesitant about entering an unfamiliar world. We shall measure success here by the number who take that first step, believing that that will engender the motivation required to master the techniques presented elsewhere.

A unique feature of the volume is its reference to all the countries that now make up the United Kingdom and Ireland. There are several reasons for this. First, we wish to encourage the study of family and community history throughout the area. Secondly, because of the massive migration within the area, we feel that much of interest to the family and community historian can only be understood within this broader context. Thirdly, we wish to draw attention to sources available in one country but not in others, such as the householder schedules of the 1901 and 1911 censuses in Ireland; the Statistical Accounts in Scotland; the language returns in the Welsh and Scottish censuses; or the poll books, so common in England and so rare elsewhere.

Another characteristic of the volume is its emphasis on contemporary sources and methods. The twentieth century is almost at an end. Much of its history remains to be captured. In fact, this could be seen as *the* most important task for present-day family and community historians. Fast disappearing are landscapes, artifacts, skills, certain aspects of familial life – marriage, for instance, is not the institution it once was. Fortunately, modern technology has eased the historian's task. Tape-recorders have transformed oral history; film and video have brought new ways of recording and presenting the past; computers have done something (and promise more!) in the field of data storage, manipulation and presentation. All are covered in this volume.

The volume stands on its own and we believe can be used with profit by all family and community historians. But it also links to the three other volumes in the series. It builds on them, in that it is there that you may have found the substantive background discussion and suggested questions for shaping your own research (and your own research, after all, is what you are using these sources and methods *for*). It also supplements them by its treatments of certain topics – maps and plans; photographs and postcards; newspapers; databases; ethical and legal issues. It complements them by completing the coverage of topics discussed there (e.g. collecting and using oral evidence; how to take a sample; source criticism).

You can use this volume in several ways, reflecting its varied content and multiple approaches. As a reference work, you will dip into it as the occasion arises: briefly, if you are after a particular source or bibliographical tool; at some length, if your research has reached a particular stage. Dare we say too that some chapters are quite a 'good read'! Whatever your needs and aspirations, you will be unlucky not to find something in the volume to satisfy them.

PART I

SOME BASICS

❖ ❖ ❖

CHAPTER 1

QUESTIONS AND STRATEGIES FOR RESEARCH

by Michael Drake (section 1) and Ruth Finnegan (sections 2 and 3)

1 GETTING STARTED: MAKING AN INVENTORY

Your first step on the research path should be to make an inventory of your strengths. In order to do this, you should draw your own *larger* version of the table shown in Table 1.1, which you can then fill in for this purpose. (I suggest that you complete the table as a working document, using a soft pencil. You will probably want to make changes to it.) Let us now discuss each of the headings in Table 1.1 with a view to seeing how to make your entries.

Table 1.1 An inventory of your research strengths (draw up a *larger* version of this table and use it to prepare an inventory)

Type of source	Time	Interests	Research strategy	Technical skills
1 Personal				
2 Local				
3 Standard				

1.1   SOURCES

Personal   Research into family and community history obviously requires sources. Fortunately, Britain and Ireland are exceedingly rich in sources, and in libraries and record offices at which they can be studied. You should start, however, by examining the sources you yourself possess. Much will depend upon whether you belong to a family that 'loves a clear out' or one that hoards everything down to pieces of string and empty margarine cartons. My own family occupied a half-way position. So I have letters, including some sent by a distant ancestor who emigrated to the USA in 1858, and some my father wrote from a troopship on the way to India at the end of the Second World War, as well as from India itself and Burma. I have quite a lot of photograph albums going back to the turn of the century, with one or two photographs going back even earlier. Miscellaneous wills, house deeds and business records have also survived.

You may have similar documents or printed ones (e.g. extracts from local newspapers, school magazines, club, church or chapel records). And you will, as likely as not, have a number of relatives and friends who not only possess similar records but are also in themselves repositories of oral evidence which you may exploit.

The two great advantages of using such personal evidence are that it is inherently interesting, simply because of its intimate nature, and that it is readily accessible, thus saving you valuable time.

Local collections   Most of us live within an hour or so of a local record office, which in some cases will be part of a public library. Such offices contain, broadly speaking, two kinds of source material. The first consists of local collections of material not to be found elsewhere (i.e. unique bodies of evidence of the past). Figure 1.1 is a facsimile of part of a guide to one local collection which happens to be close to where I grew up. It is housed in the Calderdale Central Library in Halifax.

Standard sources   Secondly, in addition to local collections, many record offices and libraries will have sources which I call 'standard' because they contain the same type of information, often in the same format. The most widely available and in many ways most valuable of these are the enumerators' books from the censuses of 1841–91 in England, Wales and Scotland and the householders' schedules for 1901 and 1911 in Ireland (both north and south). Newspapers are another source I would describe as standard and these too are commonly available, especially from the middle of the nineteenth century. Registers of baptisms, burials and marriages from the Churches of England, Wales, Scotland and Ireland as well as those of non-conformist denominations are abundant in some areas. The archive office in Calderdale's central library, for example, has a vast quantity of parochial and non-parochial registers, these being especially numerous for the nineteenth and twentieth centuries. Local government records too are widely available.

You will be especially fortunate if you live close to a library or archive office which has either printed or microfiche copies of parliamentary papers for the nineteenth and twentieth centuries. Although difficult to access – their sheer bulk is daunting enough – parliamentary papers contain much of local historical relevance. Finally, you will find many libraries and archives hold long runs of local society publications, especially of historical, archeological and parish register societies.

To start your search for archives, look up the entries for places near to you in one of the useful finding guides listed in Chapter 12, section 3.1, and make a point of visiting your local library to see what is available. One example of such a guide is Susanna Guy's excellent *English local studies handbook* (1992), which also gives the addresses of local history societies (often that of the secretary) and indicates whether or not they publish journals. If you are not already a member

WEST YORKSHIRE ARCHIVE SERVICE: CALDERDALE

The archive service in Halifax was established in 1964, building on foundations laid by the Halifax Museums Service, local public libraries and the Halifax Antiquarian Society. It moved to its present purpose-built accommodation in the Halifax town centre in January 1983. Calderdale joined the West Yorkshire Archive Service in April 1983.

Search room, Calderdale District Archives

THE RECORDS

Official records

The official archives of local government bodies in the area are well represented and comprise records from Calderdale Metropolitan Borough Council and its nine predecessor authorities, the County Borough of Halifax, the Boroughs of Brighouse and Todmorden, the Urban Districts of Elland, Hebden Royd, Queensbury and Shelf, Ripponden, and Sowerby Bridge, and the Rural District of Hepton. These Councils had themselves inherited archives from their predecessors which include records of civil townships from 1665, Improvement Commissioners from 1762 and Local Boards of Health, Boards of Guardians and Urban and Rural Sanitary Authorities which were established in the area during the course of the 19th century.

Family and estate records

The most significant deposits from private sources are the records of the Listers of Shibden Hall, Southowram 1329-1937, Stansfelds of Field House, Sowerby 1701-1920, Armytages of Kirklees Hall, Brighouse c.1200-1947 and Sunderlands of Coley Hall, Hipperholme 1197-1882. These collections include local manorial records, many of the surviving medieval documents relating to the area and, from the 17th century onwards, letters and diaries

which usefully supplement the official archives of the period. The Shibden Hall estate muniments include the notebooks of Jonathan Hall of Elland, upholsterer 1701-1761, letters of the philosopher, David Hartley 1730-1756, eye-witness accounts of battles during the American War of Independence and the extensive travel journals of Anne Lister 1806-1840.

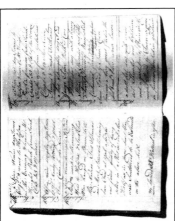

Journal of Cornelius Ashworth of Ovenden, farmer and handloom weaver 1782-83.
Ref. HAS:761

Business records

In view of Halifax's importance as an early centre for the cloth industry, the collections have an inevitable textile emphasis and include the records of Samuel Hill of Soyland, clothier 1736-1738, John Firth of Halifax, worsted manufacturer 1739-1752 and Cornelius Ashworth of Ovenden, farmer and handloom weaver 1782-1816, alongside the much bulkier deposits of the period of the Industrial Revolution. The holdings also reflect other commercial and industrial activity in the area, however, and records are available relating to local banking 1735-1959, brewing 1808-1965, clay and brick making 1800-1966, clock making 1750-1812, coal mining 1633-1937, engineering 1849-1984, printing 1832-1948, stone quarrying 1773-1970 and wire manufacturing 1868-1963. The deposited solicitors' accumulations include the papers of Robert Parker, the 18th century Halifax attorney, whose clients were scattered throughout West Yorkshire and beyond.

Ecclesiastical records

The parish records of Shelf, Diocese of Bradford 1850-1982, are held by the office, together with the archives of over 200 Baptist, Congregational, Methodist and Unitarian churches which highlight the long and dominant tradition of dissent and non-conformity in the Upper Calder Valley. Many of the parochial registers, non-parochial registers and bishop's transcripts for the area are available on microfilm.

Political and trade union records

Amongst the large numbers of political and labour organisations trade union deposits from 1834 onwards figure most prominently, but also represented in this class are the records of the Anti-Corn Law League 1839-1846, Halifax Chartism 1838-1840, local co-operative societies 1832-1972, friendly societies 1769-1981, political parties 1871-1981, trades councils 1866-1981 and working men's clubs 1877-1952.

Other records

Other collections reflect the cultural, philanthropic, convivial and educational life of the district and include the records of the Halifax Mechanics' Institute 1825-1922, Halifax Antiquarian Society 1900-1972, Halifax Loyal Georgean Society 1799-1981, Halifax Chess Club 1840-1959, Nathaniel Waterhouse Charities 1635-1868, Heath Grammar School 1585-1946, Halifax Literary and Philosophical Society 1830-1964, and Luddenden Village Library 1776-1917. The office also holds several films relating to the area and a rapidly expanding collection of oral history archives, providing a rich source of information from local informants on various aspects of social life, work, politics and religion during the 20th century.

Grant of land in Hipperholme by Jordan, son of Peter de Presteley to Roger son of Helye de Broo c.1197.
Ref. CH:1/1

Figure 1.1   A guide to West Yorkshire Archive Service, Calderdale

you should get in touch with those local societies of interest to you, both for help with sources and for ideas on how to use them. This applies too if you want information from a more distant place than your immediate locality.

As likely as not, you will draw on a number of sources in any research that you do. Having made your initial trawl through what is available, you should then seek to make entries in all three sections of the first column in Table 1.1.

One final point: before starting your research, you should at least glance through Chapters 3 to 6 in this volume, and you should also look at Chapter 12 for more advice on libraries and archives. These chapters draw your attention to a wide variety of sources, indicate where they can be found, and offer some ideas as to what can be done with them. Reading them could cause you to revise your initial thoughts.

1.2   TIME

Probably more research projects fail because of bad time management than any other single cause. It is a failing that affects all manner of researchers from full-time Ph.D. students, with the benefit of university libraries and one-to-one supervision, to part-time Open University students whose access to sources might involve a sacrificed lunch hour, the odd Saturday morning, or those evenings when late-night shopping keeps libraries open beyond normal working hours.

Under the heading of 'time', therefore, you should consider the following:

1   How long have you to complete your research – six months, a year, five years? Even if you feel time is not a factor, it is worth setting a limit simply because this will enable you to go through the invaluable process of budgeting your time.

2   What 'real' time have you available? By that I mean, within the six months or five years you have set yourself, what parts of the day, week, month, etc. are actually available? Is it five lunch hours a week, or a Saturday morning every month and three two-hour evening sessions every week, or is it? ... well I leave you to decide.

3   What time must you spend actually getting to places that you need to visit for your research? Here you need to plan your visits to coincide with your general research strategy. It is no good, say, turning up at an archive office before you have considered, to some degree, what you would like to do and have investigated some of the literature on it. It is also very easy – and pleasant – to sit in an archive office collecting data which turns out to be irrelevant to your project. 'It might just come in handy' is not a good basis on which to proceed.

4   Also, don't forget to allow time for analysing your data and for writing it up.

All this sounds rather discouraging and prescriptive advice to apply to what is likely to be an extremely exciting and pleasurable activity – if a bit fraught at times! It is not meant to be off-putting – merely friendly advice from one who has wasted more time than he likes to remember or cares to admit!

1.3   INTERESTS

Your interests in family and community history could be narrowly focused or broad in the extreme. By that I mean you may be interested in throwing light on a particular place at a particular time, or you might wish to contribute to a broader understanding of family and community history. Both are perfectly legitimate forms of enquiry. However, if your interests are of the former kind you are more of a historian, if you tend to the latter you are more of a social scientist. Not many years ago, traditional historians were very scathing of social scientific enquiries, whilst many social scientists believed historians to be antiquarians at best. But the division is not a hard and fast one nowadays, and in recent years there has been much toing and froing. Nevertheless, there is still something of a difference, and this will help determine your choice of sources, strategy and techniques. It will also affect the time you take. If your interests tend more towards the historical, you may well spend more time on searching out and analysing your sources; if you have more of a social scientific bent, the processing of your data could well occupy you more.

Your interests will, of course, depend to some extent on your education prior to beginning your research project. And 'education' here will include the informal sort acquired in work. The knowledge and technical skills acquired through work experience should be considered in directing your attention to topics of research, sources, and methods. As a local government officer, for example, you may be able to interpret local government sources more perceptively than one who has not had your experience. A doctor or nurse might well do the same with Medical Officer of Health reports. Knowledge of computing acquired at work may encourage you to embark on a more quantitative study. So, in the column headed 'interests', make notes *now* as to your current ideas. Since you will very likely modify them in the course of your investigations, use a soft pencil so you can easily rub them out!

1.4   RESEARCH STRATEGY

Two useful strategies are those which could be termed the 'hypothesis testing' and the 'questioning sources' strategies. Which of these strategies you adopt – or the one on which you lay the greater emphasis, assuming you mix them – will depend on your interests, the sources you have available, and the techniques you adopt. Broadly speaking, the 'hypothesis testing' strategy lends itself to quantitative sources and techniques; the 'questioning sources' one to qualitative techniques (e.g. oral history, the use of narrative (i.e. telling a story rather than testing a hypothesis) and literary sources).

These strategies are discussed more fully in section 2 below (and also in Volume 1, Chapter 2).

1.5   TECHNICAL SKILLS

I started this chapter by suggesting that you should make an inventory of your strengths. Implicit in this are your limitations – already we've discussed the problem of time and the accessibility of sources. The same applies to the question of your technical skills. You should examine yourself on these as objectively as possible.

What skills do you possess?

Here is a checklist you may care to go through:

o   Can you read quickly?

o   Can you make notes efficiently (i.e. get down the essence of whatever it is you read within a small space)?

o   Can you type/word process?

o   Can you plan your work?

o   Would you say you were a tidy person?

o   Have you worked before with primary sources?

o   What experience have you had of subjecting primary sources to the questioning suggested in Chapter 2?

o Have you done any interviewing? How good would you say you were at it?

o Can you take good photographs?

o Can you draw graphs and diagrams?

o Have you any computing skills?

o Are you familiar with and/or can you use appropriately any of the following quantitative techniques?

Averages; standard deviation; percentages; birth, death, marriage rates; sampling; tests of significance.

o Can you write reports people wish to read?

o Can you use a tape-recorder for interviewing?

o Can you use a video camera?

o Can you give a good talk or lecture?

Even if your answers – objectively arrived at! – are in the negative for many of these questions, this does not mean that you cannot or will not use some of these techniques in researching and presenting your project. When you have digested the rest of this book you will know why!

2 TWO WELL-TRIED RESEARCH STRATEGIES

by Ruth Finnegan

The fourth column in Table 1.1 deserves some special attention, even at this early stage, for it will affect the conduct of your work directly. Here are some additional points to note.

First, completing and presenting a piece of serious research is more than just amassing a series of facts or copying out chunks of information from documents. It also means interpreting and presenting the evidence systematically in some wider framework and relating it to comparable cases or to intelligible questions and theories which are also of interest to other researchers. There are, in consequence, certain basic steps in research which are recognized by most social and historical researchers (at least as far as the *practical* steps of actual investigation are concerned – *theorizing* always attracts controversy!). These are summarized in Schema A.

Schema A: Basic steps in research

1 Find a particular topic or question of interest (or recognize you have already found one).

2 Consult the relevant evidence, using appropriate sources and methods.

3 Consider the topic or question in some wider perspective, for example:

o comparable or contrasting cases

o current academic findings on the topic

o other theories, concepts or questions about the subject.

4 Reach a conclusion and/or present the findings.

For any research arising from the kinds of topics and questions in family and community history, *something* of all these stages is likely to arise – more, or less, emphasized in each case, and not necessarily in this order. So a second point to consider is how to put the stages together into a research strategy appropriate for *your* needs.

You have various choices, for there are several variants within this overall framework. Some are highly specialized or time-consuming, like sophisticated survey or experimental strategies, or research resulting from a lifetime's steeping in primary sources – fine for those with the time and resources but probably not realistic for many readers of this volume. Fortunately, there are other equally reputable but more limited research strategies. Out of these we are emphasizing two, as both reasonably practicable within the constraints under which you are probably working, and adaptable to shorter as well as longer studies. For the purposes of this discussion, these strategies are called 'hypothesis testing' and 'questioning sources'.

2.1   THE 'HYPOTHESIS TESTING' STRATEGY

This strategy involves starting from a topic in which you are interested, and exploring it further through discovering whether or not the evidence supports some particular view of it (a view based on current scholarly writing, on your own hunch, or on what you know about apparently similar cases). This view is then stated in the form of an explicit hypothesis, which is tested out by consulting the relevant evidence (the data) and seeing if this confirms or falsifies that hypothesis.

For example, you may be interested in a particular locality – say a small neighbourhood within a town – and have been stimulated by some of the theories about 'community' to explore whether it really *is* a 'community' in the sense, say, of sharing similar origins (one possible aspect of community; see Volume 2). So you might construct a hypothesis like: *'The majority of a community's residents at any one time will have been born in the same area'* (e.g. in a particular county or foreign country, depending on the specific area). You would then test this by consulting the relevant evidence (e.g. interviews for a recent example, or the census enumerators' books (CEBs) for the nineteenth century) and reaching your conclusion. (For a detailed discussion of an example of this strategy, see Volume 1, Chapter 2, section 2.1; other examples will be found throughout Volumes 1–3.)

Hypothesis testing is a long-established strategy in historical investigation and, more especially, in the social sciences, where it is also sometimes described as 'hypothetico-deductive' or 'positivistic'. The main stages are summarized in Figure 1.2. It has many advantages, particularly for those with limited time or resources, and some limitations (see section 2.3 below).

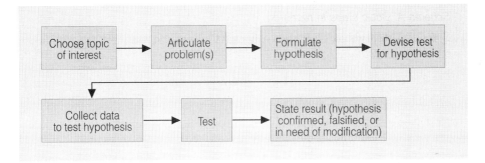

Figure 1.2   Typical steps in the hypothesis testing research strategy. The various steps (particularly those at the start and end) are also normally related to comparable studies by other researchers and/or more general or theoretical perspectives (see step 3 in Schema A)

2.2   THE 'QUESTIONING SOURCES' STRATEGY

The second approach is more like a spiral than the mainly one-way progression of the hypothesis-based strategy. It involves a constant toing and froing between sources and questions, with an emphasis on 'understanding' and 'interpretation' rather than precise 'testing'.

An example could be research starting from the same kind of topic as before: a desire to understand a local community more fully, both for its own sake and in the light of more general writing about community and communities. You might begin from similar questions but then discover from examining your initial sources or interviews, or by looking at other sources like local newspapers or directories, that other links *besides* common birthplace seem to emerge, or that it is hard to assess what importance really was attached to place of birth. So you might be led on to modify your question into, say, *'What kinds of links did bind people in this locality?'*; then find, by looking again at the kind of information available in your sources, that this wide question too could usefully be modified to, say, an exploration of the various clubs functioning in the area, or the extent of overlap between certain political and religious affiliations. Your conclusions on these questions might need to be tentative and point to yet further questions to be explored to reach a full understanding of the community – but would still have resulted in uncovering something new.

This strategy has a less clear-cut end than the hypothesis testing one. So you need to avoid being tempted ever-onwards without drawing your research together into at least an interim report and making a conscious effort to relate it to other writing. But your research can lead to new insights that you had never considered at the start. (For a detailed discussion of an example of this strategy, see Volume 1, Chapter 2, section 2.2; other examples will be found throughout Volumes 1–3.)

Once again, this is a long-established strategy among both social and historical researchers. It is sometimes also described as a 'humanistic' or 'research spiral' strategy. Its main stages are summarized in Figure 1.3.

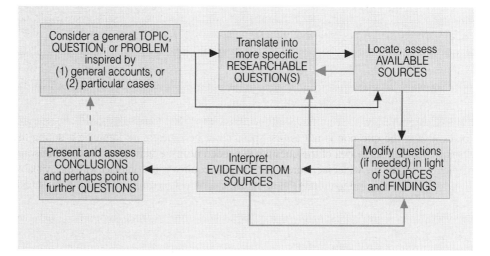

Figure 1.3   Typical steps in the questioning sources research strategy (feedback links are indicated by lightly shaded arrows). The various steps (particularly those at the start and end) are also normally related to comparable studies by other researchers and/or more general or theoretical perspectives (see step 3 in Schema A)

2.3   CONTRASTS AND COMPARISONS

It will be clear from Figures 1.2 and 1.3 that there is plenty of overlap between the two strategies, which can in turn be related back to Schema A. But differences are interesting too.

Which contrasts between the two research strategies would you identify as important?

Each strategy has its own characteristics, which are worth reflecting upon when you are considering your own plans. They could broadly be summarized as follows:

1   The initial questions or topics in the questioning sources strategy are often more *open and broad* than those in the more limited (and thus sometimes more practicable) hypothesis testing strategy.

2   Questioning sources is usually more *iterative* (i.e. there is constant feedback to modify the original question) as against the one-way direction of hypothesis testing.

3   Hypothesis testing often stresses *measuring*; questioning sources stresses *interpreting*.

4   Hypothesis testing leans more towards establishing or testing something *general* ('typical', 'representative', even a 'law'); questioning sources leans towards gaining deeper understanding of the *particular* (the difference is a matter of degree – both strategies have some interest in both ends of this continuum).

5   Both *quantitative* and *qualitative methods* are possible in both strategies, but hypothesis testing particularly emphasizes the former, questioning sources the latter.

6   The strategies have contrasting *vocabularies*. In hypothesis testing: 'hypothesis', 'test', 'data', 'collect facts', 'objective', 'scientific'. In questioning sources: 'problem', 'question', 'sources', 'consult', 'discover', 'interpret or understand', 'personal insight', 'humanistic'.

These characteristics have implications for the strengths and limitations of each strategy, and what each is good for. Here are some worth considering.

Hypothesis testing   This strategy is not necessarily based on quantification, but is often specially suited to exploiting quantifiable data. It is strong on measuring, testing and reaching a definitive conclusion within a limited time, for a *specific* hypothesis can be focused on and less time spent explaining unforeseen complexities. It looks more objective too (though this can be exaggerated). The downside is that it provides less opportunity to take on *new* discoveries and is probably less open to complexity, subjective experience and the significance of real (not just statistical) human variation.

Questioning sources   This strategy is specially appropriate for open-ended questions and topics, where the question is not at first specific but becomes more formulated during the research (though *some* idea of the question is needed near the start, often drawn from some acquaintance with the wider literature). The strategy requires you to interact with the available sources and be prepared to modify the question or problem progressively in the light of your findings. The danger is that too much time is spent with the sources so that no findings or conclusion are reached within the time available. The strategy leads to 'understanding' rather than to 'testing' or definitive conclusions. Any generalization you arrive at is likely to draw on comparative or theoretical perspectives and/or an in-depth understanding of the wider historical context, rather than being based on numerical measurement.

Despite the contrasts, do you think you might need to take similar *practical* steps within the two strategies? If so, what are these steps?

Whichever strategy you follow, similar steps are necessary: consider a topic and the likely sources (are they accessible?); relate these to some wider perspective (whether of other cases or the existing scholarly literature); and come to some conclusion. The general factors to bear in mind are summarized in Table 1.1, and, for the actual research stages, in Schema B.

Schema B: Key stages in research

1   Think about a *topic, problem* or *source.*

2   Locate and assess *available sources* and *methods* (especially important, for if it turns out that appropriate sources and methods are *not* available you may need to abandon the topic and start again).

3   Consider the specific *issue* (question, debate, generalization or usual assumption) you could explore through these sources and methods.

4   Translate the issue into a *limited researchable question/hypothesis/topic.*

5   Pursue *investigation and/or testing of evidence,* with available methods and sources, *refining* the question etc. if appropriate.

6   *Relate results back to (4)* (your specific question, hypothesis, etc.) and *compare or contrast* with any similar studies you can find.

7   Close circle by *presenting results and relating them back to (3)* (the issue, etc.): How far does your work support or challenge received views? How far has it changed your own original views? What further questions are now raised?

Note 1:   Further advice about sources, methods and modes of presentation is given in this volume; information about issues, theories, debates, and comparative cases is given throughout Volumes 1–3, together with illustrative examples.

Note 2:   There is no short-cut to discovering what research has been done already, but following through the discussions and further references in Volumes 1–3 and in Chapters 3–6 in this volume will certainly help. Remember too that a piece of related research (whether national or in a different period or locality) will be a help rather than a hindrance to your own project: you could use it as a springboard to investigate how far *your* locality or period, etc. was the same or (perhaps) interestingly different.

2.4   SOME THEORETICAL BACKGROUND

You might also be interested to note how the two research strategies tie in with some long-standing arguments about the methodology of social and historical research. Even *within* the social sciences – and increasingly within history too – there have been battles between those who emphasize generality, the search for science-like laws and/or quantified testing of hypotheses, as against those more concerned with 'understanding', interpretation and insight into personal and human qualities. Many controversies of this nature are discussed in the academic literature. Two examples of these are: the divergences between positivist approaches and Weberian 'interpretive sociology' within the social sciences; and the 'two views of history' – 'scientific or cliometric' (measuring history) as against 'traditional' history – as expressed in Fogel and Elton (1983). Many of these issues are succinctly set out in Table 1.2, taken from Ken Plummer's influential *Documents of life* (1990).

   These distinctions are sometimes taken to represent some deep divide between historical and social scientific approaches. There is some justification for this in the kinds of sources and evidence typically used in each: historians focusing on personal, unique, written sources, often

Table 1.2 A bridgeable divide?

	Towards the humanities	Towards the positivistic sciences
Foci	Unique and idiographic Human centred The inner: subjective, meaning, feeling	General and nomothetic Structure centred The outer: objective, 'things', events
Epistem-ology	Phenomenalist Relativist Perspectivist	Realist Absolutist/Essentialist Logical positivist
Task	Interpret, understand Describe, observe	Causal explanation Measure
Style	'Soft', 'Warm' Imaginative Valid – 'real', 'rich'	'Hard', 'Cold' Systematic Reliable, 'replicable'
Theory	Inductive and grounded 'Story telling'	Deductive and abstract 'Operationalism'
Values	Ethically and politically committed Egalitarianism	Ethically and politically neutral 'Expertise and elites'

Note: The table is reproduced in full as it will be of interest to those already knowledgeable about these theoretical controversies, but the basic point lies in the overall contrasts rather than a mastery of the technical terms used.

Source: Plummer (1990) p.6

(until comparatively recently) those of the literate or powerful élite; social scientists focusing on their opportunities to measure, through interviews and surveys, or through tapping less personalized data from the past.

However, two points need to be made about these somewhat simplified distinctions. First, approaches from both 'sides' have for long been accepted in *both* historical and social scientific research. Sociologists, historical geographers and (especially) anthropologists have often also emphasized 'understanding', 'human-centred' or 'case-study' approaches; correspondingly, there is an established tradition of historians relying on quantification and invoking the vocabulary of hypothesis testing. The well-known Cambridge Group for the History of Population and Social Structure, together with its associated journal *Local Population Studies,* is one illustration of this crossover. The group has included both historians and social scientists (in so far as these are different), and besides its emphasis on quantification – appropriate indeed for the demographic questions with which it is concerned – has also stimulated studies which follow more 'humanistic', case-study lines.

Secondly, there is now a marked convergence between what *could* once have been represented as two separate traditions – a convergence already hinted at in the title of Table 1.2. Social scientists are more and more interested in personal, biographical or experiential dimensions, with an increasing appreciation of historical specificity, personal life histories, and the findings of oral history; historians are increasingly turning to questions raised in *social* history, and moving outside élite studies to those of ordinary people and popular culture, approaches further reinforced by trends in recent feminist and oral-based history. This has led to a new appreciation of the role of individual lives and of the local and personal variants within what once looked like uniform and homogeneous trends such as 'industrialization' or 'modernization'. The converging approaches are well illustrated in some contemporary work within family and community history (see, for example, Hareven, 1991), and are well summed up in Brian Elliott's recent comments on 'combining the two crafts of history and sociology' (1990, p.59). (For further analysis see also Burke, 1992; Plummer, 1990, Chapter 1; and the discussion in the Introduction to Volume 1). Increasing numbers of researchers are now trying to explore that knotty but fascinating relation between the personal, local or unique on the one hand, and the more general, national or aggregated on the other.

3 A NOTE ON LEGAL AND ETHICAL ISSUES

The academic and practical points discussed so far are not the only factors in research; ethical and legal factors also need to be considered. These are mentioned at appropriate points in later chapters. It is important, however, for you to be aware from the outset that research is not just a set of impersonal scientific procedures, but a process in which you as researcher and those with whom you are collaborating are personally involved.

This human dimension is particularly obvious in family and community history, an area of research which often touches upon sensitive material with deeply felt undertones at a personal level. Moreover, unlike some other forms of social research, *individual* people and places may be identified rather than 'anonymized', and your findings may rely on active help and information from other people. So it should go without saying – except that it is sometimes forgotten – that the individuals or groups being studied in the past or, perhaps, questioned or interviewed in the present, need to be treated with dignity and understanding; and furthermore, that those cooperating in the research should not be misled about its aims or how their assistance will be used and acknowledged (for implications for interviewing, see Chapter 7, section 3).

Human awareness and openness are thus important principles, well recognized by researchers nowadays (see Homan, 1991). It is not all plain sailing, however, for researchers *also* have a duty to tell the truth as they find it, and to communicate their findings: in other words, there may be a duty not to conceal information which some informants or descendants might perhaps prefer not to have revealed – even to themselves, sometimes, let alone others. You can thus face real dilemmas in the personal choices you have to make. There are no simple answers – except to note that if such issues arise they need to be considered seriously, and that you are not the first to have to face them.

Some ethical obligations have also become enshrined in law, especially that relating to copyright and 'intellectual property rights'. This is discussed later (clearance of copyright material for publication in print in Chapter 10, section 3.1.3; and permissions for using interview material etc. in Chapter 7, section 3.2). These aspects too need to be taken seriously.

Finally, then, your research is a human activity, with the dilemmas and obligations that that entails. It has its problems and frustrations at times, and you need to keep your wits about you. But it can also be a rich and rewarding experience. You are involved in the pursuit of truth, the discovery of perhaps unexpected information and understanding, and the shared appreciation of new dimensions in human life and history.

REFERENCES

Burke, P. (1992) *History and social theory*, Cambridge, Polity Press.

Drake, M. (ed.) (1994) *Time, family and community: perspectives on family and community history*, Oxford, Blackwell in association with the Open University (Course Reader).

Elliott, B. (1990) 'Biography, family history and the analysis of social change', in Kendrick, S. et al. (eds) *Interpreting the past, understanding the present*, Basingstoke and London, Macmillan. Reprinted in Drake, M. (1994).

Fogel, R.W. and Elton, G.R. (1983) *Which road to the past? Two views of history*, New Haven and London, Yale University Press.

Guy, S. (1992) *English local studies handbook: an essential guide to sources of information for professional and amateur historians,* Exeter, University of Exeter Press.

Hareven, T.K (1991) 'The history of the family and the complexity of social change', *American Sociological Review,* 96, 1, pp.95–125. Reprinted in an abridged form as 'Recent research on the history of the family' in Drake (1994).

Homan, R. (1991) *The ethics of social research,* London, Longman.

Plummer, K. (1990) *Documents of life: an introduction to the problems and literature of a humanistic method,* London, Unwin Hyman.

CHAPTER 2

PRIMARY SOURCES: HANDLE WITH CARE

by Arthur Marwick

My biggest difficulty is not knowing what knowledge of, or views about, history you already have. Quite likely your strongest feeling is one of enthusiasm for getting on and doing some family or community history of your own. Even so, my hope here is to try to persuade you to think a little about the wider implications of historical study. (If by chance you come from a background in literary or art historical studies, I also want to make you aware that there are good reasons for preferring the approaches of mainstream historians to those of such cultural theorists as Foucault and Barthes.)

Let me, then, quickly set out the ten points I wish to establish and develop in this chapter.

1   Primary sources are absolutely fundamental to history; without primary sources there would be no history.

2   This does not mean that all you do in history is put together a clutch of primary sources and read off what you think they tell you.

3   Primary sources, in fact, are usually fragmentary, ambiguous, and very difficult to analyse and interpret. The analysis and interpretation of primary sources call for high-level skills, which can be learned, or acquired by experience, but which we are certainly not born with.

4   Primary sources come in an enormous, and constantly expanding, variety and extend far beyond the traditional written documents.

5   The actual writing of a piece of history (student essay, article, thesis, or book) requires many other talents and skills beyond those of analysing and interpreting primary sources, including theorizing, conceptualizing and generalizing.

6   However, theories, concepts, generalizations not founded in primary evidence, and not subject to amendment or abandonment in the light of further primary evidence, are fundamentally unhistorical: for historians, the words of Marx, or, for that matter, Marwick, have no force whatsoever unless the nature of the *evidence* (i.e. the primary sources) on which the words are based is open for inspection and evaluation.

7   History is a universal subject upon which almost everyone (whether qualified or not) has an opinion. Most art historians, literary critics, or musicologists believe that paintings, poems, and symphonies must be located in their historical context. Many of the most-used concepts in intellectual discourse are rooted in history: 'democracy', 'class', 'capitalism', 'ideology'. There are broad principles which govern all aspects of historical investigation, but within that broad framework, different techniques, different approaches, may very properly be applied depending upon the type of investigation.

8   While it is possible to sort out analytically the processes a historian goes through, the real-life activity is complex, iterative, and subject to disconcerting discontinuities and dazzling convergences. It is easy to jump to the naïve conclusion that historians first find the facts, and then, according to prejudice or ideology, arrange them into some design of their own. Actually, 'facts'

in history come in all shapes and sizes, and many levels of complexity (the Second World War is undoubtedly a 'fact', but one containing within it an inexhaustible range of further 'facts' – where does one begin, or end?). What, of course, the historian engages with is *sources*, teasing out from them 'facts' of all sorts: material circumstances, states of mind, motivations, decisions, assumptions, values, etc.

9   Though primary sources are frequently inadequate in offering answers to all the questions we would like to have answered, they often present the opposite problem of offering masses of information of no significance to the enquiry being pursued, and indeed, sometimes, of no significance whatsoever. Every 'fact', every quotation, culled from the documents, must pull its weight; its significance in the argument or interpretation being expounded must be made absolutely clear.

10   Only through a thorough awareness of the nature of primary sources can we be aware of the imperfections of historical knowledge. The achievements of professional historians are great, but since all history is based on sources, and since sources are fragmentary, intractable, and fallible, there will always be things about the past which we do not know with any certainty.

In order to develop and sustain these points, it will first be necessary to pay attention to some issues about the nature and purposes of historical study, and the past, before tackling the central points about handling primary sources.

1   THE NATURE AND PURPOSES OF HISTORICAL STUDY

The word 'history' is used in many ways. The most relevant and comprehensive definition for our purposes is as follows: 'The systematic and disciplined study of the human past, together with the bodies of knowledge (incomplete, often tentative, but constantly changing and expanding) produced by that study.'

I deliberately say 'bodies' of knowledge, because the human past is so extensive, so varied, that no single, integrated body of knowledge is possible. In this, as in a number of other ways, history is analogous to the natural sciences as a whole: just as science does not claim to produce an integrated account of the natural world and its relationship to the universe, nor a universal explanation embracing all the phenomena contained therein, so history does not claim to present a universal account or explanation of the past.

What do you think are the main reasons for studying history?

There are all kinds of personal reasons for studying history. You may be doing it quite simply because you enjoy it: there is something poetic, is there not, in the notion that there existed in the past families and communities, in some ways so like your own, yet, in so many other ways, utterly different? You may well feel that the skills and modes of thinking that you acquire in studying history will be of great use to you in your subsequent career, even if that has nothing to do with professional history. However, the justification for there being a history profession, for historical research and teaching being supported (however inadequately) by universities and governments, goes rather deeper. Quite simply, societies need history. What happened in the past exerts an overpowering influence upon what is happening today, and, indeed, upon what will happen in the future. Without an understanding of the past it is impossible to begin to grapple with the problems of today and tomorrow. History, let me be clear about this, does not claim to offer solutions; but without history we would not have the basic understanding which makes solutions at least attemptable.

Like all other serious scholarly disciplines, history is a cumulative subject. Individual historians work on relatively small and fairly delimited portions of the past; they benefit from the achievements of their predecessors, and learn from their mistakes. It is only within that perspective upon what history, as a profession and a discipline with clear social functions, actually is (as distinct from what philosophers and ideologists want it to be) that one can understand the role and nature of primary sources.

2 THE PAST

I have suggested an analogy between the manner in which the natural sciences study the natural world, and history studies the human past. The natural world is still all around us, even if many of its most important elements and structures are quite imperceptible to normal human observation. But the past, by definition, does not now exist; it has passed, it has gone for good. There may be a poetic truth in declaring that 'the past is another country'. But there are no boats, no jet planes, which will take us directly to that 'country'. The past can only be apprehended by the relics and traces which it has left: archaeological remains, buildings of all descriptions, field plans, folk-tales and myths, family traditions, written and printed documents and texts in all their immense variety – in other words, primary sources. If, through some cataclysmic event, resulting from natural causes or human agency, all traces of the past, prior, say, to the lives of our parents, were wiped out, it would still be possible to believe that a past had existed (because we are aware directly that our parents existed before we did, it is not difficult to imagine the existence of our parents' parents, of their parents, and so on back through time), but, beyond the history books already in existence, there would be no possibility of any further historical study. I don't think I need to make a meal of this one. Clearly, whatever else may be required for the production of history, primary sources are absolutely essential.

From all this emerges the obvious, and perhaps even banal, distinction between primary sources and secondary sources. Primary sources derive, 'naturally', as it were, or 'in the ordinary course of events', if you prefer that phrase, from human beings and groups of human beings going about their business or fulfilling their vocations in past societies; occasionally, perhaps, with an eye on the future, but generally in accordance with immediate needs and purposes. On the whole, one can say that primary sources are not created to satisfy the curiosity of future historians. Secondary sources, of course, are the very accounts produced by these future historians, using such primary sources as have survived. There are, it is true, secondary sources which for certain types of investigation serve as primary sources. There are occasional sources which contain both secondary and primary elements – where there are quotations within the text, for example. But in general this distinction between primary and secondary sources is a fundamental one – though no historian claims that mastery of this humble truth holds the magic key to all historical investigation.

3 HANDLING PRIMARY SOURCES

The commonest mistake the novice historian makes is to think: 'Great, I've got the primary source [whether it be a diary, a parish record, a book of etiquette, or whatever], now all I have to do is copy this stuff out, and I'm there.' The worst fault I find in the first drafts of dissertations and theses is the undigested presentation of great chunks from the raw sources without any evaluation of what they are saying, or why they are thought to be significant.

What steps do you think you should take in evaluating a primary source?

Experienced historians will have internalized, or perhaps never even consciously thought about, the processes one has to go through in evaluating, analysing, and interpreting the different kinds of historical source, but it can do nothing but good to set out here, in analytical, even pedantic, fashion, exactly what these steps are, what questions have to be asked.

Authenticity   Is the source authentic? Is it what it purports to be? Now we are not going to be sending you off to consult sources which have been forged, or are otherwise inauthentic. Still, the issue does come up from time to time, and it is one all historians have to keep firmly in mind. The forging of charters and wills is certainly far from unknown. Here there are various technical checks which can be employed: Do the materials used date from the appropriate period? Are the script employed, the style of language, and the legal forms as they should be, etc.? Autobiographies and biographies are important sources for family history: it is always worth endeavouring to establish that they are what they purport to be. The ghost-writing of the autobiographies of celebrities is a well-known industry today. The question of authenticity cropped up rather spectacularly in 1985 when a British Sunday newspaper published as authentic the quite cleverly faked 'Hitler Diaries'.

    An interesting and far from straightforward (things usually are far from straightforward in the analysis of historical sources) case is provided by the 'biography' of the Victorian novelist Thomas Hardy, *The life of Thomas Hardy*, 'by' his second wife (Hardy, 1928; 1930). Scholars subsequently established that the biography had in fact been written by Hardy himself, which, of course, changes its whole nature as evidence. As a relatively objective, factual account by a woman who knew him only in later life, it is not authentic; in fact, it contains the modified version of events which Hardy wished to convey to posterity. On the other hand, as an autobiography by Hardy himself it is authentic, and, where compared with the real facts as we know them, gives interesting insights into Hardy's thought processes.

Provenance   Closely connected to authenticity is the question of provenance. Where did the source come from, where was it originally found? This is particularly important in regard to physical artifacts or archaeological sources, but can also apply to written sources. In E.P. Thompson's justly celebrated study of *The making of the English working class*, much of the material on working-class figures was found by him in police files: that in itself is very significant in showing the suspiciousness, and even fear, with which the authorities looked upon working-class activism. Sometimes, therefore, provenance can throw extra light on the significance of a written document. We can be more sure about the authenticity of any type of source the more we know about its provenance.

Dating   When exactly was the source produced? Dating is absolutely central to all historical activity. Even written documents are often not dated. Only a thorough knowledge of the period and of the technical skills involved will enable the historian to produce a sustainable date. Only when the source is dated can one assess its relevance to the particular topic being investigated. One will also need to relate the date of a particular source to the dates of other relevant sources, and to other significant dates. For example, if your evidence so far is leading you towards developing the case that, *after* the onset of the long cycle of rising prices in 1849, the relationships between children and their parents became more relaxed, and you come across a very striking instance of filial independence, this will be of little help to your argument if it turns out in fact to date from *before* the onset of the long cycle of rising prices in 1849.

Type of source   What category does the particular source we are looking at fall into? Of course, we usually know before we start what sort of source we are about to consult, whether a will, or a private letter, or minutes of a committee meeting, etc. Still it is always worth keeping firmly in mind just what exactly it is one is reading. Written texts of all varieties, as well as physical artefacts, are almost always designed in conformity with certain established conventions. Only when the conventions, the codes, if you like, of the particular type of source being studied have been taken into account, can it be interpreted. Any departures from convention will, of course, be of special interest to the historian. This matter is of particular weight when it is a question of making use of literary or artistic sources. It must never be forgotten that poems, plays, and novels are *deliberately* works of the imagination. In approaching paintings, it is essential to be aware of the conventions which an artist of any particular period or style uses in representing reality – the *schemata* he employs, as E.H. Gombrich puts it. A painting of eighteenth-century French peasants eating bread, garlic and wine *may* be evidence as to their regular diet; but there is always the quite strong possibility that the artist might have been more concerned with infusing his painting with the religious symbolism of the Last Supper than with accurate sociological observation.

Origin of source: how created   More fundamental questions lie behind the need to define the category of the source being studied. How and for what purposes did the source come into existence? What person, or group of persons, created the source? What basic attitudes, prejudices, vested interests would he, she, or they have been likely to have had? Who was it created for, or addressed to? It often is very necessary to scrutinize the mechanics, as it were, of how a source comes into being. One of the most illuminating sets of sources for sexual behaviour in the *ancien régime* are the *déclarations de grossesse*, statements required by law from unwed mothers. It is easy to get carried away (as it is with all rich and colourful sources), but the historian has to keep firmly in mind that these are transcriptions, subject to the accuracy and honesty of the scribes, of what the women *said*, not necessarily always of what actually happened. Henry Mayhew's reports in the *Morning Chronicle* are a well-known source for London life in the mid-nineteenth century. Much of the value of the reports lies in the fact that they often contain verbatim accounts from the various people Mayhew interviewed. How accurately did Mayhew report them (the sentence construction of poor working–class people sometimes seems quite remarkable)? To what extent were the interviewees themselves always telling the truth? If we are dealing with a private letter, was it written with the genuine intention of conveying reliable information, or, maybe, to curry favour with the recipient? Here knowledge of the respective social positions of writer and recipient will be useful. If we are dealing with some kind of committee of investigation, it will be useful to know what the sympathies of the writers of the report were. Minutes (of committees, of town councils, etc.), technically recording what a body as a whole *agreed* its decisions to be (though usually not the full debates and arguments), can be incomplete and even slanted.

No one but the historian can comprehend the fascinating variousness of sources; no one better than the historian knows their dreadful fallibility.

Relevance: value for the particular topic   All of the preceding questions lead into a major evaluative one: how relevant to, how valuable for, the particular topic under investigation is the particular source being studied? A variety of sub-questions are involved here. Is the information being conveyed really first-hand? How close were the authors of the source to the events being described? Certain collections of letters have by now become standard literary artefacts. There will always be the question of how representative a source is; of how far a text contains accurate observation, how far merely eccentric opinion. Looking at the intended audience, (see 'Origin of source' above) can often be helpful here. One could, I believe, say that

Mayhew's readership wanted accurate information, and that he would not have survived as a journalist if he had not done his best to provide this. Conduct books, guides to social customs, etiquette, and fashion are important sources for family history, but the question will often be whether actual behaviour is being described or, perhaps, an unattainable ideal. My view, in general, would be that guides and manuals will (rather like guides to home computing today) have to be pretty accurate, or they will be of no value to their potential customers. Often, as in other aspects of historical study, there can be no final resolution. In arguing, some years ago now, that during the Second World War women in general, because of the responsibilities they had to take on, became more confident about their own abilities, and more critical of the automatic supremacy assumed by their husbands, I made considerable use of *Nella Last's war, a mother's diary 1939–45* (Broad and Fleming, 1983). In my view, what Nella Last was entering in her diary was entirely consistent with a good deal of other less specific evidence. However, in 'The effect of the war on the status of women' (in Smith, 1986), Smith questioned the representative nature of Nella Last's diary and criticized my use of it. My view remains that my interpretation was a correct one, but I have to admit that Smith has a fair point. That's history! (The argument is also referred to in Summerfield, 1988.) As already indicated, there are plenty of problems in using novels, or plays, or for that matter films or television programmes as historical sources. Full contextual study really is needed before you can decide whether such a cultural artefact has any relevance to, or significance for, your topic. The author's (director's, etc.) intentions will be important, as will the conditions of production generally. But often most important of all will be contemporary reception: if you have a bestseller on your hands you may be in business; but if, in fact, it's a case of an obscure little work that no one read … be very careful!

The golden rule in handling sources is *never to use a tangential source when there is likely to be a more central one.* For wage rates, do not use a novel, or even a political speech, when there are government or employers' statistics (which themselves, of course, may not necessarily be reliable). Some historians like quoting from novels (e.g. Best, 1973) – it shows a touch of class. The idea may be to demonstrate that a particular attitude, a particular circumstance, is so pervasive that it has permeated even into fiction. If that is the point, it is best for the historian to say so. Historical writing should be explicit, not allusive, not ambiguous, not full of hidden resonances, as one might expect in a novel or a poem. Anyway, the fundamental point is that one does not settle for *any* source, but the *best* source for the particular piece of information in question.

One of the great dangers in historical study is making some snap, smart-alec judgement without bothering with the hard work of asking questions and seeking answers. This is specially tempting with visual sources. In a famous passage in *Mythologies* (1957), Roland Barthes described how, when visiting his hairdresser, he glanced at the illustrated magazine, *Paris Match*: on the cover, a young black soldier in a French uniform was giving the military salute, his eyes raised, 'fixed, no doubt', Barthes surmised, 'on the fold of the tricolour flag'. What this image signifies, continues Barthes, is: 'that France is a great empire which all her sons, without distinction of colour, serve faithfully under her flag, and that there is no better response to the critics of French colonial rule, than the zeal with which this black is serving those who are said to be his oppressors.' Now, that may very well be the significance of this photograph, *placed as it is on the cover of this particular magazine.* Still, the true historian would want to dig a bit further into the question of editorial intentions, hoping to get access to the magazine's own minutes and records. Had the photograph been published, say, in a left-wing magazine, its significance might be very different. Then we have the question of whether the photograph is of a genuine event, or whether, perhaps, the soldier is a model taking part in a carefully contrived set-up. All I am saying here is that, while semiologists no doubt are entitled to go their own way about things, historians, before deciding upon the relevance and usefulness of any particular source to their enquiries, do have to probe as deeply as they can.

'Meaning'   Logically, the point I come to now might well have been put first. It is that no source can be interpreted until it has been fully understood, and that includes understanding it as contemporaries would have understood it. Obviously you will not have got far with a document if, in the first place, you can't even read the damn thing. For certain periods and topics, the specialist skills of palaeography and philology are essential prerequisites. All technical terms, legal phrases, or the names of particular officials or institutions will have to be fully understood. Esoteric allusions (Biblical, or classical, say), and all references to individuals will have to be fully elucidated in order that the meanings and implications of the document can come through. For historians operating outside the purely British context, translation, obviously, can be a problem, and a more fraught one than is sometimes believed. In a Second World War document, a *partisan* (resistance fighter) will usually be a hero; but in a seventeenth-century document, a *partisan* is a villain, a particularly obnoxious kind of tax farmer. These are things learned only through knowledge and experience.

Context   As an abstract, step-by-step analysis of what historians do, this has all been slightly artificial. Historians do not work from single sources, but from a whole mosaic of sources. Each single primary source will be analysed in the light of what is known from other primary sources, and also, of course, from the relevant secondary sources. No one coming to a primary source completely fresh will get much of value from it: perhaps, at best, a simple content summary, a paraphrase, but nothing of the unwitting testimony, or the significance of the source, or its relationship to other sources and to existing interpretations. One of the prime requisites for a historian, alas, is sheer knowledge. The more the historian already knows, the more he or she will get from any particular individual source.

The key steps involved in the evaluation of primary sources are summarized in Schema A.

Schema A: Evaluating a primary source

o   Authenticity: Is the source what it purports to be?

o   Provenance: Where does the source come from?

o   Dating: When exactly was the source produced?

o   Type: To what category does the source belong?

o   Origin: How and for what purpose was the source created?

o   Relevance: How relevant is the source to the topic under investigation?

o   'Meaning': Can the source be fully understood?

o   Context: How should the source be understood and analysed in the context of what is known from other relevant primary and secondary sources?

---

4   CONCEPTS IN HISTORY

The governing purpose behind the analysis and interpretation of primary sources is the production of a piece of history. The writing of history involves many problems, including the organization and structure of the overall argument or interpretation. In producing a coherent argument or interpretation, the historian will be bound to employ generalizations and concepts (whether borrowed from others, or perhaps invented specially to deal with the particular problems thrown up in an investigation).

But the two activities, analysing and interpreting sources, and producing the work of written history, are not separate. As the historian perceives that certain concepts ('legitimacy', say, or, 'class', or, perhaps, 'community') are going to be indispensable in writing up the final work, they will inevitably be applied in the actual analysis of the sources themselves.

Concepts are vital to historical study at all stages. None the less, the hallmark of the historian is to treat all concepts with caution and scepticism. If they cease to be supported by empirical evidence, they have to be modified or abandoned. Concepts should never take over, should never dominate, the sources.

EXERCISE 2.1

1   I suggest that you now go back and read the ten points with which this chapter began, making sure that you fully understand what I am saying, and my reasons for saying it.

2   Take any source on which you are currently working and assess it in the light of the eight key points discussed in section 3 and summarized in Schema A. (You will find it useful to return to this exercise from time to time for any important source you are using.)

FURTHER READING

For 'mainstream' approaches to history, see Marwick (1989) and (for the debate on the status of primary sources) Marwick (1993); for an approach building on Marx and receptive to Foucault (not essential unless you are interested), see Tosh (1991).

REFERENCES

Barthes, R. (1957) *Mythologies*, Paris, Seuil.

Best, G. (1973) *Mid-Victorian Britain, 1851–1875*, St Albans, Panther (originally published in 1971 by Weidenfeld).

Broad, R. and Fleming, S. (eds) (1983) *Nella Last's war: a mother's diary, 1939–45*, London, Sphere.

Hardy, F.E. (1928) *The early life of Thomas Hardy, 1840–1891*, London, Macmillan.

Hardy, F.E. (1930) *The later years of Thomas Hardy, 1892–1928*, London, Macmillan.

Marwick, A. (1989) *The nature of history* (3rd edn), London, Macmillan.

Marwick, A (1993) '"A fetishism of documents?"; the salience of source-based history', in Kozicki, H. (ed.) *Developments in modern historiography*, London, Macmillan.

Mayhew, H. (1981–2) *The Morning Chronicle survey of labour and the poor: the metropolitan districts*, Horsham, Caliban (five volumes).

Smith, H.L. (ed.) (1986) *War and social change: British society in the Second World War*, Manchester, Manchester University Press.

Summerfield, P. (1988) 'Women, war and social change. Women in Britain in World War II', in Marwick, A. (ed.) *Total war and social change*, Basingstoke, Macmillan.

Thompson, E.P. (1980) *The making of the English working class*, Harmondsworth, Penguin Books.

Tosh, J. (1991) *The pursuit of history: aims, methods and new directions in the study of modern history* (2nd edn), London, Longman.

PART II

USING SOURCES

⁜ ⁜ ⁜

CHAPTER 3

THE CENSUS, 1801–1991

by Dennis Mills (section 1) and Michael Drake (section 2)

The census is undoubtedly the most important source for family and community historians of the nineteenth and twentieth centuries. It thus appropriately opens this series of chapters on using sources. Taken virtually every ten years since 1801, the census contains a vast amount of information about virtually every man, woman and child in the United Kingdom and Ireland. Original copies of the census reports are comparatively rare, but facsimile or microfiche copies are available in some libraries and record offices. As for the manuscript census enumerators' books (CEBs), British law currently prohibits the release of these until 100 years have elapsed (referred to as the '100-year rule'); therefore only the CEBs for 1841–91 are available for inspection. In Ireland most of the original returns prior to 1901 have been destroyed. However, the householder schedules for 1901 and 1911 are available. Both these and the British CEBs are obtainable in a variety of formats: microfilm, transcripts, computer disks. Together they form a rich and accessible resource for researchers.

Here we shall deal with both the printed census reports and the unprinted CEBs, the analysis of which provided the material for those reports. We shall be paying less attention to locating the reports and CEBs, and more on how to assess them as primary sources (see also Chapter 2) and on how to use them for research into family and community history.

We have decided to look at the census reports first. There are several reasons for this. First, when starting a piece of research based on unprinted sources such as the CEBs, it is a good idea to see the context in which they appeared: in our case this means how the census was taken. This comes out in the reports. Secondly, the comments preceding the tabular material in the reports often draw attention to the shortcomings of the CEBs. Two examples drawn from the Scottish census reports will illustrate this. The first concerns the definition of a house. In 1861 Scotland was forced to adopt the English definition of a house, resulting in 'the returns for Scotland [being] … utterly worthless' (*Census of Great Britain, 1861*, British Parliamentary Papers (BPP), 1862, vol. L, p.971). The reason for this was that:

> *While an English town tends to spread over a great breadth of surface – the house of each family being 'a building within party walls' – the Scottish town is crowded into lesser space, and the houses are built, as it were one over another, so that they rise to a height of six or more storeys, each storey or flat being a distinct house, as independent of the others as are the separate houses of England; and moreover they are generally possessed by different proprietors.*

(BPP, 1862, vol. L, p.972)

The second case concerns the column in the CEB asking for information on the number of children aged from 5 to 15 years who were attending school. With refreshing honesty the census report noted:

> *It is difficult to say now what was the exact object sought to be attained by that inquiry; but if it meant to elicit the* number of the population of these ages receiving instruction, *it failed to accomplish its purpose. Thus, the very wording of the clause excluded,* Firstly, *all those children who from ill health or other causes were unable to attend school during the first week of April.* Secondly, *it excluded all those receiving instruction at home through tutors or governesses, and* Thirdly, *it excluded the whole children [those fit and well] attending those schools which, in several parts of Scotland, are shut during the month of April, in order to permit the children to aid in the Spring Agricultural operations.*

(BPP, 1862, vol. L, p.980)

The question was repeated in the 1871 census, although this time 'children being educated at home under a *tutor* or *governess*' were to be included and the age range changed to 5–13.

A final point to note is that there were variations in the information sought from different parts of a country. Thus, for example, the 1881 Scottish census report gave information on Gaelic speakers, though there was no column for this on the example of a completed householder schedule sent to each householder. A copy of this schedule appears in the report (see Figure 3.8).

1   PRINTED CENSUS INFORMATION 1801–1991

The first task of a community historian is to choose and define a community, a task that will vary according to the intended theme. For example, the study of an institution such as a friendly society, using its minute books, will demand much less attention to geography than a demographic analysis of half a dozen suburban streets in a growing Victorian city. Nevertheless, a friendly society did not operate in a territorial vacuum, and its history will reflect the socio-demographic characteristics of the population it served. So too will the history of a family or group of families.

A preliminary study of appropriate census reports will, therefore, frequently be useful in providing the context for specific research topics, and essential as a starting point for most projects in community history. In fact this last point cannot be stressed too much. For by examining the reports you will not only discover the background to census taking, as noted earlier; you will also get a general idea of the community you are interested in or, if not the precise community, the district of which it is a part. Through this you may well pick up pointers to matters bearing upon your specific interests. Above all you will be able to see the development of your community over a relatively long time-span.

For every administrative unit in Britain, the total population, the numbers of males and females, and varying amounts of other socio-demographic information were recorded in every tenth year from 1801 to 1991, excepting 1941 because of the war, and with the addition of the 1966 sample census. Parallel information is available for Ireland from 1821 (see Tables 3.4 and 3.5 for the complete list of dates). This section makes some suggestions about how to use the printed census reports.

1.1   WHERE TO START

Your work will almost certainly involve visits to a central public library, a county record office, or an academic library. Try to make a short first enquiry; don't be afraid to tell the librarian what you have in mind. A good starting point might be a county or town history, where the author may have done some analysis of census data.

After this refer to county trade directories, along with old Ordnance Survey maps, to get a general impression of administrative units and their boundaries. In particular, notice in which *hundred* or *wapentake* your prospective area of study was situated; these ancient administrative areas were used exclusively by the English census authorities from 1801 to 1831. Notice too in which *Poor Law union* your area was to be found, this being coterminous with the *registration district* used by the Registrar General for registering births, marriages and deaths in England and Wales in 1837 and for taking the census in 1841 and subsequently. Poor Law unions were groups of parishes brought together (hence *union*) for the effective administration of poor relief, in accordance with the Poor Law of 1834. One aspect of this was the building of a workhouse in each union.

Lewis's *Topographical dictionaries* (1831–1846) are similarly useful and are available for all parts of the British Isles in the first half of the last century. Invaluable for Scotland are the three sets of Statistical Accounts for each county (one for the 1790s, and then the mid-nineteenth-century and twentieth-century updates – see Chapter 4, section 6). In Ireland the Royal Dublin Society published statistical surveys of 23 of the 32 Irish counties between 1801 and 1832. There is also the *Parliamentary gazetteer of Ireland*, published in three volumes in 1846; the Irish Ordnance Survey memoirs (the field notebooks used by the surveyors compiling the OS maps of Ireland in the 1820s and 1830s, mostly of the northern half of the country), currently being reissued in 38 volumes (Day and McWilliams, 1991–); and the great survey by Richard Griffith, the *General valuation of Ireland*, published in over 200 parts.

The next source – the Victoria County History – is now available for most English counties. The first volumes appeared at the beginning of the twentieth century and the process goes on. The population table is generally found in Volume II of a county's history (with the reference usually being given as, for example, VCH Kent II). These tables usually cover only the period 1801–1901, with exceptions such as Kent (1801–1921) and Cheshire (1801–1971). We shall look at a few examples to give you an idea of the information available and how to use it in identifying a study population.

The population table in VCH Oxon II for the period 1801–1901 has parishes grouped in the ancient hundreds, following the editor's view that his purpose was to take the historic situation forward to 1901. The wide choice of communities by size becomes apparent very quickly, as, for example, in the Wootton Hundred in 1801, where there were populations ranging from 53 at Over Worton to 1,552 at Deddington. Comparison between directories and maps and this population table shows that some substantial hamlets like Hempton and Clifton, which lie in Deddington parish but are situated over a mile from the main village, are omitted from VCH. Similarly, use maps to help you avoid choosing a community split by a parish boundary, like Wilmington in Devon where the parish boundary between Offwell and Widworthy ran down the main street until recent decades; likewise, Woodstock in Oxfordshire had some houses in Wootton parish, and so on in many places.

Where there was considerable change because of industrialization, as in mining communities, or because of urban growth, great care has to be exercised. For instance, for Nottingham, the VCH population table carries on until 1901 as if the boundary extension of 1877 had never occurred, suggesting that Nottingham had a population total of 113,590 in 1881. Fortunately, Nottingham has at least one city history which shows that within the new boundary there were 186,575 people (Gray, 1953, p. 113; see also below in section 1.3).

Problems of this kind are alleviated by a few newer style VCH population tables, as in VCH Cheshire II, which works backwards from the 1971 boundaries, as well as forwards from those of 1801. For instance, Alderley Edge, first identified as an administrative entity in 1894 by the renaming of Chorley Urban District as Alderley Edge UD, is distinguished from the ancient parish of Alderley, with its separate townships of Nether Alderley, Over Alderley and Great Warford, all of which became civil parishes between the 1871 and 1881 censuses.

Such matters are usually resolved by recourse to the census reports themselves, but at least the VCH population tables give a good initial overview. There are similar problems concerning parish acreages, for which no really accurate figures on a standardized basis were available until the Ordnance Survey's measurements of the third quarter of the nineteenth century. These acreages are to be found in most VCH population tables, but are related back to the boundaries of 1801, so look out for subsequent changes.

For the rural historian it is desirable to use acreage figures to calculate comparative population densities, which help to differentiate the effects of soil fertility and land use practices, settlement control by landowners, and the distribution of industries and of trades/craftsmen in large numbers. Population density is generally calculated on the basis of the numbers of persons per square mile: change acreages to square miles by dividing by 640 (the more numerate may wish to calculate metric equivalents as well). Changes in acreages from the mid-Victorian period onwards help to pinpoint changes in the administrative units used for census purposes.

1.2   CENSUS REPORTS: THE GENERAL PICTURE

After preliminary investigations in directories, VCH population tables and local histories, and having made a preliminary choice of community, you are now ready to consult the census reports themselves. At this point ask about runs of reports kept in your library: many may not be on the open shelves. You should also ask if your library has copies of, or access to, the 1,000-volume facsimile reprint of the British Parliamentary Papers (BPP) published by the Irish University Press (they contain most of the census reports), or the Chadwyck-Healey microfiche edition (see Chapter 5, section 1 below on parliamentary papers). The library may hold the following guides to census reports:

General Register Office (1951) *Guides to official sources no. 2, census reports of Great Britain 1801–1931,* London, HMSO. A revised edition was published as:

Office of Population Censuses and Surveys and the General Register Office, Edinburgh (1977) *Guide to census reports, Great Britain 1801–1966,* London, HMSO; see especially pp. 270–3 for areas.

Also look out for interpretative texts, such as those dealing primarily with England and Wales:

Wrigley, E. A. (ed.) (1971) *Nineteenth-century society: essays in the use of quantitative methods for the study of social data,* Cambridge, Cambridge University Press. This is especially useful for the summary of tables in the census reports 1801–91, showing what information is available for which administrative areas (e.g. ancient parishes, county boroughs) at each census, and giving the same treatment for Scotland as for England and Wales (pp.37–46).

Lawton, R. (ed.) (1978) *The census and social structure: an interpretative guide to nineteenth century censuses for England and Wales,* London, Frank Cass. This is useful for the questions asked at individual censuses (pp. 292–3) and the principal areas (i.e. administrative levels) for which populations are given in the census reports of 1801–1931.

Higgs, E. (1988) *Making sense of the census: the manuscript returns for England and Wales, 1801–1901,* London, HMSO for the Public Record Office. As the title indicates, this book concentrates on the census enumerators' books, but in so doing discusses in detail the questions asked at the censuses, and therefore the types of information available in tabular form in the reports. See also the work of Lumas (1992a, 1992b) listed in the 'References and further reading'.

For Scotland, see Flinn, M. W. (ed.) (1977) *Scottish population history from the seventeenth century to the 1930s,* Cambridge, Cambridge University Press.

For Ireland, see Vaughan, W.E. and Fitzpatrick, A.J. (1978) *Irish historical statistics: population 1821–1971*, Dublin, Royal Irish Academy.

Comparative data for all counties in the British Isles and the principal towns of the UK appear in:

Mitchell, B.R. (1988) *British historical statistics*, Cambridge, Cambridge University Press, and previous editions under slightly different titles.

The key information in most nineteenth-century census reports at the level of the smallest administrative units appears under the following headings:

Population totals

Totals of males and females

Houses inhabited

Houses uninhabited

Houses building (i.e. being built)

Acreages (note the caveats in section 1.1 above)

Crude occupational groups in the period 1801–31

Information about language in Scotland 1881–91 and in Wales in 1891

In 1861 information about numbers of rooms per house appears for Scotland, though not until 1891 for England and Wales.

At the level of larger administrative units, such as boroughs and counties, information can also be expected on the following:

Ages

Marital status

Birthplaces, usually by county

Occupations

Number of rooms in household

Deaf, dumb, blind (1851–91), to which imbecile, idiot, lunatic added from 1871.

Information on religion and education was collected separately in 1851.

Reports may be used in conjunction with details derived from the CEBs from 1841. The smallest units appearing in the reports may take up less than one CEB for a small village, perhaps one CEB for a village of 400–800 people, while in very large towns several dozen enumerators may have been employed. The reports often contain figures for the several wards or ancient parishes within a town.

Data for Ireland vary marginally from the British norm, but the administrative hierarchy is different and more complex (see Collins, 1993). The *topographical indexes* in census reports for 1851, 1871 and 1901 are very helpful. An example is shown in Table 3.1.

Table 3.1 Extract from the 1901 census of Ireland, topographical index, townland of Tullyballydonnell

Population: 79; inhabited houses: 19

OS Sheet No.	Area	County	Barony	Parish	County District	District Electoral Division	Number in County Book
62,63	373 ac.	Antrim	Upper Massereene	Ballinderry	Lurgan No.3	Ballinderry	155

Census reports were usually published in several volumes. The earlier volumes for each census contain information at the national level and larger administrative units, such as counties and large towns. Later volumes contain data for the smallest census units down to wards or parishes. Frequently local collections contain county reports for the period from 1901; otherwise individual counties are found in larger volumes containing several counties, the whole of Scotland, and so on.

There is no room here to give the lengthy bibliographical details of the census reports. Many can be found in the 'guide books' listed above. However, it is useful to know that the likely Dewey classification number is 304.6021, and that libraries often use the heading 'Great Britain: Censuses' as the key to finding census reports in their subject index and 'Great Britain: Parliamentary Papers', 'British Parliamentary Papers', 'Registrar General' or 'OPCS' in their author index. Northern Ireland censuses after 1921 may be cited under 'Northern Ireland Registrar General', and the Irish Republic censuses under 'Eire: Department of Industry and Commerce' (1926 and 1936) and 'Eire: Central Statistical Office' (censuses of 1946 and later).

1.3   CENSUS REPORTS: A CLOSER LOOK

The use of census data may be illustrated through examples. The first involves a return to the implications of Nottingham's boundary extension of 1877. From 1871 to 1891 the Census Office for England and Wales published population tables for 'geographical counties' (Volume 1) and 'registration or union counties' (Volume 2). The former date back to time immemorial and were made up of hundreds and wapentakes. The latter stem from the Act of 1834 empowering Poor Law commissioners to create districts (or unions) for administering poor relief without necessarily taking notice of old county boundaries. They created 626 districts, and when grouped together they formed the registration or union counties. The average registration county contained a dozen or so registration districts. For Nottingham, the census report for 1881 (Volume I, Summary Table VI) indicates a population of 186,575 within the municipal borough, compared with 113,590 suggested by VCH Notts II. But the 1881 report, like Gray (1953, p.113), refers to the borough *after* the boundary extensions that took place after the census of 1871 when the borough had a population of only 86,621, so explaining the huge increase of about 100,000 people. In the same report, the main Table 3 breaks the Nottingham borough total down by civil parishes, townships and wards; Table 8 gives further information for ecclesiastical parishes and districts, revealing that the ancient parishes of St Mary and St Nicholas had been split into 15 new districts between 1845 and 1874. For the whole of Nottinghamshire, Table 7 gives information on civil parishes and townships in alphabetical order.

Volume II of the 1881 census report is set out by registration districts in a format similar to that shown in Figure 3.1. Table 4 in Volume II of the population tables shows that the Nottingham Registration District was divided into eleven sub-districts, but even this large number did not include all the extended borough. Table 5 solves the problem because it summarizes data by sanitary districts, of which the borough was one, and shows that it also included the civil parishes of Basford and Bulwell, with a population of nearly 27,000, giving the total of 186,575.

New towns have a different set of problems. For example, in 1851 Crewe Town was situated not in Crewe township, but in the township of Monks Coppenhall, with a total population of 4,571, of which some were living in the old village of that name. Exactly how many is not given in the census report, so recourse to the CEBs would be necessary to establish it, unless it has been published in a local history.

In Scunthorpe the complications of town growth in a once entirely agricultural area have been studied in some detail. Amongst other developments, Armstrong (1981) charted the several phases of administrative change culminating in borough status in 1936. Using large-scale Ordnance Survey maps, the 1918 Minutes of Inquiry into Proposed Amalgamation, and other sources, Pocock (1970) traced population change across the 1918 amalgamation, as shown in Table 3.2.

Table 3.2 Summary of population changes in Scunthorpe, 1871–1961

Old rural townships	1871	1911	1918 (est.)	New town wards	1918 (est.)	1939 (est.)	1961
Crosby	288	3339	5575	Crosby, Park	5500	12000	11189
Scunthorpe	701	10171	12312	West, Town, East	12300	14200	13146
Frodingham	577	1734	1750	Frodingham and Brumby	3600	11500	21358
Brumby	178	1197	2004				
Ashby	669	3237	3735	Ashby	3700	6200	21631
Totals	2413	19678	25376	Totals	25100	43900	67324

Source : Pocock (1970) pp.52 and 60

EXERCISE 3.1

Refer to Table 3.2 and calculate the percentage increases in total population for the periods (a) 1871 to 1911 and (b) 1918 (using the wards total) to 1961. Comment on the appropriateness of using percentage increases in a situation such as this.

Answers/comments p.298.

Notice that the two old units of Frodingham and Brumby were combined by the census authorities after 1918, thus inhibiting comparisons of population before and after that date. Pocock also discovered that 300 people in New Brumby had been misplaced in Frodingham by the 1881 census report because the boundaries between Frodingham and Brumby were not clearly understood (Pocock, 1970, p. 52). You should check for local work of this invaluable kind, as it will prevent mistakes and the wastage of time in using census reports.

A final example arises from the work of a local history class at Scopwick, ten miles south of Lincoln, to which I presented some statistics on house occupancy from the census reports of 1921 to 1971. This provided the background for a discussion of socio-demographic change and of housing conditions (also using a survey of sanitary facilities in the parish in the 1960s by the rural district council). As in many areas of rural England, the combined population of the ancient parishes of Scopwick and Kirkby Green peaked in the nineteenth century (at 558 in 1861, see Figure 3.1), and declined steadily to 426 in 1901, reviving to 468 in 1911.

Table 3.3 demonstrates a number of general problems: first, the combination of two ancient parishes into one civil parish during the 1920s; second, changes took place in the presentation of data; and third, there are complications caused by institutional populations, in this case an RAF station, which grossly inflated the parochial totals. Other places might contain, for instance, a hospital, boarding school, workhouse or prison, and these should be removed before calculating mean household size or house occupancy rates. Not all institutions are identified in the census reports, but the bigger anomalies are likely to be taken into account.

In some districts, for example fishing ports, there might be the opposite problem of residents being away on census night. In the period covered by Table 3.3 the reports take this factor into account by recording the numbers absent from private households (or private families to use the older term), making it possible to calculate the 'normal resident population' in private households, including those absent on census night.

TABLE 4.—AREA; HOUSES and INHABITANTS, 1861 and 1871, in PARISHES, &c.—*continued*.

SUPERINTENDENT REGISTRAR'S DISTRICT.			Area in Statute Acres	HOUSES.						POPULATION.					
				1861.			1871.			Persons.		Males.		Females.	
Registrar's Sub-district.	Parish, Township, or Place.			Inha-bited.	Un-inha-bited.	Build-ing.	Inha-bited.	Un-inha-bited.	Build-ing.	1861.	1871.	1861.	1871.	1861.	1871.
	419. SLEAFORD.														
1. Billinghay	North Kyme - - -	¹Township	3490	108	4	–	138	–	–	455	700	224	347	231	353
	Billinghay ³ - - -	¹Township	}6780	299	11	–	323	9	–	1403	1501	698	711	705	790
	Walcott - - -	- Hamlet		129	1	2	129	–	1	605	609	300	306	305	303
	Timberland ⁴ - -	- Township	}9190	121	2	–	113	6	–	589	563	289	277	300	286
	Martin - - -	- Hamlet		181	8	–	185	2	–	909	914	475	467	434	447
	Thorpe Tilney - -	- Hamlet		23	–	–	26	–	–	120	158	59	78	61	80
	Blankney - - -	- Parish	6000	90	4	–	94	2	–	560	568	296	292	264	276
	Scopwick - - -	- Parish	3190	79	2	–	83	4	–	383	404	204	209	179	195
	Kirkby Green - -	- Parish	437	27	1	–	28	1	1	175	141	81	76	94	65
	Rowston - - -	- Parish	1520	43	1	2	46	1	–	224	233	114	115	110	118
2. Sleaford -	Temple Bruer - -	- *Parish*	3910	13	–	1	19	6	–	104	149	67	83	37	66
	Brauncewell - -	- Parish	3470	18	–	–	24	1	–	112	139	63	81	49	58
	Bloxholme - -	- Parish	1298	23	1	–	21	–	–	115	84	55	39	60	45
	Ashby-de-la-Laund -	- Parish	2880	28	–	–	26	–	–	176	161	94	91	82	70
	Digby - - -	- Parish	2382	67	4	–	70	2	–	330	307	166	150	164	157
	Dorrington - -	- Parish	680	102	4	1	108	3	2	467	495	234	263	233	232
	Ruskington - -	- Parish	4750	240	8	1	247	7	–	1089	1156	552	569	537	587

Figure 3.1 A specimen page from the 1871 census, *Population tables, area, houses and inhabitants*, Volume II, *Registration counties* (Source: British Parliamentary Papers, vol. LXVI, Part II, Session 1872)

Notes

1 This section of the report shows part of Registration District 419, Sleaford, within the Registration County of Lincolnshire. Billinghay sub-district includes the parishes of Scopwick and Kirkby Green which are mentioned in the text. The notes indicated by the superscript numbers give additional information about population changes, house building and boundaries. The acreages given were estimates, e.g. the 6,000 acres at Blankney is corrected in later reports to 6,781 acres following the Ordnance Survey's work.

2 The order in which parishes appear in tables of this kind is generally the order in which the CEBs are stored and listed, the same order being used for microfilms. As the registration districts were based on Poor Law unions, which sometimes stretched across the boundaries of ancient counties, the registration counties differed somewhat from the latter. Parishes caught in this 'trap' are usually listed in two places, or cross-references are given.

Table 3.3 Scopwick and Kirkby Green, Lincolnshire: some population and housing data, 1921–71

Ancient parishes	Population			Households	Normal residential population	Rooms	Rooms per person	Mean household size	RAF Digby
	Persons	Males	Females						
1921									
Scopwick	423	231	192	80	353	431	1.22	4.4	70 (est.)
Kirkby Green	147	76	71	27	135	134	0.99	5.0	

Civil parish of Scopwick & Kirkby Green	Population			Households	Normal residential population	Rooms	Persons per room	Mean household size	RAF Digby
	Persons	Males	Females						
1931	1039	716	323	120	413	543	0.76	3.4	626
1951	1170	855	315	127	425	574	0.74	3.3	745
1961	783	576	207	142	430	705	0.61	3.0	353
1971	639	390	249	160	475	833	0.57	3.0	164

Source: census reports for 1921 to 1971

The main change in the presentation of data occurred between 1921 and 1931, when the ratio of rooms to persons was reversed from rooms per person to persons per room, so a little arithmetic is necessary to make a comparison between these censuses.

_____ **EXERCISE 3.2** _____

Calculate the number of persons per room in 1921, taking the figures for Scopwick and Kirkby Green together.

Answer/comments p.298.

House occupancy rates have to be seen within the context of changes in mean household size, since any fall in this index will lessen overcrowding without alteration to house structures. By 1901 mean household size in Scopwick and Kirkby Green had declined to 3.98 persons per household from a peak of well over five persons half a century before. By 1911 it had risen again to 4.3, the most likely reason being larger numbers of children, but by 1931 it had fallen to 3.4 and subsequently followed the national trend downwards.

When figures for house occupancy were first collected in 1921 (in England and Wales – earlier in Scotland) the rooms counted were: living rooms, bedrooms and kitchens, while bathrooms, sculleries and closets were excluded. Subsequent minor alterations of terminology have probably not caused any more distortions than those arising from interpretations in individual circumstances. With a figure of 0.86 persons per room in 1921, declining to 0.57 persons in 1971, house occupancy rates fell sharply. The Scopwick local history class realized that this was only partly explained by house extensions and the larger average size of new houses, and that the count of rooms does not take into account wide variations in the housing stock, which contains old farm houses, modest cottages, and modern houses.

1.4   COMPARING LOCAL WITH NATIONAL TRENDS

You will find it illuminating to compare the population characteristics of communities with those of the country as a whole. When the national population was increasing rapidly, an individual community had to move upwards at the same rate in order not to fall behind national norms. Tables 3.4 and 3.5 summarize population change in the British Isles, making possible comparisons between individual communities and national trends. The work by Mitchell (1988) and the census reports provide opportunities for other comparisons, e.g. between an individual unit and the county in which it was situated, or between urban and rural communities.

The course of population change has many social and economic implications. A declining or static community is often an ageing community, while a hallmark of most rapidly growing communities is youthfulness. In-migrants attracted by good employment prospects are likely to be predominantly young adults in the process of family formation, which also contributes to lower average ages.

The sex ratio, usually expressed as the number of females per 1,000 (or 100) males, is also a significant indicator of employment structure. Mining communities, agricultural areas without domestic industries, and manufacturing areas with male-dominant industries (e.g. shipbuilding or foundry towns) usually show a male bias, whereas old-established towns and resorts with large numbers of domestic servants show a female bias. However, the national 'surplus' of females throughout the period of the census reports must be taken into account.

Table 3.4 Summary of census data, 1801–1991, Wales and Ireland

	Wales				Ireland			
	Total population (000s)	Increase since last census (000s)	%	Females per 1000 males	Total Population (000s)	Increase since last census (000s)	%	Females per 1000 males
1801	587			1102				
1811	673	86	14.7	1089				
1821	794	121	18.0	1032	6802			1035
1831	904	110	13.9	1029	7767	966	14.2	1047
1841	1046	142	15.7	1018	8178	411	5.3	1033
1851	1163	117	11.2	999	6554	-1624	-19.9	1053
1861	1280	117	10.1	1005	5799	-753	-11.5	1044
1871	1413	132	10.3	1001	5412	-387	-6.7	1050
1881	1572	159	11.3	999	5175	-238	-4.4	1042
1891	1771	200	12.7	985	4705	-470	-9.1	1029
1901	2013	241	13.6	990	4459	-246	-5.2	1027
1911	2421	408	20.3	965	4390	-69	-1.5	1003
1921	2656	236	9.7	997				
1931	2593	-63	-2.4	1004				
1939	2487	-106	-4.1	1025				
(1939 mid-year estimates from National Registration)								
1951	2599	112	4.5	1046				
1961	2644	45	1.7	1047				
1971	2731	87	3.3	1047				
1981	2792	61	2.2	1062				
1991	2812	20	0.7	1069				
					Northern Ireland			
1926					1257			1066
1937					1280	23	1.8	1054
1951					1371	91	7.1	1053
1961					1425	54	3.9	1053
1971					1536	111	7.8	1034
1981					1533	-3	-0.2	1045
1989					1583 (estimate)			
1991					1573	41	2.7	1054
					Republic of Ireland			
1926					2972			972
1936					2968	-4	-0.1	952
1946					2955	-13	-4.4	977
1951					2961	6	0.2	965
1961					2818	-143	-4.8	990
1971					2978	160	6.0	991
1981					3443	465	15.6	991
1991					3523 (preliminary)			1011

Sources: For Wales: Williams (1985) p.7; for Ireland: Mitchell (1988) p.10, based on census reports with a few modifications. For 1989, 1991: Hunter (1992) and *Census of population of Ireland, 1991, preliminary reports, areas*, p.6 and p.10; for Northern Ireland, *Census 1991, summary report*, p.1.

Table 3.5 Summary of census data, 1801–1991, England and Wales, and Scotland

| | England & Wales | | | | Scotland | | | |
	Total population (000s)	Increase since last census (000s)	%	Females per 1000 males	Total population (000s)	Increase since last census (000s)	%	Females per 1000 males
1801	8 893			1 057	1 608			1 176
1811	10 164	1 272	14.3	1 054	1 806	197	12.3	1 185
1821	12 000	1 836	18.1	1 036	2 092	286	15.8	1 129
1831	13 897	1 897	15.8	1 040	2 364	273	13.0	1 122
1841	15 914	2 017	14.5	1 046	2 620	256	10.8	1 110
1851	17 928	2 013	12.6	1 042	2 889	269	10.3	1 100
1861	20 066	2 139	11.9	1 053	3 062	174	6.0	1 112
1871	22 712	2 646	13.2	1 054	3 360	298	9.7	1 096
1881	25 974	3 262	14.4	1 055	3 736	376	11.2	1 076
1891	29 003	3 028	11.7	1 063	4 026	290	7.8	1 072
1901	32 528	3 525	12.2	1 068	4 472	446	11.1	1 057
1911	36 070	3 543	10.9	1 068	4 761	289	6.5	1 062
1921	37 887	1 816	5.0	1 096	4 882	122	2.6	1 080
1931	39 952	2 066	5.4	1 088	4 843	-40	-0.8	1 083
1939	41 460	1 508	3.8	1 081	5 007	164	3.4	1 076
	(1939 mid-year estimates from National Registration)							
1951	43 758	2 298	5.5	1 082	5 096	90	1.8	1 094
1961	46 105	2 347	5.4	1 067	5 179	83	1.6	1 086
1971	48 750	2 645	5.7	1 058	5 229	50	1.0	1 079
1981	49 155	405	0.8	1 059	5 131	-98	-1.9	1 080
1991	48 968 (preliminary)				4 957 (preliminary)			

Source: 1801–1981: Mitchell (1988) p.9, based on census reports, with a few modifications; 1991: Hunter (1992)

1.5   SMALL AREA STATISTICS: THE CURRENT SITUATION

Starting with the 1961 census, the Census Office has made available information on a very large number of variables for individual enumeration districts, including persons present in private households and several types of institutions; age-sex data; countries of origin; employment; housing tenure and conditions; household composition; socio-economic groups; car ownership; and travel to work. This was originally made available on magnetic tape, but some libraries have acquired print-outs. Starting with the 1971 census, microfiches have become available, and are sometimes found in larger libraries. In particular it should be noted that, starting with the 1981 census, county reports have been discontinued, making it necessary to consult microfiche tables in order to find population totals for the smaller administrative units such as civil parishes. In some parts of the country, planning departments have abstracted these simple totals, sometimes with supporting information such as numbers of males and females, and printed them in booklets which may be found in public libraries.

2   THE CENSUS ENUMERATORS' BOOKS (CEBs)

As the name indicates, these books were compiled by the census enumerators. They consist of transcripts of the census forms left with and completed by each individual householder and then collected by the census enumerator – a routine essentially the same in 1991 as in 1841. Much depended in the early days on the census enumerators, when illiteracy meant they had to take a hand in completing the schedules on behalf of some householders (and the point that *any* household head might have problems is amusingly illustrated in Figure 3.2). They had also, when copying the householders' schedules into the CEBs, to add certain information, such as the address, the number of the schedule, and information on uninhabited houses or those in the process of building; in Scotland only, information was gathered on the number of rooms with windows and whether any members of the household were temporarily absent. Information was also to be provided on persons living in tents or caravans, on boats, etc. Thus there was rather more involved than merely delivering and collecting the householders' schedules.

The census authorities did not have too much faith in the enumerators, and this affected the way the forms were drawn up and the relative simplicity of the duties to be carried out. For instance, it would appear that the reason we have the name of every individual on the census forms from 1841 onwards, and why the names were written 'at length', was because otherwise 'an enumerator may sit at home and make *marks* and no examiner could detect the errors' (*History of the census of 1841*, p.5). That such suspicions were generally unfounded is indicated by the fact that in Scotland in 1871, of the 8,342 enumerators employed, only one had to be prosecuted for making false returns (*Census of Scotland, 1871*, p.1). *The Times* reported that applications for the post of enumerator in London in 1861 'were exceedingly numerous and instances occur in which clergymen, scripture readers and others, influenced by philanthropic motives, have expressed a desire to enumerate districts inhabited by the poorer classes' (5 February 1860). In 1891, however, Ogle, the Superintendent of Statistics at the General Register Office, was highly critical of the enumerators: 'on the whole rather a poor lot … very unsatisfactory … their mere handwriting and the general aspect of their work showed that a great many of them were very illiterate men' (*Report of the Committee … to inquire into … the taking of the census*, 1890, pp.30–1). In fact Ogle didn't have a good word for many other aspects of the census (the work of the registrars who supervised the enumerators was done 'very badly', while a

Figure 3.2 Taking the census, a cartoon by George Cruikshank, 1851 (Source: *The comic almanack*, second series 1844–1853, published 1878, London, Chatto & Windus)

'very large proportion of the clerks' at the central office in 1881 'turned out to be absolutely unfit for any work at all'), so perhaps he was a somewhat jaundiced character. Nevertheless, Ogle's comments and the extreme wariness of the census authorities when it came to putting any more of a burden on enumerators than was absolutely necessary, does alert us to keeping our eyes open when working with the CEBs. The instructions had to be interpreted by a temporary staff of thousands, and in advising householders it was inevitable that anomalies would occur.

2.1   WHAT IS IN THE CEBs?

Before looking at the strengths and shortcomings of the CEBs it is worth noting what geographical areas they covered (Table 3.6) and the information they contained (Table 3.7 and Figures 3.4–3.8). The enumerator was required to annotate each page according to the area it covered; for example, if in 1881 the people named on the page lived in a particular urban sanitary district he would give the name of it, and strike through the heading 'Rural Sanitary District', or vice versa. When the schedules belonging to a particular civil parish, municipal borough, urban sanitary district, etc. had been entered, the enumerator was to state, for instance, 'End of the Civil Parish of —', leave the rest of the page blank, and put the following schedule on the first line of the next page. If followed correctly (and regrettably this was not always the case) these instructions are of great value to the family or community historian, for they not only provide the limits of different types of community (ecclesiastical, political, sanitary), but they also make it easier to link information contained in the census with that provided by other sources, such as electoral registers and poll books (municipal wards and parliamentary boroughs), or registers of births or deaths, and Medical Officer of Health reports (sanitary districts).

The information sought by each census varied both over time and between countries. The differences were, however, comparatively minor (see Table 3.7 and Figures 3.6 and 3.7) and much less than some important lobbyists wanted (see Drake, 1972, pp.7–19).

Table 3.6 Area descriptions at the head of each page of the CEBs (England and Wales)

	Census of:	
1841	1851	1861
City or Borough of Parish or Township of	Parish or Township of Ecclesiastical District of City or Borough of Town of Village of	Parish or Township of City or Municipal Borough of Municipal Ward of Parliamentary Borough of Town of Hamlet or Tithing of Ecclesiastical District of
1871	1881	1891
Civil Parish [or Township] of City or Municipal Borough of Municipal Ward of Parliamentary Borough of Town of Village or Hamlet etc. of Local Board [or Improvement Commissioner's District] of	Civil Parish [or Township] of City or Municipal Borough of Municipal Ward of Parliamentary Borough of Town or Village or Hamlet of Urban Sanitary District of Rural Sanitary District of Ecclesiastical Parish or District of	Administrative County of Civil Parish of Municipal Borough of Municipal Ward of Urban Sanitary District of Town or Village or Hamlet of Rural Sanitary District of Parliamentary Borough or Division of Ecclesiastical Parish or District of

Table 3.7 Structure of a CEB, 1841–91 (England and Wales, and Scotland)

Number of householder's schedule[1]

Name of street etc. and number or name of house[2]

Houses (inhabited, uninhabited or building)

Name and surname of each person

Relation to head of family[1]

Condition [i.e unmarried, married, widowed][1]

Age[3] and sex

Occupation

Where born[4]

If deaf-and-dumb, blind, imbecile, idiot or lunatic[1,5]

Number of rooms occupied if less than five[6]

Rooms with one or more windows[7]

Employee, employed, neither employed nor unemployed[8]

Language spoken: 'English' (if English only): 'Welsh' (if Welsh only); 'Both' (if English and Welsh);[9] 'Gaelic' (if Gaelic only); 'G and E' if both Gaelic and English[10]

Attending school only, or being privately educated[11]

---

1 Not in 1841.

2 'Place' only asked for in 1841. This produced as much (or as little!) information as the more long-winded request of subsequent censuses.

3 In 1881 and 1891 'age last birthday'.

4 In 1841 whether born in same county or not, or in Scotland, Ireland or Foreign Parts.

5 Whether blind, deaf-and-dumb only in 1851 and 1861; in 1891 lunatic, imbecile or idiot put in one category. For Scotland 1861–81, four categories used: (1) deaf and dumb, (2) blind, (3) imbecile or idiot, (4) lunatic. If 'from birth', that comment to be appended. In 1891 categories (3) and (4) brought together and 'from childhood' replaces 'from birth'.

6 Only in 1891. To be entered against 'name of each occupier'.

7 Scotland only from 1861.

8 Only in 1891. Little information on women.

9 Only in Wales and Monmouthshire in 1891. A Welsh translation of the schedule had been used in Wales from 1841 onwards and in 1871 the letter 'W' placed in the first column of the CEB if this Welsh translation used.

10 Scotland only, 1861–91.

11 Scotland only, 1871.

Before using a CEB (or householder's schedule) it is necessary to examine it closely, to see what it does and does not reveal. In order to illustrate some of the things you should look out for, I have annotated a page from a CEB from each of the 1841, 1851 and 1861 censuses of England and Wales; a householder's return from the Irish censuses of 1901 and 1911; and the model schedule sent to every Scottish householder at the censuses of 1871, 1881 and 1891 (Figures 3.3–3.8). For a more comprehensive discussion of the CEBs for England and Wales, see Higgs (1989).

NOTES FOR FIGURES 3.3–3.8

Notes for Figure 3.3

1(a)   The enumerators were asked to draw a single oblique dash like this 'at the end of the names of each family' in order to separate nuclear families from so-called 'residuals', i.e. lodgers, boarders, servants, co-resident relatives.

1(b)   'At the end of the names of inmates of each house' the enumerators were asked to draw this double oblique dash.

Enumerators did not always follow these instructions and in any case it is not always clear what the distinction meant. Were, for example, the separate families also separate households looking

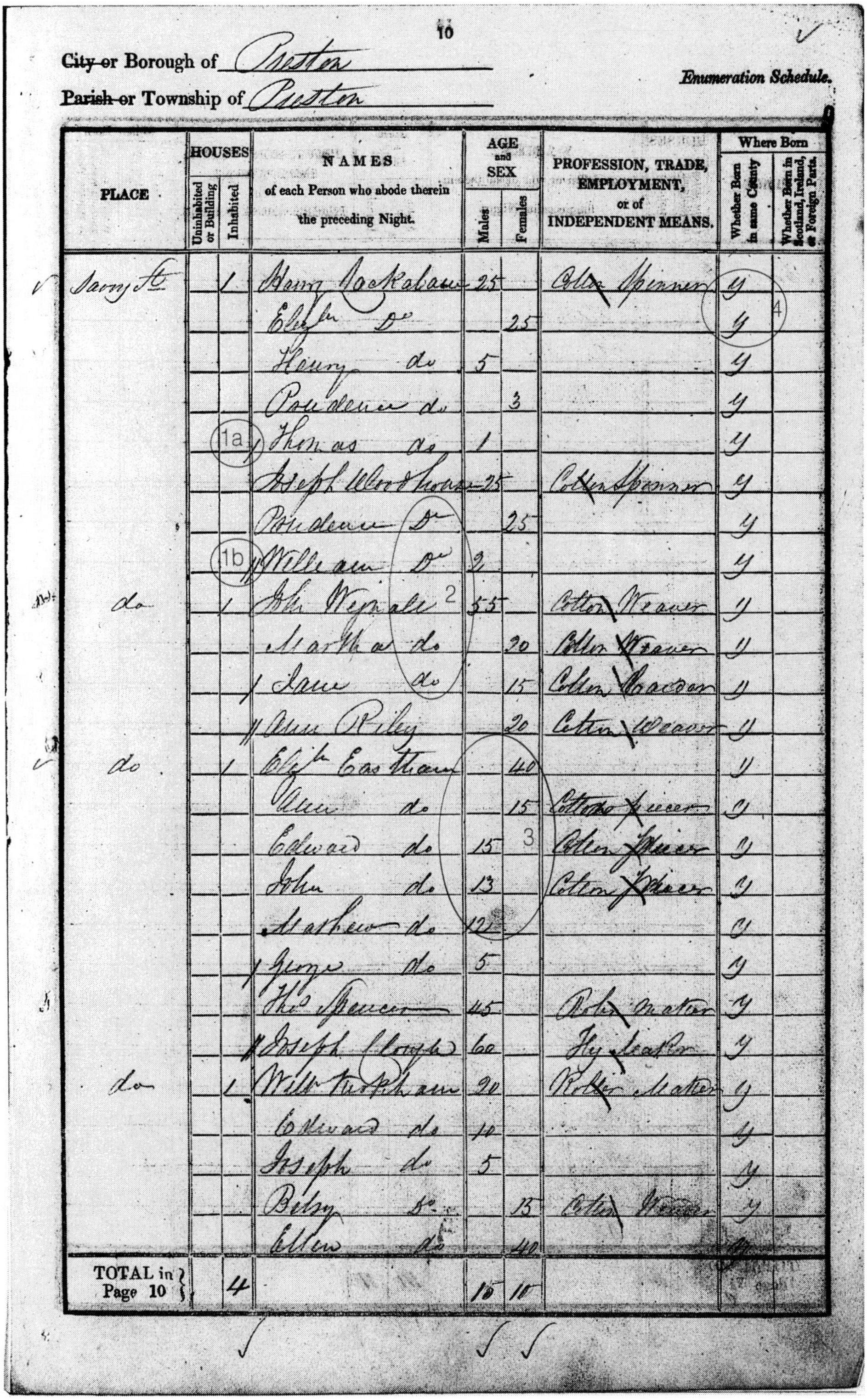
10

~~City or~~ Borough of Preston

~~Parish or~~ Township of Preston

Enumeration Schedule.

PLACE	HOUSES: Uninhabited or Building	HOUSES: Inhabited	NAMES of each Person who abode therein the preceding Night.	AGE and SEX: Males	AGE and SEX: Females	PROFESSION, TRADE, EMPLOYMENT, or of INDEPENDENT MEANS.	Where Born: Whether Born in same County	Where Born: Whether Born in Scotland, Ireland, or Foreign Parts.
Savoy St		1	Henry [illegible]	25		Cotton Spinner	y	
			Eliz^th Do		25		y	
			Henry do	5			y	
			Prudence do		3		y	
			Thomas do	1			y	
			Joseph Woodhouse	25		Cotton Spinner	y	
			Prudence Do		25		y	
			William Do	2			y	
do		1	John Wignall	55		Cotton Weaver	y	
			Martha do		20	Cotton Weaver	y	
			Jane do		15	Cotton Weaver	y	
			Ann Riley		20	Cotton Weaver	y	
do		1	Eliz^th Eastham		40		y	
			Ann do		15	Cotton Piecer	y	
			Edward do	15		Cotton Weaver	y	
			John do	13		Cotton Weaver	y	
			Mathew do	12			y	
			George do	5			y	
			Thos Spencer	45		Roller Maker	y	
			Joseph Clough	60		Fly Maker	y	
do		1	Willm [illegible]	20		Roller Maker	y	
			Edward do	10			y	
			Joseph do	5			y	
			Betsy Do		15	Cotton Weaver	y	
			Ellen do		40		y	
TOTAL in Page 10		4		15	10			

Figure 3.3 Extract from an 1841 census enumerator's book for Preston (Lancashire) (Source: Public Record Office)

after their own catering arrangements (a more modern definition of household)? The absence of the double stroke could be the result of there being further members of the household on the next page – see William Kirkham's household. The position of this household is somewhat ambiguous, since the head has no wife present and there is no single oblique dash separating the two young children (William's?) from the people (relatives?) on the last two lines.

2   The 1841 census did not ask for relationships between members of a household to be given. Thus one has to guess. In this case it would appear that Joseph and Prudence Woodhouse are man and wife and that William is their son. But what is to be made of the next family? Is Martha the wife of John, a sister, a cousin, or – more likely – the eldest daughter?

3   The enumerators were asked to 'write the age of every person under fifteen years as it is stated to you. For persons aged 15 years and upwards write the lowest of the term of five years within which the age is. Thus for persons aged: 15 years and under 20 write 15, 20 years and under 25 write 20' (those over 70 were to be rounded down to the nearest ten years). On the schedule here, it would appear that this instruction was followed. But we cannot be certain that the 'lowest of the term of five years' was always used. Also, many enumerators ignored the instruction and put down everyone's age as stated to them. It should also be noted that many people did not know their age, a fact clearly demonstrated when the same person is traced in two or more CEBs. Beginning in 1881 'age last birthday' was the question asked.

4   'Y' stands for 'yes', 'N' for 'no'. Note too that a precise statement as to place of birth was not given.

Notes for Figure 3.4

1   On this schedule we get a very precise statement of address. This is not always the case. Even when a number is given one cannot always be sure of where a house was, for the following reason:

> There are many towns containing long lines of cottage streets, formed by the gradual coalescence of buildings erected by several small proprietors; and in such streets it is not uncommon for each proprietor to give his little road a distinctive name and to number the houses it contains from one upwards, without the smallest regard to the numbers in the vicinity! In Nottingham there was formerly a long street which was said to repeat its numbers up to three no less than thirty times, and which was the despair of relieving officers and parish doctors. A resident there would give his address as 'the fifth number three on the right hand side as you go up', for such names as 'Matilda Place' or 'Eliza Cottages' had long been swept away.
>
> (The Times, 8 February 1871)

2   Enumerators were instructed:

> Under the last name in any house (i.e. a separate and distinct building, and not a mere storey or flat), he should draw a line across the page as far as the fifth column. Where there is more than one Occupier in the same house, he should draw a similar line under the last name of the family of each Occupier; making the line, however, in this case, commence a little on the left hand side of the third column, as in the example in page vi. of his book ... By the term 'house', he must understand 'a distinct building, separated from others by party walls'. Flats, and sets of chambers, therefore, must not be reckoned as houses.
>
> (Tillott, 1972, p.92)

The problem was, first, that the rule was not always followed, and second, that the complexity of some residential arrangements made it difficult to follow. For instance, on this schedule it is not clear whether Thomas and Alice Taylor at 29 Savoy Street were 'lodgers' looking after them-selves, or 'boarders' sharing the table of John Jones. If the former, then they should really be regarded as a separate household; if the latter, then they should not. Anderson (1972, pp.136–7)

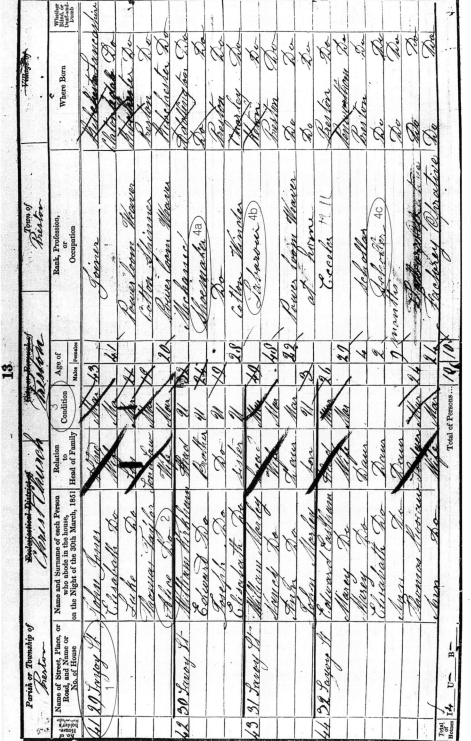

Figure 3.4 Extract from an 1851 census enumerator's book for Preston (Lancashire) (Source: Public Record Office)

suggests that, with one or two exceptions, 'the co-residing group should be defined as comprising all the names listed in an enumerator's book from one entry "head" in the column headed "relation to head of family" to the last name preceding the next entry "head"'.

Note that in the 1861 and subsequent censuses, a double oblique dash replaced the long line, followed by a '1' in the column headed 'Houses inhabited'. Together these marked the ending and beginning of a new house.

3   The term 'condition' was used to describe the marital status of each member of the population. Officially sanctioned abbreviations were 'Unm' for unmarried', 'Mar' for married, 'W' for widow, and 'Widr' for widower. You will come across others, e.g. 'M' for married or 'S' for single, in the 1891 CEBs.

4   A number of problems arise in interpreting the occupational data for the census. Several are illustrated here. The first (4a) is that although enumerators were asked to differentiate between 'masters' and 'journeymen', they rarely did so. Thus we don't know for certain whether a 'shoemaker', 'butcher' or 'baker' was, say, a shop assistant or the owner of a business, or (if the latter) the size of the business. We can, of course, get some idea from the housing and address; here, for instance, we might assume that Edward Kirkham should have been labelled a 'journeyman'. The second (4b) is that often the single designation 'labourer' is given without a qualifying adjective. We cannot therefore be sure what kind of work such men did. Also, secondary occupations are often omitted. As for the third (4c) it would appear unlikely that Preston could boast scholars as young as two years of age. Perhaps this little girl was with a child minder? Implausibly young scholars are found in many CEBs.

Notes for Figure 3.5

1   The single and double oblique strokes of the 1841 census replaced the short and long lines of 1851. The 1861 CEBs are sometimes less legible than those of 1851 as the number of lines per page was increased from 20 to 25 without a change in page size. In 1891 there were 31 lines to the page.

2   This and subsequent censuses asked employers to state the number of people they employed and, in the case of farmers, the acreage they farmed. Neither was reported consistently. Sometimes abbreviations were used (e.g. Ag Lab for agricultural labourer) though even the officially recognized ones – like Ag Lab – were not always used. For these see the instructions at the beginning of each CEB. Women's occupations appear intermittently. Nevertheless, they reveal that as many women (43 per cent) worked outside the home in 1861 as in 1971 (Hakim, 1980, p.560). In 1891 three new columns were added to the form, headed 'Employer', 'Employed' and 'Neither Employer nor Employed' (though this gave rise to a certain amount of confusion).

Notes for Figure 3.6

1   Unlike the situation in England, Wales and Scotland, the household schedules from the Irish censuses of 1901 and 1911 have been preserved as loose forms – they were not copied into volumes of census enumerators' books. The Form A household schedule has no address attached. This is obtained from the Form B reference (see top right of Form A). Form B was a tabulated form completed by the enumerators and attached to household enumeration forms for their districts. Thus Form B gave the 'Household and Building Return' and listed, under each street in turn, each household head, the address of the house, its class in terms of windows, number of rooms, etc., and the number of families in each house. This Form A is from Belfast.

2   Birthplace information was not required beyond the city or the county level, a practice reminiscent of that adopted in the rest of Britain in 1841. In practice, however, more detail was often given.

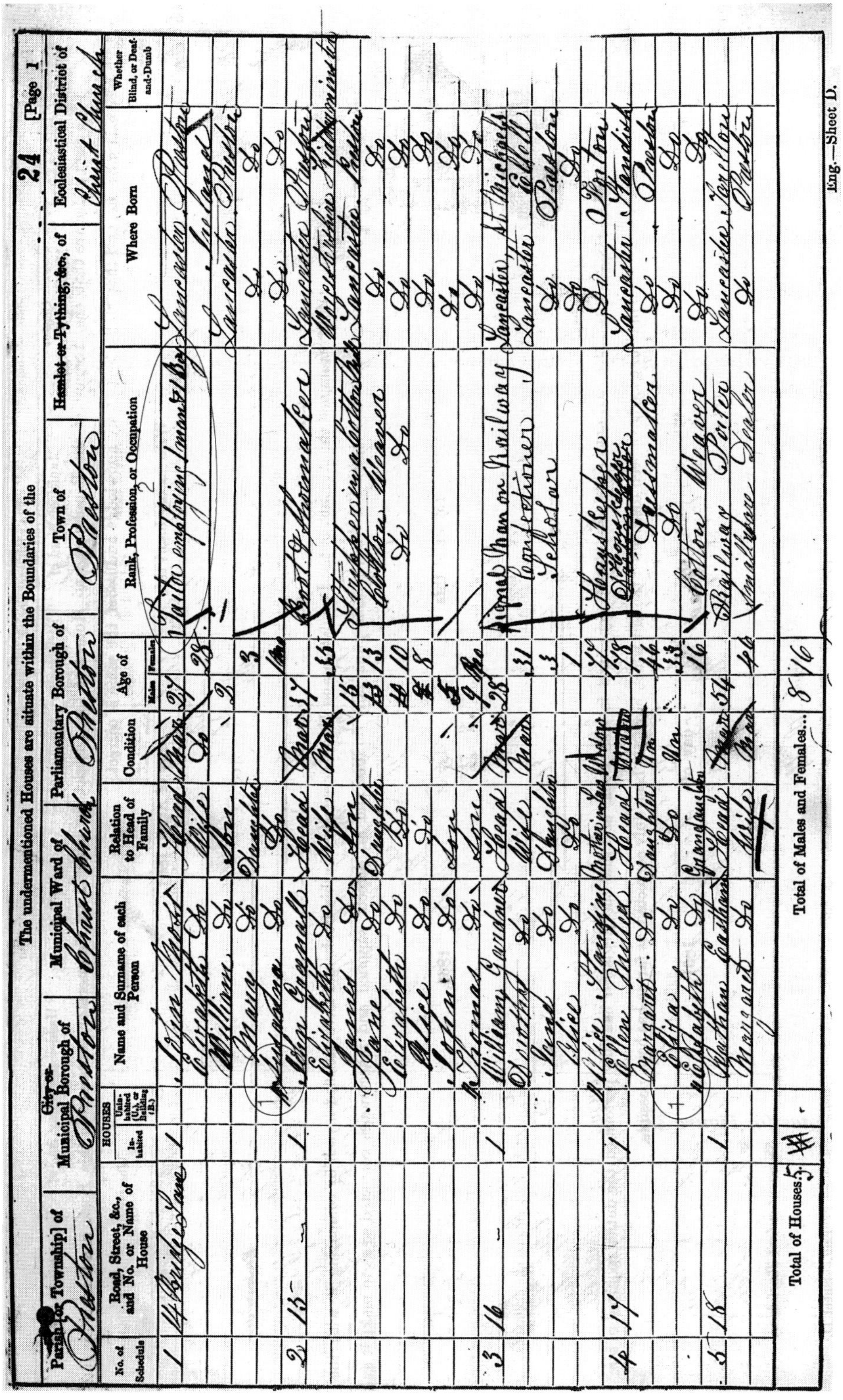
[Page 1

24

The undermentioned Houses are situate within the Boundaries of the

Parish [or Township] of | City or Municipal Borough of | Municipal Ward of | Parliamentary Borough of | Town of | Hamlet or Tything, &c., of | Ecclesiastical District of

No. of Schedule | Road, Street, &c., and No. or Name of House | HOUSES: Inhabited; Uninhabited (U.), or Building (B.) | Name and Surname of each Person | Relation to Head of Family | Condition | Age of Males / Females | Rank, Profession, or Occupation | Where Born | Whether Blind, or Deaf-and-Dumb

Total of Houses | Total of Males and Females

Eng.—Sheet D.

Figure 3.5 Extract from an 1861 census enumerator's book for Preston (Lancashire) (Source: Public Record Office)

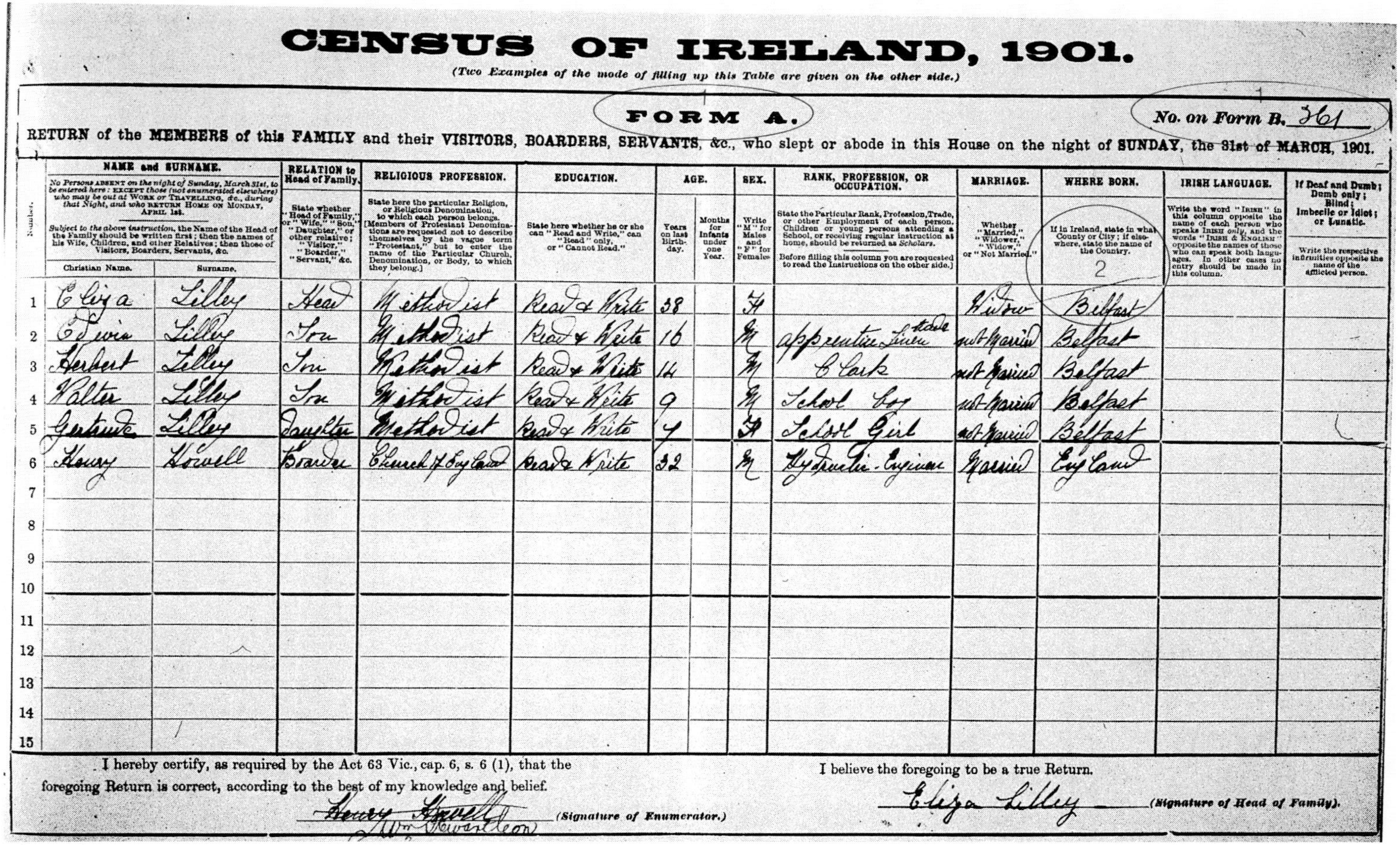

CENSUS OF IRELAND, 1901.

(Two Examples of the mode of filling up this Table are given on the other side.)

FORM A.

No. on Form B. 361

RETURN of the MEMBERS of this FAMILY and their VISITORS, BOARDERS, SERVANTS, &c., who slept or abode in this House on the night of SUNDAY, the 31st of MARCH, 1901.

Number	NAME and SURNAME. No Persons ABSENT on the night of Sunday, March 31st, to be entered here: EXCEPT those (not enumerated elsewhere) who may be out at WORK or TRAVELLING, &c., during that Night, and who RETURN HOME ON MONDAY, APRIL 1st. Subject to the above instruction, the Name of the Head of the Family should be written first; then the names of his Wife, Children, and other Relatives; then those of Visitors, Boarders, Servants, &c. Christian Name.	Surname.	RELATION to Head of Family. State whether "Head of Family," or "Wife," "Son," "Daughter," or other relative; "Visitor," "Boarder," "Servant," &c.	RELIGIOUS PROFESSION. State here the particular Religion, or Religious Denomination, to which each person belongs. [Members of Protestant Denominations are requested not to describe themselves by the vague term "Protestant," but to enter the name of the Particular Church, Denomination, or Body, to which they belong.]	EDUCATION. State here whether he or she can "Read and Write," can "Read" only, or "Cannot Read."	AGE. Years on last Birthday.	AGE. Months for Infants under one Year.	SEX. Write "M" for Males and "F" for Females.	RANK, PROFESSION, OR OCCUPATION. State the Particular Rank, Profession, Trade, or other Employment of each person. Children or young persons attending a School, or receiving regular instruction at home, should be returned as Scholars. Before filling this column you are requested to read the instructions on the other side.]	MARRIAGE. Whether "Married," "Widower," "Widow," or "Not Married."	WHERE BORN. If in Ireland, state in what County or City; if elsewhere, state the name of the Country.	IRISH LANGUAGE. Write the word "IRISH" in this column opposite the name of each person who speaks IRISH only, and the words "IRISH & ENGLISH" opposite the names of those who can speak both languages. In other cases no entry should be made in this column.	If Deaf and Dumb; Dumb only; Blind; Imbecile or Idiot; or Lunatic. Write the respective infirmities opposite the name of the afflicted person.
1	Eliza	Lilley	Head	Methodist	Read & Write	38		F		Widow	Belfast		
2	Edwin	Lilley	Son	Methodist	Read & Write	16		M	Apprentice Linen trade	not Married	Belfast		
3	Herbert	Lilley	Son	Methodist	Read & Write	14		M	Clerk	not Married	Belfast		
4	Walter	Lilley	Son	Methodist	Read & Write	9		M	School Boy	not Married	Belfast		
5	Gertrude	Lilley	Daughter	Methodist	Read & Write	7		F	School Girl	not Married	Belfast		
6	Henry	Howell	Boarder	Church of England	Read & Write	32		M	Hydraulic Engineer	Married	England		
7													
8													
9													
10													
11													
12													
13													
14													
15													

I hereby certify, as required by the Act 63 Vic., cap. 6, s. 6 (1), that the foregoing Return is correct, according to the best of my knowledge and belief.

~~Henry Howell~~ Wm Henderson (Signature of Enumerator.)

I believe the foregoing to be a true Return.

Eliza Lilley (Signature of Head of Family).

Figure 3.6 A householder's return from the 1901 Census of Ireland (Belfast) (Source: National Archives, Dublin)

CENSUS OF IRELAND, 1911.

Two Examples of the mode of filling up this Table are given on the other side.

FORM A.

No. on Form B.

RETURN of the MEMBERS of this FAMILY and their VISITORS, BOARDERS, SERVANTS, &c., who slept or abode in this House on the night of SUNDAY, the 2nd of APRIL, 1911.

No.	NAME AND SURNAME (Christian Name)	Surname	RELATION to Head of Family	RELIGIOUS PROFESSION	EDUCATION	AGE — Males	AGE — Females	RANK, PROFESSION, OR OCCUPATION	PARTICULARS AS TO MARRIAGE — Whether "Married," "Widower," "Widow," or "Single."	Completed years the present Marriage has lasted	Total Children born alive	Children still living	WHERE BORN	IRISH LANGUAGE	If Deaf and Dumb; etc.
1	Robert	Devlin	Head of Family	Roman Catholic	Read & Write	42	—	Plumber	Married	—	—	—	Londonderry		
2	Rose Anne	Devlin	Wife	Roman Catholic	Read & Write	—	38	—	Married	14	9	7	L. Derry City		
3	Mary	Devlin	Daughter	Roman Catholic	Read & Write	—	13	Scholar	Single				L. Derry City	Irish & English	
4	Michael Jos	Devlin	Son	Roman Catholic	Read & Write	11	—	Scholar	Single				L. Derry City		
5	Elizabeth	Devlin	Daughter	Roman Catholic	Read & Write	—	10	Scholar	Single				L. Derry City		
6	Patrick	Devlin	Son	Roman Catholic	Read only	8	—	Scholar	Single				L. Derry City		
7	James	Devlin	Son	Roman Catholic		6	—	Scholar	Single				L. Derry City		
8	Robert	Devlin	Son	Roman Catholic		5	—	Scholar	Single				L. Derry City		
9	Annie Rosa	Devlin	Daughter	Roman Catholic		—	1		Single				L. Derry City		
10	Mary	Doherty	Aunt	Roman Catholic	Read only	—	63	House Keeper	Single				Donegal Derry County 2		
11															
12															
13															
14															
15															

I hereby certify, as required by the Act 10 Edw. VII., and 1 Geo. V., cap. 11, that the foregoing Return is correct, according to the best of my knowledge and belief.

Thomas Bachelor, Signature of Enumerator.

I believe the foregoing to be a true Return.

Robert Devlin, Signature of Head of Family.

Figure 3.7   A householder's return from the 1911 Census of Ireland (Londonderry) (Source: National Archives, Dublin)

Notes for Figure 3.7

1 The Irish census of 1911 requested from married women information on the number of children born alive and the number still living. In practice, the information was also often supplied by widows.

2 Although birthplace information was only required at the county, city or country level, more information, as in 1901, was often given. In this case the townland (probably Balloughry in the parish of Templemore just outside the city) was noted.

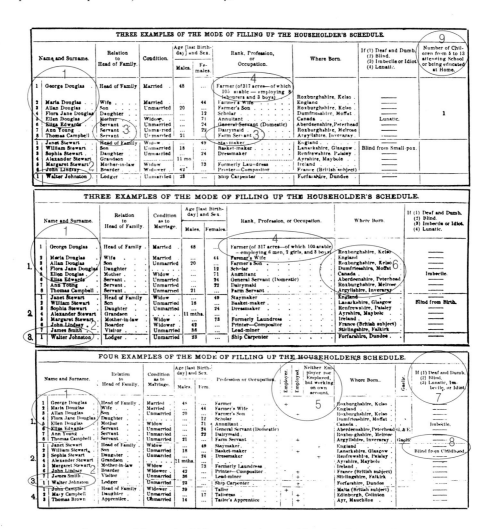

Figure 3.8 Illustration of the mode of filling out the householder's schedule provided by the Scottish census authorities in 1871 *(top)*, 1881 *(centre)* and 1891 *(bottom)* (Source: *Census of Scotland, 1871, 1881 and 1891*, in BPP, 1872, vol. LXVIII, p.64; 1882, vol. LXXVI, p.31; 1892, vol. XCIV, p.31)

Notes for Figure 3.8

1 They never died, nor did they age! The spirit of conservatism that dominated census taking extended even to the model answers provided.

2 In 1871 and 1881, the lodger Walter Johnston is separated off from the family in which – presumably – he lodged. In 1891 he was not.

3   Note that the term servant appears both in the Relation to Head of Family column and in the Rank, Profession or Occupation column. This could lead to confusion when totalling the number of servants, especially when those in the Relation column were relatives of the head of family by blood or marriage (for a discussion see Higgs, 1982).

4   An important entry if completed correctly – sadly it often was not – was that on acreage and employment on individual farms. Note that eight labourers were employed, though there is no indication as to what sex they were. And was the dairymaid included among them? Reporting on the 1841 census for England and Wales, *The Times* made great fun of the fact that in Northampton-shire in 1841 only 199 female agricultural labourers were returned (the actual number was 209, so even *The Times* was fallible – see *Census of England and Wales, 1841*, BPP, 1844, vol. XXVII, p.217) or 'one to a parish and exactly at the rate of one to a thousand persons? As there were 3,315 farmers and graziers, only one in sixteen would appear to have employed female agricultural labour' (*The Times*, 12 September 1844). *The Times* also noted that in the whole of England and Wales only 854 civil engineers were enumerated (actual figure 853), of whom 233 were in the county of Somerset! (*The Times*, 16 September 1844).

5   Note that the return on acreage and farm employment was dropped in 1891 and a return on employment status was required. The same occurred in England and Wales.

6   As in England and Wales, a local birthplace was only required for those born in Scotland.

7   Note the change in this rubric as compared with 1871 and 1881.

8   Note the change in this rubric as compared with 1871 and 1881.

9   This question had been asked in 1861, though then the age range was 5–15 and no mention was made of education at home.

2.1.1   SOCIO-ECONOMIC GROUPING (SEG)

You may wish to see where a family, or set of families, you are interested in is ranked in terms of social status. Occupations are often used as an indicator of status or class. Again, you might use the information on occupations to describe the economy of a particular community, or set of communities, at a point in time or over time. To do either of these it is necessary to group the thousands of occupations appearing in the CEBs into a manageable number of categories. There has been much argument over how to do this, and a variety of schemes have been proposed (see Mills, 1982; Mills and Mills, 1989). Here I have chosen two. The first (shown in Table 3.8) was devised by Alan Armstrong and gives a socio-economic grouping (SEG) for York in 1851. In studying other communities you will need to use your judgement as to where other occupations should be slotted into Armstrong's scheme. (Again, for a fuller discussion see Mills, 1982, pp.19–27.) The second (Table 3.9) puts occupations into economic categories, and was devel-oped by Charles Booth in 1886. Booth, in preparing his major social survey *Life and labour of the people in London* (see Chapter 4, section 6 for details), devised this classification because of his profound dissatisfaction with the official system. This changed from census to census, making comparability virtually impossible; besides, the system was full of ambiguities. Table 3.9 is an abbreviation of that produced by Booth. For fuller details of occupations and the total numbers in them in England and Wales in the period 1841–91, see Armstrong (1972) pp.255–81.

Table 3.8 Armstrong's social classification for York, 1851

Class I

Accountant	Magistrate (stipendiary, i.e. paid	Reporter
Archbishop's secretary	magistrates are classified, but honor-	Sharebroker
Architect	ary magistrates such as JPs are not)	Shipowner
Army officer	Museum curator	Solicitor
Attorney	Naval officer	Surgeon or physician
Dentist	Ordnance surveyor	Surveyor
Independent minister	Rector	Vicar

Class II

Auctioneer	Language professor	Relieving officer
Bookkeeper	Music teacher	Schoolmaster/Schoolmistress
Coal agent	Professor of music	Sculptor
Commercial teacher	Proprietor of ladies' seminary	Station master
Factor (unspecified)	Police chief constable	Translator (language)
Inland revenue collector	Railway audit clerk	Veterinary surgeon
Land agent	Railway inspector	

(Farmers should be included here, unless they have less than five acres — acreage is usually given — in which case they should go in Class III.)

Class III

Assistant (to linen draper)	Coal dealer	Girth weaver
Assistant (ordnance office)	Compositor	Glass blower
Baker	Comb-maker	Glass maker
Basket maker	Confectioner	Glass stainer
Beer retailer	Cook	Glover
Blacksmith	Cooper	Greengrocer
Boiler maker	Coppersmith	Grocer
Bookbinder	Cordwainer	Gun maker (gunsmith)
Bookseller	Corn, flour dealer	Gutta-percha merchant (broker)
Bonnet maker	Currier	Hairdresser
Boot closer	Cutler	Hatter
Brass fitter	Damask weaver	Hay and straw dealer
Bricklayer	Dentist's assistant	Hosier
Brush maker	Draper	Housepainter
Builder	Dressmaker	Innkeeper (publican)
Butcher	Eating-house keeper	Ironmonger
Cabinet maker	Engine driver	Iron-moulder
Cabman	Engineer	Iron turner
Calico weaver	Engine fitter	Joiner
Car (carriage) painter	Engine-spring maker	Law stationer
Chair maker	Engraver	Leather dresser
Chemist	Farrier	Linen spinner
Cattle dealer	File cutter (maker)	Manure dealer
Clerk (unspecified)	Fireman	Marble mason
Clockmaker	Fishmonger	Master grinder
Coach builder	Florist	Master mariner
Coach-lace weaver	French-kid stainer	Miller (flour and grain)
Coachman	Fringe weaver	Millwright
Coach trimmer	Fruiterer	Muffin maker
Coachsmith	Gas fitter	Musician
Coach-wheel maker	Gilder	

Class III (continued)

Music seller	Railway guard	Stone sawer
Nail maker	Railway pointsman	Tailor
Nurse	Railway policeman	Tea dealer
Omnibus driver	Saddler	Telegraph clerk
Optician	Saddle-tree maker	Tobacconist
Pawnbroker	Sailor	Traveller (commercial)
Perfumer	Sawyer	Upholsterer
Picture dealer	Seamstress	Victualler
Picture-frame maker	Seedsman	Waiter
Pipe maker (tobacco)	Shipbuilder	Warehouseman
Plane maker	Ship's carpenter	Watchmaker
Plasterer	Shoemaker	Weaver (textile)
Police constable	Shopman	Wheelwright
Plumber	Silversmith	Whitesmith
Pot dealer	Silver turner	Wine and spirit dealer
Pot maker (potter)	Slater	Wire worker
Poulterer	Soldier	Wood carver
Printer	Stationer	Woodsman
Railway clerk	Staymaker (corset maker)	Woodturner
Railway fitter	Stonemason	Writer

(Innkeepers with servants and tradesmen, dealers and manufacturers who were employers should be upgraded to Class II.)

Class IV

Agricultural labourer	General servant	Office keeper
Brazier	Gentleman's servant	Ostler
Brewer	Goods deliverer (railway)	Pavior
Brickmaker	Groom	Quiltress
Carter (or carrier) (horse drawn conveyance)	Herdsman	Rail stoker
Cloth dresser	Horsebreaker	Railway ticket collector
Cork cutter	Horsekeeper	Rope maker
Cowkeeper	Hotel porter	Steward (club)
Drover	Housekeeper	Stoker
Engine cleaner	Housemaid	Washerwoman
Flax dresser	Laundress	Waterman (boatman)
Gardener		

Class V

Charwoman	Messenger	Rail porter
Errand boy	News vendor	Road labourer
Hawker	Porter	Scavenger
Labourer	Rag and paper collector	

Source: Armstrong (1972) pp.215–23

Table 3.9   Charles Booth's economic grouping[1]

Code	Description	Code	Description
AG	AGRICULTURE	T	TRANSPORT
AG 1	Farming, includes farmers, labourers, etc., forestry	T 1	Warehouses and docks (excludes Manchester warehousemen)
AG 2	Land service, e.g. agricultural machine proprietors	T 2	Ocean navigation, includes ship's cooks and stewards
AG 3	Breeding, includes breeders, vets, drovers, farriers	T 3	Inland navigation
AG 4	Fishing	T 4	Railways
M	MINING	T 5	Roads, includes toll collectors
M 1	Mining	D	DEALING
M 2	Quarrying	D 1	Coals
M 3	Brickmaking, but includes sand, flint and gravel workers	D 2	Raw materials, e.g. timber, corn, wool
M 4	Salt and water works	D 3	Clothing materials, e.g. cloth merchants, Manchester warehousemen
B	BUILDING	D 4	Dress (presumably both wholesale and retail)
B 1	Management, e.g. architects, builders	D 5	Food (ditto)
B 2	Operatives, e.g. bricklayers, carpenters, thatchers	D 6	Tobacco (ditto)
B 3	Roadmaking, includes railway navvies	D 7	Wines, spirits and hotels (ditto)
MF	MANUFACTURE	D 8	Lodging and coffee houses
MF 1	Machinery	D 9	Furniture (apparently wholesalers), but includes pawnbrokers
MF 2	Tools, includes gemsmiths, pin and steel pen makers	D 10	Stationery and publications
MF 3	Shipbuilding, includes sailmakers	D 11	Household utensils and ornaments, e.g. ironmongers
MF 4	Iron and steel, includes blacksmiths	D 12	General dealers
MF5	Copper, tin, lead, etc., includes whitesmiths	D 13	Unspecified, e.g merchants, brokers, valuers, salesmen
MF 6	Gold, silver jewellery	IS	INDUSTRIAL SERVICE
MF 7	Earthenware, includes glass, plaster and cement	IS 1	Banking, insurance and accounts
MF 8	Coals and gas	IS 2	General labourers
MF 9	Chemical, includes ink and matches	PP	PUBLIC SERVICE and PROFESSIONAL SECTOR
MF 10	Furs and leather	PP 1	Administration (central)
MF 11	Glue, tallow, etc. includes soap, manure	PP 2	Administration (local)
MF 12	Hair, includes brushes, quills, combs, bone workers	PP 3	Administration (sanitary) i.e. town drainage and scavenging
MF 13	Woodworkers, excludes MF 14	PP 4	Army, officers and men, active and retired
MF 14	Furniture, includes French polishers and undertakers	PP 5	Navy (ditto)
MF 15	Harness and carriage, both road and rail	PP 6	Police and prison officers
MF 16	Paper	PP 7	Law
MF 17	Floorcloth and waterproof	PP 8	Medicine, includes dentists, chemists
MF 18	Woollen, includes knitters of wool	PP 9	Painting, i.e. art, but includes animal preservers
MF 19	Cotton and silk	PP 10	Music and amusements, e.g. performers, games service
MF 20	Flax, hemp, etc., includes rope and net workers	PP 11	Literature, i.e. authors, editors, journalists, etc.
MF 21	Lace	PP 12	Science
MF 22	Dyeing	PP 13	Education
MF 23	Dress, includes hosiery, hat, glove, footwear	PP 14	Religion
MF 24	Sundries connected with dress, e.g. umbrellas, buttons	DS	DOMESTIC SERVICE
MF 25	Food preparation, includes cattle food	DS 1	Indoor service, includes institutional servants
MF 26	Baking	DS 2	Outdoor service
MF 27	Drink preparation, includes maltsters	DS 3	Extra service, appears to be self-employed, e.g. chimney sweeps
MF 28	Smoking, includes pipes		RESIDUAL POPULATION
MF 29	Watches, instruments and toys	I	Property owning
MF 30	Printing and bookbinding	II	Indefinite, includes vagrants, lunatics, etc.
MF 31	Unspecified manufacturers, artisans, apprentices, factory labourers	III	Dependent classes, e.g. children, housewives

[1] Brenda Collins tells me that the groupings shown in Table 3.9 are similar to those used in the published reports of the Irish census of 1901 and 1911.

Source: based on the work of Charles Booth, 1841–1891

2.2   WHAT CAN YOU DO WITH THE CEBS?

If you haven't worked with the CEBs it is a good idea to limber up on them by doing an exercise on one column. A simple exercise would be first to read the appropriate census report for the topic you have chosen, e.g. occupation, age, etc., to see what the situation was in the little world (registration district or county, say) of which your chosen area forms a part. Then analyse your column by, for example, totalling the different ages and putting them into the groups used by the census authorities. You can then compare your area with the somewhat larger one analysed by the census authorities, and speculate on the similarities or differences. Do there seem to be more people in some age groups than expected (the effect of migration, perhaps?); more women in certain age groups than men (reflecting a build-up of domestic servants?). Such an exercise will not only increase your familiarity with 'your' CEBs; it will also introduce you to the important practice of comparing your findings with others and probably will trigger off ideas as you work your way through the material. It is amazing how things will catch your eye, believe me!

After working on one column you will probably see how much more information you can acquire by working on two together. For instance, knowing how many people are single, married or widowed is not very illuminating, but seeing how many are in these various states in the different age groups certainly is. Combining occupations with ages is equally illuminating.

_____ **EXERCISE 3.3** _____

Can you think of three other projects that could be based on linking one CEB column with another?

Comments p.298.

At the start I suggested that you nest your research – however elementary and limited – in the census reports. As you advance you should set it in the context of numerous articles and books based primarily on the CEBs. You will be helped in this by Mills and Pearce's (1989) comprehensive bibliography, which covers over 400 studies. This bibliography has two strong points. First, it annotates each study according to location, topic(s) and method(s), and gives references to the publication in which it can be found (see Figure 3.9). Secondly, the bibliography is continually being updated by the Cambridge Group for the History of Population and Social Structure, 27 Trumpington Street, Cambridge, CB2 1QA. The Group will supply a computer print-out of studies categorized according to topic, place, year of publication, etc. for a modest fee.

As your work advances you will feel the need to acquire various skills. Some will be simple. For example, if you are doing a study involving social or industrial stratification you will find it helpful to categorize your occupations in some way, probably using the Armstrong or Booth classification systems discussed above. To adopt either of these will carry the added advantage that you will be able to compare your findings with those of others. Quantitative techniques (see Chapter 8) are likely to prove indispensable. These need not be highly complex: much can be gleaned by compiling tables using percentages, rates or ratios, and through sampling and correlation. The ever cheaper and increasingly friendly computer may well tempt you to embark on a study using this tool, though if you do, take heed of Kevin Schürer's advice (Chapter 9, section 1).

Finally, you should always remember that the basic qualities required for all historical research are imagination and patience. The former is often enhanced through practice. You will be surprised how replicating a study in a different area or period will spark off new ideas, leading to fresh insights.

CARTER, H., 1980
Transformations in spatial structure of Welsh towns in the nineteenth century
Transactions of the Honourable Society of Cymmrodorion, pp 175-200
Census used   1851 1871
Locality   GLAMORGAN   Merthyr Tydfil, Industrial (1851 census only)
                                                      Neath,   Industrial (1871 census only)
                    CARDIGAN   Aberystwyth, Resort (1871 census only)
Social structure studies
Stratification scheme   Not specified
                                            Related to area of residence
Migration studies
Calculation of native born
Classification of birthplace   by name of area
                                            Related to occupation
Segregation studies
Variables to describe segregation   Occupation, social class, rateable value or housing quality, house occupancy
Techniques   Map

DALY, M., 1982
Social structure of the Dublin working class 1871-1911
Irish Historical Studies, vol 23, no 90
Census used   1871 1911
Locality   LEINSTER   Dublin, pop 250,000, Capital city, trade, manufacturing
Other sources   Marriage registers
Note: Explores differences between skilled and unskilled occupations, and movements between them
Demographic topics
Special studies   Age difference between spouses
Family studies
Family elements   Mean size
                                            Children by birthplace of head
Occupation studies
Classification   Industrial
                                            Related to religion
Social structure studies
Stratification scheme   Registrar-General's scheme as modified by Armstrong
Social mobility studies   Inter-generational
Migration studies
Calculation of native born
Classification of birthplace   Related to occupation
Special studies   Compares birthplaces of married couples
Segregation studies
Variables to describe segregation   Rateable value or housing quality, age of head, birthplace, sex of head,
                                            occupation, social class, mean household size
Special studies   Comparisons between dwellers in tenement, corporation and artisan dwellings

MILLS, D.R., 1978A
The residential propinquity of kin in a Cambridgeshire village, 1841
Journal of Historical Geography, vol 4, pp 265-76
Census used   1841
Locality   CAMBRIDGESHIRE   Melbourn, pop 1608, Rural, agricultural
Other sources   Tithe map 1839, Congregational and Anglican registers
Note: Study of residential propinquity of kin
Methodology
Special techniques   House repopulation
Segregation studies
Special studies   Propinquity of kin
                                            Comparisons with Anderson's (1972A) methodology

Figure 3.9   Some sample entries from the bibliography by Dennis Mills and Carol Pearce, *People and places in the Victorian census* (1989)

2.3   FINDING THE CEBs

As mentioned earlier, the CEBs are widely available on microfilm in record offices and libraries (for specific locations see Gibson, 1990), especially for the local areas served by them. Currently those for the 1841, 1851, 1861, 1871, 1881 and 1891 censuses of England, Wales and Scotland are open to public scrutiny. For Ireland it is possible to examine the 1901 and 1911 householders' schedules – quite a bonus! There are no CEBs for these censuses. Unfortunately, most of the earlier Irish returns, though thankfully not all, were destroyed (see Royle, 1978, and ffolliott, 1987). Paper copies of the English, Welsh and Scottish CEBs can often be obtained on a self-service basis at local record offices and libraries. The prices vary considerably. Copies of the Irish returns for the whole of Ireland for 1901 and 1911 can be obtained from The National Archives, Bishop Street, Dublin, Ireland. Copies of the 1901 census only can be obtained for the six counties of Northern Ireland from the Public Record Office of Northern Ireland, 66 Balmoral Avenue, Belfast, Co. Antrim, BT9 6NY.

A computer print-out of the 1851 CEBs for a large sample (it covered some 400,000 individuals) of English, Welsh and Scottish CEBs was produced by Michael Anderson and is now available from the ESRC Data Archive, University of Essex, Wivenhoe Park, Colchester, Essex, CO4 3SQ. For those with access to a computer the Data Archive will also supply machine-readable CEB data files either as 'raw data' (i.e. data with no software dependency) or set up in a number of popular software packages, including *Paradox, PC-File, Reflex* and *DBase* versions 2–4. The cost is modest.

Before starting work on any particular community or topic involving the CEBs, it would pay to consult Schürer and Anderson (1992). Here you will find a description of numerous projects that have used both British and overseas CEBs. Again, much of the material underpinning these projects is available from the ESRC Data Archive at cost.

Mention must also be made of the British 1881 Census Project. Funded and directed by the Genealogical Society of Utah (a part of the Church of Jesus Christ of Latter-Day Saints), the project involves transcribing *all* the CEBs with information on over 26 million people. After transcription the data is entered on computers and indexed (by surname, birthplace and as enumerated); initially this is being done by county, though eventually it will be done for Britain as a whole. The work of transcription is being carried out almost entirely by family historians, most of whom are members of local family history societies. When completed, possibly by 1996, copies will be available in record offices and at the family history libraries of the Church of Jesus Christ of Latter-Day Saints.

Finally, there are CEB transcripts and indexes for many local areas. Enquiries as to the availability of these should be made to a library, record office or family history society in the area of interest to you. Issues of the *Family History News and Digest*, published by the Federation of Family History Societies, also give details of these transcripts and indexes.

_____ *EXERCISE 3.4* _____

1   Use the checklist of key issues for evaluating primary sources given in Schema A in Chapter 2 (p.22) to review your understanding and evaluation of the material on CEBs in this section. Comment on as many of these key issues as you can in relation to using CEBs as a source.

2   Note down (a) any ideas you have so far about making use of CEBs in research, and (b) where you might turn for further ideas.

Comments p.299.

2.4 USEFUL ADDRESSES

The census office addresses for enquiries are as follows:

Census Customer Services, Office of Population Censuses and Surveys (OPCS), Segensworth Road, Titchfield, Fareham, PO15 5RR.

Census Customer Services, General Register Office (GRO Scotland), Ladywell House, Ladywell Road, Edinburgh, EH12 7TF.

General Register Office, Oxford House, 49–55 Chichester Street, Belfast, BT1 4HL.

Central Statistics Office, Demography Branch, Ardee House, Rathmines, Dublin 6.

General Register Office, Joyce House, 8–11 Lombard Street East, Dublin 2.

REFERENCES AND FURTHER READING

Note: entries marked with an asterisk are of particular value for those researching the CEBs for the first time.

Anderson, M. (1972) 'Standard tabulation procedures for the census enumerators' books 1851–1891', in Wrigley (1972) pp.134–45.

Armstrong, M. E. (ed.) (1981) *An industrial island: a history of Scunthorpe*, Scunthorpe, Borough Museum and Art Gallery.

Armstrong, W.A. (1972) 'The use of information about occupation', in Wrigley (1972) pp.191–310.

Census of England and Wales, 1841, BPP, 1844, vol. XXVIII, pp.13ff.

Census of Scotland, 1871, Report, BPP, 1872, vol. LVIII, pp.1ff.

Census of Great Britain, 1861, Report, BPP, vol. LXXVIII, pp.1ff.

Collins, B. (1993) 'The analysis of census returns: the 1901 census of Ireland', in *Ulster Local Studies*, 15, 1, pp.38–46.*

Collins, B. and Pryce, W. T. R. (1993) 'Census returns in England, Ireland, Scotland and Wales', audio-cassette 2A in Braham, P. (ed.) *Using the past: audio-cassettes on sources and methods for family and community historians*, Milton Keynes, The Open University.*

Day, A. and McWilliams, P. (eds) (1991–) *Ordnance Survey memoirs of Ireland 1830–9*, Belfast, Institute of Irish Studies, Queen's University of Belfast in association with the Royal Irish Academy, Dublin.

Drake, M. (1972) 'The census, 1801–1891', in Wrigley (1972) pp.7–46.

ffolliott, R. (1987) 'Irish census returns and census substitutes', in Begley, D. F. (ed.) *Irish genealogy: a record finder*, Dublin, Heraldic Artists Ltd.

Flinn, M. (ed.) (1977) *Scottish population history from the seventeenth century to the 1930s*, Cambridge, Cambridge University Press.

Gibson, J.S.W. (1990) *Census returns 1841–81 on microfilm: a directory to local holdings in Great Britain*, 5th edition, Birmingham, Federation of Family History Societies. This book is being continually updated to take account of the release of CEBs under the 100-year rule.

Gibson, J. (1992) *Marriage, census and other indexes for family historians*, 4th edition, Birmingham, Federation of Family History Societies.

Gray, D. (1953) *Nottingham: settlement to city*, Nottingham, Nottingham Co-operative Society Ltd.

Griffith, R. (1858–64) *General valuation of (rateable property in) Ireland*, Dublin, General Valuation Office.

Hakim, C. (1980) 'Census reports as documentary evidence: the census commentaries 1801–1951', *Sociological Review*, 28, 3, pp.551–80.

Higgs, E. (1982) 'The tabulation of occupations in the nineteenth-century census with special reference to domestic servants', *Local Population Studies*, 28, pp.58–66.

Higgs, E. (1989) *Making sense of the census: the manuscript returns for England and Wales, 1801–1901*, London, HMSO.*

History of the census of 1841, manuscript held in the Library, General Register Office.

Hunter, B. (ed.) (1992) *The statesman's year book 1992–93*, London, Macmillan.

Irish University Press (1970) *British Parliamentary Papers* (BPP), *Population*, vol. 17, Shannon, Irish University Press.

Lawton, R. (ed.) (1978) *The census and social structure: an interpretative guide to the nineteenth century censuses*, London, Frank Cass.

Lewis, S. (1831) *Topographical dictionary of England*, 4 vols and supplement, London, S. Lewis and Co.

Lewis, S. (1833) *Topographical dictionary of Wales*, 2 vols, London, S. Lewis and Co.

Lewis, S. (1846) *Topographical dictionary of Scotland*, 2 vols, London, S. Lewis and Co.

Lewis, S. (1837) *Topographical dictionary of Ireland*, 2 vols, London, S. Lewis and Co.

Local Population Studies (1991) *Special census issue*, LPS, Tawney House, Matlock, Derbyshire, DE4 3BT.

Lumas, S. (1992a) *Making use of the census*, Public Record Office Reader's Guide No.1, London, PRO.*

Lumas, S. (1992b) *An introduction to the census returns of England and Wales*, Birmingham, Federation of Family History Societies.*

Mills, D.R. (ed.) (1973) *English rural communities: the impact of a specialized economy*, London, Macmillan.

Mills, D.R. (1982) *A guide to the nineteenth-century census enumerators' books*, Milton Keynes, Open University Press.

Mills, D.R. and Mills, J. (1989) 'Occupation and social stratification revisited: the census enumerators' books of Victorian Britain', *Urban History Yearbook 1989*, pp.63–77.

Mills, D. and Pearce, C. (1989) *People and places in the Victorian census: a review and bibliography of publications based substantially on the manuscript census enumerators' books 1841–1911*, Historical Geography Research Series no.23, Department of Geography, The College of St. Paul and St. Mary, Cheltenham, Glos., GL50 2RH.*

Mitchell, B.R. (1988) *British historical statistics*, Cambridge, Cambridge University Press.

Pocock, D.C.D. (1970) 'Land ownership and urban growth in Scunthorpe', *East Midlands Geographer*, 5, pp 52–61.

Report of the Committee appointed by the Treasury to inquire into certain questions connected with the taking of the census (1890), BPP, vol. LVIII, pp.13–154.

Royle, S.A. (1978) 'Irish manuscript census records: a neglected source of information', *Irish Geography*, II, pp.110–25.

Schürer, K. (1991) 'The 1891 census and local population studies', *Local Population Studies*, 47, pp.16–29.

Schürer, K. and Anderson, S.J. with the assistance of Duncan, J.A. (1992) *A guide to historical data files held in machine-readable form*, Association for History and Computing, c/o Department of History, Royal Holloway and Bedford New College, University of London, Egham, TW20 0EX.

Tillott, P.M. (1972) 'Sources of inaccuracy in the 1851 and 1861 censuses', in Wrigley (1972) pp.82–133.

Williams, L. J. (1985) *Digest of Welsh historical statistics*, vol.1, Cardiff, HMSO for Welsh Office.

Wrigley, E.A. (ed.) (1972) *Nineteenth-century society: essays on the use of quantitative methods for the study of social data*, Cambridge, Cambridge University Press.

CHAPTER 4

USING WRITTEN SOURCES: SOME
KEY EXAMPLES

The census is undoubtedly among the sources most extensively used by family and community historians. But other sources also have much to offer. Some further examples are analysed in this chapter, ranging from partly standardized directories and parish registers to more personal and 'qualitative' sources like autobiographies and diaries.

We have not tried to be comprehensive, but rather to illustrate how these and other sources can best be exploited. As our title indicates, the emphasis is on *using* sources. You will find something about how to locate them, but this is not pursued in detail (information about the range of excellent, detailed finding aids for particular sources is given in the lists of references and further reading following relevant sections in this and later chapters; see also Chapter 13). Our central aim, rather, is to provide examples, drawn from some particularly useful and widely available sources, of how sources can be critically and constructively assessed, and of the ways in which they can be exploited to carry out interesting projects in family and community history: the sorts of questions that can be tackled, the pitfalls that await the unwary, and some research findings. These documents are products of the interplay between many thousands of men and women in many differing situations and of varying degrees of honesty, competence and diligence. That is why you should always check them out in the ways suggested in Chapter 2.

You will certainly come across and want to use many other sources not discussed in these chapters. The Medical Officer of Health reports, for example, are included as just one example of the hundreds of other reports coming out of local government. Likewise, though the census was rightly given pride of place in the last chapter, central government has also produced thousands of other inquiries (published in the British Parliamentary Papers (BPP), see Chapter 5, section 1). Many of these too would repay analysis. There is much that waits to be done! So you should regard the discussion and exercises in this and the following chapter as a means of deepening your critical experience of using sources and increasing your confidence to deal with sources in your own research, whether or not those sources happen to coincide with the examples discussed here.

1   DIRECTORIES

by W.T.R. Pryce

A directory is a list of persons or institutions who, in some way or other, share corporate interests, identities, occupations and professions. For example, *Crockford's clerical directory*, published annually since 1858, is the definitive listing of Anglican clergy in England, Wales and Ireland; and ministers of the Episcopal Church in Scotland. Directories have been published for other professions and organizations (see Rogers, 1989, pp.43–4). The *Medical directory*, another example, goes back to 1845. *Who's who* (first issued in 1849) and *Who was who* (lists of the famous who have died – first issued in 1920) are probably the best known of all directories.

But for community historians, with their specific research focusing on place and locality, town or county directories are of prime importance. Also known as trade or commercial directories, these exist as printed lists of local tradesmen, professionals and public-office holders. Usually, these *local* directories include the names of the 'principal inhabitants': that is, members of the clergy (especially Anglicans), and local 'bigwigs' (including owners of land) with residences in the town or district. Directories may be small, just a few pages devoted to a single town; or encyclopaedic, covering all towns in a region; or they may be national in scope. Women are included in many directories, especially among the landowners, farmers and gentry, but their names also occur in lists of retailers, traders and craftspeople. However, unlike men, often no occupation or trade is stated – presumably because they were widows carrying on the family business after the loss of a husband or after they had been abandoned. There is even a national directory with classified lists of women in specialist crafts and trades: the *Women workers directory*, published in London in 1909 by Bale and Danielson. Regrettably, this does not seem to have been developed into a regular series like many other directories. Copies are now very rare but they can be consulted in major copyright libraries (see Shaw and Tipper, 1989, p.386).

Hillam's (1991) book on the dental profession is an example of a study that draws extensively on a wide range of directories, both local and national. Dating from 1879, but probably more useful from the 1930s, old directories of telephone subscribers, where they have survived, are another source of local information (see Robson, 1973, pp.165–77). Virtually a complete collection of these can be consulted at British Telecom Archives, Room GO9, Telephone House, 2–4 Temple Avenue, London, EC4Y OHL.

Usually, local trade directories include details of postal services; passenger transport facilities; cultural institutions such as schools, chapels and churches, clubs and societies; and details of communication media – telegraph and telephone facilities and local newspaper circulation. Invariably, retail, distributive and specialist craft trades and professional services are well represented. The distinguishing character of the local directory is that its purpose was overtly commercial – to aid in the promotion of business activities (see Figures 4.1 and 4.2).

Since prominent individuals in a town, tradesmen, shopkeepers and professionals are listed by name, directories are of much interest to family historians. Moreover, they offer considerable scope for writing community histories – especially in aggregate studies of local occupational structures. Directories may turn out to be the only means of finding out, virtually for any town, large or small, details as to market functions, the sphere of influence that a specific centre had carved out from the surrounding areas, or for tracing developments over time (see, for example, the discussion in Volume 2, Chapter 5).

Although the earliest directories appeared in the late seventeenth century, it was not until the second half of the eighteenth century that towns outside London began to be covered. The *Universal British directory* (published in parts between 1790 and 1798), despite being incomplete, is widely regarded as the first serious attempt to compile a 'national' directory. This was followed by a more comprehensive series of local and regional listings from the 1830s. Coverage of Scotland dates from 1772 (Shaw and Tipper, 1989), and of towns in Ireland from 1788 (Dublin from 1751) (ffolliott and Begley, 1987).

Directories were produced by commercial publishers – some of whom soon became household names (e.g. Kelly, Pigot). Apart from supplying information to local people,

Figure 4.1 (opposite) Entry for Llanfair Caereinion, Powys, in Slater's *Royal national and commercial directory and topography of the counties of Gloucestershire, Monmouthshire, and North and South Wales*, Manchester, 1858, p.47. The directories published by James Pigot, starting in 1814, at Manchester, and continuing in partnership with Isaac Slater from 1839 to 1853, provide unrivalled coverage of towns in northern England, Scotland, Ireland and Wales. The firm was later incorporated in Kelly's directories, but Pigot's name was still used until 1882. (See Shaw and Tipper, 1988, p.9.) (Source: National Library of Wales)

Directory. LLANERCHYMEDD. **North Wales.**

PLACES OF WORSHIP AND THEIR MINISTERS.	CONVEYANCE BY RAILWAY ON THE CHESTER AND HOLYHEAD LINE.	MAIL CARTS.
SAINT MARY'S CHURCH——Rev. Hugh Owen, M. A. incumbent		To ALMWICH, a *Mail Cart*, every morning about half-past nine
BAPTIST CHAPEL, ministers various	The nearest *Station* is BODORGAN, about 12 miles distant.	To BANGOR and LLANGEFNI, a *Mail Cart*, every afternoon at ten minutes past five
CALVINIST CHAPEL, ministers various		
INDEPENDENT CHAPEL, ministers various		

LLANFAIR,

OR *Llanvair*, is a small market-town, in the parish of Llanfair-Caereinion, hundred of Mathrafel, county of Montgomery; 178 miles N.W. from London, 7 w. by s. from Welchpool, about 11 N. from Newtown, and 25 w. by s. from Shrewsbury; pleasantly seated in a fertile valley, nearly surrounded by a chain of hills, and on the banks of the Verniew stream. It consists of three small streets, through the principal one of which, the high road from Shrewsbury (by way of Welchpool and Machynlleth) to Aberystwith passes. Most of the houses are ancient, but an air of neatness pervades the whole town. The greater number of the inhabitants are employed in agricultural concerns, and others in spinning and weaving yarn into a kind of coarse striped woollen generally worn by the humbler classes.—

Flannel is also manufactured here; the currying of leather, malting and tanning are among other branches of trade, pursued, and there are several corn mills. Viscount Clive is lord of the manor, and holds, by his steward, leet courts twice in the year, at one of which certain officers are appointed for the government of the town. The places of worship are the parish church of St. Mary, and a chapel each for Baptists, Independents, Calvinists and Methodists. The market is held on Saturday, and the fairs on Shrove Tuesday, the Saturday before Palm Sunday, May 18th, July 26th, October 3rd, November 1st, and the Friday next before Christmas day. The population of the parish in 1841, was 2,747 inhabitants, and in 1851, 2,727.

POST OFFICE, Elizabeth Griffiths, *Post Mistress*.—Letters from LONDON and all parts arrive (from WELCHPOOL) every morning at half-past eight, and are despatched thereto every afternoon at half-past four.—*Money Orders granted and paid here.*

GENTRY AND CLERGY.
Davies Captain —, Brynglas
Howell Rev. Griffith, Cao office
Jones Rev. Cadwallader, Brynhiarth
Jones Rev. David, Llanfair
Jones Fredk. Lloyd, Esq. Garthlurydd
Jones Price, Esq. Cyfronydd
Jones Rev. Richard, Llanfair
Jones Rev. Richard Abel, Llanfair
Jones Rev. Robert, Llanfair
Jones Mr. William, Llanfair
Lewis Mrs. —, Brynglas
Pugh Rev. —, Vicarage
Watkin Rev. William, Llanfair

SCHOOLS.
BRITISH AND FOREIGN SCHOOL, Edward Roberts, master
Evans Margaret [master
NATIONAL SCHOOL, Thomas Argyle,

BLACKSMITHS.
Evans William
Jehu Morris
Jones Robert
Jones Samuel
Roberts John, Mellynddol

BOOT AND SHOE MAKERS.
Breese John
Edwards John
Jones John
Lewis John
Williams Thomas

BUTCHERS
Goodwin David
Jones Benjamin
Price Richard

CORN & FLOUR DEALERS
Evans Edward | Jones Evan
Evans Morris | Lewis David
Evans Price | Price Richard
Jehu David | Richards John

DRESS AND STRAW BONNET MAKERS
Baxter Elizabeth | Hughes Mary
Davies Elizabeth | Lewis Margaret
Davies Esther | Roberts Mary

FLANNEL MANUFACTURERS
Jones James
Thomas Evan

GROCERS, DRAPERS AND DEALERS IN SUNDRIES.
Bebb Evan
Ellis Hugh
Evans Edward
Evans Humphrey

Evans Maurice
Evans Samuel
Griffiths Elizabeth (and druggist)
Hughes Thomas [druggist
Humphreys Jane (& ironmonger &
Humphreys John Lloyd
Jones Evan
Jones Jeremiah
Price Richard
Watkin William

HAIR DRESSERS
Baxter Thomas
Roberts Harriet

INNS & PUBLIC HOUSES
Black Lion, John Morris
Boot, John Evans
Crown, David Lewis
Eagle, Maurice Evans
Goat Inn, Jane Evans
Powis Arms, David Davies
Red Lion, Evan Nightingale Owen
Swan, Evan Evans
Wyunstay Arms Inn, Daniel Hughes

JOINERS & CARPENTERS
Ellis David
Ellis Hugh (& builder)
Ellis John
Jones John
Thomas David

MALTSTERS
Bebb John
Hughes Daniel
Morris Edward
Morris John

MILLERS.
Evans John, Hemarth
Evans Mary, White Lion Mill
Jehu Thomas
Richards John, Dolrhydefald
Whittaker James, Mellynddol

PLUMBERS & GLAZIERS.
Evans Thomas
Griffiths Richard
Jones Richard & Son

SADDLERS
Edwards Richard
Williams David
Williams John

SKINNERS
Davies John (& tallow chandler)
Morgans Richard

STATIONERS.
Baxter Thomas (& bookbinder)
Davies John

SURGEONS.
Jones John
Theodore William

TAILORS
Brees Richard
Gittons Christopher
Richards Evan
Thomas Evan

WHEELWRIGHTS
Ellis John
Evans Richard
Jehu David
Roberts Thomas

Miscellaneous
Humphreys Charles, registrar of births, deaths, and marriages
Jones Christopher & John, curriers
Jones John, tanner
Jones Richard & Son, bookbinders

PLACES OF WORSHIP, AND THEIR MINISTERS.
ST. MARY'S PARISH CHURCH—Rev. — Pugh, vicar; Rev. David Jones, curate
BAPTIST CHAPEL Rev. Richd. Abel J
INDEPENDENT CHAPEL—Rev. Cadwallader Jones
METHODIST (Calvinist) CHAPEL, Rev. Richard Jones
METHODIST (Wesleyan) CHAPEL —Rev Robert Jones

POOR LAW UNION.
WORKHOUSE, at Llanfyllin.
Governor—Evan Evans
Matron—Mary Evans
Schoolmaster—David Rowlands
Schoolmistress—Jane Rowlands
Chaplain—Rev. — Thompson
Surgeons—David Evans, Thos. Edwards and John Jones [Jones
Clerk to the Board of Guardians—Wm.
Relieving Officers—Maurice Jones, Geo. Jones, and Charles Humphreys

RAILWAY.
The nearest *Station* is at SHREWSBURY, twenty-five miles distant.

CARRIERS
To WELCHPOOL, Thomas Davies and David Jenkins, Monday and Friday.

47

Figure 4.2 Broad Street, Llanfair Caereinion, early 1860s. Carte-de-visite photograph (original size: 4⅛×2½in., 104×63mm.) by P. Jones, photographer, Hope Street, Wrexham, taken soon after Llanfair town appeared in Slater's *Directory*, 1858 (see Figure 4.1). The double-fronted shop in the mid-distance (centre right, person wearing white apron standing outside) is that of Jane Humphreys, listed in the directory under 'grocers, drapers and dealers in sundries' (Source: Pryce, 1991, p.61)

directories were used by travelling salesmen and commercial travellers working on behalf of the larger wholesalers who supplied local shops. Clearly, for the printers and publishers (often separate companies), profit maximization was the immediate goal. From the dates of publication, as well as from general similarities in the presentation of data, it is clear that stiff competition existed between publishers. Moreover, there is evidence that some compilers plagiarized entries from better-established publications; and there were numerous takeovers by rival publishers.

1.1 PROBLEMS OF INTERPRETATION AND ANALYSIS

A series of trade directories can yield valuable insights as to the changes occurring in specific towns during the nineteenth and twentieth centuries – for example, the rise and fall of different industries or types of employment, or the changing functions of towns. But *rigorous techniques and consistent standards have to be applied to their analysis.* Close attention needs to be directed to specific matters of data quality and comparability.

Accuracy of compilation   In general, the reliability of the data improves during the nineteenth century. In later editions, only rarely do we find no entries for a specific town, but coverage in the early directories was much more sporadic: some villages and, frequently, whole counties were left out. Moreover, even when a town was included, some traders refused to allow their names to be included for fear of being recruited, unwittingly, into the county militia, or because it would give a competitor knowledge of their business activities! Others seem to have been concerned lest their tax liabilities were increased when their names had been published!

When new editions were prepared it seems, as one directory put it, that the first revisions were completed as 'a matter of voluntary co-operation on the part of local gentlemen'. In consequence, in some localities the number of entries reflected local attitudes, elements of snobbery, and whims as to who should be included. It was not until after 1850 that comprehensive revisions were carried out systematically; but the continued reliability of the directory information appears to have fallen off considerably after World War II, especially in their coverage of small towns.

Difficulties of relating entries to specific places   The publication of directories seems to have been a lucrative business. However, as Lewis (1975) points out, directory compilers (at least those publishing on a national basis) were sometimes uncertain as to the exact limits of particular settlements. Thus, it is not at all unusual to find entries relating to small centres (especially subtowns and villages – see Volume 2, Chapter 5) subsumed with those of the nearest market town. This can give false impressions as to the regional importance of a town.

Multiple entries   Duplication of entries seems to have been widespread. For example, this occurred when business partners were listed separately, or when an established business had several branches. Again, as in studies of central place functions (see Volume 2, Chapter 5, section 1.2), this can result in more services being attributed to a particular town than, in reality, it discharged. On the other hand, where the focus is on the individual or a family business, multiple entries do reveal interesting new information on the range of entrepreneurial or public service activities.

Classification of traders   In the directories, individual entrepreneurs are listed either (a) in broad trade categories (e.g. under 'butchers' or 'booksellers'), or (b) alphabetically by name, with the trade indicated after the name. There does not seem to be any consistency of approach. Because, in urban historical geography, the final indication as to the relative importance (i.e. functional status) of an urban centre depends on how its central place activities are grouped for the purposes of the research, it is essential that the individual entrepreneur is counted as a single enterprise.

On the other hand, *depending on the research topic under investigation*, persons with dual occupations may need special consideration. Thus, if a man or woman is listed as 'shoemaker and publican', his/her activities will need to be counted under each of these categories because both activities relate to the central place functions discharged at that location.

Part-time occupations and services   When the population was small, business people adjusted to local circumstances by: (a) combining a range of goods and service activities in one enterprise; (b) restricting business *at any one centre* to specific days/times so that the entrepreneur could meet the needs of customers at several different locations; and/or (c) taking a stall at the local weekly market or a monthly fair. In extracting information from the trade directories, it is important to record details of part-time functions so that these can be allocated appropriate weightings in the analysis.

Spatial and temporal coverage   If a research project involves comparisons amongst different towns, it may turn out that the directories covering these places were compiled at different dates. Occasionally, entries for small centres may be deficient, listing, perhaps, just post-office details and places of worship when, in reality, more activities were discharged from that same location. In these circumstances, it may be necessary to extract information from rival directories published by competitors, from directories that appeared within two or three years of the date under consideration, or from alternative sources such as rent lists and books, poll books or newspaper advertisements. The extent to which supplementary data have been used should be indicated clearly in the final research report.

_____ **EXERCISE 4.1** _____

Evaluate the directory entries for the town of Llanfair Caereinion, Powys, 1858, reproduced in Figure 4.1. Which of the following can you identify as potential problems for the researcher?

1   Individuals cannot be identified by name.

2   Multiple/repeated entries.

3   Cannot identify service functions.

4   No information on how the town related to other centres.

5   Cannot identify the exact number of trade outlets.

6   Craft, trade and service outlets are better represented than retail traders.

7   Inadequate locational information (individual businesses).

Answers/comments p.299

1.2   FURTHER INFORMATION

Details of the directories covering specific towns and localities can usually be obtained from local reference libraries and record offices. For information concerning their publication and coverage up to 1856, see Norton (1950). More up-to-date information on England and Wales (1850–1950), and Scotland (1772–1950), is provided in Shaw and Tipper (1989). For Irish directories, see ffolliott and Begley (1987). The scope of local directories and their validity as sources is covered in Lewis (1975), Shaw (1982), and Shaw and Tipper (1989).

REFERENCES AND FURTHER READING (SECTION 1)

Armstrong, J. (1993) 'Local directories: exploring change and continuity in business activity', audio-cassette 4A in Braham, P. (ed.) _Using the past: audio-cassettes on sources and methods for family and community historians_, Milton Keynes, The Open University.

Atkins, P.J. (1990) _The directories of London, 1677–1977_, London, Cassell.

Crockford's clerical directory, London, Church House Publishing (first published 1858).

ffolliott, R. and Begley, D.F. (1987) 'Guide to Irish directories', in Begley, D.F. (ed.) _Irish genealogy: a record finder_, Dublin, Heraldic Artists Ltd.

Hillam, C. (1991) _Brass plate and brazen impudence: dental practice in the provinces, 1755–1855_, Liverpool, Liverpool University Press.

Lewis, C.R. (1975) 'Trade directories: a data source in urban analysis', _The National Library of Wales Journal_, 19, pp.181–93.

Norton, J.E. (1950) _Guide to national and provincial directories of England and Wales (excluding London) published before 1856_, London, Royal Historical Society.

Pryce, W.T.R. (1991) _The photographer in rural Wales_, Llanfair Caereinion and Welshpool, The Powysland Club.

Robson, B.T. (1973) _Urban growth: an approach_, London, Methuen.

Rogers, C.D. (1989) *The family tree detective* (2nd edn), Manchester, Manchester University Press.

Shaw, G. (1982) *British directories as sources in historical geography*, London, Institute of British Geographers, Historical Geography Research Series, No.8.

Shaw, G. and Tipper, A. (1989) *British directories: a bibliography and guide to directories published in England and Wales, 1850–1950; and Scotland, 1773–1950*, Leicester, Leicester University Press.

The medical directory, London, Modern Book Company (first published 1845).

Who was who, London, A. & C. Black (first published 1920).

Who's who, London, A. & C. Black (first published 1849).

Women workers directory (1909) London, Bale and Danielson.

2   POLL BOOKS AND ELECTORAL REGISTERS

by Michael Drake

2.1   POLL BOOKS

Until the Secret Ballot Act came into force in 1872, voting in parliamentary elections was carried out in public. On polling days (voting often took more than one day to complete), the vote of each elector was entered in the poll book. Most manuscript poll books were destroyed in 1896. This was not as grievous a blow as it might have been because it was not unusual for a local printer to publish a copy immediately after the poll had closed. For the period 1832–72, around 40 per cent of all contested elections produced a poll book, sometimes as a special supplement to a local newspaper. Prior to 1832, coverage was less complete. Poll books show considerable variation in the amount of material they contain. At the very least they give the name of the elector and the way he cast his vote or votes (many constituencies had two members). Some, however, contain much more than this. For instance, *The Bath poll book for 1855,* as well as giving the name and address of each elector and the way his vote was cast, also gives his occupation and the amount he was assessed for the poor rate. *The Newry poll book for 1868* gives the religious affiliation of voters. Most also give the names of electors who did not cast their votes; some go further, indicating if the reason for this was their having died or having been removed from the electoral register for other reasons (see Figure 4.3).

Naturally, poll books are immediately of use for psephological studies (i.e. for such questions as who voted and who abstained and who voted for whom): always bearing in mind that in the 'poll book era' only men had the vote, and a minority of men at that (see Table 4.1). Examples of questions which could be investigated are as follows. In the larger urban constituencies, can one find some areas supporting one candidate rather than another? Did people from different occupations or religious affiliations support particular candidates (see Vincent, 1967; Walker, 1989)? Using the rate books (carefully!) as a surrogate for wealth, can one detect better off electors supporting different candidates from the less well off? Are there indications of bribery or other illegitimate forms of influence? Inquiries – printed in the British Parliamentary Papers (see Chapter 5, section 1) – into allegations of corruption are a useful additional source here, as are local newspapers. Linking the evidence of one poll book with that of another, using individual voters' records as the linking device, can produce a sort of political genealogy of the electorate. Family historians might care to produce these in the form of psephological (voting) trees, akin to

THE
BATH REFORM POLL BOOK

FOR

1841

PARISH OF BATHWICK.

	1832. Pmr. Rbk. Hse.	1835. Pmr. Rbk. Dby.	1837. Pmr. Rbk. Pct. Bgs.	1841. Dcn. Rbk. Pot. Bgs.
r Adams Richard Leonard, Henrietta-street ..	—	—	--	
Alleson William, 46 Pulteney-street ..				
Andrews Augustus, Vellore, Sydney-gardens ..	1			1
Aust James, Villa-field	—	—	1 1	1 1
Awdry Jeremiah, 7 Johnstone-street ..	—	—	—	1 1
Ayerst Robert Gunsley, 20 Pulteney-street ..	—	—	—	1 1
r Barratt Samuel, 12 Sydney-place	1	1	1 1	
Barlow Edward, 102 Sydney-place	1 1	1	1 1	1 1
Batchelor Thomas, 9 Raby-place	1 1	1		1 1
Ball Henry, 1 Sydney-buildings	—	—	1 1	1 1
Barnard James, 60 Pulteney-street	—	—	1 1	1 1

THE

BATH POLL BOOK.

1841.

☞ *The greatest pains have been taken in the compilation of this Book. If, however, it should contain any errors, the Publisher will be most happy to rectify them, on their being pointed out.*

Name.	Description.	Where situate.	P	B	R	D
Aberfield William	policeman	1, Bridewell lane	1	1		
Abraham John	optician	1, St. Andrew's terrace				
Abraham Robert Thomas	gentleman	1, Rivers street			1	1
Abrahams George	gardener	Sussex pl., Widcombe	1	1		
Abrey William	policeman	Lansdown road, West	1	1		
Ackland Thomas (disqualified)	baker	3, Southgate street				
Adams George	coach spring maker	52, New King street	1	1		
Adams John	butcher	2, Piccadilly place			1	1
Adams Joseph	beer seller	42, Avon street			1	1
Adams Rich. L. (disqualified)	clerk	Henrietta street				
Adams Samuel	coachmaker	10, Seymour street	1	1		
Adams Thomas	pastrycook	21, Cheap street			1	1

Figure 4.3 Extracts from poll books for Bath showing styles typical of the 1832–72 period. The letters in the column headings stand for the names of the candidates (e.g. 'R' or 'Rbk' stands for J.A. Roebuck; 'D' or 'Dcn' stands for Lord Viscount Duncan) (Source: Bath Public Reference Library)

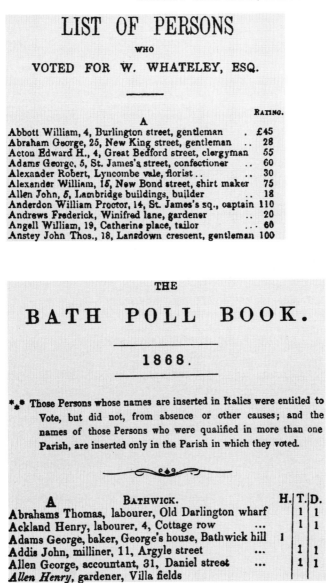

LIST OF PERSONS

WHO

VOTED FOR W. WHATELEY, ESQ.

A

	RATING.
Abbott William, 4, Burlington street, gentleman	£45
Abraham George, 25, New King street, gentleman	28
Acton Edward H., 4, Great Bedford street, clergyman	55
Adams George, 5, St. James's street, confectioner	60
Alexander Robert, Lyncombe vale, florist	30
Alexander William, 15, New Bond street, shirt maker	75
Allen John, 5, Lambridge buildings, builder	18
Anderdon William Proctor, 14, St. James's sq., captain	110
Andrews Frederick, Winifred lane, gardener	20
Angell William, 19, Catherine place, tailor	60
Anstey John Thos., 18, Lansdown crescent, gentleman	100

THE

B A T H   P O L L   B O O K.

1 8 6 8.

₊ Those Persons whose names are inserted in Italics were entitled to
Vote, but did not, from absence or other causes; and the
names of those Persons who were qualified in more than one
Parish, are inserted only in the Parish in which they voted.

A BATHWICK.	H.	T.	D.
Abrahams Thomas, labourer, Old Darlington wharf		1	1
Ackland Henry, labourer, 4, Cottage row ...		1	1
Adams George, baker, George's house, Bathwick hill	1		
Addis John, milliner, 11, Argyle street ...		1	1
Allen George, accountant, 31, Daniel street ...		1	1
Allen Henry, gardener, Villa fields			

Figure 4.3 (continued)

family trees (see Figure 4.4). Such longitudinal studies indicate not only the loyalty of individual voters to one candidate (set of principles, promises or party label) but also the extent of the turnover of voters in a particular constituency. Many of these exercises involve *nominal record linkage* (NRL) (see Chapter 9, section 1.3, and Schürer, 1993).

Quite apart from political behaviour, poll books offer an insight into community life generally. Today, political parties dominate political behaviour. In the poll book era, however, some historians believe that local factors were the determining ones (e.g. the proclivities of particular leading families, landed or industrial; traditions of radicalism or deference; or the personality of a 'sitting' MP). But what of national issues – the Poor Law, Corn Law repeal, parliamentary reform, the Crimean War – which bulk so large in our traditional political histories? Can these be seen operating at the constituency level? Can the people who changed their

Table 4.1 Voting qualifications: the growth of the parliamentary franchise

	Boroughs	Counties outside boroughs	Comments
Pre-1832	Boroughs always elected their own MP(s) – the qualification varied from borough to borough	Counties outside boroughs were always represented separately. The *county franchise* was based on the ownership of freehold land assessed as worth 40 shillings or more a year to its owner	In 1831, on the eve of the Reform Act, about 478,000 men (out of a population aged 21 or over in England and Wales of ten million) had any say in the choice of their MP – perhaps 1 man in 10
1832	The traditional franchise of each borough continued, with the addition of householders (i.e. occupier, whether owner or tenant) of property assessed as worth £10 a year	Freeholders with property worth 40*s* a year. Copyholders renting property at £10 a year. £10 leaseholders with at least 60 years leases. £50 leaseholders with at least 20 years leases. Any tenant paying more than £50 a year	By 1833, about 814,000 voters – richer industrialists, merchants and substantial farmers Voters – 1 man in 7
1867	Every adult male householder resident for a year and heads of families lodging in unfurnished rooms paying £10 a year in rent	Any owner or leaseholder of property rated at £5 a year, or tenant of property rated at £12 a year	1,430,000 in 1866 2,500,000 in 1868 This now included most working men in towns and cities but excluded rural labourers Voters – 1 man in 3
1884	No change	Same voting qualifications as granted to the boroughs in 1867	3,200,000 in 1883 5,900,000 in 1885 Most rural labourers now received the vote but still excluded were heads of households who shared houses; adult males living with parent(s); soldiers in barracks; and women Voters – 2 men in 3
1918	All males over 21 (residents or owners); women over 30 who were householders or wives of householders – 6 women in 10 Plural voting was limited to one residential and one business or university qualification (previously a man could vote in any constituency where he met the property qualification)		Voters – 5 people in 6 over 21
1928	Every resident or owner over 21		97% of the adult population
1948	Abolition of business/non-resident ownership vote and university seats		
1969	Everybody over 18		

Source: based on Todd (1989) pp.54–5

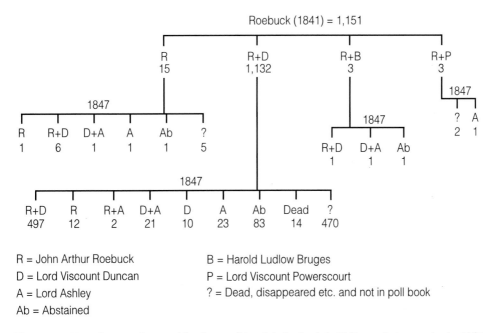

R = John Arthur Roebuck   B = Harold Ludlow Bruges
D = Lord Viscount Duncan   P = Lord Viscount Powerscourt
A = Lord Ashley   ? = Dead, disappeared etc. and not in poll book
Ab = Abstained

Figure 4.4   How electors who voted for the candidate J.A. Roebuck in 1841 cast their votes in the 1847 election (Source: based on *The Bath poll book for 1847*)

allegiance plausibly have done so for reasons of this kind? And was there a halfway house between local and national politics – namely, regional politics (Nossiter, 1975)?

Because poll books frequently – though not universally – give detailed addresses, it is possible to use them for purposes other than politics. For instance, one could get some idea of movement within a community – at least of how long people stayed at a particular address. However, in this regard poll books are less useful than electoral registers, since they only appeared after an election had taken place, and of course only included those qualified to vote (see Table 4.1). If occupation and address are given, then studies of residential distribution by occupation can be carried out. Given a surrogate for income/wealth, such as rate books, then this can also be used to map residential segregation. And of course the poll books can be linked with the CEBs (Schürer, 1993). For a selection of studies involving the use of poll books, see the references and further reading at the end of this section. There are also a number of unpublished MA and Ph.D. theses based on poll book studies, available in university libraries.

Poll books are widely available in England, less so in Wales, Scotland and Ireland. Having been little used either by historians or political scientists, they can usually be studied in their original printed form. To see whether or not there are poll books for a community which interests you (and which libraries and record offices have them), see Gibson and Rogers (1990). You should not, however, give up if a poll book is not listed. They are still being rediscovered – as are manuscript poll books or facsimiles.

2.2   ELECTORAL ROLLS OR REGISTERS

Annually published lists of electors can sometimes provide appropriate source material for the study of population turnover and, by implication, migration. As they give no indication of voting behaviour, they are little use for psephological study. Before 1918, however, only males enjoying certain property qualifications had the right to vote in parliamentary elections and so were included in these lists of names (see Table 4.1). Unmarried women, however, could participate in

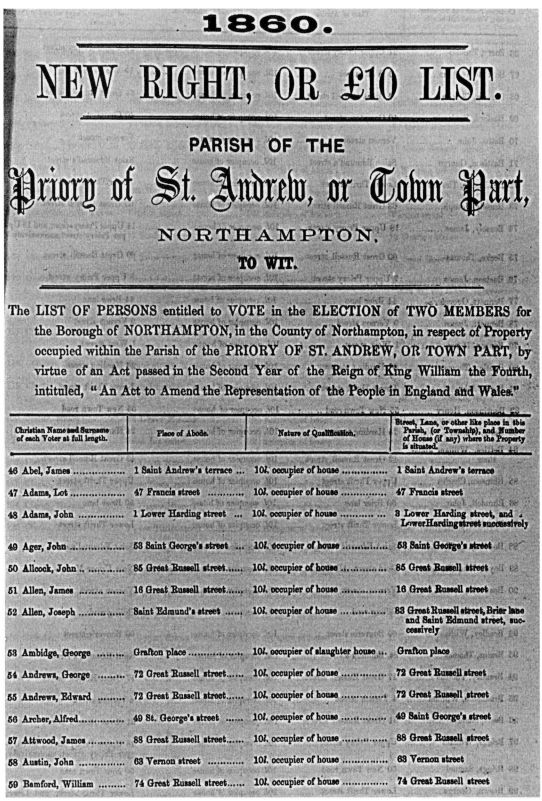

1860.

NEW RIGHT, OR £10 LIST.

PARISH OF THE

Priory of St. Andrew, or Town Part,

NORTHAMPTON,

TO WIT.

The LIST OF PERSONS entitled to VOTE in the ELECTION of TWO MEMBERS for the Borough of NORTHAMPTON, in the County of Northampton, in respect of Property occupied within the Parish of the PRIORY OF ST. ANDREW, OR TOWN PART, by virtue of an Act passed in the Second Year of the Reign of King William the Fourth, intituled, "An Act to Amend the Representation of the People in England and Wales."

Christian Name and Surname of each Voter at full length.	Place of Abode.	Nature of Qualification.	Street, Lane, or other like place in this Parish, (or Township), and Number of House (if any) where the Property is situated.
46 Abel, James	1 Saint Andrew's terrace	10l. occupier of house	1 Saint Andrew's terrace
47 Adams, Lot	47 Francis street	10l. occupier of house	47 Francis street
48 Adams, John	1 Lower Harding street	10l. occupier of house	3 Lower Harding street, and Lower Harding street successively
49 Ager, John	53 Saint George's street	10l. occupier of house	53 Saint George's street
50 Allcock, John	85 Great Russell street	10l. occupier of house	85 Great Russell street
51 Allen, James	16 Great Russell street	10l. occupier of house	16 Great Russell street
52 Allen, Joseph	Saint Edmund's street	10l. occupier of house	83 Great Russell street, Brier lane and Saint Edmund street, successively
53 Ambidge, George	Grafton place	10l. occupier of slaughter house	Grafton place
54 Andrews, George	72 Great Russell street	10l. occupier of house	72 Great Russell street
55 Andrews, Edward	72 Great Russell street	10l. occupier of house	72 Great Russell street
56 Archer, Alfred	49 St. George's street	10l. occupier of house	49 Saint George's street
57 Attwood, James	88 Great Russell street	10l. occupier of house	88 Great Russell street
58 Austin, John	63 Vernon street	10l. occupier of house	63 Vernon street
59 Bamford, William	74 Great Russell street	10l. occupier of house	74 Great Russell street

Figure 4.5   Examples of nineteenth- and twentieth-century electoral registers (Source: Northamptonshire Record Office)

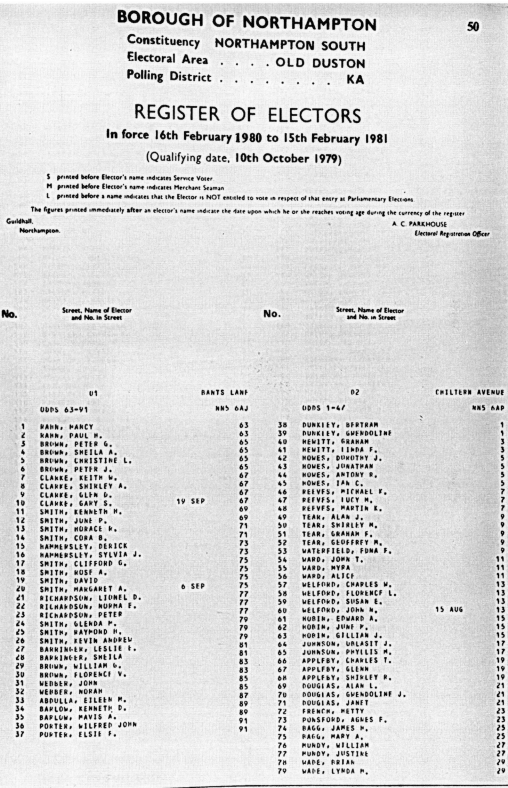

BOROUGH OF NORTHAMPTON   **50**

Constituency   NORTHAMPTON SOUTH

Electoral Area . . . .OLD DUSTON

Polling District . . . . KA

REGISTER OF ELECTORS

In force 16th February 1980 to 15th February 1981

(Qualifying date, 10th October 1979)

S printed before Elector's name indicates Service Voter.

M printed before Elector's name indicates Merchant Seaman.

L printed before a name indicates that the Elector is NOT entitled to vote in respect of that entry at Parliamentary Elections.

The figures printed immediately after an elector's name indicate the date upon which he or she reaches voting age during the currency of the register

Guildhall,   A. C. PARKHOUSE

Northampton.   *Electoral Registration Officer*

No.	Street, Name of Elector and No. in Street		No.	Street, Name of Elector and No. in Street	
	01	BANTS LANE		02	CHILTERN AVENUE
	ODDS 63-91	NN5 6AJ		ODDS 1-47	NN5 6AP
1	RAHN, NANCY	63	38	DUNKLEY, BERTRAM	1
2	RAHN, PAUL M.	63	39	DUNKLEY, GWENDOLINE	1
3	BROWN, PETER G.	65	40	HEWITT, GRAHAM	3
4	BROWN, SHEILA A.	65	41	HEWITT, LINDA F.	3
5	BROWN, CHRISTINE L.	65	42	HOWES, DOROTHY J.	5
6	BROWN, PETER J.	65	43	HOWES, JONATHAN	5
7	CLARKE, KEITH W.	67	44	HOWES, ANTONY R.	5
8	CLARKE, SHIRLEY A.	67	45	HOWES, IAN C.	5
9	CLARKE, GLEN D.	67	46	REEVES, MICHAEL K.	7
10	CLARKE, GARY S. 19 SEP	67	47	REEVES, LUCY M.	7
11	SMITH, KENNETH H.	69	48	REEVES, MARTIN K.	7
12	SMITH, JUNE P.	69	49	TEAR, ALAN J.	9
13	SMITH, HORACE R.	71	50	TEAR, SHIRLEY M.	9
14	SMITH, CORA B.	71	51	TEAR, GRAHAM F.	9
15	HAMMERSLEY, DERICK	73	52	TEAR, GEOFFREY M.	9
16	HAMMERSLEY, SYLVIA J.	73	53	WATERFIELD, EDNA F.	9
17	SMITH, CLIFFORD G.	75	54	WARD, JOHN T.	11
18	SMITH, ROSE A.	75	55	WARD, MYRA	11
19	SMITH, DAVID	75	56	WARD, ALICE	11
20	SMITH, MARGARET A. 6 SEP	75	57	WELFORD, CHARLES W.	13
21	RICHARDSON, LIONEL D.	77	58	WELFORD, FLORENCE L.	13
22	RICHARDSON, NORMA F.	77	59	WELFORD, SUSAN E.	13
23	RICHARDSON, PETER	77	60	WELFORD, JOHN N. 15 AUG	13
24	SMITH, GLENDA M.	79	61	HOBIN, EDWARD A.	15
25	SMITH, RAYMOND H.	79	62	HOBIN, JUNE P.	15
26	SMITH, KEVIN ANDREW	79	63	HOBIN, GILLIAN J.	15
27	BARRINGER, LESLIE F.	81	64	JOHNSON, URLASIT J.	17
28	BARRINGER, SHEILA	81	65	JOHNSON, PHYLLIS M.	17
29	BROWN, WILLIAM G.	83	66	APPLEBY, CHARLES T.	19
30	BROWN, FLORENCE V.	83	67	APPLEBY, GLENN	19
31	WEBBER, JOHN	85	68	APPLEBY, SHIRLEY R.	19
32	WEBBER, NORAH	85	69	DOUGLAS, ALAN L.	21
33	ABDULLA, EILEEN M.	87	70	DOUGLAS, GWENDOLINE J.	21
34	BARLOW, KENNETH D.	89	71	DOUGLAS, JANET	21
35	BARLOW, MAVIS A.	89	72	FRENCH, NETTY	23
36	PORTER, WILFRED JOHN	91	73	PUNSFORD, AGNES F.	23
37	PORTER, ELSIE F.	91	74	BAGG, JAMES H.	25
			75	BAGG, MARY A.	25
			76	MUNDY, WILLIAM	27
			77	MUNDY, JUSTINE	27
			78	WADE, BRIAN	29
			79	WADE, LYNDA M.	29

Printed by the Electoral Registration Officer of the Borough of Northampton

Figure 4.5 (continued)

local government from 1869 onwards, if they had the appropriate property qualifications (see Gibson and Rogers, 1993).

Unlike modern electoral registers, nineteenth-century electoral rolls cannot therefore be regarded as representative of all adults in the population. Nevertheless, there have been several studies which demonstrate the utility of these sources (Dickinson, 1958; Werbner, 1979) whilst we await the further release of CEBs under the hundred-year rule (see the introduction to Chapter 3).

For example, electoral rolls have been effectively drawn on in a study of housing and social mobility in Leicester since the Industrial Revolution (Pritchard, 1977). This focuses on three aspects of social behaviour:

1   the creation and dissolution of households;

2   movements of established households within the city; and

3   migration into and out of the city.

Some of Pritchard's conclusions themselves provide appropriate topics for further research. For instance, he states that, in general, 'the poorer the area, the more closely intermeshed are its migration flows. High mobility in poor areas is associated with very short-distance moves which have the minimum directional bias. As one moves up the social scale, so this directional bias appears to be closely connected with suburban development' (Pritchard, 1977, p.59). Similarly, although conducted on a much smaller, village scale, Robin's (1980) study of Elmdon (Essex) includes sections on migration which draw on local lists of voters as well as other sources like the census returns and birth/death/marriage certificates. Like Pritchard's work on Leicester, this research relies on nominal record linkage (NRL) between the electoral rolls, various other records and more recent surveys. Amongst many interesting findings, Robin's study reveals that, in the decade 1949–59, Elmdon recorded slightly fewer migratory movements than a hundred years ago. Analysis of the electoral registers decade by decade shows that it was from the 1920s that the numbers of strangers coming to live in the village community first began to outstrip the numbers of young, native-born 'Elmdoners' reaching the age of 21 years. Moreover, whilst in the mid-nineteenth century it was lack of employment opportunities that drove out the young, today it is the unavailability of housing due to the constraints imposed by market forces and official planning policies.

Although electoral registers were reproduced annually, they are not as readily available as one might have expected. For current availability, see Gibson and Rogers (1993).

REFERENCES AND FURTHER READING (SECTION 2)

Cox, G. (1987) *The efficient secret: the Cabinet and the development of political parties in Victorian England*, Cambridge, Cambridge University Press.

Davis, R.W. (1972) *Political change and continuity 1760–1885: a Buckinghamshire study*, Newton Abbott, David and Charles.

Dickinson, G.C.D. (1958) 'The nature of rural population movement – an analysis of seven Yorkshire parishes based on electoral returns from 1931–1954', *Yorkshire Bulletin of Economic and Social Research*, 10, pp.96–105.

Drake, M. (1970) 'The mid-Victorian voter', *Journal of Interdisciplinary History*, 1, 3, pp.473–90.

Drake, M. (ed.) (1994) *Time, family and community: perspectives on family and community history*, Oxford, Blackwell in association with The Open University (Course Reader).

Fraser, D. (1976) *Urban politics in Victorian England*, Leicester, Leicester University Press.

Gibson, J. and Rogers, C. (1990) *Poll books c.1695–1872: a directory to holdings in Great Britain,* Birmingham, Federation of Family History Societies.

Gibson, J. and Rogers, C. (1993) *Electoral registers since 1832; and Burgess Rolls: a directory to holdings in Great Britain,* Birmingham, Federation of Family History Societies.

Hanham, J.J. (1971) *The reformed electoral system in Great Britain 1832–1914,* London, The Historical Association.

Hanham, H.J. (ed.) (1972) *Charles R. Dod's electoral facts from 1832 to 1853 impartially stated,* Hassocks, Harvester Press.

Mclean, I. (1992) 'Rational choice and the Victorian voter', *Political studies,* 40, 3, pp.496–515.

Moore, D.C. (1975) *The politics of deference,* Hassocks, Harvester Press.

Neale, R.S. (1972) *Class and ideology in the nineteenth century,* London, Routledge & Kegan Paul.

Nossiter, T.J. (1975) *Influence, opinion and political idioms in reformed England. Case studies from the North-east 1832–74,* Hassocks, Harvester Press.

Pritchard, R.M. (1977) *Housing and the spatial structure in the city: residential mobility and the housing market in an English city since the Industrial Revolution,* Cambridge, Cambridge University Press.

Robin, J. (1980) *Elmdon: continuity and change in a north-west Essex village, 1861–1964,* Cambridge, Cambridge University Press.

Schürer, K. (1993) 'Nominal lists and nominal record linkage', audio-cassette 2B in Braham, P. (ed.) (1993) *Using the past: audio-cassettes on sources and methods for family and community historians,* Milton Keynes, The Open University.

Todd, A. (1989) *Basic sources for family history: back to the early 1800s,* Allen and Todd, 9 Square Street, Ramsbottom, Bury, Lancashire, BL0 9BE.

Vincent, J.R. (1967) *Pollbooks: how Victorians voted,* Cambridge, Cambridge University Press.

Walker, B.M. (1976) 'Irish election pollbooks, 1832–1872 (1)', *Irish Booklore,* 3, 1, pp.8–13.

Walker, B.M. (1989) *Ulster politics: the formative years, 1868–86,* Belfast, Ulster Historical Association and The Institute of Irish Studies.

Werbner, P. (1979) 'Avoiding the ghetto. Pakistani migrants and settlement shifts in Manchester', *New Community,* 7, 3, pp.376–89. Reprinted in Drake (1994).

3   CHURCH AND CHAPEL REGISTERS

by Michael Drake

Forty years ago, the small industrial town in which I grew up had ten places of worship for a population of 8,000. There were also eleven fish and chip shops – but that's another story! There was a Church of England parish church and a Roman Catholic church; three Methodist chapels; a Congregationalist chapel; a Christadelphian ecclesia; a Church of Christ; a Salvation Army meeting place and a Gospel Temperance Hall (see Table 4.2). Of these, only the Church of England and the Methodists appear to have had congregations in the town before 1800.

Table 4.2   Some statistics of religion in Birstall (West Riding, Yorkshire), January 1955

Place of worship	Seating capacity	Members	Sunday school attendance
St. Johns (Methodist)	1,200	111	200
Church of England	1,000	400	150
Temperance Hall	650	90	60
Mt. Tabor (Methodist)	550	65	50
Roman Catholic	400	650	–
Congregationalist	200	55	50
Salvation Army	150	109	80
'Mount Top' (Methodist)	100	67	25
Church of Christ	50	30	20(?)
Christadelphian	50	28	30(?)

Source: Drake (1955) personal investigation

So not all of the town's population could have been accommodated even had they so wished. The crush could have been smaller in the nineteenth century, though two of the larger buildings (the Gospel Temperance Hall and the Roman Catholic Church) were not built until the first decade of the twentieth century.

Oral history, membership lists, and reports of activities in the local press will tell us about these congregations in the recent past. But what of earlier periods? For that one must turn to the documentary evidence, of which registers of baptisms, marriages and burials are likely to be the most easily accessible. These were the responsibility of religious bodies prior to the introduction of civil registration in the early to mid-nineteenth century (see dates in Chapter 5, section 1).

3.1   BAPTISM REGISTERS

In England before 1700, the Church of England's parish registers provide a good indication of the numbers of births in communities throughout the country. This is because baptisms appear to have taken place within a week of birth and parish registers covered most of the population (Wrigley and Schofield, 1981). By 1800 this was no longer the case. For the country as a whole, it has been estimated that some 30 per cent of births did not appear in a Church of England baptism register. This was partly because of the rise of nonconformity; partly because of the inability of the Church of England to cater for the rapidly rising populations of the new industrial areas; and partly because the gap between birth and baptism appears to have widened to a month or so, thus increasing the likelihood of infants dying before being baptized.

The situation in Wales, Scotland and Ireland was worse (i.e. an even higher proportion of births did not find their way into a baptismal register). Registration by the established churches was never as efficient as in England. In Ireland the majority of the population were members of the Catholic church, which did not have an efficient registration system (Connolly, 1985, pp.7–18). Though the picture nationally may appear bleak in each of these countries, at the local level there are likely to be registers which cover the population sufficiently to allow measures of fertility to be calculated.

BAPTISMS ſolemnized in the Pariſh of *Wendover* in the County of *Bucks* in the Year 18*17*

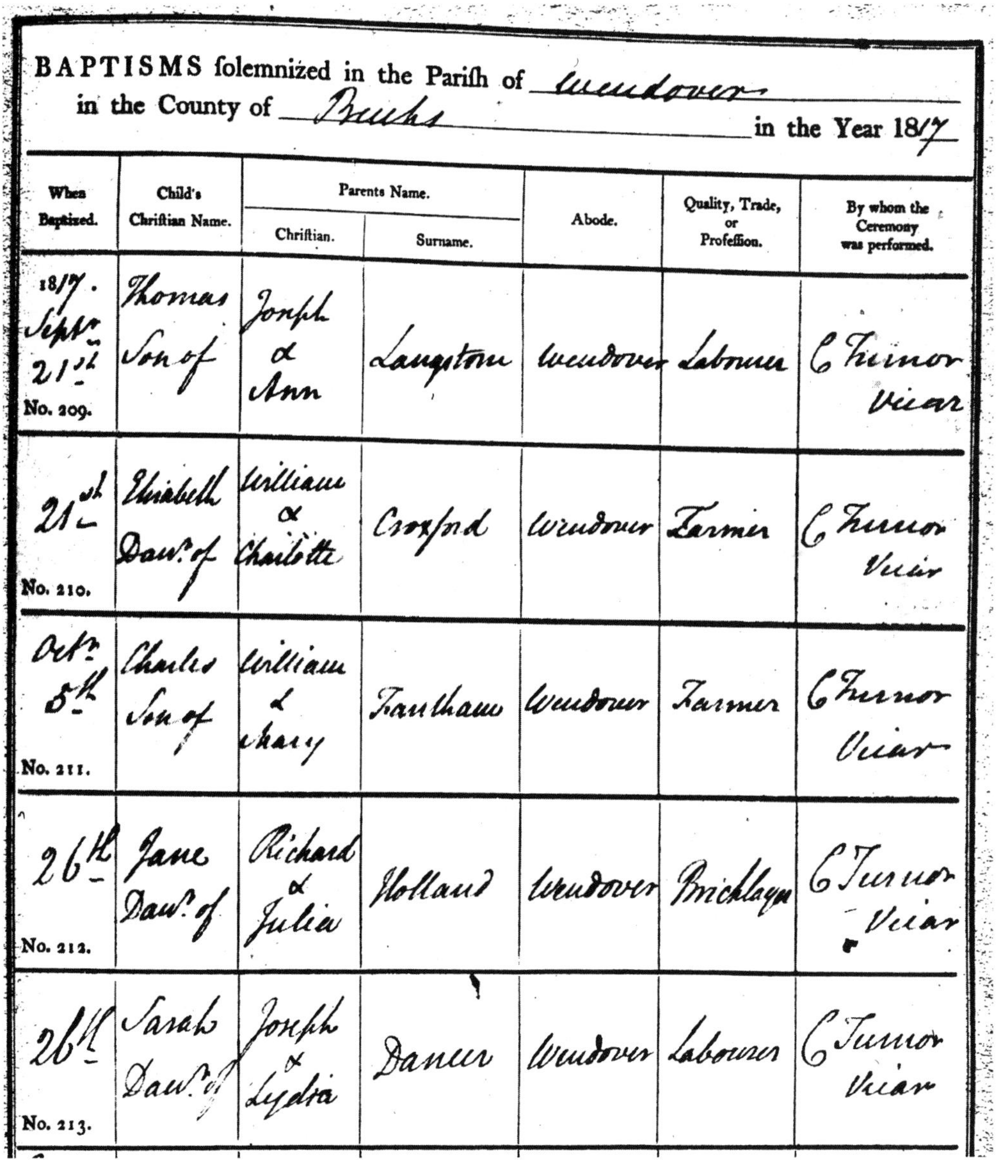

When Baptized.	Child's Chriſtian Name.	Parents Name. Chriſtian.	Parents Name. Surname.	Abode.	Quality, Trade, or Profeſſion.	By whom the Ceremony was performed.
1817. Septr 21st No. 209.	Thomas Son of	Joseph & Ann	Langston	Wendover	Labourer	C Turnor Vicar
21st No. 210.	Elizabeth Daw^r of	William & Charlotte	Croxford	Wendover	Farmer	C Turnor Vicar
Octr 5th No. 211.	Charles Son of	William & Mary	Fantham	Wendover	Farmer	C Turnor Vicar
26th No. 212.	Jane Daw^r of	Richard & Julia	Holland	Wendover	Bricklayer	C Turnor Vicar
26th No. 213.	Sarah Daw^r of	Joseph & Lydia	Dancer	Wendover	Labourer	C Turnor Vicar

Figure 4.6 Example from Wendover, Bucks Parish register of baptisms, 1817 (Source: Bucks County Record Office, Aylesbury)

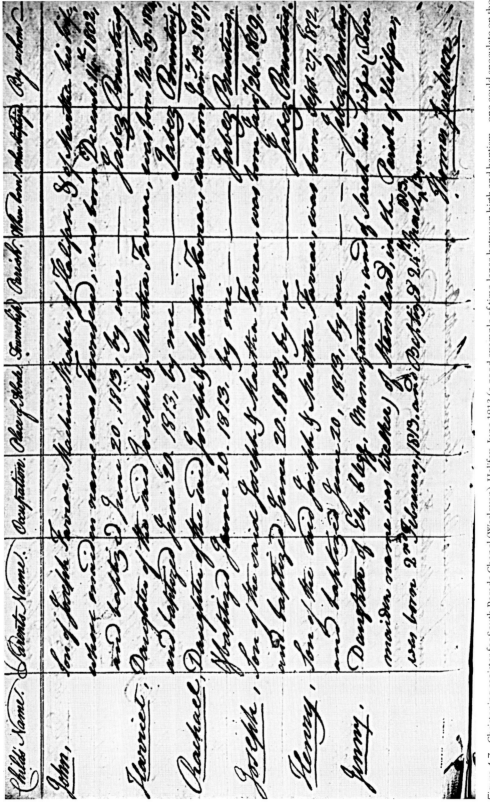

Figure 4.7 Christening register for South Parade Chapel (Wesleyan), Halifax, June 1813 (a good example of time-lapse between birth and baptism – one could speculate on the reasons) (Source: Public Record Office)

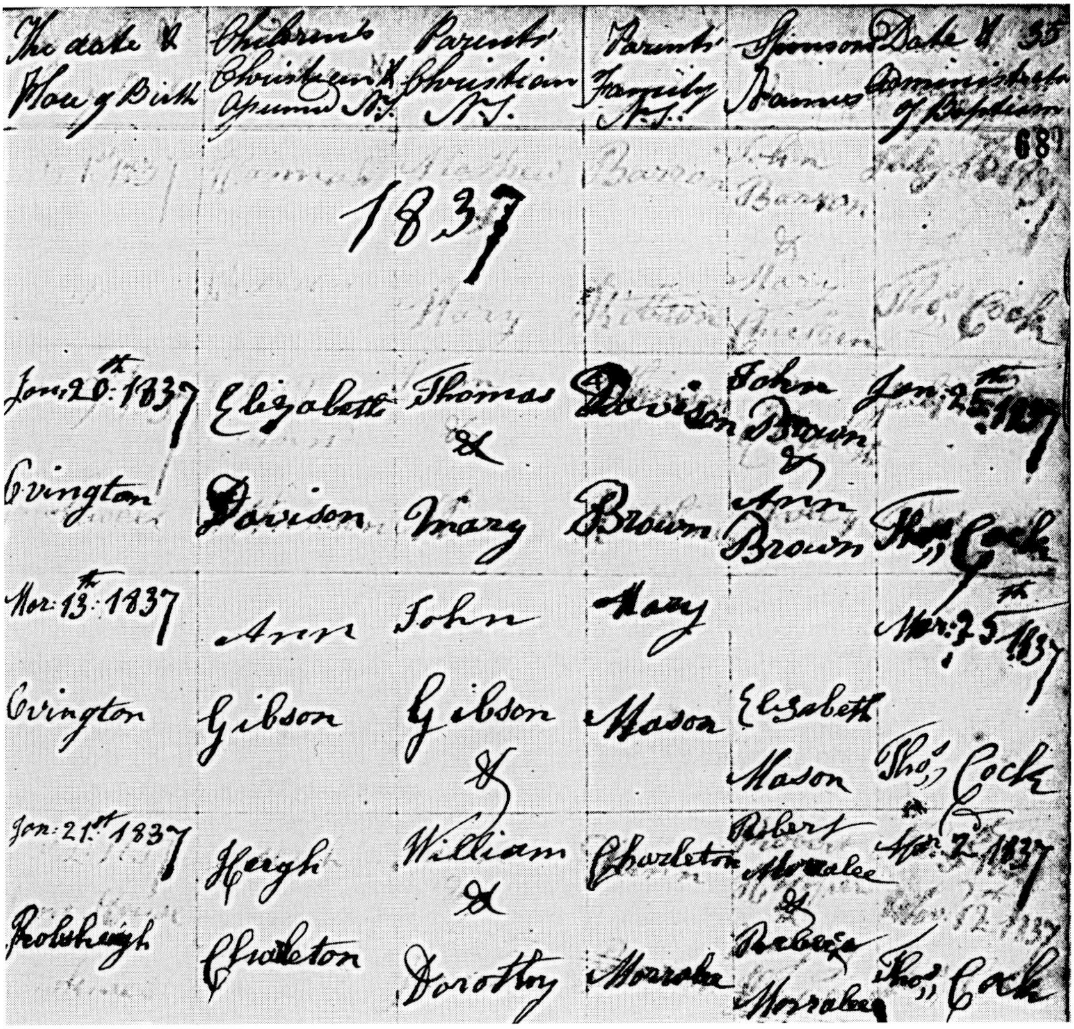

The date & Place of Birth	Children's Christian & Surname N.S.	Parents' Christian N.S.	Parents' Family N.S.	Sponsors Names	Date & Administrator of Baptism
		1837			
Jan: 20th 1837 Ovington	Elizabeth Davison	Thomas & Mary	Davison Brown	John Brown & Ann Brown	Jan: 25th 1837 Thos Cock
Mar: 13th 1837 Ovington	Ann Gibson	John Gibson &	Mary Mason	Elizabeth Mason	Mar: 25th 1837 Thos Cock
Jan: 21st 1837 Rolshaugh	Hugh Charleton	William & Dorothy	Charleton Morralee	Robert Morralee & Rebecca Morralee	Mar: 7th 1837 Thos Cock

Figure 4.8 Extract from Roman Catholic baptismal register of the Chapel of Cheeseburn Grange in the Parish of Stamfordham, Northumberland, 1837

EXERCISE 4.2

Take a nineteenth-century baptism register, produced for a parish of the Church of England, Wales or Scotland (see section 3.5 below on location of registers). Total the number of baptisms over a three-year period, centred on a census year (e.g. 1800–2; 1810–12, etc.). Calculate the mean number per year (i.e. divide the total by three), and then work out the number of baptisms per 1,000 population. (Note that this exercise does not apply to Ireland, since the Church of Ireland registers never pretended to cover the whole population.)

Example:

Baptisms 1810 to 1812 = 87

Mean no. of baptisms = 87 ÷ 3 = 29

Population in 1811 = 1,120

Baptisms per 1,000 population =

Were you to come up with a figure like this, for this date, it would indicate that the register was not accounting for all the births in the population of the community it supposedly covered. You may be able to combine entries from two or more registers (e.g. one from the Church of England, another from the Methodists). This may give you a figure closer to the expected 30–40 per 1,000. If your figure is much less than this, you are witnessing a crack in the ideal of one church baptizing all infants and efficiently recording the event. By 1800 this was no longer true of the whole of any one of the countries under consideration here. And as time passed the divisions within the Christian denominations increased and became more acute. The Birstall experience (see Table 4.2) was repeated throughout much of England, and though religious antagonism never reached the Irish pitch it was not negligible. It is into this, rather than the demographic experience of a community, that the nineteenth- and twentieth-century registers offer insight. The newer nonconformist congregations did not fit into the parish boundaries of the established churches. Aggregating data is, therefore, hazardous.

The extent to which the registers reflect differences in a community depends upon their content. Let us suppose that you have a register of baptisms containing the following: baptismal date; child's first name(s); parents' first names and surname; address; 'quality, trade or profession of father'; and the name of the person conducting the ceremony. The baptismal date is of interest as indicative of the timing (i.e. the day of the ceremony). Was one day more popular than others? If so, did this change over time (Drake, 1982, pp.22–47)? Was there any indication that 'better off' people (inferred from father's occupation) baptized their children at different times from the less well off? Turning to address: what relationship had this – in terms of distance, accessibility – to the church/chapel where the baptism took place? Was there evidence of 'localism' (choosing the nearest place for the ceremony) or its converse (travelling miles to a fashionable church)? And what about the choice of first name? Were there any patterns to be discovered here? Were biblical names popular (Joshua, Joseph, Mary) or secular ones (Albert, William, George)? And again, were there changes over time? Or were there differences in the names chosen by the better off as against the less well off, again inferred from father's occupation?

The extent to which exercises of this sort can be carried out will depend upon the amount of information the registers contain. For instance, some Methodist registers contain the date of birth and baptism on specially printed schedules from about 1819. It would be interesting to see whether the average gap of a month or more between birth and baptism – characteristic of Church of England registers giving this information in the early years of the nineteenth century (Berry and Schofield, 1971; Drake, 1982) – was repeated amongst the Methodists.

3.2 MARRIAGES

Let us assume you have a marriage register which gives the date of the ceremony; the first names and surnames of bride and groom; their ages (in years, not just in the form 'of full age': i.e. over 21 years); the civil status of the couple (i.e. bachelor, spinster, widower, widow); the 'rank or profession' of bride and groom (in practice, often only that of the latter); residence of bride and groom at the time of marriage; and first names and surnames of the fathers of bride and groom, together with their 'rank or profession'.

Depending upon how full the information is, the marriage registers provide numerous opportunities for exercises likely to cast light on community life. Take, for instance, the time of year at which a marriage takes place. This has been associated with a community's economic character. Pastoral areas tended to have an upsurge of marriages after the spring lambing and calving was over; in corn-producing areas, this increase might be after the harvest was completed (Kussmaul, 1990). In the west of Ireland, the end of a calendar year and the beginning of the next might see a peak in the number of marriages, if the men were seasonal migrants on the farms and building sites of England and Scotland (Brody, 1973). Other factors might be the avoidance of

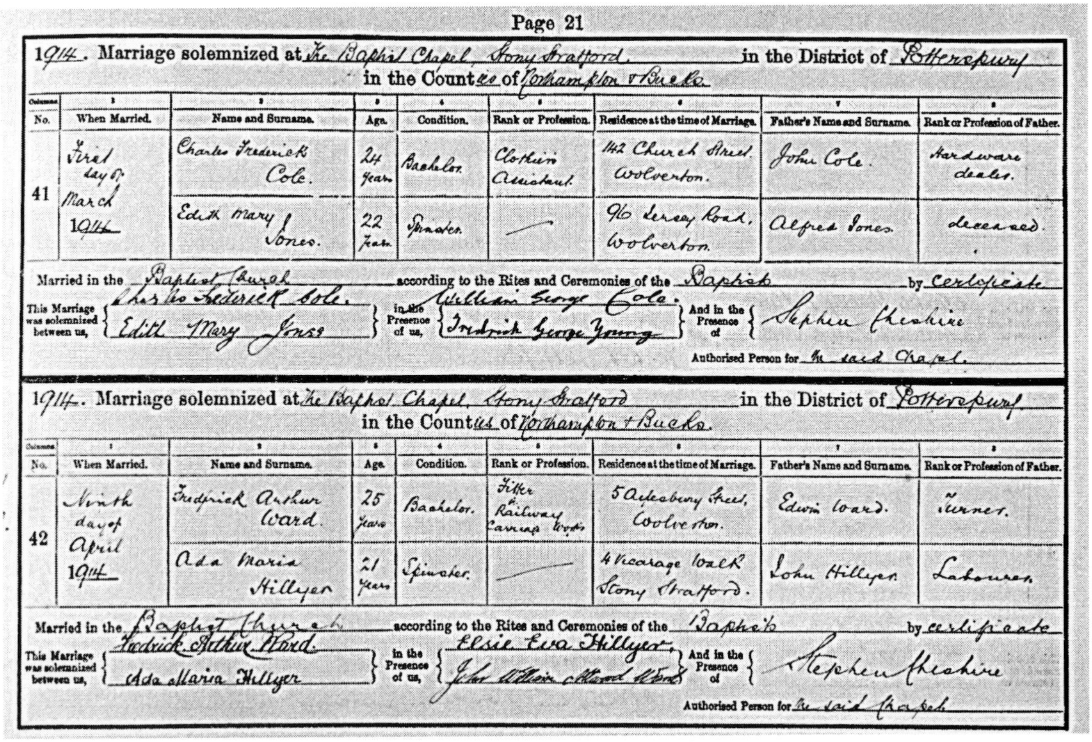

Page 21

1914. Marriage solemnized at The Baptist Chapel, Stony Stratford in the District of Potterspury in the Counties of Northampton & Bucks

No.	When Married.	Name and Surname.	Age.	Condition.	Rank or Profession.	Residence at the time of Marriage.	Father's Name and Surname.	Rank or Profession of Father.
41	First day of March 1914	Charles Frederick Cole.	24 years	Bachelor	Clothier Assistant	142 Church Street, Wolverton.	John Cole.	Hardware dealer.
		Edith Mary Jones.	22 years	Spinster	—	96 Jersey Road, Wolverton.	Alfred Jones.	deceased.

Married in the Baptist Church according to the Rites and Ceremonies of the Baptists by certificate

This Marriage was solemnized between us, Charles Frederick Cole. Edith Mary Jones

in the Presence of us, William George Cole. Fredrick George Young

And in the Presence of Stephen Cheshire Authorised Person for the said Chapel.

1914. Marriage solemnized at The Baptist Chapel, Stony Stratford in the District of Potterspury in the Counties of Northampton & Bucks

No.	When Married.	Name and Surname.	Age.	Condition.	Rank or Profession.	Residence at the time of Marriage.	Father's Name and Surname.	Rank or Profession of Father.
42	Ninth day of April 1914	Frederick Arthur Ward.	25 years	Bachelor.	Fitter Railway Carriage Works	5 Aylesbury Street, Wolverton.	Edwin Ward.	Turner.
		Ada Maria Hillyer	21 years	Spinster.	—	4 Vicarage Walk Stony Stratford.	John Hillyer.	Labourer.

Married in the Baptist Church according to the Rites and Ceremonies of the Baptists by certificate

This Marriage was solemnized between us, Fredrick Arthur Ward. Ada Maria Hillyer

in the Presence of us, Elsie Eva Hillyer. John William Ward

And in the Presence of Stephen Cheshire Authorised Person for the said Chapel

Figure 4.9 Example from the marriage register of a nonconformist chapel, 1914 (Source: Stony Stratford Baptist Church, Bucks)

Lent or the popularity of traditional holidays. Merely totalling the number of marriages on a monthly basis, making an allowance for months of different lengths, will provide a crude measure of marriage seasonality (for how to calculate a more sophisticated measure, see Chapter 8, section 5).

Age at first marriage is also a matter of interest. Did workers in industrial occupations marry earlier than those in agriculture or traditional crafts where 'waiting on dead men's shoes' might play a part? In Ireland, after the Famine, did the system of arranged marriages ('the match') lead both to later marriage and a significant gap between the ages of bride and groom (Connell, 1968; Fitzpatrick, 1987)?

Social mobility can be illuminated through occupational information available in marriage registers. One can get some idea of inter-generational mobility by comparing the occupation of fathers and sons. A problem here is that because one is looking at people at different times in their life, literally a generation apart, intra-generational mobility may play a role. For instance, a father aged 50 may have a higher occupation, socially speaking, than his son, marrying at the age of 25. This would suggest the son was downwardly mobile. Had they been compared at the same age, this may not have been the case. Another form of social mobility can, however, be measured by comparing the occupations of the fathers of the bride and the groom. Here one would be seeing whether, through marriage itself, either the bride or the groom was moving up or down the social scale – or staying put – judged in terms of social *origins*.

In both these enquiries, one has to battle with the question of what the occupational description actually meant. It is of interest in this connection that so many registers (and census forms, for that matter) ask for rank, trade, quality or profession, rather than occupation. Moreover, such documents rarely give information about multiple occupations – not at all uncommon in the nineteenth century; or avoid ambiguities, such as whether a butcher, say, is the owner of a butcher's shop or an employee. Comparing occupational descriptions for the same person in different registers, census returns and trade directories can throw some light on this.

Another line of research concerns women's occupations. Because these were often of an auxiliary nature (e.g. being a farmer's or a shopkeeper's wife), or were part-time and domestic (e.g. sewing, charring, laundering), they were omitted from both registers and census forms. Fuller returns are found in areas where women worked full-time outside the home. Where an occupation is given, you could explore the relationship between it and that of the groom or the bride's father. For marriages occurring in a census year, checks can be carried out to see what, if any, differences there are between the occupation given in a register and in a census. Changes over time are also worth recording.

3.3 BURIAL REGISTERS

Because transportation problems still ensure that most people are buried relatively near to where they die, and because, for health and decency reasons, burial grounds are regulated with some strictness, one might assume that by the middle of the nineteenth century most deaths were registered. This was certainly not the case in the opening decades of the century, at least not in England (Wrigley and Schofield, 1981). Burial registers giving age at death and cause of death (not by any means universal and often of doubtful accuracy) have, nevertheless, been used for demographic studies (Hinde, 1987; Williams, 1992). It is preferable, however, to use the civil

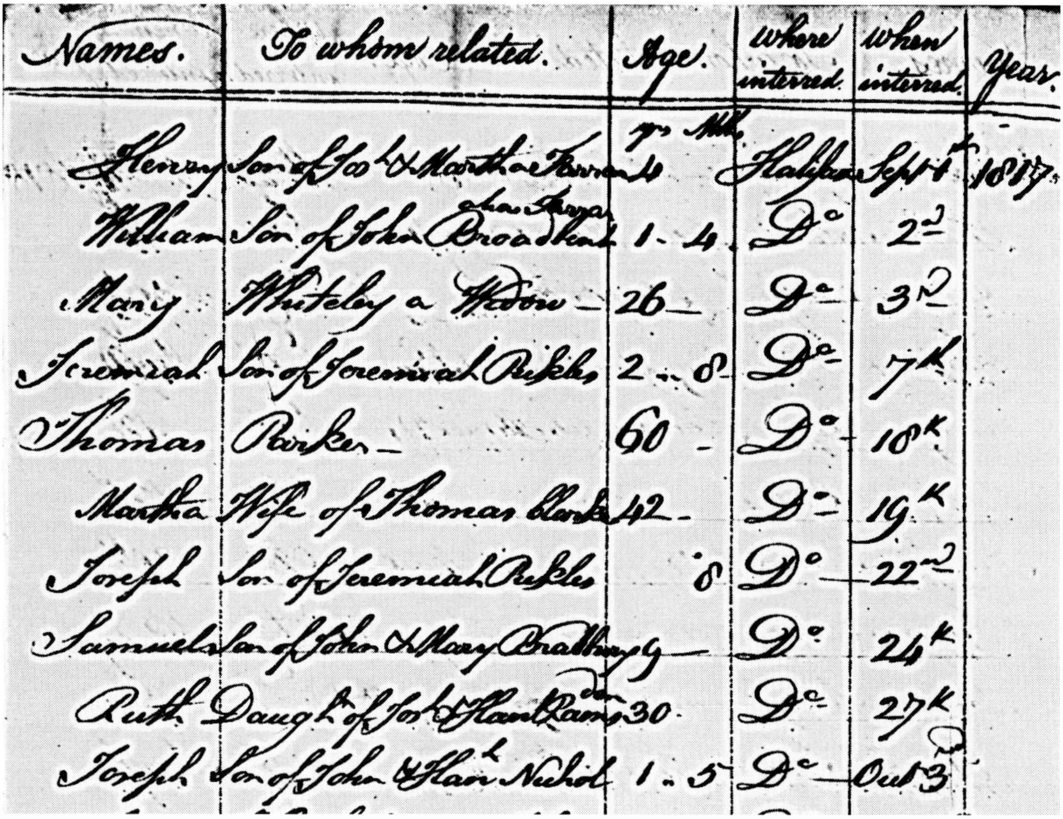

Names.	To whom related.	Age.	where interred.	when interred.	Year.
Henry	Son of Jos & Martha [illegible]	Yrs. Mth. 4	Halifax	Sept 1st	1817.
William	Son of John & Ann Broadbent	1 - 4	Do	2nd	
Mary	Whiteley a Widow	26	Do	3rd	
Jeremiah	Son of Jeremiah Pickles	2 .. 8	Do	7th	
Thomas	Parker	60	Do	10th	
Martha	Wife of Thomas Clarke	42	Do	19th	
Joseph	Son of Jeremiah Pickles	8	Do	22nd	
Samuel	Son of John & Mary Bradbury	9	Do	24th	
Ruth	Daughr of Jos & Hannah Ramsden	30	Do	27th	
Joseph	Son of John & Hannh Nichol	1 .. 5	Do	Oct 3rd	

Figure 4.10 Burial register for South Parade Chapel (Wesleyan), Halifax, 1817 (you may like to compare the first entry with the christening register shown in Figure 4.7) (Source: Public Record Office)

registers (if this is possible – see Chapter 5, section 1), since those who compiled them were, by law, obliged to cover the entire population.

Although some idea of changes in mortality can be gathered by totalling the ages of all who died and then dividing by the number of deaths, at two points in time, the result could be meaningless if the age distribution of the population also changed. Suppose, for example, one did the exercise in 1890 and 1990. The average age at death would be much higher in the latter year than in the former. Much of the change is the result of dramatic falls in the infant mortality rate (i.e. deaths under the age of one year per 1,000 live births in the same year). But part of the change is because the birth rate has also dropped dramatically, resulting in an older population. Thus, even if infant mortality had not fallen *at all* between 1890 and 1990, the average age at death would have risen, because the number of children *at risk* of dying under the age of one year would be smaller.

3.4   REGISTERS AND OTHER RECORDS

I've already suggested that linking registers to census returns can increase our knowledge. The same applies if one looks at them together with other documents. Church rolls or chapel membership lists spring to mind here. The returns of the 1851 Religious Census carried out in Britain are another source. Censuses in Ireland carried a question on religious affiliation, thus providing information not available elsewhere. In the nineteenth century and for most of the twentieth, local newspapers gave extensive coverage to church and chapel affairs, thus alerting one to the people who took a prominent role therein. Local and national religious bodies also sometimes reported on individual congregations (e.g. visitation returns prepared for the bishops of the Church of England), which can provide further insight.

3.5   WHERE TO FIND THE REGISTERS

Finally, where are church and chapel registers to be found? Local record offices may contain not only original registers that have been deposited for safe keeping but also microfilms of locally relevant registers now housed in national collections (like the pre-1837 nonconformist registers held at the Public Record Office in London). Many libraries also house catalogues indicating the existence and whereabouts of registers. Family history societies have transcripts of some registers, and the library of the Society of Genealogists has a unique collection. There are also a number of indexes, the most extensive being the International Genealogical Index (IGI) of baptisms and marriages, compiled by The Church of Jesus Christ of Latter-day Saints from its filmed copies of parochial and non-parochial registers. The IGI is listed by county and widely available on microfiche (at least for the local county or counties) in many local libraries. However, this index is not comprehensive, and it needs to be used with caution. (For a selection of the many finding aids to parochial and non-parochial registers, and related material such as bishops' transcripts, see the list below.)

REFERENCES AND FURTHER READING (SECTION 3)

Berry, B.M. and Schofield, R.S. (1971) 'Age at marriage in pre-industrial England', *Population Studies*, 25, pp.453–63.

Brody, H. (1973) *Inishkillane: change and decline in the west of Ireland,* London, Allen Lane, The Penguin Press.

Connell, K.H. (1968) 'Catholicism and marriage in the century after the famine', in *Irish peasant society: four historical essays,* Oxford, Clarendon Press.

Connolly, S.J. (1985) *Religion and society in nineteenth-century Ireland*, Dublin, Economic and Social History Society of Ireland.

Dennis, R. and Daniels, S. (1981) ' "Community" and the social geography of Victorian cities', *Urban History Yearbook*, pp.7–20. Reprinted in Drake (1994).

Drake, M. (ed.) (1982) *Population studies from parish registers: a selection of readings from Local Population Studies*, Matlock, Local Population Studies.

Drake, M. (ed.) (1994) *Time, family and community: perspectives on family and community history*, Oxford, Blackwell in association with The Open University (Course Reader).

Fitzpatrick, D. (1987) 'The modernization of the Irish female', in O'Flanagan, P. et al. *Rural Ireland: modernization and change 1600–1900*, Cork, Cork University Press.

Hinde, P.R.A. (1987) 'The population of a Wiltshire village in the nineteenth century: a reconstitution study of Berwick St. James, 1841–71', *Annals of Human Biology*, 14, 6, pp.475–85.

Humphery-Smith, C. (1984) *The Phillimore atlas and index of parish registers*, Chichester, Phillimore.

Kussmaul, A. (1990) *A general view of the rural economy of England, 1538–1840*, Cambridge, Cambridge University Press.

Mullett, M. (1991) *Sources for the history of English nonconformity, 1660–1830*, London, British Records Association (*Archives and the user*, no.8).

Palgrave-Moore, P. (1988) *Understanding the history and records of nonconformity* (2nd edn), Norwich, Elvery Dowers Publications.

Southall, H. (1991) 'The timing of marriage in mid-nineteenth century industrial communities', *Local Population Studies*, 47, pp.77–80.

Williams, N. (1992) 'Death in season: class, environment and the mortality of infants in nineteenth century Sheffield', *Social History of Medicine*, 5, 1, pp.71–94.

Wolffe, J. and Golby, J. (1993) 'Religious records as sources', audio-cassette 5A in Braham, P. (ed.) *Using the past: audio-cassettes on sources and methods for family and community historians*, Milton Keynes, The Open University.

Wrigley, E.A. and Schofield, R.S. (1981) *The population history of England 1541–1871: a reconstruction*, London, Edward Arnold.

FINDING PAROCHIAL AND NON-PAROCHIAL REGISTERS: A SELECTION OF AIDS

Begley, D.F. (1984) 'Irish parish registers', in Begley, D.F. (ed.) *Handbook on Irish genealogy*, Dublin, Heraldic Artists Ltd.

Breed, G.R. (1988) *My ancestors were Baptists: how can I find out more about them?*, London, Society of Genealogists.

Clifford, D.J.H. (1992) *My ancestors were Congregationalists – in England and Wales – with a list of registers*, London, Society of Genealogists.

Gandy, M. (1983) *My ancestor was Jewish: how can I find out more about him?*, London, Society of Genealogists.

Gibson, J.S.W. (1992) *Bishops' transcripts and marriage licences, bonds and allegations: a guide to their location and indexes*, Birmingham, Federation of Family History Societies.

Gibson, J.S.W. and Hampson, E. (1992) *Marriage, census and other indexes for family historians,* Birmingham, Federation of Family History Societies.

Grenham, J. (1992) *Tracing your Irish ancestors,* Dublin, Gill and Macmillan. Lists location of Irish registers.

Leary, W. (1990) *My ancestors were Methodists: how can I find out more about them?,* London, Society of Genealogists.

Local Population Studies (1974–82) *Original parish registers in record offices and libraries* (first edition plus four supplements), Tawney House, Matlock, Derbyshire, DE4 3BT. Useful, but some information is now out of date.

McLaughlin, E. (1988) *Parish registers,* Birmingham, Federation of Family History Societies.

Milligan, E.H. and Thomas, M.J. (1990) *My ancestors were Quakers: how can I find out more about them?,* London, Society of Genealogists.

Steel, D.J. (1964–) *National index of parish registers,* London, Society of Genealogists. Several volumes, including: (1) *Sources of births, marriages and deaths before 1837* (1973); (2) *Sources for nonconformist genealogy and family history* (1973); (3) *Sources for Roman Catholic and Jewish genealogy and family history* (1974).

Williams, C.J. and Watts-Williams, J. (1986) *Cofrestri Plwyf Cymru: parish registers of Wales,* Aberystwyth, National Library of Wales and Welsh County Archivist Group.

4   MEDICAL OFFICER OF HEALTH REPORTS

by Michael Drake

The nineteenth-century obsession with death produced a vast number of initiatives from 1831–32 onwards, including the setting up of Boards of Health and the appointment of inspectors covering communities of various types and sizes. This led to reports, two collections of which – covering hundreds of communities that are well indexed – have been published on microfiche (Pidduck, 1978; Thomas, 1979). The Public Health Act of 1872 established sanitary authorities in rural and urban areas and these in turn appointed Medical Officers of Health who reported to them annually.

4.1   CONTENT

The reports vary in what they cover. Those I have examined, dating from towards the end of the nineteenth century and the beginning of this, can be divided into two parts. First, there are standard items dealing with births, deaths, and diseases over time (each report commonly gives figures for a run of years), for various districts within the authority's boundaries. Secondly, there are special investigations or discussions of particular topics (arising from the particular interests of the Medical Officer of Health), or events in the district, or current preoccupations.

To give the flavour of these reports, here is a brief summary of the contents of the report for the Borough of Northampton for the year ending 31 December 1904 by James Beatty MA, MD, DPH, Medical Officer of Health, Superintendent of the Borough Hospitals for Infectious Diseases, and Police Surgeon for the Borough of Northampton. With a title like this, he was obviously a significant figure in the community! The report is to be found in a printed volume at the Northamptonshire Record Office (Beatty, 1905).

The report opens with a table giving the estimated population for 1904 (on this more later); area; density of population (per acre and per house); totals of births and deaths and corresponding crude birth and death rates (see Chapter 8, section 5); deaths from various diseases and per quarter. Two non-standard items then follow: an account of 'the physiography and geology' of the area; and a very interesting discussion of four different ways of estimating the 1904 population. The discussion of population estimation is interesting, not only for demographic reasons, but for the light it throws on various aspects of the community. Thus, the author rejects the Registrar General's recommended method of estimating populations between censuses by extrapolating from the growth/decline rate between the two previous censuses; in this case 1891 and 1901. The reason given is that the late 1890s was a boom period for the town, the early 1900s one of depression. A second method of estimating population size was based on the numbers enjoying the municipal franchise. This leads to a discussion of the impact of the depression on the numbers on relief, for in accepting relief one lost the franchise. Additionally, people giving up their houses and going into lodgings lost their vote. Evidence on these points is discussed, including impressionistic remarks. The third method was to estimate the population 'by comparison of the numbers of inhabited houses in 1901 and in 1904'. The fourth and final method was an admittedly 'simple one', being 'the excess of births over deaths during the three years from the spring of 1901 to that of 1904, adding this to the census population and making a further addition for the second quarter of 1904'. In fact, this last method was chosen, since, for a variety of reasons, migration into and out of the town was considered to be negligible.

There follows a series of tables giving the number of inhabitants per house in the various wards of the town, and also birth rates (within and outside marriage and by ward). Crude death rates and infant mortality rates can also be found for different districts within the town. The latter ranged from 97.6 to 194.4 per 1,000 live births (Beatty, 1905, p.105).

Infant mortality (death under one year of age per 1,000 live births) is given very extensive treatment. This was, of course, the heroic age in the conquest of infant mortality and something of the excitement this struggle engendered amongst Medical Officers of Health comes through in the prose. (Present-day concerns have shifted to the elderly.) Thus, in Northampton, the rate had dropped from 188.4 per 1,000 in 1878 to 137.7 in 1904. The reasons for this fall can be derived in part from the information on the cause of death given for the years 1894–1904 (the fall was not a constant one by the way), as well as from the age at death from various causes. This information was given for infants who died in the first, second, third or fourth week of life, and thereafter at monthly intervals. There is also a discussion of whether those who died were breast or bottle fed (still a major issue), or a mixture of both; the kind of bottle used (the long tube or boat shape – the former apparently lethal!); the physique of the victims; and the condition of the houses in which their short lives were spent.

Direction for the feeding of infants was the title of a pamphlet written by the Medical Officer of Health and distributed by the Health Visitor and the Registrars when a birth was registered.

Much of the data on infant mortality was collected by the Health Visitor, Miss Gough, praised by the Medical Officer of Health for her tact and discretion in making her enquiries. This was very necessary because 'a proportion of the mothers seemed to fear that the enquiries were being made owing to an idea that they had neglected their children' (Beatty, 1905, p.31).

The report also looks at individual diseases, there being a detailed account of a particularly widespread epidemic of scarlatina with 2,224 cases reported (the estimated population of the town was 90,340).

The Medical Officer of Health also draws attention to the recently published *Report of the Committee on Physical Deterioration*. This committee had been set up when the appalling physique of many of the men who had volunteered to serve in the Boer War was discovered. The report's 53 listed recommendations are repeated in the Medical Officer of Health's report, with a plea that they be followed up in Northampton. He ends with this comment:

> At this point I would like to emphasize how much may be done by private, apart from municipal or state effort. The public health is not the care alone of the municipality or the state, private individuals who have the time at their disposal can and ought to make the advancement of the health of the community one of their duties. An enormous amount of good could be done by someone who is not an official, and who is not looking for a seat on the Council, and who could not therefore be accused of having an axe to grind. Such men exist in other towns e.g. Mr Rowntree in York. Why should there not be such men in Northampton?
>
> (Beatty, 1905, p.102)

(For the pertinence of the reference to Mr Rowntree, see section 6 below, on social surveys.)

The report, which runs to 158 pages plus a number of pull-out graphs, concludes with a survey of the sanitary administration of the town (with reports on insanitary dwellings; factories and workshops; bakehouses; offensive trades; drains; food administration; milk supply; common lodging houses, etc.). A page summarizing the 'routine work carried out by the Health Department during the year 1904' records a heroic endeavour in what must often have been far from pleasant circumstances.

4.2   HOW CAN WE USE THE REPORTS?

The reports are obviously very useful for straightforward demographic exercises on fertility and mortality, especially the latter (see Chapter 8, section 5). However, they need to be interpreted with care. They were inevitably coloured by the interests and enthusiasms of individual Medical Officers of Health and by the sources they themselves relied on. Dr Beatty appears to have been particularly energetic. Other local authorities were not so fortunate. Thus, some reports can be rich in supporting, non-quantitative evidence, others not. For a fascinating report by a Scottish Medical Officer of Health, see Russell (1888). The extent of the non-standard items in the reports also varies considerably. Again, Dr Beatty's report appears to be particularly rich. Analysed over a ten- or twenty-year period, the reports can provide the basis for a series of studies into fertility, mortality, disease, housing, working conditions, child care, etc., which can also be set in a national or regional context. Indeed, many reports provide such a context, presumably to see how well or badly the area covered was doing.

One should not, however, confine oneself simply to the contents of the reports. Taken with other sources – the census, electoral returns, rate books, directories, etc. – the reports can provide an entrée into neighbourhoods, through the information they sometimes give on wards. That a town like Northampton was far from homogeneous — viewed from the Medical Officer of Health's standpoint – raises the possibility of interesting enquiries into other forms of intra-urban diversity (e.g. politics, social segregation, residential patterns, etc.).

Finally, the reports, like other similar documents, provide an insight into what is now commonly called the *mentalité* of the writers and their informants. This comes out indirectly through what is chosen for emphasis; through the use of language to describe the various phenomena discussed; and through emotive appeals like the one cited above, in which Dr Beatty appeals for a 'Mr Rowntree' to step forward in Northampton.

4.3   LOCATION

The annual reports of the Medical Officers of Health are commonly found in local authority archives, which in turn are now often deposited in county municipal archives. Usually the reports are printed and so pose no problems of legibility. Even where reports – and correspondence – are not printed, the quality of handwriting is usually good to excellent. The detailed example above comes from an English borough at the beginning of this century. Comparable reports – but of varying quality – are to be found throughout the UK and Ireland down to the present day.

REFERENCES AND FURTHER READING (SECTION 4)

Beatty, J. (1905) *Annual report on the health of the county borough of Northampton for the year ending December 31, 1904* (ref.X7517), Northampton, Northamptonshire Record Office.

Pidduck, W. (1978) *Urban and rural social conditions in industrial Britain, series one. The local reports to the General Board of Health, 1848–57. A complete listing and guide to the Harvester Press microform collection with an introduction by H.T. Smith,* Hassocks, Harvester Press.

Porter, S. (1990) *Exploring urban history: sources for local historians,* London, Batsford.

Riden, P. (1987) *Record sources for local history,* London, Batsford.

Russell, J.B. (1888) *Life in one room: or, some serious considerations for the citizens of Glasgow,* Glasgow, James Maclehose and Sons.

Thomas, M. (1979) *Urban and rural social conditions in industrial Britain, series two. The reports of the Local Government Board 1869–1908. A complete listing and guide to the Harvester microfiche collection,* Hassocks, Harvester Press.

The following academic and local authority libraries hold the Harvester Press microfiche collections of reports (edited by Pidduck and Thomas): Brotherton Library, Leeds; Hertfordshire County Council; Somerset County Council; National Library of Wales; Cambridge University; Royal Library, Denmark; Bristol University; Strathclyde University; Loughborough University; Sussex University; Nottingham University; Rolle College, Exmouth; Bradford Metropolitan Council; Manchester Public Library; Kingston University; Leeds Metropolitan University; Warwick University; Teesside University; Open University; British Library, Boston Spa; Roehampton Institute; Crewe and Alsager College; PRO, Kew; Chester College; London School of Economics; Southampton University; Bolton Institute of Technology; Hull University; Bath College of Higher Education; Lancaster University; Wellcome Institute. Individual fiche for particular places can be bought relatively cheaply from Research Publications International, PO Box 45, Reading, RG1 8HF.

See also the references and further reading at the end of section 6.

5   BUSINESS, TRADE UNION AND OCCUPATIONAL RECORDS

by Peter Braham

5.1   BUSINESS RECORDS

Business records contain a great deal to interest the student of family and community history. For example, company archives may include not only details of staff, directors and shareholders, but also information about products and services, prices, customers, changes in the structure of an industry and in markets, and so on.

Business historians will wish to situate the history of a given firm in a wider context by asking, for example, what factors gave rise to the growth of such a firm or to its disappearance. But it seems curious that family and community historians researching into business records have not really ventured much beyond tracing the 'genealogy' of a company or setting down a company chronology. There may be good reasons for beginning at the more modest end of the continuum: to show *what* happened in a particular company. But there is no need to remain rooted at that level of enquiry. A study of an individual company might yield useful information, not merely about that company, its organization and working conditions, but also new perspectives about the changing world of commerce and industry more generally.

In many instances, business records – ranging from prospectuses to ledgers – remain with the companies that created them or with their successor companies. Although access is then at the discretion of the company concerned, would-be researchers have often found that such companies welcome rather than deflect those interested in studying their corporate past. Where company records have found their way into the public domain (notably in the PRO and at local record offices), there may still be conditions of access attached. Apart from these sources, a number of institutions, like the Business Archives Council, are specifically devoted to business history, and The Royal Commission on Historical Manuscripts have substantial holdings of business records. In addition, a valuable but often neglected source is the plethora of trade journals.

In compiling his bibliography of British businesses, Goodall wrote to county and district librarians whose responses enabled a great deal of material to be included, the existence of which would not otherwise have been suspected – but many more company histories are probably waiting to be discovered (Goodall, 1987, p.12). He did not attempt to encompass a further range of materials – technical brochures, annual reports, reports of a company's efforts in the Second World War, press cuttings, and so on – which, though disparate, might yield valuable information and insights to the student of family and community history.

Even where there are records for a given company, problems may remain. Because many company histories were privately printed and circulated, their existence may not be known. In addition, although the quality of recently produced company histories has tended to improve, older histories were often intended to celebrate an anniversary rather than to be works of substance, and so may be incomplete, unreliable, or otherwise lacking. It is therefore important to consider how reliable and comprehensive a particular set of business records are, and whether they need to be compared with more complete records of a similar company.

How then should you start your search? The records of many local businesses may still be held locally, so this may be a good place to begin. Among general surveys, one of the most comprehensive is Richmond and Stockford's (1986) survey of all 710 companies, registered in England and Wales between 1856 and (May) 1884, that were still surviving in 1980. They also surveyed 296 companies, registered between (June) 1884 and (May) 1889, that were still surviving in 1980 (60 per cent of the surviving companies registered during the latter period). The 'survivors' represented a mere 4 per cent of the 30,334 companies registered in the period 1856–1889. The survey's compilers believed that if the companies themselves had survived, then their records were more likely to have survived as well. Nevertheless, besides producing a *general* register of business archives held by existing firms and encouraging research, they also believed that, by locating these archives, they were helping to preserve records that might otherwise be destroyed. They claim that most of the records that they detail had not previously been *available* for research because of ignorance of their existence. Your research in this area may thus be pioneering.

Richmond and Stockford's survey was sponsored by the Business Archives Council (BAC) whose library – open to all researchers by appointment – contains 4,500 business histories, covering the United Kingdom and abroad. It publishes its own periodical, *Business Archives*, and a regular newsletter.

As might be expected, some sectors or industries are better served than others. For example, if your interest is in banking in the late nineteenth and early twentieth centuries, you can begin with Presnell and Orbell's (1985) guide. This can be supplemented by Parker's study of nineteenth-century banking in Hertfordshire (1986), which, apart from its substantive information about one area, probably gives a reliable indication of the kind of material that may exist in other localities: for example, absorbed banks' records held in the central archives of clearing banks; banking solicitors' records and other material held in county record offices; and relevant material in the Guildhall Library (London).

5.2   TRADE UNION AND LABOUR RECORDS

Unfortunately, the trade unions' pride in past struggles and achievements has not been matched by a propensity to preserve their records. In short, surviving material is patchy. Where local trade union records *have* been deposited in record offices, their extent and value is quite variable. On the other hand, national records of trade unions include a great deal about local events and so may help to compensate for the dearth of local records. It is the very paucity of documentation about the local party or trade union branch which underlines the value of obtaining personal recollections of events. Such recollections may not only supplement existing documents, but might also enable us to examine such documents with new insights.

The indispensable guide to locating records of the labour movement is Cook's six-volume *Sources in British political history* (1975–8), the most relevant for our purposes being volumes 1 and 6. Though the vast majority of trade unionists will *not* have left behind private papers about their involvement and will not therefore be mentioned in the collections of papers of prominent individuals (such as Cook, volumes 2–5), where such biographies survive they can provide a valuable insight into the part played by individuals in wider campaigns. (See, for example, Burnett, 1974 and Burnett et al., 1984, 1987.)

5.3   OCCUPATIONAL RECORDS

As entire books have been written about *single* occupations, what follows must be almost entirely indicative and illustrative (for further references to specific occupations, see Raymond, 1992, and Storey, 1987; see also section 1 above on directories).

Before the nineteenth century, occupational statistics on any large scale are scarce. We rely instead on local studies using very detailed sources and studies of particular groups or industries. All this changed, however, with the coming of the census, which had as a central aim the compilation of detailed occupational data at an individual level, and thus gave us a much more reliable picture of the economic geography of Britain (Glennie, 1990, p.4). The division of occupations in the 1851 and subsequent censuses into 27 classes (which remained unchanged until 1901) eases the task of large-scale statistical comparisons over time. But we should not assume that the *facility* to make such comparisons overcomes all potential problems, because shifts in occupational structure also reflect social and cultural changes. In reading occupational labels and then compiling statistics about the rise and fall of certain occupations, we should remember not only that the meanings of particular labels have changed, but that the meaning of having an *occupation* has changed. In particular, what is the nature and degree of specialization? Is 'work' full-time or part-time? Must 'work' be paid? (See Glennie, 1990, pp.10–11.)

If we take postal workers as an example, matters seem quite straightforward: their employment clearly belongs to the mainstream economy, there is a single employer, and the archives are readily identifiable (see Daunton, 1985; Clinton, 1984; and Farrugia, 1969). There is a guide to the Post Office Archives (Farrugia, 1987), and important postal history collections are housed at the

National Post Museum and in the Morton Collection (owned by the Union of Communication Workers). An insight into the nature of a postman's life at work and at home is given in the diary of Edward Harvey (Storey, 1982). On the other hand, research in this area may be complicated by the need to reconcile the different *types* of records: those of the Post Office itself, trade union records, and the experiences of postal workers.

By contrast, domestic servants present very different problems for researchers. The greatest single class of workers throughout the nineteenth century, domestic servants were ignored in parliamentary papers and were the subject of just one official inquiry (see Volume 3, Chapter 3, section 1). Perhaps this was because domestic servants were distributed in small units, formed no unions, nor otherwise expressed organized discontent (Higgs, 1983, p.202).

As Horn (1975) shows, there is a wide range of primary and secondary sources about domestic servants. For example, most county record offices will contain useful material in family and estate papers (these may include details of wages, applications, references and so on). Storey provides details of the records that may be obtained from the Warwickshire County Record Office (1987, p.11). Apart from this, the local press may indicate the market in servants' posts and may include letters from those seeking servants or employment as servants.

Much of the research into domestic service has been designed to illuminate the relationship between master ('upstairs') and servant ('downstairs'), and within this tradition there has been a bias towards collecting the experiences of servants in upper-class houses. For example, 60 per cent of the employers quoted in Horn (1975) and Burnett (1974) belonged to the titled or landed classes (Higgs, 1983, p.203). But these 'micro-level' sources are unlikely to be representative of servant-employing Victorian households.

Higgs (1983) offers a different analysis of the role of domestic servants in Victorian England. He points out that the widely quoted wages for domestic servants take no account of the large number of servants recruited from the workhouse who were paid little or nothing; and he warns of inconsistencies in calculating numbers of servants between censuses which render the occupational tables in the nineteenth-century census of 'dubious validity': for example, the 1891 census included all women 'helping at home' as domestic servants. He argues that changes in numbers of domestic servants ought to be seen in terms of the changing technology of the household and the *relocation* of employment out of the home; thus, the rise in retailing employment may reflect 'differentiation of this activity out of household production' whereby 'general servants' are replaced by 'shop assistants' in the census (Higgs, 1983, pp.201–2, 203–4 and 209).

We can see from this example that, as well as identifying primary sources, we need to think carefully about how such source material can best be evaluated.

5.4   SOME USEFUL ARCHIVES AND RESOURCES

Established collections of trade union records include those at the Bishopsgate Institute (230 Bishopsgate, London, EC2M 4QM); the Brynmor John Library at the University of Hull, whose holdings are summarized in Saville and Dyson (1989) and are available on-line via HUMAD (Hull University Manuscript and Archives Database), access to which is via JANET, EXLIB or home computer with modem; the Modern Archives Centre (University of Warwick, Coventry, CV4 7AL), which is where the Trades Union Congress is gradually transferring its records, and which holds important collections of nineteenth-century trade union records; and the Morton Collection (Bruce Castle Museum, Lordship Lane, Tottenham, London, N17 8NU).

Important collections of business records are held at the Business Archives Council (185 Tower Bridge Road, London, SE1 2UF) and in the company reports collection in the Guildhall Library, London.

REFERENCES AND FURTHER READING

Armstrong, J. (1993) 'Local directories: exploring change and continuity in business activity', audio-cassette 4A in Braham, P. (ed.) *Using the past: audio-cassettes on sources and methods for family and community historians*, Milton Keynes, The Open University.

Armstrong, J. and Jones, S. (1987) *Business documents: their origins, sources and uses in historical research*, London, Mansell.

Armstrong, W. (1972) 'The use of information about occupation', in Wrigley, E. (ed.) *Nineteenth century society: essays in the use of quantitative methods for the study of social data*, Cambridge, Cambridge University Press.

Bellamy, J. (1970) *Yorkshire business histories: a bibliography*, Bradford, Bradford University.

Burnett, J. (ed.) (1974) *Useful toil: autobiographies of working people from the 1820s to the 1920s*, London, Allen Lane.

Burnett, J., Vincent, D. and Maynall, D. (eds) (1984, 1987) *The autobiography of the working class: an annotated critical bibliography*, 3 vols, Hassocks, Harvester.

Clinton, A. (1984) *Post office workers: a trade union and social history*, London, Allen and Unwin.

Cook, C. (ed.) (1975–8) *Sources in British political history:* vol.1, *A guide to archives of selected organizations and societies* (1975); vol.2, *A guide to the private papers of selected public servants* (1975); vols.3,4, *Papers of MPs* (1977); vol.5, *Papers of selected writers, intellectuals, publicists* (1978); vol.6, *Supplement* (1978), London, Macmillan.

Daunton, M. (1985) *Royal Mail: the Post Office since 1840*, London, Athlone Press.

Ebury, M. and Preston, B. (1976) 'Domestic service in late Victorian and Edwardian England, 1871–1914', *Reading Geographical Papers*, 42.

Farrugia, J. (1969) *The letter box: history of Post Office pillar and wall boxes*, Fontwell, Centaur Press.

Farrugia, J. (1987) *A guide to Post Office Archives*, London, Post Office Archives.

Fowler, S. (1991) *Sources for labour history*, Richmond, Surrey, Labour Heritage.

Gerard, J. (1984) 'Invisible servants: the country house and local community', *Bulletin of the Institute of Historical Research*, 57, November, pp.178–88.

Glennie, P. (1990) *Distinguishing men's trades: occupational sources and debates for pre-census England*, University of Bristol, Historical Geography Research Series, no.25.

Goodall, F. (1987) *A bibliography of British business histories*, Aldershot, Gower.

Higgs, E. (1983) 'Domestic servants and households in Victorian England', *Social History*, 8, May, pp.201–10.

Higgs, E. (1989) *Making sense of the census: the manuscript returns for England and Wales, 1801–1901*, Oxford, Basil Blackwell.

Historical Manuscripts Commission (1990) *Records of British business and industry, 1760–1914: textiles and leather*, Guide to Sources for British Industry, 8, London, HMSO.

Horn, P. (1975) *The rise and fall of the Victorian servant*, Dublin, Gill and Macmillan.

Horrocks, S. (1971) *Lancashire business histories*, Manchester, Manchester University Press.

Jeremy, D. and Shaw, C. (eds) (1986) *Dictionary of business biography* (5 vols and supplement), Sevenoaks, Butterworth.

Lee, C. (1979) *British regional employment statistics, 1841–1971*, Cambridge, Cambridge University Press.

Modern Records Centre (1991) *Trade union and related records in repositories*, Warwick, University of Warwick Library.

Orbell, J. (1987) *A guide to tracing the history of a business*, Aldershot, Gower.

Pain, G. and Bennett, J. (1985) *A bibliography of British industrial relations: supplement*, Cambridge, Cambridge University Press.

Pain, G. and Woolven, G (1979) *A bibliography of British industrial relations*, Cambridge, Cambridge University Press.

Parker, J. (1986) *Nothing for nothing for nobody: banking in Hertfordshire,* Hertfordshire Publications.

Pelling, H. (1992) *A history of British trade unionism*, London, Macmillan.

Presnell, L. and Orbell, J. (1985) *A guide to the historical records of British banking*, Aldershot, Gower.

Prochaska, F. (1981) 'Female philanthropy and domestic service in Victorian England', *Bulletin of the Institute of Historical Research*, 54, May, pp.79–85.

Raymond, S. (1992) *Occupational sources for genealogists: a bibliography*, Birmingham, Federation of Family History Societies.

Richmond, L. and Stockford, B. (1986) *Company archives: a survey of 1,000 of the first registered companies in England and Wales*, Aldershot, Gower.

Richmond, L. and Turton, A. (1987) *Directory of corporate archives: some corporate members of the British Archives Council which maintain archives facilities* (2nd edn), London, Business Archives Council.

Ritchie, L.A. (1992) *The shipbuilding industry: a guide to historical records*, Manchester, Manchester University Press for Business Archives Council.

Rowe, D. (ed.) (1979) *Northern business histories: a bibliography*, London, The Library Association.

Saville, J. and Bellamy, J. (1992) *Dictionary of labour biography*, 9 vols, London, Macmillan.

Saville, J. and Dyson, B. (1989) *The labour archive at the University of Hull*, Brynmor John Library, University of Hull.

Shaw, G. and Tipper, A. (1988) *British directories: a bibliography and guide to directories published in England and Wales (1850–1950) and Scotland (1773–1950)*, Leicester, Leicester University Press.

Slaven, A. and Checkland, S. (1986, 1990) *Dictionary of Scottish business biography*, 2 vols, Aberdeen, Aberdeen University Press.

Storey, R. (1980) 'Labour archives in the United Kingdom', *Archivum*, 27, pp.147–67.

Storey, R. (ed.) (1982) *A postman's round, 1858–1861: selected abstracts from the diary of Edward Harvey,* Warwick, University of Warwick Library.

Storey, R. (1987) *Primary sources for Victorian studies: an updating,* Victorian Studies Centre, University of Leicester.

Storey, R. (1980) 'Records of the working man', *Genealogists Magazine,* 20, 1, pp.5–10.

Waterson, M. (1980) *The servants' hall: a domestic history of Erddig,* London, Routledge.

Zarach, S. (1987) *Debrett's bibliography of business history,* London, Macmillan.

6   SOCIAL SURVEYS

by Michael Drake and David Englander

Hardly a day goes by without the results of some social survey or other being reported in the newspapers. Almost invariably, these surveys are based on interviews (see Chapter 6, section 7, and Chapter 7) with a sample of the population (on sampling and its problems, see Chapter 8, section 6). The subjects covered run the whole gamut of social life, from soap powder preferences to political inclination, TV viewing to spending habits. Two of the largest, most accessible and useful present-day surveys are the British government's *General Household Survey* (annual since 1971) and its *Family Expenditure Survey* (annual since 1953–4), both invaluable for the family and community historian. First, they suggest areas of interest that can be pursued in the more recent or distant past. Secondly, although the results are often presented for different regions of the country (variously defined) and rarely come down to the 'community level', they do provide a yardstick against which to set one's own findings. And replicating the surveys on a smaller scale could highlight even greater variation in behaviour than the regional figures suggest.

The contrast between these current surveys and those of the pre-Second World War period is very marked. Today's surveys are carried out by large private or public bodies (e.g. Gallup, Mori, government departments). Early surveys were associated with individuals – Henry Mayhew, Charles Booth, Seebohm Rowntree; with members of the numerous statistical societies in the 1830s and 1840s; or 100 years later with that new breed, professional social scientists. A partial exception would be inquiries carried out in connection with the census and the registration of births, marriages, and deaths. Of course, Charles Booth and Seebohm Rowntree had assistants – very distinguished ones in some cases (e.g. Beatrice Webb).

Another major feature of early social surveys was that their focus was wider than that of present-day ones. One example would be the Scottish Statistical Accounts, a remarkable series of volumes describing contemporary society in the 1790s, the 1830s to 1840s, and the 1940s to 1960s. The first, the Old Statistical Account (OSA) was initiated and compiled by Sir John Sinclair, who persuaded ministers throughout Scotland to submit detailed returns on their parishes (some of their comments need to be received with due caution, however). His questionnaire, one of the earliest of its kind, covered all aspects of social and economic life, producing invaluable data on every locality during an era of dramatic change in social, agricultural and industrial life. Sinclair also produced an overview and update in his *Analysis of the Statistical Account of Scotland* (1825). The OSA can be used comparatively alongside the Second (or New) Statistical Account, a comparable but more systematic and detailed exercise in the late 1830s and early 1840s, resulting in a total of fifteen volumes. The Third Statistical Account (late 1940s onwards) provided some valuable portraits of post-Second World War society, urban and rural (the later volumes (1950s and 1960s) were of variable usefulness) (see Donnachie and Hewitt, 1989, p.185). For examples of research building on the eighteenth- and nineteenth-century Statistical Accounts, see Volume 2, Chapter 2; Volume 3, Chapter 4. (For some surveys on Ireland, see Chapter 3 in this volume, section 1.1.)

A second striking example of an early survey with a wide focus is Charles Booth's monumental seventeen-volume work, *Life and labour of the people in London* (1889–1902). This was divided into three series – Poverty, Industry and Religious Influences – concerned with social, productive and cultural relations under varying conditions. The Booth survey addressed the Labour Question or Social Question, a subject area broader than the measurement of poverty with which Booth is customarily, and erroneously, identified.

In addition to the valuable published volumes, most of the materials relating to the Booth survey still exist. The originals are held at the British Library of Political and Economic Science at the London School of Economics, and there is a microfilm facsimile which might be obtainable by your local library. The Booth Collection resists simple summary (for a detailed description and evaluation of the archive, see O'Day and Englander, 1993). For our purposes, the single most important component is the 392 notebooks which record the interviews, impressions and raw data on which the published volumes rest. The first eighty are connected with the Poverty Series, with information on the street survey – 13,600 streets in all were included – and the special investigations of selected areas. The notebooks surveying the streets of East London are the most informative: the name of the street headed the page and there followed detailed tabulated information for each house and household or family, including occupation, probable income, number of children and number of occupants in each room. Alas, the unit changed from the family to the street when Booth proceeded to compare the East End with other areas. Each family was still classified, but without comparable material on income, occupation and poverty.

A striking feature of the Booth survey was the attempt to supply an areal representation of poverty. Each street was classified according to the general condition of its inhabitants and given a colour code. The Poverty Map, prepared by Booth and his associates in 1889 (see Figure 4.11), was then revised and enlarged with the aid of the local police. The metropolis was divided into a number of beats, each patrolled jointly by an interviewer and a police respondent. 'During these walks', wrote Booth, 'almost every social influence was discussed, and especially those bearing upon vice and crime, drunkenness and disorder'. These police notebooks not only disclose the difficulties in identifying the predominant social character of individual streets, but are a mine of information on particular localities and perceptions of community.

For the Industry Series, the whole population was grouped by trade and divided into sections. In some 81 octavo notebooks are transcribed the reports of interviews with workers and employers, together with miscellaneous notes on industrial processes, work design and health risks, as well as assorted press-cuttings, digests and summaries. Institutional analysis fills many pages, including notes on the origins, structure and function of selected trades and benefit societies, often with supporting documentation pasted in.

Booth's concern to represent the whole population within his scheme of industrial classification found expression in seven notebooks devoted to inmates of institutions. These consist of some 1,457 case histories transcribed from the Relieving Officer's records of the Stepney Poor Law Union. Booth, allowed privileged access to these records, obtained particulars of the name, age, status and occupation of applicants for relief, together with details of their personal circumstances and family histories. These records take us as close as we are likely to get to the voice of the very poor.

Having tested poverty by various indices – incomes, crowding, educational attainment, servant-keeping, and so on – Booth felt impelled to extend his survey to incorporate other non-quantifiable social influences which 'form part of the very structure of life', without which it was

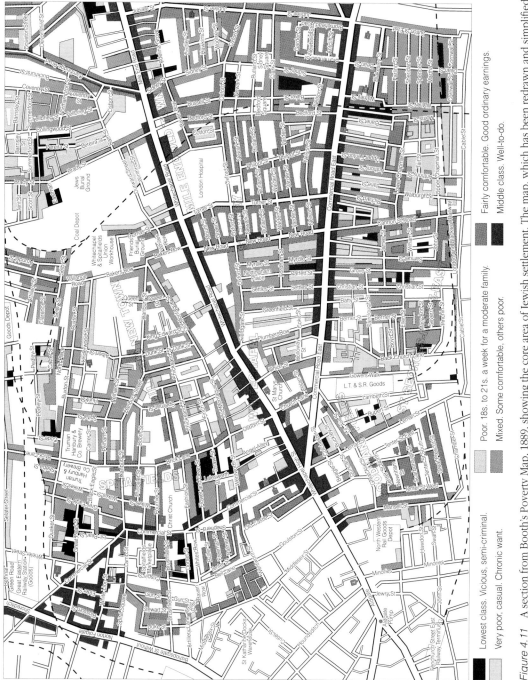

Figure 4.11   A section from Booth's Poverty Map, 1889, showing the core area of Jewish settlement. The map, which has been redrawn and simplified, shows the predominant social class composition of the streets of the area (Source: Booth, 1889–1902, maps volume)

Lowest class. Vicious, semi-criminal.

Very poor, casual. Chronic want.

Poor. 18s. to 21s. a week for a moderate family.

Mixed. Some comfortable, others poor.

Fairly comfortable. Good ordinary earnings.

Middle class. Well-to-do.

not possible 'to complete the picture of things as they are'. The seven densely packed volumes that comprise the Religious Influences Series embody Booth's extraordinary attempt to probe the spiritual and moral health of the people. The notebooks for this series include 1,450 structured interviews with ministers from all denominations and 350 interviews with local officials, charity administrators, educationalists and others. The specimen schedule for Booth's interviews on religion printed below gives some idea of the wealth of the data.

The Church of England
Life and Labour of the People in London,
Religious Influences. (Mr Charles Booth's Inquiry)

1   What is the general character of the population?

2   What portion do the ministrations of the Church touch?

3   What persons are employed? (stating duties and whether paid or not)

4   What buildings are used? (including missions rooms, schools and clubs)

5   What services or other religious meetings are held and by whom and how many attended?

6   What social agencies are connected with the Church? – institutes, societies, clubs, entertainments, meetings, etc.

7   What educational work is done?

8   To what extent are the people visited? (by Clergy or District Visitors)

9   What arrangements are there for nursing the sick?

10   To what extent is charitable relief given or administered by the Church?

General Questions

Under what other religious, charitable or philanthropic influences do the people come?

What co-operation is there between the Church and other bodies?

Remarks with reference to the district are wanted on –
    Local Government (including Poor Law Administration)
    Police
    Drink
    Prostitution
    Crime
    Marriage
    Thrift
    Health
    Housing and Social Conditions generally

[signature]

(Where possible, a comparison should be made between Past and Present).
It is not intended that this Form should be filled up, but it may be found useful for making notes to an interview.

(Booth Collection, B222, fo.81)

Name of Householder......... Catherine A. Elliott.

Street and Number ...... 4, Micklegate Court,(out of Micklegate).

Number of rooms in House....... 2 & K.   Number of bedrooms....... 2   Bathroom...... No
    (*State kitchen or scullery separately*).   (No sink or water tap in house).

Rent .... 6/2d p.w. clear.   Total number of occupants 3
                                            (*Including lodgers*).

Rates ....

Members of Household.	Age.	Sex.	Occupation and where employed.	Wage.
Widow	62		Gets Widow's Pension 10/- States her Husband worked as a Boilersmith on the L&M.S.Railway, but he has now been dead over 21 years. Prior to his death, was ill, & off work 13 years. Widow here, would like an Almshouse, if she could get one.	10/-
Marrd. Dghter. Mrs. Ralph Wilson	24		At home. (Has just got married).	
Husb. " "	27		Tempy. Labourer at the Fortifex Rubber Factory Clementhorpe: Has had pretty regular work of late, but has been on Dole a good deal. (Gets about £2-5-10d p.w. wage). Also is in receipt of Army Reserve Pay, having served in the Northumberland Fusiliers: Is on his last year of Army Reserve Pay.	

    (*Say if children are at school, and if over 14 and unemployed, if they are attending any classes*).   45/10.

Do the children receive Free Meals at School? ....   7/-.

    Do.   Milk at School? ....   62.10.

Amount received from sub-tenants and boarders ....

Unemployment Insurance ....   Public Assistance...............   Health Insurance ....

Sick Clubs...............   War Pension ....   Widow's Pension...... 10/-

Old Age Pension ....   Total Family income ....

ALLOTMENT (Size and rent) ...... No   Garden attached to house...... No
    (*Say if a private or Corporation Allotment*).

Estimated value of produce raised on Allotment ....

GENERAL OBSERVATIONS ON HOUSEHOLD:—

    Widow & Daughter complain about the damp state of house, & also the inconvenience, there being no sink or water tap in house: Also they have to share lavatories.
    Not in Poverty.   (*continue overleaf*)

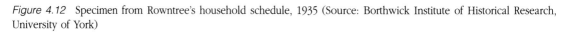

Figure 4.12 Specimen from Rowntree's household schedule, 1935 (Source: Borthwick Institute of Historical Research, University of York)

A further major characteristic of early social surveys was their focus on particular places. The importance of this for community historians is indicated in Seebohm Rowntree's comment introducing his famous survey of the town of York, *Poverty: a study of town life* (1903):

> At the outset I had to decide whether to collect information on the 'extensive' method or on the 'intensive'. In other words, the choice lay between gathering together and analysing such statistics regarding towns in the United Kingdom as were to be found in Government Returns, Reports of Medical Officers of Health, the records of the various branches of the Charity Organization Society etc., etc., or studying in detail the conditions of a single typical town.
>
> A very little inquiry sufficed to show that any picture of the condition of the working classes of provincial England based on the former method would be very incomplete and of doubtful service. On the other hand, the great value of Mr Charles Booth's classical work on the *Life and labour of the people in London* led me to hope that a similar investigation made for a provincial town might be of use, as it was impossible to judge how far the general conclusions arrived at by Mr Booth in respect of the metropolis would be found applicable to smaller urban populations. Having satisfied myself that the conditions of life obtaining in my native city of York were not exceptional, and that they might be taken as fairly representative of the conditions existing in many, if not most, of our provincial towns, I decided to undertake a detailed investigation into the social and economic conditions of the wage-earning classes in that city.
>
> (Rowntree, 1903, pp.xvii–xviii)

EXERCISE 4.3

What do you think are the strengths and weaknesses of the 'extensive' and 'intensive' methods of social enquiry?

Answers/comments p.300

Many surveys of particular communities were carried out in the first half of the twentieth century (see the reference and further reading list at the end of this section). There had also been a flowering of such studies in the 1830s and 1840s, a period when many felt the collection of quantitative data would, of itself, provide the solutions to society's problems. As a result, statistical societies were founded in many towns (Cullen, 1975). Many had short lives. Nevertheless it is always worth enquiring in your local library or record office to see whether any such surveys exist, either in manuscript or printed form (see the reference and further reading list below for examples).

Social surveys should, therefore, be in the arsenal of all family and community historians, providing ideas, data, techniques, and a tradition of which to be proud.

REFERENCES AND FURTHER READING

Baird, C.R. (1838) 'Observations upon the poorest classes of operatives in Glasgow in 1837', *Journal of the Statistical Society*, I, pp.167–72.

Beamish, N.L. (1844) 'Statistical report on the physical and moral condition of the working classes in the parish of St. Michael, Blackrock, near Cork', *Journal of the Statistical Society*, VII, pp.251–4.

Bell, C.R. (1968) *Middle class families: social and geographical mobility* (based on Swansea), London, Routledge & Kegan Paul.

Booth, C. (ed.) (1889–1902) *Life and labour of the people in London*, 17 vols, London, Macmillan.

Bowley, A.L. and Burnett-Hurst, A.R. (1915) *Livelihood and poverty: a study in the economic conditions of working-class households in Northampton, Warrington, Stanley and Reading*, London, Bell.

Bowley, A.L. and Hogg, M.H. (1925) *Has poverty diminished?: a sequel to 'Livelihood and poverty'*, London, King.

Bulmer, M., Bales, K. and Sklar, K.K. (eds) (1991) *The social survey in historical perspective 1880–1940*, Cambridge, Cambridge University Press.

Chart, D.A. (1914) 'Unskilled labour in Dublin: its housing and living conditions', *Statistical and Social Inquiry Society of Ireland*, XIII, pp.160–75.

City of Edinburgh (1906) *C.O.S. report on the physical condition of 1400 school children in the city; together with some account of their homes and surroundings*, London, P.S. King.

Cullen, M.J. (1975) *The statistical movement in early Victorian Britain: the foundations of empirical social research*, Hassocks, Harvester Press.

Donnachie, I. and Hewitt, G. (1989) *A companion to Scottish history*, London, Batsford.

Durant, R. (1939) *Watling: a survey of social life on a new housing estate*, London, King.

Edmonds, R. Jnr (1839) 'A statistical account of the Parish of Madron, containing the Borough of Penzance in Cornwall. Digested from the first series of questions circulated by the Statistical Society of London', *Journal of the Statistical Society*, II, pp.198–233.

Family Expenditure Survey (annual since 1953–4) London, HMSO.

Felkin, W. (1838) 'An account of the situation of a portion of the labouring classes in the township of Hyde, Cheshire', *Journal of the Statistical Society*, I, pp.416–20.

Felkin, W. (1839) 'Statistics of the labouring classes and paupers in Nottingham', *Journal of the Statistical Society*, II, pp.457–9.

Ford, P. (1934) *Work and wealth in a modern port: an economic survey of Southampton*, London, Allen and Unwin.

Frankenburg, R. (1966) *Communities in Britain: social life in town and country*, Harmondsworth, Penguin.

Fripp, C.B. (1839) 'Report of an inquiry into the condition of the working classes of the City of Bristol', *Journal of the Statistical Society*, II, pp.368–75.

General Household Survey (annual since 1971) London, HMSO.

Griffin, D. (1840) 'An enquiry into the mortality occurring among the poor of the city of Limerick', *Journal of the Statistical Society*, III, pp.305–30.

Grundy, F. and Titmuss, R.M. (1945) *Report on Luton*, Luton, Gibbs, Bamforth.

Hennock, E.P. (1987) 'The measurement of poverty: from the metropolis to the nation, 1880–1920', *Economic History Review*, 40, pp.208–27.

Heywood, J. (1838) 'Report of an enquiry conducted from house to house, into the state of 178 families in Miles Platting, within the borough of Manchester in 1837', *Journal of the Statistical Society*, I, pp.34–6.

Hindmarsh, L. (1838) 'On the state of agriculture and the condition of the agricultural labourers of the northern division of Northumberland', *Journal of the Statistical Society*, I, pp.397–414.

Jones, D.C. (ed.) (1934) *The social survey of Merseyside*, 3 vols, Liverpool, Liverpool University Press and Hodder and Stoughton.

Jordan, T. (1857) 'The present state of the dwellings of the poor, chiefly in Dublin', *Statistical and Social Inquiry Society of Ireland*, II, pp.12–19.

Kay, J.P. (1838) 'Earnings of agricultural labourers in Norfolk and Suffolk', *Journal of the Statistical Society*, I, pp.179–83.

Mayhew, H. (1861–62) *London labour and the London poor; a cyclopædia of the condition and earnings of those that will work, those that cannot work and those that will not work*, 4 vols, London, Griffin, Bohn.

McKenzie, D. (1981) *Statistics in Britain 1865–1930: the social construction of scientific knowledge*, Edinburgh, Edinburgh University Press.

Moser, C.A. and Kalton, G. (1971) *Survey methods in social investigation* (2nd edn), London, Heinemann Educational.

Neild, W. (1841) 'Comparative statement of the income and expenditure of certain families of the working classes in Manchester and Dukinfield, in the years 1836 and 1841', *Journal of the Statistical Society*, IV, pp.320–34.

O'Day, R. and Englander, D. (1993) *Mr Charles Booth's inquiry: life and labour of the people in London reconsidered*, London, Hambledon Press.

Rawson, R.W. (1843) 'Results of some inquiries into the conditions and education of the poorer classes in the parish of Marylebone in 1838', *Journal of the Statistical Society*, VI, pp.44ff.

Rees, A.D. (1951) *Life in a Welsh countryside: a social study of Llanfihangel yng Ngwynfa* (2nd edn), Cardiff, University of Wales Press.

Rosser, C. and Harris, C. (1965) *The family and social change: a study of family and kinship in a South Wales town*, London, Routledge & Kegan Paul.

Rowntree, B.S. (1903) *Poverty: a study of town life*, London, Thomas Nelson and Sons.

Rowntree, B.S. (1941) *Poverty and progress: a second social survey of York*, London, Longman.

Rowntree, B.S. and Lavers, G.R. (1951) *Poverty and the welfare state: a third social survey of York dealing with economic questions*, London, Longman.

Sheffield Social Survey Committee (1931–33) *Reports on various aspects of life in Sheffield*, 9 vols, Sheffield, Sheffield Social Survey Committee.

Sinclair, Sir J. (1791–99) *The Statistical Account of Scotland*, 21 vols, Edinburgh, William Creech […]. In 1975–83, a reissue of *The Statistical Account of Scotland*, 20 vols, general editors Donald J. Withrington and Ian R. Grant, was produced by EP Publishing, Wakefield.

Sinclair, Sir J. (1825) *Analysis of the Statistical Account of Scotland*, 2 parts, Edinburgh, A. Constable & Co. Reprinted in 2 vols in 1970 by Johnson Reprint Corporation, New York (*Reprints in social and economic history*).

Smith, H.L. (1930–35) *The new survey of London life and labour,* 9 vols, London, P.S. King.

Stacey, M. (1960) *Tradition and change: a study of Banbury,* London, Oxford University Press.

Statistical Committee of Leeds Town Council (1839) 'Report upon the condition of the town of Leeds and its inhabitants', *Journal of the Statistical Society,* II, pp.397–424.

Statistical Society of Bristol (1838) 'An account of an enquiry into the state of 275 poor families in the City of Bristol', *Journal of the Statistical Society,* I, pp.86–8.

Statistical Society of London (1840) 'Report … on the state of the working classes in the parishes of St. Margaret and St. John, Westminster', *Journal of the Statistical Society,* III, pp.14–24.

Statistical Society of Manchester (1839) 'Report on the condition of the population in three parishes of Rutlandshire in March 1839', *Journal of the Statistical Society,* II, pp.297–302.

Statistical Society of Manchester (1841) 'Report on the condition of the working classes in the town of Kingston-upon-Hull', *Journal of the Statistical Society,* IV, pp.212–21.

Weld, C.R. (1843) 'On the condition of the working classes in the inner ward of St. George's Parish, Hanover Square', *Journal of the Statistical Society,* VI, pp.17–23.

Wells, A.F. (1935) *The local social survey in Great Britain,* London, Allen and Unwin.

Willmott, P. (1963) *The evolution of a community: a study of Dagenham after forty years,* London, Routledge & Kegan Paul.

Willmott, P. and Young, M.D. (1960) *Family and class in a London suburb,* London, Routledge & Kegan Paul.

Wybrow, R.J. (1989) *Britain speaks out, 1937–87: a social history as seen through the Gallup data,* London, Macmillan.

Young, M.D. and Willmott, P. (1962) *Family and kinship in East London,* Harmondsworth, Penguin.

Young, T. (1934) *Becontree and Dagenham. The story of the growth of a housing estate,* London, Samuel Sidders.

7 NEWSPAPERS

by John Golby

Newspapers are one of the most easily accessible of primary sources. Local libraries often have runs of local newspapers, some dating back to the early years of the nineteenth century and, very occasionally, even earlier. Newspapers are valuable and much underrated sources. They can be of help to the family historian, with their announcements of births, marriages and deaths. In this respect, obituary columns can be particularly useful. Newspapers often report, sometimes in great detail, particular local events and occasions, and their many advertisements provide all sorts of information concerning the sale of lands and properties, news of forthcoming events, and particular offers made by local retail outlets.

Unfortunately, apart from *The Times,* few newspapers are indexed. Consequently, unwary researchers can spend an enormous amount of time browsing through columns of small print and, although there are always absorbing stories and snippets of information to read, they will find at the end of the day that they have added very little, if anything at all, to their overall research aims. So, newspapers must be treated with care, and time will very often be best spent when searching for information about particular known events, such as a local election, a local scandal, or the death of a relative.

Before going on to discuss in more detail the ways in which local newspapers can be used profitably in your research projects, it is important to understand something about the development of the newspaper press, especially during the nineteenth century. Technological constraints, economic and political circumstances, and the fact that newspaper proprietors and editors have been interested in different things at different periods have all been important factors in explaining why the coverage of local news and particular types of news in the local press has varied so much during this period.

7.1   THE DEVELOPMENT OF THE NEWSPAPER PRESS IN THE NINETEENTH CENTURY

The period from 1800 onwards has been a period of growth and change for newspapers: growth in the number of newspapers published, in pages printed, and in circulation figures. However, in 1800 the only daily papers were those printed in London. Provincial newspapers were produced weekly and, for the most part, they merely provided a compendium of news taken from the London dailies. This news consisted primarily of international and parliamentary events, court news and other odd snippets of information; usually, there was little space devoted to local events. What is worse for the local historian, the news was printed in columns with very few headings, so that it is difficult to identify or isolate individual items quickly.

The provincial press took on this particular role of passing on the London news partly because there was no way London dailies could be distributed throughout the country quickly. Furthermore, they did not possess the technology to print vast runs of papers. It took a compositor about five hours to make up a page of print (twenty hours work for a four-page newspaper), and it took about one hour for about 200 copies of a four-page newspaper to be printed. It was a slow and costly business. Costs were high because distribution was by stagecoach, and because during the wars with France the government imposed heavy stamp duties. In 1797, the duty was $3d$ per copy and in 1815 it was raised to $4d$ per copy. In that year, the provincial newspaper the *Northampton Mercury* cost $7\frac{1}{2}d$.

With the introduction, in the early years of the nineteenth century, of the iron frame press and Gamble's paper-making machine (which not only halved the cost of paper but improved its quality), the number of provincial newspapers increased. Further stimulus was given to the press when the government reduced the stamp duty on newspapers to $1d$ in 1836 and abolished the duty altogether in 1855. Also, distribution costs were reduced with the availability of rail transport from the 1840s on. So, by the mid-1850s, the *Northampton Mercury*, although dependent on advertising revenues for its profits, was sold for $3\frac{1}{2}d$, under half the price for which it was sold in 1815.

These changes meant that editors were able to increase the size of their papers and so, as well as continuing to report London and international news, they now had more space to devote to local news items. Many local newspapers were set up in the middle years of the century. Some were short-lived, but most major towns had one, if not two or more, local weekly newspapers by the 1850s. Local libraries will have information concerning the newspapers local to their areas, but if there is a need to research further afield, West (1983) contains an extensive list of the dates when local newspapers were started, ended or were taken over.

By the 1850s, local newspapers were providing much more of a local news service. Indeed, some were employing their own shorthand reporters to cover local events. But care must be taken in using local newspapers dating from this period. First, as has already been mentioned, many towns had more than one newspaper. These papers very often represented differing political viewpoints, so it is important to check up on the politics, ownership and editorship of particular papers. The *Newspaper press directory,* published annually from 1846, provides this sort of information (note that this is now called *Benn's media directory*).

Secondly, some local editors were highly selective about what matters they reported. Thus, one should not automatically assume, just because the local press did not report certain local events, for example theatre events, that there were no such activities going on in the locality. Again, some editors refused to report certain controversial activities which might cause offence among their potential readership. Trinder (1982, p.5) quotes from a report which appeared in the *Banbury Advertiser* in 1856, during a dispute in the town over how the Sabbath should be kept:

> *On some questions which from time to time have agitated the town, we have deemed it right to maintain a discreet silence. The Sabbath Question has been thus passed by, because thought unsuitable to the columns of a newspaper.*

Thirdly, special care needs to be taken by those researching villages or small towns which did not possess their own local paper. Although papers such as the *Nottingham Journal* reported activities in the villages within the county of Nottingham and, indeed, even some areas of Derbyshire and Leicestershire, the editor of the paper was invariably dependent for reports upon someone living within each village, usually the local schoolmaster or a clergyman. Consequently, the reports very often reflect the particular interests of the local reporter and do not necessarily give anything like a full picture of the activities within the village. However, there is one consolation for the village researcher. Reports from outside the main town are very often grouped in columns specifically devoted to local news, and the names of each village are given a small headline so that it is comparatively easy to discover reports for particular villages.

The repeal of the stamp duty in 1855 not only brought an increase in the number of provincial weekly papers printed but also an increase in the number of daily provincial newspapers produced – both morning and evening papers. Few provincial daily newspapers were published before 1855, the *Liverpool Telegraph and Shipping Gazette* (1826) probably being the oldest. But between 1855 and 1870, 78 new provincial dailies were started, of which 17 were evening papers. By no means all survived for very long but, understandably, the vast majority of these dailies were published in towns with populations of over 80,000, and in areas furthest away from London. Of the 58 provincial dailies in existence in 1870, all, apart from the two in Brighton and Norwich, were published in towns 'to the north and west of a line drawn from Exeter to Hull' (Lee, 1976, p.68).

Evening papers became particularly popular towards the end of the century. They were able to produce up-to-date local news and they also aimed to satisfy the growing national interest in sport by devoting about a quarter of their news space to football, cricket and racing.

Further important changes took place in the structure of the newspaper industry. The introduction of steam presses and other capital intensive equipment, together with improved methods of distribution, had inevitably resulted in comparatively large amounts of capital being needed to float new papers. Whereas in 1844 the *Northern Star* had broken even financially with a circulation of just over 6,000, by 1918 the *Sunday Express* was running at a loss, even with circulation figures of around 250,000 (Curran, 1978). By the end of the nineteenth century, there was a marked shift in the control of newspaper ownership away from the small proprietor. The development of newspaper empires was under way and has continued throughout the twentieth century. But for those researching and using newspapers in the twentieth century, local news is fuller and local events are more widely advertised in the local press. This is particularly true for the last decade or so, with the growth of free local newspapers.

7.2 HOW CAN WE USE NEWSPAPERS?

Remember, few newspapers are indexed, so that if you are not clear what you are looking for before you start work on newspapers, you can waste a great amount of time. But newspapers can be particularly useful if, for example, you have established at least the rough dates of particular births, marriages or deaths of members of your family or of local notables. Very often obituary notices can be especially helpful because age at death is often given, and, if the individual is a person of some local standing, names of people attending the funeral may be listed, together with the church or chapel at which the service was held.

Newspapers can also be useful if you wish to explore a particular local event, perhaps in order to see what actually happened, whether and to what extent any members of your family were involved, or, in a broader sense, to see what light this event threw upon the local community. With respect to this latter point, Hammerton and Cannadine (1981) relied heavily on reports, leaders and advertisements from various local newspapers to investigate 'the links and shared assumptions which bound the community' of Cambridge together during the planning and celebration of the Diamond Jubilee of Queen Victoria in the town in 1897. Clearly, care has to be exercised here because newspapers very rarely report what people other than news editors are thinking. However, Yeo (1976, pp.x–xi) argues that, at least during the late nineteenth and early twentieth centuries, 'there was a far greater proportion of straight, often verbatim reporting, of sermons, speeches, the proceedings of annual meetings, "annual courts" of hospitals and the like. There were correspondingly less over-written, slanted "news" items'.

A perhaps more straightforward approach would be to take a local election and examine the various press reports, preferably from more than one paper, detailing the events leading up to the election. This could be done with profit for any period, but it would be particularly rewarding to examine an election before the introduction of the Secret Ballot Act in 1872. The reports could shed considerable light on how a particular town was divided along political lines. You should be able to discover, not only who the principal local supporters of the political parties were, but also where local events were held, which particular pubs and inns were centres for the political parties, and which particular bands and organizations supported particular candidates. Remember, it is important when using newspapers to make sure you know who owned the papers and their political allegiances.

Local newspapers, particularly twentieth-century papers, can play a vital role in helping you to assess the extent of cultural activities within a town. As we have seen, more activities were reported as the nineteenth century progressed. By going through the editions of a weekly paper for one particular year and taking note of reports and advertising material, you should get a good idea of the range of activities available within a given town, organized by both formal and informal associations.

7.3 LOCATION AND FINDING AIDS

by Paul Smith

Public libraries often have good runs of local newspapers (often on microfilm), and local newspaper offices often have facilities for viewing past copies. Never forget that the local history library or the record office covering your area may have published or maintain a finding-list or similar of the local press. The area local and/or family history societies may also have a list. All nineteenth- and twentieth-century newspapers are also collected at the British Library's Newspaper Library, Colindale Avenue, London, NW9 5HE.

The British Library's NEWSPLAN programme for the microfilming and preservation of UK local newspapers is surveying the UK by area. The British Library and local libraries are cooperating in this project, the final goal of which is the preservation on microfilm of all UK newspapers. The reports published so far are: Northern Region (1989), North Western Region (1990), West Midlands (1990), Yorkshire and Humberside (1990), and East Midlands (1989). The pilot project report on the South West appeared in 1986. The NEWSPLAN surveys are now outpacing the BBN volumes (see below) in speed of publication but, where both cover an area, use both.

Should you need to investigate the national or local press currently or retrospectively, you will find the following useful:

Willings press guide (annual from 1874) East Grinstead, Reed Information Services Ltd. The main alphabetical sequence gives full information about the newspapers and periodicals listed. Preceding it is the 'Newspaper index' which groups newspapers by place. Of its two volumes, (1) deals with United Kingdom titles.

Benn's media directory (annual from 1846) Tonbridge, Benn Business Information Services Ltd. This is the current title of the oldest directory or guide to the press in the world. First published as the *Newspaper press directory* in 1846, it became *Benn's press directory* in 1978 and now bears the above title.

There is also the ongoing series *Bibliography of British newspapers* (BBN), published by the British Library Board in London. The pioneer here was the Wiltshire volume published by the Library Association Reference Special and Information Section in 1975. Other volumes available are: Cornwall and Devon (1991), Nottinghamshire (1987), Kent (1982), Durham and Northumberland (1982), and Derbyshire (1987). Each volume covers its county or counties using pre-1974 boundaries.

Catalogue of the newspaper library Colindale (1975) London, British Museum Publications for the British Library Board. Of the eight volumes, (1) covers London, (2) covers England, Wales, Scotland and Ireland. Newspapers are listed alphabetically by title within an alphabetical list by place of publication. The final four volumes comprise a title index.

Dixon, D. (1973) *Local newspapers and periodicals of the nineteenth century: a checklist of holdings in provincial libraries*, Leicester, University of Leicester Victorian Studies Centre (*Victorian Studies Handlist*, no.6).

Ferguson, J.P.S. (1956) *Scottish newspapers held in Scottish libraries*, Edinburgh, Scottish Central Library.

Gibson, J.S.W. (1989) *Local newspapers, 1750–1920: England and Wales; Channel Islands; Isle of Man: a select location list*, Birmingham, Federation of Family History Societies. Describes, by county and local area, what newspapers were published, when, and where they can be consulted.

Gurnet, J. (1983) 'Newspaper indexes for the family historian', *Genealogists Magazine*, 21 pp.109–12.

Linton, D. and Boston, R. (eds) (1987) *The newspaper press in Britain: an annotated bibliography*, London and New York, Mansell Publishing.

McLaughlin, E. (1989) *Family history from newspapers* (2nd edn), Birmingham, Federation of Family History Societies.

Munford, A.P. (1976) *South Yorkshire newspapers 1754–1976*, South Yorkshire County Council (*Archive Handlists*, no.1).

Tercentenary handlist of English and Welsh newspapers, magazines and reviews, 1620–1920 (1920) London, The Times.

The Waterloo directory of Victorian periodicals, 1824–1900, Phase I (1976) Ontario, Wilfred Laurier University Press (*Waterloo Directory,* no.1). Lists alphabetically 'the newspaper and periodical titles published in England Ireland Scotland and Wales at any time between 1824 and 1900' (Preface, p.vii).

West, J. (1983) *Town records,* Chichester, Phillimore. See especially Chapter 10.

REFERENCES (SECTION 7)

Curran, J. (1978) 'The press as an agency of social control', in Boyce, G., Curran, J. and Wingate, P. (eds) *Newspaper history from the seventeenth century to the present day,* London, Constable (etc.) for the Press Group of the Acton Society.

Hammerton, E. and Cannadine, D. (1981) 'Conflict and consensus on a ceremonial occasion: the Diamond Jubilee in Cambridge in 1897', *The Historical Journal,* 24, 1, pp.111–46.

Lee, A.J. (1976) *The origins of the popular press in England 1855–1914,* London, Croom Helm.

Trinder, B. (1982) *Victorian Banbury,* Chichester, Phillimore.

Trinder, B. and Golby, J. (1993) 'Local newspapers as sources', audio-cassette 4B in Braham, P. (ed.) *Using the past: audio-cassettes on sources and methods for family and community historians,* Milton Keynes, The Open University.

West, J. (1983) *Town records,* Chichester, Phillimore.

Yeo, S. (1976) *Religion and voluntary organisations in crisis,* London, Croom Helm.

8 AUTOBIOGRAPHIES, LETTERS AND DIARIES

by John Golby

Most of us, when we think about autobiographies, reminiscences and memoirs, associate them with the famous, powerful and rich. In the nineteenth century, autobiographies of statesmen, eminent soldiers, explorers and clergymen abounded. In the twentieth century, sports, film and television stars have been added to these ranks. Very few of us studying family and community history have forebears or existing relatives who fall within these categories, so perhaps a reasonable question to start off with is, why include autobiographies at all in this volume? There are a number of answers.

First, there are many more autobiographies and memoirs in existence which have been written by 'ordinary' men and women than was believed even ten years ago. Leaving the rich and famous aside, Burnett et al. (1984, 1987, 1989) discovered, listed and provided abstracts of some 1,800 autobiographies written by working men and women between the years 1790 and 1945. (There may be many more yet to be discovered.) These writings (the vast majority by men) provide valuable information about the family, work and leisure experiences of men from all over England, Scotland and Wales. So, although we would deem ourselves very fortunate to find an autobiography by a member of our own family, the likelihood of discovering a work which relates to the region in which our family lived or the occupations which they undertook is relatively high.

Secondly, autobiography is one of the few historical sources in which we can learn of the direct experiences of individuals. (This point is discussed further in section 8.1 below.)

Thirdly, the growing popularity of the genre of autobiography, memoirs and reminiscences in the nineteenth century tells us incidentally a great deal about developments within that society.

For example, most, but by no means all, autobiographies were written for publication. This suggests that there was a growing literate reading public and a public interested in reading about the experiences of working people. Also, the fact that working men were able to publish their memoirs, even if helped by local subscriptions, suggests that publishing was becoming cheaper as the nineteenth century progressed. There has also been a great efflorescence of locally published autobiographies in more recent years, perhaps associated with the increasing attraction of local history and family history, and the impact of the feminist and oral history movements.

Although the writers of the nineteenth-century autobiographies come from a very wide range of backgrounds and occupations, it is perhaps not surprising that the majority are written by skilled workers. Also, of the 804 working-class autobiographies listed as having been written in the period up to 1900, only 70 are written by women (see Burnett et al., 1984, 1987, 1989). Few of the latter were published in the nineteenth century and many still remain unpublished. Considering that by the mid-nineteenth century there was very little difference in the literacy rates between men and women, and that by 1884, more women in England were literate than their menfolk (Vincent, 1989, p.24), one can only conclude that the small percentage of working women writers reflects not their ability to write but their relatively low status within Victorian society – a contrast to the large number of autobiographies and memoirs by women in more recent years.

Although we have concentrated on discussing the autobiographies of 'ordinary' men and women, we must not forget entirely those written by the rich and famous. They can often be useful in filling in details about particular events and descriptions of the localities in which they lived.

Diaries and letters are relevant for the same kinds of reasons as autobiographies. These are sources which you may be lucky enough to have within your own family. Again, it is surprising how many diaries not intended for publication are in existence or are still coming to light. In my own limited experience, within the groups of students I have been teaching over the past two years, one student possessed a diary kept by a relative who was on active service in the first few months of World War I and another discovered in the attic of his house a marvellous collection of diaries written by a female relative covering the period 1937-45. Unfortunately, with the development of the phone, and improved transport communications, the need for family letter-writing has diminished. The custom of maintaining a diary, except for noting appointments and special dates, has also declined during this century. Nevertheless, if you are fortunate enough to have family letters or diaries in your possession, then you should attempt to make use of these valuable personal sources. If you do not possess any family diaries, but wish to explore the possibilities of using these important qualitative sources, Burnett et al. (1984, 1987, 1989) list and give abstracts for 121 diaries written by working people which are available in libraries and record offices (see also Huff, 1985; Matthews, 1950; and, for an example of a case study building on a journal, Abramson, 1992).

Diaries of a slightly different kind, covering the period 1939 to 1963, can be found in the Mass-Observation archives at the University of Sussex. Mass-Observation was founded in 1937 by, among others, Tom Harrisson, Charles Madge and Humphrey Jennings (see Sheridan, 1993). Their aim was to investigate various aspects of British social life by the means of interviews, surveys and questionnaires. They also recruited voluntary observers to record their views on various topics and their activities on certain dates, often special days such as Christmas, Easter Sunday, and the Coronation of George VI. By 1939, as well as writing reports on special events and topics, many of the volunteers were encouraged to keep diaries. From 1939 to 1963, some 500 men and women wrote diaries which they sent in to Mass-Observation at regular intervals. A few of the diarists cover most of the period; other diary contributions are detailed but are only maintained for short periods of time; but it is the period from 1939 to 1945, the years of the Second World War, which is best covered by the Mass-Observation diarists. These diaries are now available to researchers, although space at the the archive is limited.

8.1   EVALUATING AUTOBIOGRAPHIES, LETTERS AND DIARIES AS SOURCES

Unlike most of the other sources you will consult during the course of your research, autobiographies, letters and diaries can convey *directly* the experiences of people living through particular events, describing their own personal, working and leisure experiences, and revealing their own particular attitudes and values. In one important sense, these are the most useful *qualitative* historical sources available. Of course, other sources such as newspaper reports, parliamentary commissions, and the writings of social investigators, like Henry Mayhew and Charles Booth, provide a great deal of useful information for the social historian, but these sources are one stage removed from the lives of the individuals under consideration. The reporters, commissioners and investigators all, to some extent, interpret the evidence relating to the lives of other individuals, before writing their reports and articles. Even oral historians, however talented, impose their own values and attitudes on their interviewees by the very questions they ask. The issues they raise, while pertinent to their own researches, may not have been the major concerns and worries of the interviewees at a certain date or a certain time in their lives. However, generally speaking, the writers of autobiographies, diaries and letters are writing about their particular interests and concerns at a particular time. In the process, they provide factual information but, perhaps more importantly, they convey their own interpretations of events and at the same time reveal, wittingly or unwittingly, their own attitudes, values and beliefs.

Nevertheless, these sources have to be treated with care. Autobiographies are often, but not always, written by people in their later years. Memories can become clouded, and while factual evidence can usually be checked, qualitative statements are sometimes harder to assess. Letters and diaries possess the advantage of usually dealing with events and experiences which have occurred in the last few days and, particularly in the case of diaries, sometimes in the last few hours. Also, whereas most letters and diaries are personal and private and are not written with publication in mind, most, but by no means all, autobiographies and memoirs are written with the intention that they are to be read by at least certain sections of the public. So it is important to understand why an autobiography was written, and at what groups within the reading public it was aimed. For example, a number of nineteenth-century autobiographies describe how working men improved their condition by their own efforts: by self-help and by self-education. Clearly, a major reason for publishing these autobiographies was a missionizing one, and we must take this into account. Nevertheless, the details within the autobiographies about the home lives of the writers, their childhood, their education, if any, and the sort of work they did is of immense importance to the family and community historian.

You should also bear in mind that most people wish to show themselves in the best possible light, and will be prepared to put a gloss on or interpret events to their advantage. This applies to published autobiographies, to the Mass-Observation diaries, and also, perhaps to a lesser extent, to letter writers and diary keepers, even if they had no intention of publishing their writings.

In addition, the writers of diaries and letters, and even more of autobiographies, are inevitably affected by current literary conventions and stock images. Vincent, in his study of nineteenth-century working-class autobiographies (1981), shows how these conventions and images shape the way in which the writers represent their experiences of, for example, childhood and the pursuit of 'useful knowledge'.

Finally, personal sources can often be infuriating because they do not discuss the subjects in which you, the researcher, are particularly interested. Despite these defects, these sources provide subjective accounts of personal experiences which are so often missing from other accounts of the past, and in this sense they offer special insight into how people felt and acted in the past. But the very fact that they are personal accounts about particular people, living in particular towns and villages and doing particular sorts of work, leads to another problem: to what extent can one use these sources to make any generalizations about society at a given time? Clearly, there are not enough of these personal sources to support the making, with any confidence, of wide, quantifiable judgements. Nevertheless, they contain vast amounts of valuable factual information. This information, together with the views and attitudes expressed by the writers, can be used to help confirm or throw doubt on previously held beliefs about the community or families you are researching and, in addition, may raise new questions to explore. Above all, personal sources provide an experiential dimension which cannot be acquired from many other sources.

Just one example can show the merits and problems of using these types of personal sources. I have chosen an entry from the diary of Hannah Cullwick, a general servant, working in the house of the Henderson family, in Gloucester Crescent, London, in 1871:

Wednesday 10 may [1871]

I got up early. Did the sweeping & clean'd the hall & watercloset on my knees before breakfast. Shook the mats. Wash'd me & got out breakfast. Did the dusting after & to prayers at 9. Wash'd up & clean'd the hearth. Put straight & dusted the potboard on my knees. Miss M gave me orders for an early dinner, & give me the things out in the storeroom, but I wouldn't ax leave of her, to go out, 'cause the last time I did she scrupled, & said she would ask Mrs Henderson, but never give me any answer. So when Missis was alone in the dining room afore the dinner went up, I tidied myself & knock'd at the parlour door & went in. I aske'd if I may go out, & Missis said, 'What's going on tonight? I don't think the ladies are going out to want you – *yes*, if you can manage for tea.' I said, 'Yes, Ma'am, I can fry the fish afore I go.' She said, 'very well,' & I said, 'Thank you ma'am,' & come down again pleas'd enough that the asking part was over, what I always *do* so dislike.

(Stanley, 1984, p.163)

How would you assess this as a source?

Cullwick did not write her diaries solely for her own eyes (Stanley, 1984, p.8), and so we would need to discover why she kept her diaries, when they were written (what about hindsight?), and for whom (for further comments on interpreting Hannah Cullwick's diaries, see Swindells, 1989). Also, this extract has the defect common to many personal written sources of not telling us what we want to know. Cullwick says she got up early, but what exactly does this mean? However, the diary entry provides a good deal of factual information concerning the work that this particular general servant undertook, and in the process we learn details about the house itself and the place of the servant within the house. But perhaps the major value of this particular extract is not as a record of work undertaken but as an account of the relationship between servant and mistress and the anguish involved in this servant asking for time off. Autobiographies, diaries and letters record facts, but they also have the unique merit of describing attitudes, feelings and experiences.

8.2   LOCATION

The nearest local history library should list any published autobiographies, diaries and letters relating to your area. Some will also possess unpublished materials. You should also consult Burnett et al.'s three volume bibliography (1984, 1987, 1989), for the period 1790 to 1945, covering both autobiographies and published diaries. The editors provide background details on writers as well as publishers and publication dates, and (for unpublished works) on where they are lodged. They also provide a superb series of subject indexes, including ones for occupations and place names. The drawbacks are that these volumes relate only to England, Scotland and Wales, exclude memoirs written in Gaelic and Welsh, and end in 1945 (see also the bibliographies in *The Cambridge bibliography of English literature*, 1966 and 1974–7, and (for diaries) Huff, 1985 and Matthews, 1950). There is no systematic guide to the huge numbers of locally published autobiographies appearing in recent years, but scanning local bookshops and libraries, and consulting local history and family history societies in the area can be helpful, as can journals such as *Oral History* which regularly note such publications.

Letters are more difficult to track down. There are some published collections on which you could draw (e.g. Erickson, 1972; Foy, 1989; see also *The Cambridge bibliography of English literature*, 1966 and 1974–7). But otherwise, unless you know, through your reading or through information gleaned from your library, the whereabouts of a collection of letters which you think would be extremely relevant to your work, it would be best to give up searching for this type of source.

The 500 Mass-Observation diaries kept at the University of Sussex are available in microfilm, arranged in monthly batches. Information about the various diary writers, together with a geographical index relating to the addresses of the diarists, is available at the Mass-Observation Archive. It is perhaps worth mentioning here that other Mass-Observation materials – reports, surveys, questionnaires, etc. – have been collected together under various topic headings, of which housing, family planning, work, employment, unemployment and demobilization are just a few. The full list and further information in a Mass-Observation records guide for researchers is available from: The Tom Harrisson Mass-Observation Archive, Arts Building D, The University of Sussex, Falmer, Brighton BN2 9QN, East Sussex. For published Mass-Observation anthologies, see Gross (1980) and Sheridan (1990).

REFERENCES AND FURTHER READING (SECTION 8)

Abramson, P.R. (1992) *A case for case studies: an immigrant's journal,* Newbury Park, Sage.

Barker, G. (1980) *Buckinghamshire born,* Milton Keynes, The People's Press of Milton Keynes.

Burnett, J. (ed.) (1974) *Useful toil: autobiographies of working people from the 1820s to the 1920s,* London, Allen Lane.

Burnett, J. (ed.) (1982) *Destiny obscure: autobiographies of childhood, education and family from the 1820s to the 1920s,* London, Allen Lane.

Burnett, J., Vincent, D. and Mayall, D. (eds) (1984, 1987, 1989) *The autobiography of the working class: an annotated critical bibliography,* Hassocks, Harvester. Vol.1, *1790–1900* (1984); Vol.2, *1900–1945,* (1987); Vol.3, *Supplement, 1790–1945* (1989).

Caliban library of working-class autobiography, Llanybydder, Dyfed, Caliban Books. Caliban Books is publishing a series of working-class autobiographies, starting in 1993. In 1993, 23 titles will be published, and there are plans to publish six titles a year from 1994.

Erickson, C. (1972) *Invisible immigrants: the adaptation of English and Scottish immigrants in nineteenth-century America,* London, Weidenfeld & Nicolson.

Foy, R.H. (1989) *Dear uncle: immigrant letters to Antrim from the USA. 1843–1852,* Antrim, Antrim & District Historical Society.

Gross, G. (ed.) (1980) *Worktowners at Blackpool: Mass-Observation and popular leisure in the 1930s,* London, Routledge.

Harrisson, T. (1976) *Living through the Blitz,* London, Collins.

Haythorne, E. (1991) *On Earth to make the numbers up,* Castleford, Yorkshire Art Circus.

Huff, C. (1985) *British women's diaries: a descriptive bibliography of selected nineteenth century women's manuscript diaries,* New York, AMS Press (*AMS Studies in Social History,* no.4). The diaries are arranged by social class and, within those divisions, by occupation of the head of household.

Matthews, W. (1950) *British diaries: an annotated bibliography of British diaries written between 1442 and 1942,* Berkeley and Los Angeles, University of California Press/London, Cambridge University Press. Arranged by year, and well indexed.

Sheridan, D. (ed.) (1990) *Wartime women: an anthology of women's wartime writing for Mass-Observation 1937–45,* London, Heinemann.

Sheridan, D. (1993) 'Writing to the archive: mass-observation as autobiography', *Sociology,* 27, pp.27–40.

Stanley, L. (ed.) (1984) *The diaries of Hannah Cullwick, Victorian maidservant,* London, Virago Press.

Swindells, J. (1989) 'Liberating the subject? Autobiography and "women's history": a reading of *The Diaries of Hannah Cullwick*', in Personal Narratives Group (ed.) *Interpreting women's lives,* Bloomington, Indiana University Press.

The Cambridge bibliography of English literature (1966) Cambridge, Cambridge University Press. Its *Supplement* in the same year, and *The new Cambridge bibliography of English literature* (1974–7) are excellent aids to tracing English, Scottish and Irish diaries, biography, autobiography, memoirs and letters. The subject indexes make their use easy and they are widely available in libraries.

Vincent, D. (1981) *Bread, knowledge and freedom: a study of nineteenth-century working class autobiography,* London, Europa Publications.

Vincent, D. (1989) *Literacy and popular culture: England 1750–1914,* Cambridge, Cambridge University Press.

White, D. (1981) *D is for Doris, V is for victory,* Milton Keynes, The People's Press of Milton Keynes.

CHAPTER 5

USING WRITTEN SOURCES: SOME FURTHER EXAMPLES

by Dennis Mills and Michael Drake

In this chapter we discuss some further written sources which, for a number of reasons, are dealt with more briefly than those in Chapter 4. Some, for example civil registers of births, marriages and deaths, and parliamentary papers and government reports, are not readily available throughout the United Kingdom and Ireland. Others, such as wills, pose particular problems of interpretation and coverage. However, the purpose of the chapter is to give some further hints on finding your way through the key written sources and also to alert you to the kinds of questions you could ask about additional sources that you will no doubt come upon. As in the other chapters in Part II, the aim is not to present a comprehensive listing of all possible sources, but rather to indicate the kinds of data you can expect to get from different types of written sources, and thus the range of research projects for which each is most likely to be useful.

Of course, the same general points apply as in previous chapters, in particular the need to treat any source critically and knowledgeably (following the points about source criticism summarized in Chapter 2), to look at it in its context, and, wherever possible, to supplement the information it provides by using additional sources.

These chapters on written source material represent navigational aids for the apprentice historian. As you will have noticed, the sources are of many different types, and are generated and compiled in different ways. It is worth reflecting further on these differences and what they might mean for your research project.

1   STANDARD AND LOCAL SOURCES

Sources like the published and unpublished *census material* (see Chapter 3), *trade directories* (Chapter 4, section 1) and in some ways *poll books and electoral registers* (Chapter 4, section 2), certainly have an (essential) local dimension; but they were largely compiled following categories developed outside the local community, and from a national perspective. This leads to a number of problems and ambiguities. But because these sources were generated in most parts of the British Isles over long periods, they have the huge advantage of allowing comparative studies both over time for a particular locality and between different localities. Not all have survived universally, but these widely available standard sources should be high on the checklists of all family and community historians.

The *civil registers* of births, marriages and deaths, together with the associated reports by the Registrars General, are another example of a widely applicable, long continued and standardized official source. The civil registration systems were started early enough to capture the dramatic changes in fertility, mortality and nuptiality over the last 150 years: the system in England and Wales began in 1837; Scotland's began in 1855 (information in this year is particularly rich – see Drake, 1982); while in Ireland civil registration was introduced in 1845 for non-Catholic marriages and was extended to cover all marriages, as well as births and deaths, in 1864. Unlike

Births (top):

No.	When and where born	Name, if any	Sex	Name and surname of father	Name, surname and maiden name of mother	Occupation of father	Signature, description and residence of informant	When registered	Signature of Registrar	Name entered after registration

Marriages (centre):

No.	When married	Names & surnames of each party	Condition[2]	Ages	Rank or profession of each party	Residence at time of marriage	Both fathers' names and surnames	When registered	Rank or profession of both fathers

Place of marriage and ceremony performed

Signatures of parties who were married

Signatures of witnesses

Deaths (bottom):

No.	When & where died	Name & surname	Sex	Age[3]	Occupation	Cause	Signature, description & residence of informant	When registered	Signature of Registrar

Figure 5.1 Data given in civil registers of births *(top)*, marriages *(centre)* and deaths *(bottom)*[1] (Source: based on Pelling, 1990, pp.29, 35)

[1] In Scotland the birth certificate gives the date and place of parents' marriage (for 1855 and then 1861 onwards); on marriage certificates the names of both mothers are given, while on death certificates both parents' names appear. For the one year 1855 much more information was given (see Drake, 1982).

[2] For example, bachelor or spinster.

[3] Often only approximate.

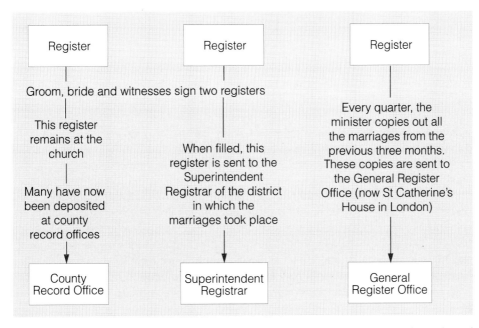

Figure 5.2   How Anglican marriages are registered in England and Wales. A similar though not identical system operates for other marriages, with one transcript being sent to the relevant General Register Office (in London, Edinburgh, Dublin or Belfast)

the registers kept by religious bodies (themselves a useful source – see Chapter 4, section 3), civil registers had a standard format which varied only slightly from country to country and changed little over time. Figure 5.1 shows the information that is given in the registers.

However, the registers are not without their weaknesses. Although, at least in England, Wales and Scotland, they soon covered the bulk of the population, they did not always include everyone, particularly in the early years, e.g. illegitimate births and Roman Catholics, especially Irish immigrants. Sometimes too there are inaccuracies both in the original entries and in their transcription for the central records (see Figure 5.2 for an indication of the procedure; for further discussion see Nissel, 1987; Todd, 1989, pp.62–77; Pelling, 1990, Chapter 5). But the registers do provide detailed demographic, residential and occupational data about individuals in standard format, and are potentially valuable for demographic and related studies of the nineteenth and twentieth centuries (e.g. Drake, 1982; Vincent, 1983), as well as for comparative studies of such topics as literacy (measured by the proportion of brides and grooms able to sign their names in the marriage register), and social mobility (through a comparison of the occupations of brides and grooms and of their respective fathers or siblings) – see Volume 3, Chapter 5.

Although the registers themselves are generally well preserved, they present serious access problems for researchers concerned with wider trends or comparisons (as distinct from those interested in buying copies of individual certificates). In England and Wales there is no general access to the civil registers for research purposes: *indexes* are available at the General Register Office in London (St. Catherine's House) and to some extent on microfiche elsewhere, but these provide no direct access to the registers themselves. Some collections made by researchers who obtained special permission from the Registrar General are available, however (some of these are discussed in Schürer and Anderson, 1992). Scottish registers can be used for a daily fee at the General Register Office in Edinburgh, whereas in Ireland the registers remain with the local registrars. As there is no general policy on access it is necessary to negotiate with them. Unlike the registration of births and deaths, the registration of marriages was left in the hands of the clergy (except for civil and certain nonconformist marriages). These marriage registers are often available in local record offices. Any possibility of civil registers becoming more widely available would be a huge advantage for research projects in family and community history.

Standard sources are clearly of great potential for comparative studies across different areas. For individual localities, however, there are also many different kinds of sources which historians may already know about or stumble across. It would be impossible to describe all of these, even in a much larger book, but it is relevant to consider the kind of light that such local sources can provide for family and community research. Many have some standard aspects, but being generated locally they are often more useful for extending a local study over time than for comparing between different localities. We will consider a few categories of documents and then draw out some general principles.

Take, for instance, the *records of the Charity Organization Society*, later the Family Welfare Association, which was operating in large cities in the first half of the present century. The Leicestershire Record Office has some 20,000 case histories, which were generated in Leicester between 1904 and 1914 (see Page, 1987, p.521). These contain a wide range of social, demographic and economic information about families applying for relief from poverty, and have been used to trace the migration of poor families within the city (Page, 1991). The methodology adopted by the Society means that comparable data exist for a very large number of families, representing a major group within the population of Leicester. How far these records are available elsewhere is something you might care to look into. They certainly exist for some parts of London.

The *records of the Poor Law authorities* are another major source for family and community historians and are widely available in county record offices. The records of out-relief have survived for many Poor Law unions (i.e. groups of parishes responsible for administering Poor Law relief). Using this source for Birmingham, Parton and Matthews (1984, pp.28–9) were able to draw up age and sex profiles of recipients in 1847 and to quantify the kinds of employment in which they were normally engaged. As thousands of people were involved, their addresses provide one means of establishing socio-spatial patterns of residence across a major city. Broadly similar documents, the *General Registers of Poor*, have survived for a few areas in Scotland and have been used, for example, to plot patterns of migration (Withers, 1986; Withers and Watson, 1991). A list of all holdings of parochial boards (the responsible bodies for out-relief in Scotland) can be found in the Scottish Records Association's 'Summaries of Archival Holdings' (for a recent survey of Poor Law records, see Gibson *et al.*, 1993).

A third example of local sources are *local government records,* which naturally include long runs of committee and council minutes. Of direct interest to the community historian, because they involve large numbers of families, are the records of housing departments. For instance, the Horncastle Rural District Council records deposited in the Lincolnshire Archives Office include various rate books and valuations, a record of rate reductions in the period 1940–8 for reasons of poverty, and 21 files probably relating to the national Overcrowding Survey of 1935–6.

Apart from the rate books just mentioned, these three examples of sources are heavily biased towards the poor, and their problems are bound to figure heavily in the records of a social and communal nature. Of a different bias are records relating to property, which in general are heavily weighted towards the rich and powerful, especially large landowners.

However, there are some important exceptions in England and Wales, and others in Scotland and Ireland. *Land tax assessments* survive in large quantities down to 1832 and sometimes beyond, and include data on tax paid by all but the very smallest proprietors, and details of most occupiers (see Gibson and Mills, 1993; Turner and Mills, 1986). The conversion of Anglican tithes into corn rents took place mostly in the early Victorian period, except where they had been totally extinguished by Enclosure Acts. This process involved *tithe awards*, which detailed the names and acreages of each owner and occupier by individual land parcels, the value of the land, and the use to which the land was put (Kain and Prince, 1985; Kain, 1986). Similarly in Scotland, the post-1854 valuation rolls are a major source of information about property, its use, rateable value, and the names and occupations of proprietors and tenants. When used imaginatively these can provide a great deal of local information. The size, structure, distribution and wealth of population can be monitored; changing economic activity can be studied through an analysis of occupations, with the rolls being used effectively alongside census enumerators' books (CEBs). The development of a village or town can be traced by recording new houses, shops, factories, churches and streets as they appear in the record (see Moody, 1986, pp.99–100; and, for Ireland, Griffith's *General valuation*, 1858–64).

Rate books are another example worth noting. Rates levied on property by various local authorities, initially for such purposes as the relief of the poor or the maintenance of roads or bridges and then for local government expenditure generally, have a long history. The nature and contents of rate books changed over the years, but they can contain the address of the property; the names of the owner and occupier; a description of the property (e.g. house, garden, shop, factory); who was assessed; the annual value of the property; the size of the rate levied; and details of the payment. Rate books are available in large numbers in local record offices mainly for urban areas, and are relatively easy to use. (For rural areas, however, nineteenth-century rate books are rare, country parishes being less bureaucratic than boroughs.)

Rate books can thus be an excellent source for studies of urban morphology, provided one remembers that they do not include all residents, only property owners (not all of whom may themselves be permanent residents). The coverage of rate books is therefore less than that of the census; to investigate how much less would itself be an interesting comparative exercise. Taken in conjunction with an appropriate map, it might be possible to plot the property values of different parts of a community either at a point in time or over time given a run of rate books, though due both to weeding in record offices and to the lack of any requirement to deposit rate books, you cannot count on this. Rate books also allow research on the property owners of a community (many or few? increasing or decreasing? were owner-occupiers important?), or, by comparing sequential rate books, migration within an area as well as to and from it – not, of course, for the whole population, but an important segment nonetheless. By linking the names of people in the rate book with entries in, for example, CEBs or poll books (nominal record linkage – further discussed in Schürer, 1993) you can find out more about them, such as their age, marital status, occupation, dependants, place of birth, and voting behaviour (Drake, 1974). Rate books can show both the number of firms in an area and give an estimate of their size. By using a local directory to find out to which industry the firms belong, you can build up a view of the local economy, again at a point in time or over time (see Lewis and Lloyd-Jones, 1987).

Another important source of local information is provided in the *British Parliamentary Papers* (BPP). These comprise the texts of Bills, and reports from royal commissions, select committees and departments of state; they cover England, Wales, Scotland, the whole of Ireland (until 1922), Northern Ireland (after 1922), the Empire and, to a lesser extent, other parts of the world. Due to their geographical scope, content and quantity, they are one of the most important sources for historians (see Powell, 1962). Together they cover, often with much local detail, the whole range of issues coming before parliament – education, health, religion, conditions of work, taxation, the franchise, censuses, economic affairs, births, marriages and deaths, and so on. Some of their material is aggregative, i.e. not broken down by local areas or household, and so it is of use primarily for background understanding of the period. But family and community historians may find rich sources in locally based investigations or in the references to detailed local examples. In addition to text, they also include maps (often in colour), plans and technical drawings.

Quarrying the BPP involves two problems. The first, availability, has been eased by the publication of facsimiles of a thousand of the nineteenth-century volumes (a selection only) by the Irish University Press (1972), and the publication of *all* the BPP up to the present day by Chadwyck-Healey on microfiche (Cockton, 1988 and 1991). The second problem, the lack of an index of places and persons mentioned in the BPP, remains. Ask your local library or archive office about the availability of the BPP. It would, incidentally, be an extremely useful service if local history societies could go through the BPP, systematically noting references to places of interest *to them*. The guide for Liverpool is a useful model (Taylor, 1972); so is that by Pidduck (1978) for the Harvester microfiche editions of local reports to the General Board of Health 1848–57 and by Thomas (1979) for the reports of the Local Government Board 1869–1908, both of which supply enormous amounts of local detail for hundreds of communities. Finally, a word of warning: BPP, especially Royal Commission reports, are not purely 'objective'. Through the selection of witnesses and questions a pre-conceived result could be assured.

Some of these sources obviously have some standardized features in their framework, categories or assumed concepts, but the amount and nature of the detailed information they contain varies widely between different areas and different periods (the same is true of some other of the sources discussed in Chapter 4, for instance the *Medical Officer of Health reports,* and *newspaper reports*). Consequently the opportunities for directly comparative or longitudinal work between different localities or historical periods are likely to be less predictable than from sources like the census, trade directories or, provided one can get at them, civil registers.

These locally based sources make up a kind of microscope for analysing the social characteristics of a particular community in some detail. But the resulting studies can also provide another vantage point for putting the more national trends into perspective. In a sense, one can perhaps mount a telescope *from* any purely local and esoteric records to bring into focus the kinds of questions to which we are led from the major classes of national documentation.

Drawing these examples together, we can argue that standard and local records of particular value to family and community historians relate either to all households, dwellings or (preferably) individuals in a territorial community, or to a large number of them representing particular social groups. Data on age, sex, indications as to prosperity or poverty, type of employment, type and conditions of housing, area of residence, length of residence, origins, or religious affiliation are offered in varying measure.

2   PERSONAL AND SPECIFIC SOURCES

Moving along the scale from standard and (partially standardized) local sources, we need also to bear in mind the more personal, idiosyncratic and special-interest sources to which historians sometimes have access. These too can lead to interesting studies, provided they are used with caution and the implications of their less standardized information is appreciated.

Among these are *wills*, which in many ways are a rather special case in that they are at once standard in framework and general function, but at the same time highly personal. For genealogical investigation and for earlier periods when inventories were common, they have been a source of prime interest. But for the more general family and community historian concerned with nineteenth- to twentieth-century research they present some real problems. Their interpretation is not always straightforward (for example, differential bequests might indicate previous disposals rather than attitudes to particular individuals). Their survival and location varies between countries (for instance, many Irish nineteenth-century wills were destroyed), periods, and even according to the size of the inheritance. More important, only a small minority of the population made wills (only about 10 per cent in the mid nineteenth century – Vincent, 1967).

Well-founded comparative studies are thus difficult – a point that is often forgotten given the richness of the personal data sometimes found in wills. Nevertheless, the move from ecclesiastical to civil probate in 1858 facilitated the gathering of wills in one place (Somerset House in London for English and Welsh wills), and the creation of national indexes which allow for more general studies (although these indexes are often not accessible *locally*). Community historians can draw on these indexes – which give information about the value of the estate – for an indication of wealth and its distribution, though arguably the BPP can be a better source of information on, for example, income taxes or property in individual parishes or parliamentary constituencies – see Rubinstein, 1981, pp.16–18. The indexes of wills are also useful in determining people's standing in the community, and the nature of the community itself.

The wills themselves can be illuminating sources for family relationships. Bequests to the testator's nuclear family apparently increased over time: does this suggest a growth in the importance of the nuclear family as against wider kin and the community in general? How much went to different categories of relatives? Was wealth passed on in trust so that whoever inherited had only a lifetime interest – was the *family* viewed as more important than its individual members? Answers to such questions varied over time and between different classes, as is illustrated in Davidoff and Hall's (1987) study of wills. They concluded that families with land tended towards primogeniture (i.e. inheritance by the first-born child), whereas the middle class favoured partible inheritance. (For further discussion of the complex questions relating to the nature and location of wills see Gibson, 1989 or 1993; Camp, 1974; and, for Ireland, ffolliott and O'Byrne, 1987.)

There are also sources produced by particular interest groups or institutions. Some of these, for example the records of particular business firms or occupational groups, were discussed in Chapter 4. Similarly there may be records – scattered perhaps but sometimes recoverable – from specific religious, cultural or ethnic groups stretching beyond a single locality. Other local institutions too may have their own records, which may (or may not) be preserved in local collections: there may be records of *particular local churches or other religious bodies,* of *schools,* or of *local recreational* or *mutual aid societies.* Some clubs preserve files of their own records, which may sometimes be fairly comprehensive and – with long-established brass bands, for example – extend back over many years. Such records are worth exploiting: a study of the cultural life of a particular community could include an investigation of its clubs and associations. During the last twenty years research into voluntary associations has developed rapidly (see Yeo, 1976, on Reading; Harrison and Trinder, 1969, and Trinder, 1982, on Banbury; Etherington, 1990, on Lewes; and for a general account Morris, 1990; also Volume 3, Chapter 9). This is in part due to the enormous increase during the twentieth century in the number of voluntary associations, especially those relating to hobbies. Tracing these is not easy, but local libraries sometimes hold lists of existing local societies (in 1991 the Voluntary Action History Society was formed to support the preservation of voluntary sector archives: for the Society's address see Chapter 13, section 2.1.2; and, for school records, Rubinstein, 1993).

Chapter 4 has already discussed other qualitative or special-interest sources, such as *local newspapers* and *autobiographies, letters and diaries,* and the kinds of studies to which they can lead. To these we could add some of the unwritten sources mentioned in Chapter 6, including *buildings, photographs* and *people's personal memories.* All such sources have their own conventions and (in some ways) recurrent patterns – it would be a mistake to think that only 'standard' or 'official' sources impose constraints on the way people generate and structure their research, or that studies of comparative themes are out of the question when you are faced with personal sources (consider, for example, Vincent's 1983 study of recurrent images in nineteenth-century working-class autobiographies). But clearly they do not provide the same range of comparative data or timescale offered by the standard sources, nor in most cases the local community coverage to be found in the locally focused sources.

Comparative or longitudinal studies in a more quantitative and direct sense are thus difficult from such sources. But they still have the potential, if well used, to take us further than just the rich details of a particular case study – fascinating for its own sake as this might be. For they can also provide both a testing ground for the kinds of perspective we get from more standard sources and themselves suggest questions and insights which can in turn be applied to the more general national and local sources. To reiterate, they can give us not just the benefits of a microscope but also the potential of using what we see through that microscope as the basis for a longer and more questioning view of what we glimpse through the telescope.

3   A COMPASS

Changing the metaphor, this chapter concludes with a table which may act as a 'compass', pointing you in the best direction for the purpose in hand. It is *an attempt to place the main sources in a hierarchy of importance and availability,* and to indicate to which of the major strategies they can be applied. Of course, the hierarchy is subjective and approximate, and much will depend on the theme of the intended research, as well as local and personal circumstances. Some sources are mostly significant as background material which mentions very few individuals, but they are likely to be of greater relevance than many published local histories (although these should also be consulted carefully, especially their references).

The right-hand column of Table 5.1 requires a little more explanation. Where the word 'territorial' appears, the source is particularly useful for studies of territorially defined communities. In country areas, villages and small market towns are implied, and these need relatively little definition by the historian. In larger towns the situation is different, since the town itself, although qualifying as a relatively easily defined territorial population, is too big for studies involving the handling of nominative data. Therefore, armed with maps (see Chapter 6), the historian needs to define a territory for study, perhaps by means of a mixture of objective social criteria (e.g. housing types), administrative divisions and the arbitrary drawing of boundaries.

Some sources (marked 'X-Terr') are useful for making comparisons between territorially defined communities, indicating the relationships between them, or tracing changes over time. Trade directories are the most obvious example, but any source which shows membership of groups across more than one 'communal territory' can be drawn into similar enquiries. For 'members', read 'customers', 'employees', and so on according to context.

Conversely, some sources will fail to give a picture of all individuals, or even households, within a communal territory, no matter how small a unit is taken. Yet it can be argued that membership of a nonconformist congregation, or of a friendly society or trade union, was to be a member of a scattered community, because its members shared interests in a manner comparable to neighbours within a territory. Also, such diverse memberships *and the links between them* may form part of the constitution of communities. Similarly, groups such as various categories of the poor, defined by the authorities to some extent rather than self-selected, shared certain characteristics and interests. These are examples of groups to which the table alludes. Again, it would be impossible to list all the different kinds that might be encountered: what matters most is that the sources should go beyond generalities of the kind so often found in minute books, and get down to telling the historian something about the members as individuals, and about the role of these groups in the wider community.

Table 5.1 'Compass bearings' for family and community historians

Source	Period and extent of availability	Who included	Types of study suggested
Census: printed	E, W, S from 1801 I from 1821	All	Aggregative background
Census: manuscript (CEBs)	E, W, S 1841–91; Ireland 1901–11 and other erratic survivals	All	Territorial, Groups
Trade directories	c.1840–1940 Others later and earlier, esp. towns	Many householders	Territorial, X-Terr
Poll books	To 1872, survival erratic	All voters, but qualifications varied	Territorial, Groups
Electoral registers	From 1832, but erratic	All electors	Territorial, Groups
Tithe awards	c. 1838–55 W, E, esp. outside East and South Midlands & East Yorks	Most householders	Territorial
Land tax assessments	E, W, esp. before 1832 and esp. outside boros	Owners and many occupiers	Territorial
Rate books	Erratically available; mostly c.1840–1940 and for towns	Most householders	Territorial
Anglican registers	Throughout period, in principle for all parishes	Declining proportion of families	Territorial, Groups
MOH reports	Mostly post-1850 and for towns	Mostly aggregative material	Territorial
Poor Law records	To 1930	Much nominal material on the poor and officials	X-Terr, Groups
Housing Dept records	Some 19th cent. but many more after 1918	Mostly working-class householders	Territorial, Groups
Government reports	From c.1840	Mostly aggregative material	Territorial
Social surveys	Especially from 1900		
Company records	From c.1850, but erratic	May include employees	Groups, X-Terr
Trade Union records	Ditto	May include members	Groups, X-Terr
Nonconformist registers	Erratic and declining over time	Nonconformists	Groups
Associational records	Continuous, but quite erratic	May include members	Groups, X-Terr
Probate records: wills and inventories	Wills continuous; inventories early 19th century	Individuals, but not all	Difficult to group
Local newspapers	Especially from c.1855; few indexed, therefore difficult	Various	General background
Autobiographies, letters, diaries	Erratic	Various	Various
Civil registers	E, W 1837 onwards S 1855 onwards I 1864 onwards	All	Difficult or impossible to get groups

Abbreviations and explanations
E = England, I = Ireland, S = Scotland, W = Wales.
Territorial = can be used for territorially defined communities.
X-Terr = can be used for studies across several such communities.
Groups = can be used for groups which nest within or extend across territorially defined communities, e.g. members of congregations, workforces, members of associations, or arbitrarily defined groups of streets.

Availability to the public, as opposed to survival, will obviously vary from one type of source to another and according to confidentiality rules laid down when documents were deposited. Readers will therefore need to check for themselves locally, but some references on finding aids etc. are given either below or in the longer discussions of particular sources in Chapters 3–6 (see also the general advice in Chapters 12 and 13).

REFERENCES

Camp, A.J. (1974) *Wills and their whereabouts,* London, Society of Genealogists.

Cockton, P. (1988) *Subject catalogue of the House of Commons Parliamentary Papers 1801–1900,* Vols.I–IV, Cambridge, Chadwyck-Healey.

Cockton, P. (1991) *House of Commons Parliamentary Papers 1801–1900. Guide to the Chadwyck-Healey microfiche edition,* Cambridge, Chadwyck-Healey.

Davidoff, L. and Hall, C. (1987) *Family fortunes. Men and women of the English middle class, 1780–1850,* London, Hutchinson.

Drake, M. (1974) *Introduction to historical psephology,* Units 9–12 of D301 *Historical data and the social sciences,* Milton Keynes, Open University Press.

Drake, M. (1982) 'The remarriage market in mid-nineteenth century Britain', in Dupaquier, J. (ed.) *Marriage and re-marriage in populations of the past,* Academic Press, London,.

Etherington, J. E. (1990) 'The community origin of the Lewes Guy Fawkes' Night celebrations', *Sussex Archaeological Collections,* 128, pp.195–224.

ffolliott, R. and O'Byrne, E. (1987) 'Wills and administrations', in Begley, D.F. (ed.) *Irish genealogy: a record finder,* Dublin, Heraldic Artists Ltd.

Gibson, J. (1989) *A simplified guide to probate jurisdictions: where to look for wills,* 3rd edn, Birmingham, Federation of Family History Societies.

Gibson, J. (1993) *Probate jurisdictions: where to look for wills,* 4th edn, Birmingham, Federation of Family History Societies. Supersedes Gibson (1989).

Gibson, J. and Mills, D. (1993) *Land tax assessments 1690–1950,* 2nd edn, Birmingham, Federation of Family History Societies.

Gibson, J., Rogers, C. and Silverthorne, E. (1993) *Poor Law union records (in England and Wales),* 4 parts, Birmingham, Federation of Family History Societies.

Griffith, R. (1858–64) *General valuation of (rateable property in) Ireland,* Dublin, General Valuation Office.

Harrison, B. and Trinder, B. (1969) *Drink and sobriety in an early Victorian town: Banbury, 1830–60,* London, Longman.

Irish University Press (1972) *Checklist of British Parliamentary Papers in the Irish University Press 1,000-volume series 1800–1899,* Shannon, Irish University Press.

Kain, R.J.P. and Prince, H.C. (1985) *Tithe surveys of England and Wales,* Cambridge, Cambridge University Press.

Kain, R.J.P. (1986) *Atlas and index of the tithe files of mid-nineteenth-century England and Wales*, Cambridge, Cambridge University Press.

Lewis, M.J. and Lloyd-Jones, R. (1987) 'Rate books: a technique of reconstructing the local economy', *Local Historian*, 17, pp.277–80.

Moody, D. (1986) *Scottish local history, an introductory guide*, London, Batsford.

Morris, R.J. (1990) 'Clubs, societies and associations', in Thompson, F.M.L. (ed.) *Cambridge social history of Britain 1750–1950*, vol. 3, Cambridge, Cambridge University Press.

Nissel, M. (1987) *People count: a history of the General Register Office*, London, HMSO.

Page, S.J. (1987) 'A new source for the historian of urban poverty – a note on the use of charity records in Leicester 1904–29', *Urban History Yearbook*, pp.51-60.

Page, S.J. (1991) 'The mobility of the poor: a case study of Edwardian Leicester', *Local Historian*, 21, pp.109–18.

Parton, A.G. and Matthews, M.H. (1984) 'The returns of Poor Law out-relief – a source for the local historian', *Local Historian*, 14, pp.25–31.

Pelling, G. (1990) *Beginning your family history*, Birmingham, Federation of Family History Societies.

Pidduck, W. (1978) *Urban and rural social conditions in industrial Britain, series one. The local reports to the General Board of Health, 1848–57. A complete listing and guide to the Harvester Press microform collection with an introduction by H.T. Smith*, Hassocks, Harvester Press.

Powell, W. (1962) *Local history from Blue Books*, London, Historical Association.

Rubinstein, D. (1993) 'School board records', audio-cassette 5B in Braham, P. (ed.) *Using the past: audio-cassettes on sources and methods for family and community historians*, Milton Keynes, The Open University.

Rubinstein, W.E. (1981) *Men of property: the very wealthy in Britain since the Industrial Revolution*, London, Croom Helm.

Schürer, K. and Anderson, S. J. with the assistance of Duncan, J. A. (1992) *A guide to historical data files held in machine-readable form*, Association for History and Computing, c/o Department of History, Royal Holloway and Bedford New College, University of London, Egham, TW20 0EX.

Schürer, K. (1993) 'Nominal lists and nominal record linkage', audio-cassette 2B in Braham, P. (ed.) *Using the past: audio-cassettes on sources and methods for family and community historians*, Milton Keynes, The Open University.

Taylor, I. (1972) *Liverpool social history 1820–1870. An annotated guide to the use of government reports and papers*, Liverpool, Liverpool History Resources Committee, University Archives, Liverpool University, Senate House, Abercromby Square, PO Box 147, Liverpool, L69 3BX.

Thomas, M. (1979) *Urban and rural social conditions in industrial Britain, series two. The reports of the Local Government Board 1869–1908. A complete listing and guide to the Harvester microfiche collection*, Hassocks, Harvester Press.

Todd, A. (1989) *Basic sources for family history: back to the early 1800s*, Allen and Todd, 9 Square Street, Ramsbottom, Bury, Lancashire, BL0 9BE.

Trinder, B. (1982) *Victorian Banbury*, Chichester, Phillimore.

Turner, M. and Mills, D. (eds) (1986) *Land and property: the English land tax 1692–1832*, Gloucester, Alan Sutton.

Vincent, D. (1983) 'Marriage, religion and class in South Fermanagh, Ireland, 1846–1920', in Lynch, O.M. (ed.) *Culture and community in Europe. Essays in honour of Conrad Arensberg*, Delhi, Hindustan Publishing Corporation.

Vincent, J. (1967) *Pollbooks. How the Victorians voted*, Cambridge, Cambridge University Press.

Withers, C.W.J. (1986) 'Poor relief in Scotland and the General Register of Poor', *Local Historian*, 17, 1, pp.19–29.

Withers, C.W.J. and Watson, A.J. (1991) 'Stepwise migration and highland migration to Glasgow, 1852–1898', *Journal of Historical Geography*, 17, pp.35-55.

Yeo, S. (1976) *Religion and voluntary organisations in crisis*, London, Croom Helm.

CHAPTER 6

USING NON-WRITTEN SOURCES

Although the term 'sources' may immediately bring to mind the model of a written document studied in the library, field research and unwritten media also have a great deal to offer – as this chapter shows.

As with any other sources, non-written sources have to be used critically as well as constructively. Thus, many of the points discussed in earlier chapters will also apply here. The key steps in evaluating a source, summarized in Chapter 2, Schema A, still apply: for example, questions concerning dating and provenance (treated in particular detail here in the case of pictorial and photographic sources); or type of source (the photographic *album* and its interpretation, for example); or how a source came into being (important throughout and specially noted in the discussions of maps, of audio and video, and of interviews).

Two themes emerge as particularly important.

First, as with any sources, but perhaps above all with unwritten ones, their message is not transparent but depends essentially on *interpretation*. This comes out again and again in this chapter. Paul Thompson and Gina Harkell put it even more strongly, in words that could be applied not just to photographs but to most of the cultural artefacts discussed here:

> *The camera may not lie. But what kind of truth does it tell? ... The picture has to be interpreted. What were the people doing, why were they in the picture, why was it taken? Photographs are silent, but we cannot rest with that; we need to see meaning in them. And where no message is given, we invent one. Most old photographs, therefore, are half pieces of history, half out of our own minds.*
>
> (Thompson and Harkell, 1979, p.7)

Secondly, none of these sources is complete in itself. As will be clear in the discussions below, their full potential is most effectively exploited when they are used in combination with a range of other sources.

1 LANDSCAPES, BUILDINGS AND PHYSICAL ARTEFACTS

by Ian Donnachie

The majority of sources on which the family and community historian draws are what we might describe as 'traditional' or 'conventional' primary or secondary sources – archives or printed material – found in record offices or libraries. But for the historian with the motivation and skills to abandon books for boots there is also an important world waiting to be discovered beyond the walls of the library. Such field excursions or studies can take you into the 'real' world of families and communities living and working in the past – if you have the eyes and imagination to reconstruct it. We have space here merely to list the main items that might be of value to such a research project, and provide a few examples of how physical relics can be deployed in the historian's toolkit. But I hope at the very least to indicate the possibilities and enthuse you with the idea of using such sources in your own research projects.

1.1   LANDSCAPE AND COMMUNITIES

The historic landscape (partly interpreted by maps, see section 2 below) often holds the key to a better understanding of why and how communities developed. For example, a study of the rural landscape surrounding nineteenth-century enclosure villages in, say, the East Riding of York-shire, adds enormously to the picture given by estate and census records about changing land-use patterns, settlements, demography, as well as working and living conditions; and field research around the North Wales slate quarrying communities (perhaps deploying some knowl-edge of the local geology and geomorphology) can reveal a great deal about the location of quarries, techniques of extraction, transport, and working and living conditions in the associated communities. Settlement patterns and town layouts are also much influenced by physical geography (see Figure 6.1 for an example). In short, the *environment* sets the context in which families and communities grow, and although it is constantly changing it can help answer some of the questions raised by your own research.

1.2   INDUSTRIAL ARCHAEOLOGY

The study of industrial buildings and artifacts, which embraces field research as well as the more detailed investigation made possible by techniques of excavation more typical of 'traditional' archaeology, presents enormous possibilities for the family and community historian.

Figure 6.1   New Lanark as seen in an early nineteenth-century print. The view shows, in considerable detail, the layout of the community with the mills in the foreground and workers' housing in the background – all built on a narrow and constrained site by the edge of the River Clyde. This is a good illustration of the kind of detail that can be picked out from prints and archive photographs for comparison with existing buildings and settlements (Source: Davidson, 1828)

Industrial archaeology is more than a study of the remains of manufacturing industry, for it is concerned with *all* the physical relics of economic development: warehouses and workshops as well as factories; windmills and water-wheels as well as steam engines; rural trades, craft and agricultural implements as well as urban industrial remains; transport and other public utilities; workers' housing and other social relics (see Figure 6.1). It can help answer questions about the *raison d'être* of communities, and about the workplaces, work patterns and leisure activities of those who lived in them. For example, one of my research degree students, Dr Roger Holden, who worked on the history of a family firm of cotton mill engineers and the communities they helped create, found that industrial archaeology greatly aided his project because fieldwork could explain things to which there was no obvious answer in such documentary sources as family and business papers, maps and plans, and archive photographs.

1.3   OTHER BUILDINGS

What can be described as 'social archaeology' or 'social heritage' also presents considerable research possibilities. An enormous range of buildings (such as dwelling houses, workhouses or poorhouses, churches, pubs, clubs, working men's institutes, libraries, cinemas, dance halls, and the like) and associated facilities or artifacts (like burial grounds, monuments, war memorials, sculptures, etc.) often offer the researcher further 'non-archival' possibilities for studying family and community history. Housing tells us much about the social status of families and the conditions in which our ancestors lived – from the town or country houses of the gentry at one extreme to the handloom weavers' cottages at the other. The layout of towns and villages (the basic road-patterns, for example, residential clusters, or location of churches) may still, despite changes over the years, provide clues about earlier social, religious or political groupings. Place of abode also gives an obvious link into vital registers, census enumerators' books, poll or valuation returns, which help pin down families at particular points in time. While many big country houses in both Britain and Ireland have long decayed, and much working-class housing and other buildings fallen victim to development, a valuable heritage remains to be exploited in family and community projects almost everywhere.

The local burial ground can also be a good starting-point for social and demographic research. As an example, a survey of the simple gravestones in the burial-ground at New Lanark provided a great deal of information about early villagers and their families unavailable from documentary sources (for further details about New Lanark, see Volume 3, Chapter 4). Genealogical societies have produced voluminous listings of inscriptions on tombstones and memorials – and, of course, such data can sometimes be married up to vital registers.

1.4   MEMORABILIA

Finally, an enormous range of other physical artifacts could be important in your project: what we might simply call family or civic memorabilia. These include personal objects like lockets (often containing the photographs of a loved one), jewellery, rings, and watches (all often engraved with names or initials); celebrational memorabilia, such as pottery items like wedding jugs and plates, and christening cups; military memorabilia, notably medals, uniforms and weapons; and work-related memorabilia like apprenticeship completion gifts, gifts of esteem, presentational gifts (on resignation or retiral for example), or work related mementoes, again usually engraved with useful information. For example, I have in my possession a portable escritoire engraved as follows: 'Presented to Mr Dunsmore, Tentor, by a number of weavers under his charge in the factory of Messrs. Wm. B. Watson & Co as A Token of Esteem. 10th May 1870.' It would be an

interesting bit of historical detective work to follow this up in trade directories and other 'conventional' sources. Civic memorabilia and those of related bodies like guilds can often help chart the history of a community.

The study of the past, using the evidence provided by physical remains, buildings and artifacts, is a well-established part of historical research. But fieldwork (and even the inspection of artifacts in museums) also comprehends a wider range of activities arising from its primary purpose, because *interpretation* is a fundamental aspect of the study. Fieldwork is not an end in itself, but the beginning of an end. Interpretation means assessing the significance of what has been located and recorded and, in turn, this task demands that documentary or oral evidence should be added to and weighed against what has been discovered in the field. An interplay between all forms of evidence is vital if the best results are to be achieved. Field study and conventional research should walk hand in hand, as they could well do in many of the research projects suggested throughout the volumes in this series.

REFERENCES AND FURTHER READING (SECTION 1)

Aston, M. and Bond, J. (1976) *The landscape of towns,* London, J.M. Dent & Sons Ltd.

Butt, J. and Donnachie, I. (1979) *Industrial archaeology in the British Isles,* London, Paul Elek Ltd.

Davidson, H. (1828) *A history of Lanark and guide to the scenery,* Lanark.

Holden, R.N. (1987–8) 'Pear Mill, Stockport: an Edwardian cotton spinning mill', *Industrial Archaeology Review,* 10, pp.162–74.

Industrial Archaeology Review. Journal published by the Association for Industrial Archaeology (The Wharfage, Ironbridge, Telford, Shropshire TF8 7AW), which regularly publishes material dealing with the history of industrial communities, and advises on good practice and methods of analysis.

Thompson, P. and Harkell, G. (1979) *The Edwardians in photographs,* London, Batsford.

2   MAPS AND PLANS

by John Hunt

Maps and plans provide important evidence of changes in settlement and the shaping of the landscape by human activity. Together with other data, they provide a spatial structure on which to construct enquiry and research. Early maps and plans were created for a wide variety of purposes and in varying degrees by tradesmen, craftsmen, artists and surveyors.

The best starting-point in seeking out maps and plans is usually the town library or county record office. Some of these have acquired large numbers of maps and plans related to their area. In addition, a number of specialist publications have been issued, reflecting the dramatic growth of interest in the printed maps of the past, and compiled not only for the general reader but also for local historians and those specializing in cartography. Atlases also represent very useful compilations and presentations of data. Whilst the most familiar show global political and physical patterns, there is also a wide range of special interest, single-theme publications (see the

list of further reading at the end of this section). Nineteenth-century 'topographical dictionaries' and atlases can also provide useful historical maps and other data, notably those by Samuel Lewis (1831–48).

2.1   TOWN MAPS AND PLANS

Town maps and plans are particularly useful where a sequence exists enabling comparison of growth and change over time. Pictorial representations and artistic embellishments are often encountered. Few early plans took any account of true ground dimensions, although from the 1840s onwards the Ordnance Survey (founded in 1791) began its publication of town plans at scales of 1:1056, 1:528 and 1:500.

(Note: By Ordnance Survey (OS) definition, a plan is at a sufficiently large scale for all topographical features to be shown true to scale, usually 1:2500 scale or larger. The smaller the number after the colon, the larger the scale of the map. A scale of 1:2500 means (approximately) '25 inches to one mile'. A scale of 1:1056 is a '60 inches to one mile' scale. Scale can be expressed in three ways: (a) as a Representative Fraction (e.g. 1:63,360 means that one inch on the map represents 63,360 inches (i.e. one mile) on the ground, and the map is known as a 'one-inch' map); (b) in words (e.g. 'one inch to one mile'); and (c) as a linear scale bar where a line on the map is annotated to show the lengths of units on the ground.)

Rapid town growth in the mid-nineteenth century made great demands on cartographers. Street plans sometimes showed a mixture of urban and rural features. For example, in Figure 6.2, proposed streets are aligned along the enclosed strips of the town fields.

Plans sometimes only include part of a town. An example is property maps, which record the sale of houses and show development schemes. Such plans were often accompanied by details of rents, owners, occupiers and estate records. In the late nineteenth century, maps and plans were being used as scientific and sociological tools. The Booth maps of London are particularly rich examples (see Chapter 4, section 6, Figure 4.11). Figure 6.3 shows a concentration of pubs and beerhouses in the poorer areas of Oxford, with others near Carfax and the cattle market catering for suburban visitors and traders, and others along the main roads. There is a dearth of public houses in the more polite northern suburbs and in the better-class central streets. It is interesting to note that Ordnance Survey plans of the period (e.g. see Figure 6.4) showed the location and names of public houses, and also gave detailed information on church capacity and type of membership.

2.2   ESTATE MAPS AND PLANS

Estate maps primarily delineate the property of one land owner. Many are in colour and extremely large. Collections range from the 700 maps of the Downshire estates in Ireland (115,000 acres in four counties) to a single map in private hands. The landed estates in Scotland provide an important source of such maps and other relevant material.

Pre-1850 estate plans fall into two categories, rural and industrial. Rural maps can show house ownership, tenants' names, acreage, land use, number of rooms, type of outbuilding, field boundaries, woodland, gardens, hop yards, crops (and rotation) – they provide nothing less than an inventory of the rural landscape. Industrial plans (of which there were far fewer) became relatively more important as issues such as mineral rights were taken up and land values rose. Industrial plans could be classified into those showing underground mine workings, and surface plans depicting evidence of industrial activity.

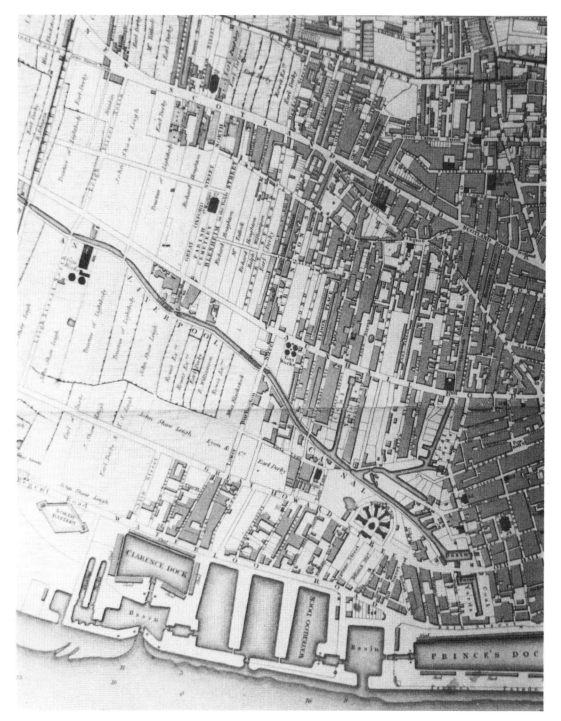

Figure 6.2   Detail from Jonathan Bennison's Map of Liverpool, 1835 (Source: Liverpool Record Office)

126

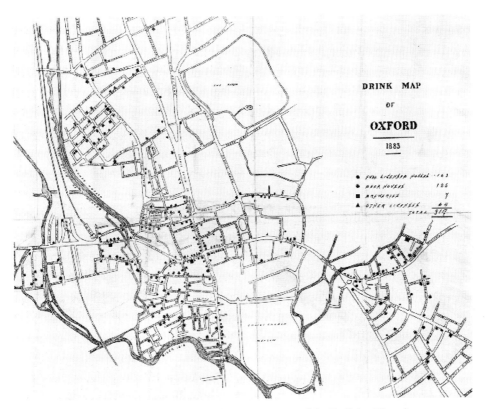

Figure 6.3   The Drink Map of Oxford, 1883 (Source: Curators of the Bodleian Library)

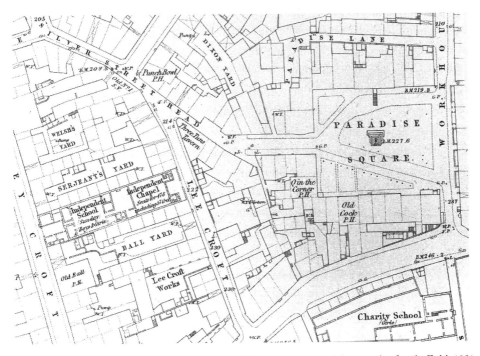

Figure 6.4   Detail from an Ordnance Survey 1:1056 (60 inches to one mile) town plan for Sheffield, 1851 (not shown to scale) (Source: Royal Geographical Society)

2.3 ENCLOSURE AND TITHE MAPS

Enclosure and tithe maps were first drawn in the eighteenth century to accompany the thousands of awards made under separate Private Enclosure Acts for individual parishes. They provide a historical record of settlements, boundaries and land ownership, and may act as legal authority on road alignment, rights of way, as well as the territorial rights of schools and charities. Most were made by 1851, at large scale and with a large range of sheet sizes. Their accuracy varied depending on the skill of the many local surveyors employed to undertake the mapping. After 1850, the manuscript surveys of private practitioners were replaced by Ordnance Survey plans. The use of such maps and plans in a research project is shown in Figure 6.5.

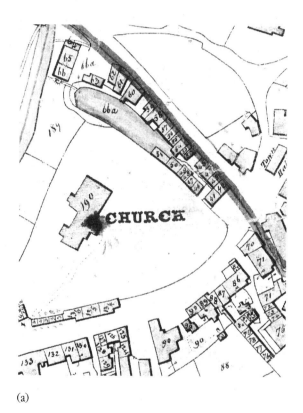

(a)

Figure 6.5 The evolution of a research map: Figure 6.5(c) was based in part on the tithe map shown in Figure 6.5(a) and the Ordnance Survey plan shown in Figure 6.5(b)

(a) Detail from a tithe map of 1845 based on a survey of 1842. This is the earliest known cartographic record of the town of Llanfair Caereinion, Powys, Wales. In preparing map (c), the researcher matched house numbers with the 1851 census enumerators' books and extracted information from accompanying schedules as well as from trade directories (Source: National Library of Wales)

(b) Detail from a first edition Ordnance Survey 1:2500 plan, 1886, showing the township of Llanfair Caereinion. Used by the researcher for plotting purposes, it provides accurate detail as to the urban layout but few clues to property ownership or development. Ornamentation gives some qualitative feel. Land parcels and acreages are shown (Source: National Library of Wales)

(c) Detail from a research map, showing urban layout and functions of Llanfair Caereinion in the mid-nineteenth century. Many inns and taverns are named, together with landmarks, public buildings and roads. Buildings are classified by shading (commercial, religious, houses, barns) and many functions are letter keyed (e.g. C=currier, M=malthouse, W=wheelwright, SM=blacksmith) (Source: Pryce and Edwards, 1979)

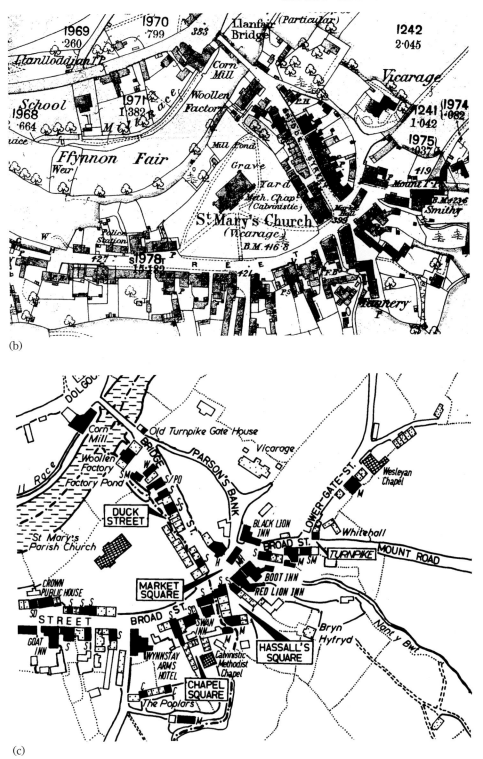

(b)

(c)

Figure 6.5 (continued)

2.4   MAPS OF TRANSPORT

Routeways are an integral feature of many maps and plans. There are, however, specialized maps of transport which are particularly useful for studies of urban growth and development. Lt. H.D. Harness produced maps (see Figure 6.6) for the Irish Railway Commission in 1837, and pioneered several techniques for graphically presenting statistical data which remain fundamentally the same today. Harness used shaded 'flow-lines' to symbolize the volume of traffic and freight along railways.

Towards the end of the nineteenth and the beginning of the twentieth century, road atlases and maps were published in great numbers, coinciding with the pioneer days of the bicycle and motor car. Improvements to turnpikes, as well as their later decommissioning, were the concern of local surveys which produced large-scale strip maps, often incorporating adjacent buildings, field names, owners and occupiers. Maps showing the navigation of rivers and canals also became popular, the most familiar series being that produced by George Bradshaw, later famous for his railway guides.

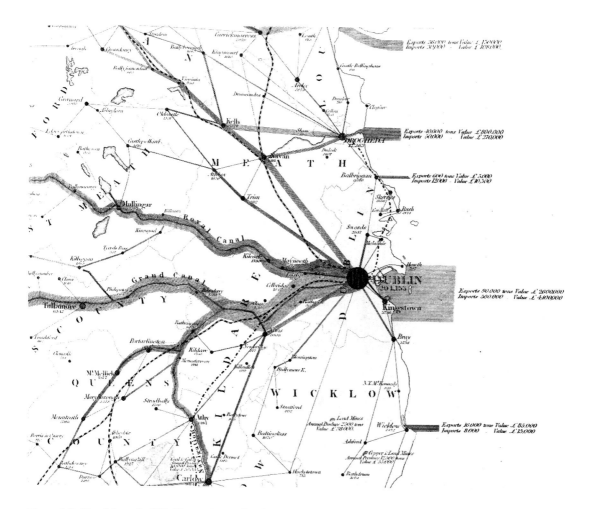

Figure 6.6   Detail from Lt. H.D. Harness's map for the Irish Railway Commission, 1837 (Source: British Library)

2.5   COUNTY MAPS

The nineteenth century saw a continuous proliferation of small-scale county maps. You might find it useful to compare maps of the same period to see if any standardization exists between different cartographic products. However, county maps can seldom be regarded as definitive; contentious issues include poor dating, reliability of source material, completeness, and bias. Some maps took over seven years to complete; one took twenty-five years!

2.6   ORDNANCE SURVEY MAPS AND PLANS

From 1824, the Ordnance Survey embarked on a uniform programme of large-scale mapping. The survey of Ireland between 1824 and 1840 showed that the 1:10,560 scale (i.e. six inches to one mile) was too small for some purposes, whilst the 1:2500 (i.e. approximately twenty-five inches to one mile) allowed the exact shape of every enclosure to be shown and area calculated with accuracy. These series were known as the '6-inch' and the '25-inch', and their importance should not be underestimated. The series covered virtually the whole of the British Isles with regular revisions. There was great controversy as to which scale was best until 1856, when it was decided to make the 25-inch series countrywide. The 25-inch plans supply very detailed topographic information with great accuracy. Many categories of roads are shown, and agricultural land is distinguished by ten different symbols. Administrative boundaries, civil and ecclesiastical, are depicted, as well as those for Poor Law Unions and Parliamentary Divisions. Hundreds of place names qualified by type style are shown and dozens of features symbolized. To appreciate such a cartographic marvel you need to peruse one at your local library or record office.

Between 1805 and 1873, the Ordnance Survey also prepared and published (in 110 sheets) a one inch to one mile map series (see Plate 15 in the plates section). These were finely engraved on copper, printed in black and represented a major achievement in the national survey of Britain. Excellent reproductions of these are available commercially, each map being accompanied by descriptive notes. There was no exact equivalent of the English one-inch series for Scotland, although 131 maps were published between 1856 and 1887. The first Irish one-inch map appeared in 1855, as part of a series of 205. These were based on earlier OS six-inch surveys. The construction of a new railway was often the cause of a new revision or edition. One special printing of the English one-inch showed the names and boundaries of those parishes for which tithe surveys were prepared – the first reliable source for those boundaries.

Plate 16, which shows a detail from an Ordnance Survey third series one-inch map, demonstrates far-reaching development in the design of the one-inch series. Compare it with Plate 15 which shows the same area. Six-colour lithographic printing was used for the first time in the third series maps, and the sheet size was extended to 27 by 18 inches. The map shows both hachures (slopes) and contours, uses colour to indicate road networks and categories, and highlights wooded areas and water features. A considerable increase in the number of names is very apparent, and included on the full map is a comprehensive key to all the features shown.

In 1938, The Davidson Committee brought about extensive changes to the Ordnance Survey with its major recommendation, the introduction of The National Grid. After the Second World War, surveying was metricated, culminating in 1974 with the 1:50,000 Landranger map series.

2.7   CONCLUSION

Maps and plans add greatly to our knowledge of the past. They may have the qualities of both a portrait and a photograph – and that of course is their strength as a source. They are as much perceived as measured and attempt to embody concepts about the real world whilst simultaneously recording factual detail. The map user should carefully assess accuracy, sustain a critical attitude and be aware of symbolic distortion. Every map will have some deficiencies, but many can usefully serve qualitative and quantitative research studies.

REFERENCES AND FURTHER READING (SECTION 2)

Andrews, J.H. (1974) *History in the Ordnance map: an introduction for Irish readers,* Dublin, Ordnance Survey Office.

Gilbert, M. (1976) *Jewish history atlas,* London, Weidenfeld & Nicolson.

Harley, J.B. (1972) *Maps for the local historian: a guide to the British sources,* London, National Council of Social Service.

Harley, J.B. (1975) *Ordnance Survey: a descriptive manual,* London, HMSO.

Harley, J.B. and Phillips, C.W. (1964) *The historian's guide to Ordnance Survey maps,* London, National Council of Social Service.

Hindle, P. (1988) *Maps for local history,* London, Batsford.

Humphery-Smith, C. (1984) *The Phillimore atlas and index of parish registers,* Chichester, Phillimore.

International Conference on the History of Cartography (1971) *The mapping of Scotland,* Edinburgh, Bartholomew.

Langton, J. and Morris, R.J. (1986) *Atlas of industrializing Britain, 1780–1914,* London, Methuen.

Lewis, S. (1831) *A topographical dictionary of England ... and the islands of Guernsey, Jersey and Man ... with maps ... and a plan of London, etc.,* 4 vols, London (also later editions, and a separate 'atlas' volume, 1842, 1848). One of a series which also included: *A topographical dictionary of Ireland* (2 vols and an atlas, 1837, 1842; facsimile re-publication 1970); *A topographical dictionary of Scotland* (with Supplementary Map volume, 1846); *A topographical dictionary of Wales* (2 vols, 1833, and later editions).

Muir, R. (1969) *Muir's historical atlas: ancient, mediaeval and modern,* London, George Philip.

Pope, R. (ed.) (1989) *Atlas of British social and economic history since c.1700,* London, Routledge.

Pryce, W.T.R. and Edwards, J.A. (1979) 'The social structure of the embryonic town in rural Wales: Llanfair Caereinion in the mid-nineteenth century', *The Montgomeryshire Collections,* 68, pp.45–90.

Rogers, A. (1972) *This was their world,* London, BBC Publications.

Smith, D. (1988) *Maps and plans for the local historian and collector,* London, Batsford.

The Village London Atlas (1986) *The growth of Victorian London, 1822–1903,* London, Alderman Press.

Wilkes, M. (1991) *The Scot and his maps,* Motherwell, Scottish Library Association.

3 PHOTOGRAPHS AND PICTURE POSTCARDS

by W.T.R. Pryce

Photographs, picture postcards – indeed, any pictorial records – should be drawn on much more extensively by family and community historians. Old photographs can be used to illustrate a written research report but, as this section shows, they are also original sources in their own right, and offer considerable potential.

3.1 PHOTOGRAPHS AS SOURCES: WHAT TO EXPECT

Although even the novice family historian soon amasses a clutch of old family photographs, these are mostly pictures of people, rarely of their homes or everyday work. This is because, before the general availability of roll film and the snapshot camera in the late 1880s (Ford, 1989, p.62), almost all family photographs were taken by specialized photographers. As they did not come cheaply, for the great majority photographs recorded only important family occasions – weddings and christenings, rarely funerals. Overwhelmingly, then, old photographs are of individuals or groups, occasionally with a glimpse of a family residence or small corner of garden. Until the introduction of the flash-bulb in the 1920s (Ford, 1989, p.84), lighting difficulties meant few domestic interiors or workplaces were photographed. Only possible with long exposures, early indoor photographs tend to record quiet scenes like church interiors. Moreover, photographers in the past, as today, recorded only glimpses of reality, the pictures not always being very representative of actual conditions (Becker, 1979).

You need to be realistic in your expectations of early photography. Don't waste time and effort seeking photographs of people and scenes that predate key technical developments in the medium (see below). Early photography had a restricted clientele: members of the aristocracy, gentry and higher professions. So if, like mine, your ancestors were, for many generations, tenant hill farmers eking out a frugal living on the Welsh uplands, then you should not expect to find family photographs until the arrival of popular snapshot photography in the late 1920s.

When, however, it comes to pictures of local scenes, family and community researchers should be able to find photographs from the earliest years of the medium, after the invention in 1839 by the Parisian painter, L.J.M. Daguerre, of the first successful photograph – the *daguerreotype*. Henry Fox Talbot soon followed with the *calotype*. Although superior in quality and cheaper than the daguerreotype, both had given way, by the early 1860s, to techniques based on the *collodion* wet-plate process. By then, photographers recorded scenes throughout Britain, mostly outdoors, and the images they recorded are still available. By the 1870s, 'family' photographers had established their studios throughout the UK (Hannavy, 1980). A number of these acquired regional, even national, renown: George Washington Wilson of Aberdeen (1853–93) (Taylor, 1981); the Yorkshireman, Frank Sutcliffe (1853–1941), who recorded many scenes of contemporary life in the vicinity of Whitby and Eskdale, and in London (Hiley, 1985); John Thomas (1838–1905), with his scenes from rural Welsh communities and Liverpool spanning half a century (Woollen and Crawford, 1977); and the Quaker, Francis Frith (1822–98) of Reigate, whose photographic expeditions took him, or his assistants, to virtually every part of the country and abroad (Wilson, 1985). It is in national collections like these that you may find photographs directly relevant to your research.

From the mid-1890s a busy trade in local views, sold as picture postcards, existed. By 1909–11, an average 860 million were sent each year. Some 20 million cards are thought still to exist from the 'golden age' of the postcard, 1894–1915. Mainly reproducing scenes from contemporary photographs, these postcards often provide the only pictorial record of some places, and, as such, are an important source.

3.2   IDENTIFICATION AND DATING OF PHOTOGRAPHS

Photographs are sources that need to be interpreted with care (see the quotation from Thompson and Harkell (1979) at the beginning of this chapter). But an essential first step is to identify and date them. This information can be derived from the photographic processes used, or from the format used, or from internal evidence in the picture.

3.2.1   PHOTOGRAPHIC PROCESSES

Table 6.1 provides a summary of the technical processes according to their date of introduction and (approximate) demise.

Original negatives are very rare before *c*.1900. Most are now in specialized collections in national archives and major museums. When an early photograph still survives, with the exception of the tintype, almost invariably it will be in the form of a positive print. For research purposes these are now our originals. Because of space restrictions, I will deal briefly with only the four categories of photographic print that you are most likely to encounter. For further information, consult Martin (1988), pp.70–95; Pols (1992); Oliver (1989); Reilly (1986); Steel and Taylor (1984), pp.74–110; or, for example, Wills and Wills (1980).

Albumen prints (1850–c.1910)   These can be identified by the white areas (the highlights of the picture) which tend to be somewhat yellow in appearance (see Plate 3(a) in the plates section). Some photographers applied gold chloride solution to improve the colour rendering, so endowing the print with a purple brown hue (see Plate 4(a)). Albumen prints tend to fade from the edge inwards and, if not fixed on a stout card, are likely to curl. They appear as cartes-de-visite (Plates 3(a) and 4(a)), cabinet prints (Plate 5(a)), and stereoscopic prints (see Table 6.2).

Ambrotype photographs (1851–c.1884)   These achieved great popularity between 1855 and 1865. When viewed against the light (as with a slide), an ambrotype is in the form of a negative; when viewed in reflected light, the same image appears as a normal positive photograph. Normally, therefore, the glass plate which carries the image is mounted in a frame over a dark background. The image is sharp and the highlights tend to be creamy-white in appearance with a restricted tonal range. Ambrotypes were widely used for portraits (sometimes, as in Plate 1, improved by hand tinting) but only rarely for landscapes and urban scenes. For protection they were normally placed in a *union case* (see section 3.2.2 below), as was the much rarer daguerreotype. To distinguish the two, note that the daguerreotype has a mirror-like surface which alternates between a positive and a negative image as the angle of illumination is changed. The ambrotype image is positive when viewed in reflected light *from any direction*. Both tend to be small, usually quarter plate ($4\frac{1}{4} \times 3\frac{1}{4}$ in.; 108×82 mm.) or one-sixth plate ($3\frac{1}{4} \times 2\frac{3}{4}$ in.; 83×71 mm.).

Tintype (or ferrotype) photographs (1852–c.1946)   Tintypes were produced by one of the cheapest methods, a process widely used by itinerant photographers, especially at the seaside. The pictures were produced almost immediately. Many families have small tintype photographs with their somewhat dark, murky images, lacking in tonal contrast. To enhance their size and appearance, tintypes were displayed in decorative mounts (see Plates 2(a) and 2(b)), though, like the ambrotype, more expensive ones appeared in small decorative union cases. To distinguish the two you will find that a small magnet adheres to the glass front of the

Table 6.1 Dating photographs via the major photographic processes since 1839. (Processes leading directly to positive images are in coloured text; processes leading to intermediate negative images are in black text.)

Process	First introduced	1839–40	1841–50	1851–60	1861–70	1871–80	1881–90	1891–1900	1901–10	1911–20	1921–30	1931–40	1941–50	1951–60	1961–70	1971–80	1981–90
1 DAGUERREOTYPE — Positive image on copper plate	1839	█	█														
2 CALOTYPE (TALBOTYPE) — Negative and positive images on paper	1840		█	█													
3 SALTED PAPER PRINT — Positive image on paper	1839	█	█														
4 ALBUMEN NEGATIVE — Negative image on glass	1848		█	█	█	█											
5 ALBUMEN PRINT — Positive image on paper	1850			█	█	█	█										
6 WAXED PAPER PRINTS — Negative image on paper	1851			█													
7 COLLODION WET-PLATE PROCESS — Negative image on glass	1851			█	█												
8 AMBROTYPE — Positive image on glass	1851			█	█												
9 COLLODION DRY-PLATE PROCESS — Negative image on glass	1854			█	█												
10 TINTYPE — Positive image on an enamelled plate	1852 (USA) / 1856 (UK)			█	█	█	█	█	█	█	█	█					
11 CARBON PRINT — Positive image on paper	1860s?					█	█	█	█	█	█						
12 CARBON TRANSFER — Positive image on ceramic, glass, enamel, leather or paper	1864				█	█	█	█	█	█	█						
13 WOODBURY TYPE — Positive image on paper	1865				█	█	█										
14 GELATINE DRY PLATE — Negative image on glass	1870s					█	█	█	█	█	█	█	█	█	█	█	█
15 PLATINUM PRINT — Positive image on paper	1873					█	█	█	█	█	█						
16 GELATINE PAPER PRINT — Positive image on glass	1880s						█	█	█	█	█	█	█	█	█	█	█
17 GUM BICHROMATE — Positive image on paper	1890s						█	█	█	█	█						
18 AUTOCHROME — Positive image in colour on glass	1904								█	█	█	█					
19 BROMOIL PRINT — Positive image on paper	1907								█	█	█	█					

Source: based, in part, on Martin (1988) pp.70–95

tintype, its name being a misnomer, as the photograph was on thin enamelled iron plates. Tintypes – usually small, typically $2\frac{1}{2} \times 2$ in. (65×50 mm.) or smaller, because they were aimed at the cheaper end of the market – are also found in finger rings and similar items of cheap souvenir jewellery. In some countries – in parts of Wales, and especially in France and the USA – tintypes, showing the dead person, are embedded in gravestones.

Gelatine paper prints   Introduced in the 1880s, gelatine paper prints produce black and white pictures, which are commonly termed 'bromides'. Subsequent improvements gave purple-brown enlarged pictures similar to albumen prints, but, unlike them, invariably with white highlights. Various other tones were produced on a wide variety of surfaces – glossy, matt, egg shell, stippled finishes – and gelatine paper prints remain popular to this day.

3.2.2 THE FORMAT OF PHOTOGRAPHS

Photographs can also be identified and dated by means of their format (see Table 6.2).

The union case   This small case with a hinged or swivel cover (see Plate 1) seems to have been copied from the cases used by painters of miniature portraits. Invariably used for daguerreotype and ambrotype photographs (and some tintypes, especially in the USA), few were sold after the 1880s. (For an illustration of a tintype in a union case, see Volume 1, Chapter 2, Figure 2.3.)

The carte-de-visite   So-called because its size matched that of a conventional visiting card ($2\frac{1}{2} \times 4\frac{1}{4}$ in.; 65×105 mm.), the carte-de-visite, a small photograph mounted on card, was a very popular format during the second half of the nineteenth century. Until the 1870s, the photographs used were usually albumen prints, which tended to fade. However, later cartes used better-quality photographs, often with a brown-black image that retained its definition. Cartes were produced in enormous numbers as souvenirs of the famous and for family and private purposes, though rarely for views (but see Plate 3(a)). Invariably the back contained an advertisement, at first somewhat plain, but more elaborate later on (see Plates 3(b) and 4(b)).

The cabinet print   This format originated in the 1860s: a high quality print, usually half plate ($4\frac{1}{4} \times 6\frac{1}{2}$ in.; 108×165 mm.) on a stout card, and carrying the photographer's own advertisement. Intended as a luxurious keepsake, complete with gold edging (see Plates 5(a) and 5(b)), these have become treasured items in many families. Like the cartes-de-visite, they tend to show people in studio settings, rarely outdoors. Still popular *c.*1914 and later, these were the products of the ubiquitous professional studio-based photographer.

Postcard prints   These were a cheaper version of the cabinet print, and are easily recognized by the standard postcard information printed on the back which helps to date the scene (see Tables 6.6 and 6.7, pp.144 and 145). Handwritten details of the scene (written by the photographer on the glass negative after it had been developed) were often provided, sometimes with the photographer's name and date (see Figure 6.7, p.138). From 1914, until the 1930s, Kodak's autographic camera was popular. This had a special flap in the back through which information could be written directly on to the film immediately after the picture had been taken, using a special metal stylus (Coe, 1989, pp.68–9).

Table 6.2   Dating photographs by format

	First introduced	1839–40	1841–50	1851–60	1861–70	1871–80	1881–90	1891–1900	1901–10	1911–20	1921–30	1931–40	1941–50	1951–60	1961–70	1971–80	1981–90
1 PHOTOGRAPHS IN UNION CASES Daguerreotypes, ambrotypes, tintypes	1854 (USA)			███													
2 CARTE DE VISITE ('CARTES') $2\frac{1}{2} \times 4\frac{1}{8}$ in. (65 × 105 mm.)	1854 (France)			██████													
3 STEREOSCOPIC PHOTOGRAPHS Twin photographs viewed through special lenses	1849			██████████													
4 TINTYPES IN PAPER MOUNTS Small dark photographs in decorative paper mounts	1852 (USA) 1856 (UK)			██████████████													
5 CABINET PRINTS IN MOUNTS Usually $4\frac{1}{4} \times 6\frac{1}{2}$ in. (108 ×165 mm.); sometimes $6\frac{1}{2} \times 8\frac{1}{2}$ in. (165 × 216 mm.)	c.1866				██████												
6 LANTERN SLIDES Monochrome transparencies on glass plates, $3\frac{1}{4} \times 3\frac{1}{4}$ in. (82 × 82 mm.) (British); $3\frac{1}{2} \times 4$ in. (88 × 102 mm.) (USA, Europe)	1850			██████████													
7 PRINTING OUT PAPERS Images with sepia-brown tones	1864				██████████												
8 DEVELOPING OUT PAPERS Images with brown, brown-black, black tones	1879						████████████████										
9 CIRCULAR PHOTOGRAPHS $2\frac{1}{2}$ in. (60 mm.) diameter. From Kodak No.1 Camera	1888 (USA)						██										
10 SMALL CONTACT PRINTS $2 \times 1\frac{1}{2}$ in. (50 × 40 mm.). From Kodak Pocket Camera	1895							██████									
11 POSTCARD PRINTS $5\frac{1}{2} \times 3\frac{1}{2}$ in. (140 × 89 mm.)	1899							██████████									
12 SNAPSHOT PRINTS $2\frac{1}{4} \times 2\frac{1}{4}$ in. (60 × 60 mm.); later $2\frac{1}{4} \times 3\frac{1}{4}$ in. (60 × 90 mm.) From Kodak Brownie Cameras	c. 1900								██████								
13 AUTOGRAPHIC PRINTS Contact prints with handwritten captions made directly on film in camera	1914									███							
14 PRINTS FROM 35mm. NEGATIVES Mainly by enlargement	1932											██████████					
15 POLAROID PRINTS Monochrome, sepia-coloured with deckle-edges	1947												████████				

Source: based, in part, on Martin (1988); Ford (1989); Steel and Taylor (1984) pp.74–110

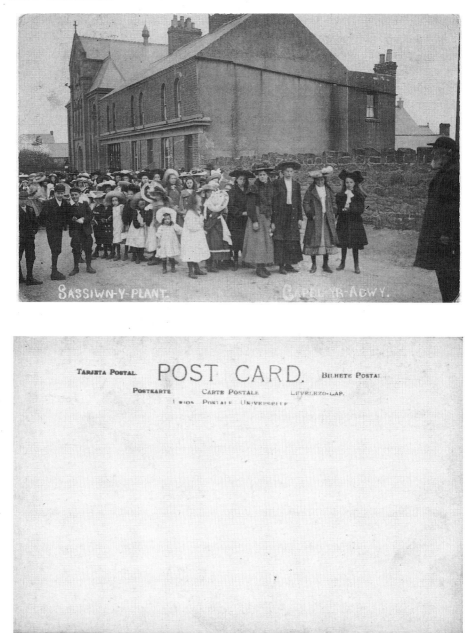

Figure 6.7 Postcard-size contact print (both sides shown), *c*.1900. Sunday school gathering at Coedpoeth, near Wrexham. The undivided back, introduced in 1902, and the statement 'Union Postale Universalle' help to date the scene (see Tables 6.5 and 6.6). Original size: $5\frac{1}{2} \times 3\frac{1}{2}$ in. (140×89 mm.) (Source: Mrs M.H. Pryce)

Snapshot prints   Snapshot photography became the principal means of making family photographs from the early 1900s (see Figures 6.8, 6.9, 6.10). Invariably printed with a clear white border, these often carried the trade or brand name of the manufacturer of the photographic paper on the back. The first Kodak pocket camera (1895) produced small pictures, but these increased in size with the arrival of the Kodak Brownie box camera (see Coe and Gates, 1977, pp.138–9). With minor variations, the snapshot remained the preferred format for much popular photography until the development of the 35mm. film camera for amateur use in the years following World War II, when it became standard procedure to produce enlarged prints from the small negatives (see Figure 6.11).

Figure 6.8 Contact print snapshot photograph, 1935. The picture was taken by the author's grandmother, using a Kodak No.2 Brownie box camera, on 120 film, soon after his birth. The author's father, James William Pryce (left) and visiting District Nurse Pryce (right, in uniform), are seated on a Coventry Eagle 147 cc motor cycle, first registered in Montgomeryshire, 1 October 1932 (see Riden, 1991). Original size: 2 ¼ × 3 ¼ in. (60 × 82 mm.) (Source: Mrs E.M. Pryce)

Figure 6.9 Contact print snapshot photograph taken in 1939 on 127 roll film, showing author (left) with his father, James William Pryce (farmer), David Sidney Pryce (brother), and sheepdog. Original size: 1½ × 2½ in. (40 × 65 mm.) (Source: Mrs E.M. Pryce)

Figure 6.10   Contact print snapshot photograph, probably taken on No.124 film, dated (from internal evidence) *c.*1917, showing New Inn, Y Foel, Llangadfan, Powys. Original size: $3\frac{1}{4} \times 4\frac{1}{4}$ in. (82×110 mm.) (Source: Pryce, 1991, p.103)

Figure 6.11   Standard size enlargement from 35mm. film negative, showing author (left) with fellow university student Paul Taylor at Aberystwyth, 1956. Original size: $3\frac{1}{4} \times 4\frac{3}{4}$ in. (84×120 mm.) (Source: W.T.R. Pryce)

Polaroid instant photographs   The Polaroid Land Camera appeared in 1947, but early results were sepia coloured and of poor clarity. Despite their relative recency, few of these seem to have survived.

Colour photographs   Colour photography first appeared in 1904 in the form of colour slides for projection, although colour tinting of monochrome photographs had taken place from the early days of the daguerreotype and the ambrotype (see Plate 1). Colour prints, as opposed to negatives or slides, only became generally available for amateur use during the 1950s and 1960s (see Table 6.3).

Table 6.3 Colour photography

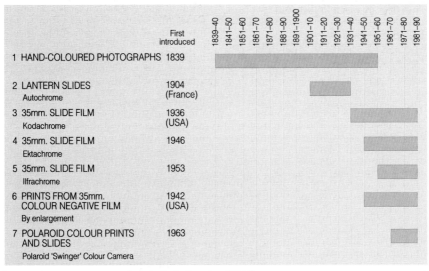

Source: based, in part, on Coe (1989); Crawley (1989)

Further guidance on identifying old photographs, especially from content, can be obtained from Lansdell (1985, 1986, 1990); Martin (1988); Pols (1992); Reilly (1986); Steel and Taylor (1984); Wills and Wills (1980). Motor cars and motor cycles are key date indicators, and pictures containing these can be dated using Riden (1991), Sedgwick and Gillies (1986, 1989), and Tragatsch (1989). The National Museum of Photography, Film and Television in Bradford (well worth a visit) and the Royal Photographic Society at Bath offer specialist advice to researchers.

3.3   MAKING COPIES OF OLD PHOTOGRAPHS

Most local photographers are prepared to make copies of old photographs that are as good as the work done by the specialists who advertise in journals such as *The Local Historian* or *Family Tree Magazine*. But costs can mount rapidly, especially if special techniques are involved. For these reasons, you may want to do your own copying. Often, the quality of the images from office photocopiers can be acceptable, especially if monochrome originals are reproduced on the special machines for copying in colour.

Many researchers, however, can use their own equipment. The modern single-lens reflex camera, with its facility for automatic and accurate setting of exposures, is recommended for making copies of old photographs, using appropriate film. Most camera manuals provide instructions for close-up work and advice on the selection and use of appropriate filters. For most copying work a macro lens is desirable, although, if suitable close-up supplementary lenses are fitted, adequate results can be obtained with a standard 50 mm. lens. If you are intent on obtaining good quality pictures, use either a small tripod to steady the camera or, better still, a copy stand. Even, balanced illumination, by artificial light, is essential. For suggestions on procedures and equipment see Pols (1992), Steel and Taylor (1984), or Shull (1988).

3.4   THE PICTURE POSTCARD ARRIVES

Not until 1894 did the post office in the UK allow private individuals to send postcards through the post, though they had been used in continental Europe (beginning in Germany) and for advertising since *c*.1870. Costing little and enjoying a lower postal rate until 1968 (see Table 6.4), postcards soon became the most popular means of written communication for virtually every-one. Useful reference books on the picture postcard include Byatt (1978, 1982), Hill (1978, 1987), Holt and Holt (1978), Lund (1985) and especially Willoughby (1992).

Table 6.4   British inland postage rates for postcards, 1870–1980

		1st class mail	2nd class mail
1870	Oct 1:	$\frac{1}{2}d$	
1918	June 3:	1*d*	
1921	June 13:	$1\frac{1}{2}d$	
1922	May 29:	1*d*	
1940	May 1:	2*d*	
1957	Oct 1:	$2\frac{1}{2}d$	
1965	May 17:	3*d*	
1968	Sept 16:	5*d*	4*d*
Decimal currency introduced			
1971	Feb 17:	3p	$2\frac{1}{2}$p
1973	Sept 10:	$3\frac{1}{2}$p	3p
1974	June 24:	$4\frac{1}{2}$p	$3\frac{1}{2}$p
1975	March 17:	7p	$5\frac{1}{2}$p
1975	Sept 29:	$8\frac{1}{2}$p	$6\frac{1}{2}$p
1977	June 13:	9p	7p
1979	August 20:	10p	8p
1980	Feb 4:	12p	10p

Sources: Parker (1976); Post Office Archives Leaflet 10A 'Letter postage rates from 1635'

As a source the advantage of postcards over one-off photographs is their general availability. Today, many opportunities still exist for building up collections of old postcards on aspects of community life: the great majority of serious collectors can offer us much advice and guidance; fairs for collectors take place in many towns; the magazine *Picture Postcard Monthly* (obtainable at fairs or from the editor – see further reading at the end of section 3) is replete with information and will take advertisements for your specific requirements; local libraries and museums have collections, as do national archives. Using the modern single-lens reflex camera, copies of individual postcards can be made easily and at relatively low cost. But begin your collections by asking members of your own family to make a search in their homes. The volume and variety of old postcards is huge – partly because of intense competition between suppliers, both locally (amongst photographers and stationers) and nationally. The largest national suppliers were Valentine and Sons of Dundee (1878–1967), and Raphael Tuck and Sons of London (1870–1972) (see Byatt, 1978, pp.287–322).

Known published studies based substantially on postcards tend to take the form of pictorial documentaries, one of the best known being *A social history of Britain in postcards, 1870–1930* (Evans and Richards, 1980). Much less common are studies that link picture postcards to other sources. Historical geographers attempting to plot changes in settlement layout, buildings, population, etc. over time, have led in this field of research. One example is a study of the 'embryonic town' in Wales, defined as settlements that grew throughout the nineteenth century but failed to develop into fully fledged urban centres (Pryce and Edwards, 1979). The authors aimed to show the changes in urban layout and social structure of Llanfair Caereinion in northern Powys. But there were no maps covering this town for the crucial years between the tithe survey of 1842 and the 25-inch to the mile Ordnance Survey plans of 1886. This information gap was filled, in part, from picture postcards, especially one showing the town in *c.*1860 reproduced in this volume as Figure 11.1(a) in Chapter 11. Individual buildings and the street layout shown on that picture were compared with later photographs taken in the 1880s and 1890s. This enabled a map to be drawn of the town in mid-century, together with notes of the subsequent changes (see also Pryce, 1991).

3.5   IDENTIFICATION AND DATING OF PICTURE POSTCARDS

Table 6.5   Identification and dating of picture postcards

1	Dating from internal evidence in the picture (e.g. buildings, street layout, events shown, etc.). This can be linked to personal/local knowledge, contemporary records, local newspapers, detailed maps and plans, evidence from oral history.
2	Postage rates printed on the card in the square reserved for the stamp.
3	Identification and date of the postage stamp.
4	Town, date and time shown in the postmark.
5	Overall dimensions and size of the postcard.
6	Up to December 1901, no messages were permitted on the back of the card, only details of the addressee. From January 1, 1902 the back is divided by a printed line with separate spaces for the address (right) and correspondence (left).
7	Printed instructions concerning correspondence (on the back, left side).
8	Manufacturer's name/trademark.
9	Name of retailer.
10	Manufacturer's reference number (if the original view register can be consulted).
11	Printing process used: lithographs/monochrome/colour overprint/'real photograph'.

Table 6.5 summarizes the various ways of dating postcards. For the postage rates (i.e. point (2) in Table 6.5), see Table 6.4 above. Stamp catalogues (Gibbons, 1992 and subsequent years) are of considerable help with (3). The postmark (4) is a less reliable guide, since stationers often purchased large stocks of cards and it may have taken many years before they were all sold. The size of the card (5) is dealt with in Table 6.6.

However, a *caveat* should be entered here: having made up their printing blocks to meet earlier official size requirements, some publishers continued to use them after 1899 when use of the larger European-size card was allowed. Such cards can be recognized by their wide plain borders, indicating photographs of an earlier age intended originally for use on smaller cards. The vertical printed line, introduced on the back of postcards in 1902 (6) is another clue for

Table 6.6   Dimensions and format of the picture postcard in Britain, 1870–1926

1870: $4\frac{3}{4} \times 3$ in. (122 × 75mm.)

The first 'official' postcards, with embossed stamps, were introduced by the Post Office, October 1, 1870. With the addressee and address shown on one side, the postal regulations stated that the message was to be written on the other side. These early cards were intended solely for sending brief messages. No pictures were allowed.

1894: $4\frac{3}{4} \times 3$in. (122 × 75mm.)

Privately printed postcards (but still with no pictures) were allowed to be sent in the UK from September 1, 1894, using adhesive postage stamps.

1894: $3\frac{1}{4} \times 2\frac{1}{4}$in. (82 × 57mm.)

George Steward & Co., Edinburgh, and F.T. Corbett, Leicester, published probably the first picture postcards in Britain. Post Office regulations stipulated that no correspondence was to be written on the address side. In consequence, brief messages were written on the other side, usually below or at the side of the picture.

1895: $4\frac{1}{2} \times 3\frac{1}{2}$in. (115 × 89mm.)

'Court postcards', decorated with small pictures, intended for personal correspondence, were introduced from 21 January 1895. Official regulations stated that these cards had to be enclosed in an addressed envelope for sending through the post.

1899: $5\frac{1}{2} \times 3\frac{1}{2}$ in. (140 × 89mm.)

Full size postcards, as approved for use by the Universal Postal Union (UPU), were allowed to be used from 1 November 1899 for internal mail within the UK. This European size was justified by publishers because the format meant that larger pictures could be reproduced. Messages were still to be written only on the picture side, not on the address side.

1902: Divided backs introduced

The Post Master General approved, in January 1902, the use of picture postcards with divided backs for sending through the post. From this date, provided they were kept clear of the address by a dividing line, messages could be included on the address side, giving more space on the reverse side for the reproduction of pictures and photographs.

1907: $4 \times 2\frac{3}{4}$in. (101 × 70mm.)
In April 1907 the Post Office raised the *minimum* permitted size for post cards to $4 \times 2\frac{3}{4}$ in. (101 × 70 mm.)

1926: $4 \times 2\frac{3}{4}$in. (101 × 70mm.) *minimum*; $5\frac{7}{8} \times 4\frac{1}{8}$ in. (148 × 103 mm.) (international size) *maximum*
Adoption of new minimum and maximum sizes for postcards in the UK.

Source: based, in part, on Parker (1976), Holt and Holt (1978), and Byatt (1978, 1982)

dating. However, some thrifty local publishers overprinted old stock: this can often be detected because the line is not the same colour as the other (earlier) printing on the card; and, owing to problems of registration, neither is it parallel to the sides of the card (Holt and Holt, 1978, p.192). Because postcards with a dividing line (a British first!) were not initially acceptable to postal authorities in continental Europe, publishers printed instructions (7) on their cards (see Table 6.7).

Table 6.7   Printed instructions on picture postcards

	Inscription	Dates
1	'For Inland Postage, this space, as well as the back*, may now be used for communication.'	1902–04
2	'For Inland Postage only, this space may be used for communication.'	1902–06
3	'This space may be used for communication.'	1904 onwards
4	'This space may be used for communication in the British Isles or to France at Postcard Rate.'	1904–07
5	'This space, as well as the back*, may be used for Inland Communication Postcard Rate, and for Foreign at Letter Rate.'	1906 onwards
6	'This space for communication.'	1907 onwards
7	From *c*.1908, it ceased to be a *requirement* to put instructions on the correspondence side, although instructions often still appeared.	*c*.1908 onwards

* The side carrying the picture.

Source: based on Holt and Holt (1978) p.193

Most, but not all, postcards carry the name/trademark of the manufacturer and/or publisher (point (8) in Table 6.5). When a special series was produced for a local retailer, his name was often shown, with a copyright attribution (Table 6.5, point (9)). Byatt (1978) gives short histories, details of trademarks, trade names and named series with dates of publication for virtually all the major firms in the business in mainland Britain from 1894 to 1939. For the dates of many local publishers, printers, stationers and retailers, consult local trade directories (see Chapter 4 of this volume). Every publisher probably kept detailed records of their postcard views (Table 6.5, point (10)). Two well-known registers have survived. One is that of the Dundee firm, Valentine and Sons (from 1878 to 1967), which can be consulted at the Department of Manuscripts, in the Library of the University of St Andrews, Scotland (for further details see Smart, 1987, and Pryce, 1991, pp.18–19). Each card has a unique number and the register contains details of the photographer, location, and the date when the negative was entered – but not the date when the picture was actually taken. The other known register is that of the Francis Frith Company of Reigate, Surrey (Wilson, 1985, pp.20 and 192). You should seek out other registers in local archives and reference libraries, but don't be too optimistic.

Other methods of dating are: questioning long-settled residents about a particular scene; checking features against 6-inch and 25-inch to the mile Ordnance Survey maps; searching local papers for reports of public events depicted on a postcard; looking at the clothing worn by people shown on cards (see Lansdell, 1985, 1986 and 1990).

3.6   THE LIFE AND TIMES OF A PICTURE POSTCARD

This is the story of just one postcard. Because it was sold for forty years and the photograph from which it originated was reproduced for twenty years, it provides a glimpse into changing technology (our eleventh way of dating postcards – see Table 6.5) and an insight into local business practices. Plate 6(a) in the plate section is a half-plate bromide contact print taken from a glass negative by Levi Jones (1858–1949), local photographer, bookseller and postmaster of

Llanfair Caereinion, Powys, Wales. It captures the valley of the River Banw on a fine day in spring, *c.*1898. A man of enterprise, Levi Jones had his print made into a picture postcard for sale in his post office. Because it was sent away to specialist printers, interesting information appears on the back of the print.

_____ *EXERCISE 6.1* _____

Examine Plate 6(b) and see if you can find the following:

1 Levi Jones' business address.

2 The proposed caption.

3 In the series of views published by Jones, the number of this particular one.

4 The nature of the original print.

5 Instructions for printing.

6 Number of copies ordered.

7 Number of reprints.

Answer/comment p.301

Of the presumed five printings of the river scene, three have been located. A close examination of Plates 7 to 9 confirms they all come from the same photograph.

Plate 7 was probably for the first or second printing, since it was produced by the improved lithographic printing process known as *mezzography* which gave a grainy image, not the regular dot patterns of early commercial lithography (Holt and Holt, 1978, p.188). Other date indicators include the divided back introduced in 1902 (see Plate 10); 'This space may be used for communication' introduced in 1904 (see Table 6.7); and the halfpenny yellow-green Edward VII postage stamp issued on 24 November, 1904 (Gibbons, 1992, p.21). Other cards, reliably dated, used the same printing process and had the same appearance. As stocks of postcards in a small town like Llanfair took some time to clear, the 1911 postmark could be a red herring.

Plate 8 shows the view enhanced by three-colour overprinting, producing what was known as a *chromolithograph, oleograph* or simply a *chromo.* This was not introduced into Britain until after 1900; from *c.*1908 it was not necessary to put instructions on the space used for correspondence (see Plate 11); the halfpenny green George V postage stamp was first issued on 22 June, 1911 (Gibbons, 1992, pp.24–5); the local postmark was 1915. All this suggests 1913 or 1914 as the likely printing date for this postcard.

Like Plate 8, the postcard shown in Plate 9 used the three-colour *chromolithographic* process, but the colours were allocated to different features (e.g. note the application of red). The colours seem more out of register in Plate 9 than in Plate 8, have a grainier appearance, and, by using a magnifying glass on the original card, a regular pattern of dots can be seen. All this suggests that a cruder and cheaper process was used, indicating a printing during the 'doldrums period' of picture postcard production (i.e. 1919–39), with its falling sales. That the card was probably printed either in 1922 or 1923 is indicated by the George V stamp, issued between 1912 and 1924 (Plate 12); the fact that postage on picture postcards was not raised to one penny until June 1918 (Table 6.4); and the postmark of nearby Welshpool, 1925.

3.7 TWO FURTHER EXAMPLES OF PICTURE POSTCARD DETECTION

Plate 13(a) carries Valentine's Register No. 50473 (see section 3.5 above). From this we learn that the original picture was recorded in the register on 21 August 1905 as having been taken by the travelling photographer and stationer T. Leigh, Caxton House, Abergele, North Wales. Leigh

Plate 1 Ambrotype in union case, *c*.1860. Studio portrait, subject and photographer unknown, to which hand tinting has been applied. Original size: quarter plate ($4\frac{1}{4} \times 3\frac{1}{4}$in.; 108×82mm.) (case size when closed: $4\frac{3}{4} \times 3\frac{3}{4}$in.; 120×95mm.) (Source: A. Francombe, Newport Pagnell)

Plate 2(a) Early tintype in embossed paper mount, *c*.1860, showing girl with hand-tinted cheeks. Original size (mount): $2\frac{3}{8} \times 4$in. (60×102mm.) (Source: B. Vossburgh, London)

Plate 2(b) Later tintype in souvenir coronation mount, 1937, showing young man and woman. Tintype images are dark, hence the colourful mount to enhance the appearance of the product. Original size (mount): $3\frac{1}{4} \times 4\frac{7}{8}$in. (82×124mm.) (Source: B. Vossburgh, London)

(a)

Plates 3(a) and 3(b)   Early carte-de-visite (both sides shown) with albumen print of Broad Street, Llanfair Caereinion, Powys. Dated *c*.1860 from internal evidence. The photographer's plain advertisement on the back is typical of early cartes. Original size (mount): $2\frac{1}{2} \times 4\frac{1}{8}$in. (65×105mm.) (Source: Pryce, 1991, p.59)

(b)

(a)   (b)

Plates 4(a) and 4(b)   Late carte-de-visite (both sides shown). Studio portrait showing David Pryce, farm labourer, and Martha Mills, after their wedding at Newtown, Powys, 24 November 1904 (paternal grandparents of author). Albumen print. The photographer's elaborate advertisement on the back and the rounded corners are features of later cartes. Original size (mount): $2\frac{1}{2} \times 4\frac{1}{8}$in. (65×105mm.) (Source: W.T.R. Pryce)

Plate 5(a) Cabinet print: studio photograph by H.C. Pilkington, Wellington Street, Burton-on-Trent, 1901, showing PC41, Thomas Henry Allen (author's maternal grandfather), who served in Staffordshire County Constabulary 1901–3. Police pension records at Stafford state that he was 'required to resign and hand in his uniform' on 14 October 1903! He later became a farm labourer. Albumen print. Original size (mount): 4¼×6½in. (108×165mm.) (Source: Mrs E.M. Pryce)

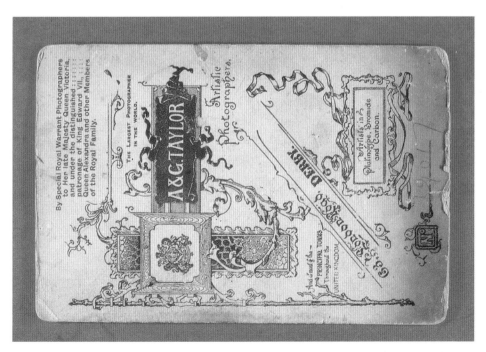

Plate 5(b) Photographer's elaborate advertisement on the back of a cabinet card print. Dated *c.*1904 from picture content. Further copies could be obtained by quoting the negative number (bottom). Original size: 4¼×6½in. (108×165 mm.) (Source: Mrs E.M. Pryce)

Plate 6(a)   Llanfair Caereinion river scene, *c*.1898. Bromide contact print from half-plate glass negative. Original size: $4\frac{1}{4} \times 6\frac{1}{2}$in. (108×165mm.) (Source: W.T.R. Pryce)

Plate 6(b)   Inscriptions on the reverse side of Plate 6(a) above

Plate 7 Plate 6(a) reproduced by lithography (mezzograph) as a monochrome postcard, *c*.1905. Original size: $5\frac{1}{2} \times 3\frac{1}{2}$in. (140×89mm.). See also Plate 10 (Source: W.T.R. Pryce)

Plate 8 Plate 6(a) reproduced by chromolithography as a colour postcard, *c*.1913. Original size: $5\frac{1}{2} \times 3\frac{1}{2}$in. (140×89mm.). See also Plate 11 (Source: W.T.R. Pryce)

Plate 9 Plate 6(a) reproduced by a cheaper form of chromolithography as a colour postcard, *c*.1922. Original size: $5\frac{1}{2} \times 3\frac{1}{2}$in. (140×89mm.). See also Plate 12 (Source: W.T.R. Pryce)

Plate 10 Address side of postcard shown as Plate 7

Plate 11 Address side of postcard shown as Plate 8

Plate 12 Address side of postcard shown as Plate 9

Plate 13(a) Monochrome lithographic postcard with hand-applied colour wash, published by Valentines of Dundee, 1905. Original size: $5\frac{1}{2} \times 3\frac{1}{2}$in. (140×89mm.) (Source: W.T.R. Pryce)

Plate 13(b) Address side of postcard shown as Plate 13(a) above

Plate 14 'Real photograph' postcard, published for advertising purposes, c.1913. Original size: $5\frac{1}{2} \times 3\frac{1}{2}$in. (140×89mm.) (Source: W.T.R. Pryce)

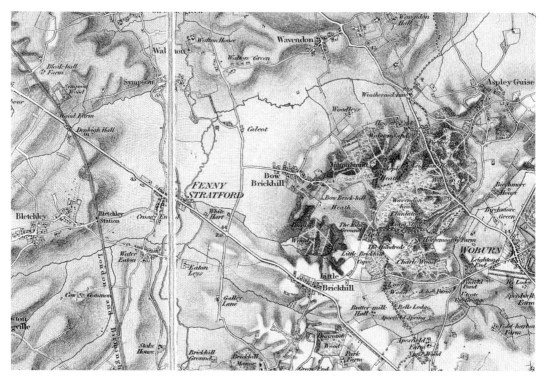

Plate 15 Detail from Ordnance Survey first edition one-inch map, Plate XLVI, 1834 (Source: Royal Geographical Society)

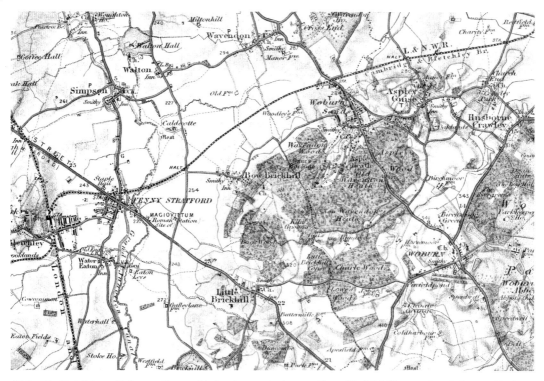

Plate 16 Detail from Ordnance Survey third series one-inch map, Sheet 96, 1913 (Source: Royal Geographical Society)

supplied numerous views to Valentine's on a commission basis. This suggests that the photograph was taken in 1905: the yellow-green Edward VII stamp (first issued on 26 November 1904) confirms this (see Plate 13(b)). The 1908 postmark is a red herring, like the postmark on Plate 7. The print was hand coloured. This is revealed when the original card is tilted, revealing local variations in the amount of light reflected from the areas carrying the different colours. Only two colours (green and blue) were used, as against three (yellow, red, blue) on the postcards shown as Plates 8 and 9. Though Valentine's were amongst the first to install colour printing, they first tried to meet growing competition from Germany by hand colouring existing stocks of monochrome cards.

Higher quality images occur on those postcards which carry the inscription 'A real photograph' or something similar. Showing fine detail, these were produced on rotary presses using the platino-bromide process from 1901 (Byatt, 1978, p.235). 'Real photograph' cards were expensive to produce and, in consequence, were used primarily when fine detail (portraits, technical pictures) or short runs were required. They tend to curl when exposed to heat or light owing to the emulsions used on the picture side of the card. Plate 14 shows a local Llanfair Caereinion garage owner and taximan, Llewelyn Jehu, in his model T Ford, *c.*1913. It was produced as a memento and advertisement for customers. When shown, as here, car numbers can be checked in the original motor vehicle registration records to provide details of the make, model, various owners and dates (see Riden, 1991).

3.8   FURTHER INFORMATION

In addition to local record offices, libraries and museums, the following institutions have large collections of old photographs and interesting exhibits:

The National Museum of Photography, Film and Television, Princes View, Bradford, West Yorkshire, BD5 OTR.

Royal Photographic Society, The Octagon, Milsom Street, Bath, BA1 1DN.

National Library of Scotland, George IV Bridge, Edinburgh, EH1 1EW.

National Library of Wales, Aberystwyth, SY23 1BR.

National Museum of Wales, Welsh Folk Museum, St Fagans, Cardiff, CF5 6XB.

National Library of Ireland, Kildare Street, Dublin 2.

Ulster Museum, Botanic Gardens, Stranmillis Road, Belfast, County Antrim, BT9 5AB.

Information on all aspects of the history of postal services, stamps and picture postcards can be obtained from:
      Post Office Archives, Freeling House, Mount Pleasant Complex (Phoenix Place Entrance), London, WC1A 1BB.

In addition to its postal history collection, the important Frank Staff Collection of picture postcards can be consulted at:
      Bath Postal Museum, 8 Broad Street, Bath, BA1 5LJ.

REFERENCES AND FURTHER READING (SECTION 3)

Note: entries marked with an asterisk are recommended for further reading.

Becker, H.S. (1979) 'Do photographs tell the truth?', in Cook, T.D. and Reichardt, C.S. (eds) *Qualitative and quantitative methods in evaluation research*, London, Sage.

Byatt, A. (1978) *Picture postcards and their publishers: an illustrated account identifying Britain's major postcard publishers, 1894 to 1939*, Malvern, Golden Age Postcard Books.[*]

Byatt, A. (1982) *Collecting picture postcards: an introduction*, Malvern, Golden Age Postcard Books.

Coe, B. (1989) 'The rollfilm revolution', in Ford, C. (ed.) (1989).

Coe, B. and Gates, P. (1977) *The snapshot photograph: the rise of popular photography 1888–1939*, London, Ash and Grant.[*]

Crawley, G. (1989) 'Colour comes to all', in Ford, C. (ed.) (1989).

Evans, E.J. and Richards, J. (1980) *A social history of Britain in postcards, 1870–1930*, London, Longman.

Ford, C. (ed.) (1989) *The story of popular photography*, North Pomfret, Vermont, Trafalgar Square Publishing.

Gibbons, S. (1992) *Great Britain concise stamp catalogue*, London, Stanley Gibbons Publications.

Hannavy, J. (1980) *The Victorian professional photographer*, Princes Risborough, Shire Publications.

Hiley, M. (1985) *Frank Meadow Sutcliffe 1853–1941*, London, The British Council.

Hill, C. (1978) *Discovering picture postcards*, Princes Risborough, Shire Publications.

Hill, C. (1987) *Shire album No. 208: picture postcards*, Princes Risborough, Shire Publications.

Holt, T. and Holt, V. (1978) *Picture postcards of the Golden Age: a collector's guide*, London, Postcard Publishing Company.

Lansdell, A. (1985) *Fashion à la carte, 1860–1900*, Princes Risborough, Shire Publications.

Lansdell, A. (1986) *Wedding fashions, 1860–1980*, Princes Risborough, Shire Publications.

Lansdell, A. (1990) *Seaside fashions, 1860–1980*, Princes Risborough, Shire Publications.

Lund, B. (1985) *Postcard collecting: a beginner's guide*, Keyworth (Nottingham), Reflections of a Bygone Age.

Martin, E. (1988) *Collecting and preserving old photographs*, London, Collins.[*]

Oliver, G. (1989) *Photographs and local history*, London, Batsford.[*]

Parker, E.K. (1976) 'The progress of the post card', *Stamp Collecting*, 26 August, pp.21–9.

Picture Postcard Monthly, the current issue can be obtained by post from the editor (B. Lund), 15 Debdale Lane, Keyworth, Nottingham, NG12 5HT.

Pols, R. (1992) *Dating old photographs*, Birmingham, Federation of Family History Societies.[*]

Pryce, W.T.R. (1991) *The photographer in rural Wales*, Llanfair Caereinion and Welshpool, The Powysland Club.

Pryce, W.T.R. and Edwards, J.A. (1979) 'The social structure of the embryonic town in rural Wales: Llanfair Caereinion in the mid-nineteenth century', *The Montgomeryshire Collections*, vol.68, pp.45–90.

Reilly, J.M. (1986) *Care and identification of nineteenth-century photographic prints*, Rochester, New York, Eastman Kodak Company.

Riden, P. (1991) *How to trace the history of your car: a guide to motor vehicle registration records*, London, Academy Books.*

Sedgwick, M. and Gillies, M. (1986) *A–Z of cars, 1945–1970*, Bideford, Bay View Books.

Sedgwick, M. and Gillies, M. (1989) *A–Z of cars of the 1930s*, Bideford, Bay View Books.

Shull, W.S. (1988) *Photographing your heritage*, Salt Lake City, Ancestry (PO Box 476, Salt Lake City, UT 84110, USA).

Smart, R. (1987) '"Famous throughout the world": Valentine & Sons Ltd, Dundee', *Review of Scottish Culture*, 4, pp.75–87.

Steel, D. and Taylor, L. (eds) (1984) *Family history in focus*, Guildford, Lutterworth Press.*

Taylor, R. (1981) *George Washington Wilson: artist and photographer, 1823–93*, Aberdeen, University of Aberdeen Press.

Thompson, P. and Harkell, G. (1979) *The Edwardians in photographs*, London, Batsford.

Tragatsch, E. (ed.) (1989) *The illustrated encyclopaedia of motor cycles, 1894 to the present day*, London, New Birlington Books.

Willoughby, M. (1992) *A history of picture postcards: a pictorial record from the turn of the century to the present day*, London, Studio Editions.*

Wills, C. and Wills, D. (1980) *History of photography: techniques and equipment*, London, Hamlyn.*

Wilson, D. (1985) *Francis Frith's travels: a photographic journey through Victorian Britain*, London, J.M. Dent & Sons Ltd.

Woollen, H. and Crawford, A. (1977) *John Thomas 1838–1905: photographer*, Llandysul, Gomer Press.

4   THE FAMILY ALBUM: PAST, PRESENT AND ABSENT

by Gill Kirkup

The family album is not just a record of people connected through ties of blood and friendship; it is a deliberately constructed narrative of family life, a family's autobiography. In addition to giving pride of place to photographs of events that are significant in marking stages in the creation and development of a family, the keeper of the album has also carefully selected the photographs to present to the world, and to the family itself, the story of its success. For example, Victorian albums often began with engagement photographs, followed by wedding pictures in pride of place, then babies lying on bearskin rugs, and then seaside holiday photographs and children in groups in various uniforms. Modern albums are likely to include mother and baby photographs taken in maternity wards, children opening Christmas presents, and adults a bit the worse for wear at a barbecue on a Mediterranean beach.

Some of the new subject matter is due to improved technology, such as flash photography; other events were once private, or even secret, such as childbirth, and it would have been considered improper to photograph them. Some subjects, such as the deathbed picture (see Figure 6.12), have become the new secrets. But the ideology of family life presented over this

Figure 6.12 'My dying husband Archibald Rough aged 37, April 1864, Blairgowrie' (Source: Claire Grey Archive)

century in albums is characterized more by continuity than by change. What a historian must remember is that the ideology is not the reality; it is a careful, but not always a conscious, construction.

Recent writers on the family album note that it is nearly always women who keep the album, attach the pictures and write the captions, although men may have taken the photographs in the first place. By the mid-nineteenth century, making decorated photograph albums became, like flower pressing and water colour painting, another female pastime (Warner, 1992). But women are in control of more than the decoration: Jeremy Seabrook, talking about using photographs in an oral history project, calls women 'custodians of the feelings' (Seabrook, 1991, p.172). Photographs which produce the 'wrong' feelings, for example embarrassment or shame, are not selected. Rosy Martin (1991) describes how women in their role as family archivists are concerned to create a picture of 'good mothering', of family cohesion. Photographs which contradict this image, such as miserable children or dirty or untidy domestic interiors, may be the life-blood of a public photographic archive, but they will never be selected for a family album. Others, for example estranged relatives or ex-partners, may be removed from albums in which they once had pride of place. This means that a historian using a family album must look beyond the surface subject of a photograph to find out what events and relationships are disguised in it, and what the absences are that surround it.

4.1   MULTIPLE READINGS OF A PHOTOGRAPH

There are many ways to read a photograph. Sue Isherwood demonstrated this when she gave a photograph from her own family album (see Figure 6.13) to three other people and compared what they could read from it. What follows are excerpts from the responses of two of these people, plus Sue Isherwood's own comments:

Brian Coe – photographic historian

This is a typical family shot printed in postcard format with pre-printed back for posting. This suggests that it was taken on a Kodak 3A folding camera which took this size of roll film. This

*camera was first sold in this country in 1903 and proved very popular between then and 1914.
The picture could have been taken either by a family member or a local professional photographer …*

Penelope Byrd – costume historian

*I would date this picture about 1900 by the style of the younger women's dresses. I am very
surprised that it is as late as 1911. These styles were old fashioned then even for a rural area. They
are all in mourning and the old lady is wearing a Victorian widow's cap which was quite an
anachronism by then … I cannot tell much about their class except that they are very plainly
dressed. The old woman certainly seems to dominate the other two, who look like sisters …*

Sue Isherwood – only daughter of the baby

*My mother was very proud of this picture, showing four generations of women; herself, Molly
(but christened Marjorie) Kendall, her mother Evelyn Kendall, her grandmother Mary Tidy and
her great grandmother Jane Tidy (nee Saxby). My grandmother was illegitimate, something I
learned only a few years before my mother's death in 1984, when talking about this photograph
… No wonder Mary Tidy is absent from the mother's stories of childhood, away in London and
stigmatised at home …*

*When I look again at the photograph I speculate on the family dramas it conceals, but mainly
on the absence of men.*

(Isherwood, 1988, p.3)

Figure 6.13   Family group, 1911 (Source: Isherwood, 1988, p.2)

4.2   THE CAPTION: PART OF THE FAMILY NARRATIVE

The caption on a photograph can be crucial to its placement in the narrative of a family or individual, and the persons who wrote the original caption may bring to it a particular personal perspective which leads others to misinterpret either the caption or the photograph. Annette Kuhn (1991) describes how a photograph of herself as a child, captioned by her mother 'Just back from Bournemouth (Convelescent) [sic]' conflicted with her own memories since she knew that she had convalesced in Broadstairs after an illness and also that she had been older than the age she was in the picture when that happened. It was possible that one of them was misremembering, but Kuhn also discovered that the caption might not have referred to herself – the subject of the photograph – but to the time in her mother's life when it was taken, a time when she, the mother, was convalescing from an accident at work. The caption works with the image to produce the family narrative, but it may be a particular narrative that would be contradicted by other members.

4.3   THE PLACE OF WORK IN THE FAMILY ALBUM

Well I've got plenty of me with the GIRLS from work, when we went out, but nothing in the factory, you know. Well, you wouldn't. Why bother?
(Quotation from one of the women interviewed by Jo Stanley for a community history project: Stanley, 1991, p.60)

Family albums, both past and present, contain few photographs of family members working at their paid employment. As discussed in section 3.1, at the beginning of the century it would have been technically very difficult to take photographs in most industrial environments. Many firms also had explicit prohibitions about photography, and the only photographs allowed were carefully posed for publicity purposes for employers and for trade unions. But it is not only these explicit barriers which explain why people usually only have pictures of themselves outside work, in the yard or at the gate, or on a special occasion. We do not choose to have images of ourselves looking distracted, busy or untidy, and this is especially the case with women. There are unlikely to be any photographs in the family albums you find of women doing domestic work in their own homes. This leads to family albums under-representing the role of work, both paid and unpaid, in the lives of the men and women pictured there.

4.4   CLASS, RACE AND DIFFERENCE

Before the invention of the Kodak Brownie camera, photography was a hobby for the middle classes, although we can see from Sue Isherwood's photo (Figure 6.13) that working-class people did have pictures taken by professionals on special occasions. However, if you are using the archive of a working-class family you will have a more limited source of photographs to draw on. You will also have photographs of people posed and wearing their best in a way that disguises class difference. For example, in Sue Isherwood's photo the class of the women is not obvious now (Mary Tidy was a cook), even to the costume historian. The indication of class is the fact that the two younger women are wearing clothes which for the period were very outdated. They could probably not afford to dress in the most fashionable style.

Tracing a family history which includes immigration may provide a rich source of photographs. As Stuart Hall (1991) argues, photographs provided an important connection between geographically divided families. New immigrants to the UK sent back photographs to illustrate their success (see Figure 6.14), and received pictures of growing children and those relatives left behind. But these pictures too are hard to interpret, argues Hall, because they use the stereotypical imagery of middle-class white portraiture and disguise the actual social conditions and experiences of the people depicted.

Figure 6.14   Images of success (Source: Derek Bishton archive)

Other forms of difference are also likely to have been disguised in family photographs. Homosexual relationships are not likely to be represented, and people with disability will probably have been posed so that their disability is disguised by clothing and position. Family albums, in their attempt to present a family narrative of success, even success against adversity, render invisible many aspects of their subjects' lived experience; it is the historian's job to render some of these visible again.

4.5   PHOTOGRAPHS AND ORAL HISTORY

Despite their problems, family photographs can play an important part in gathering oral history. They are an extremely powerful way of accessing memories and emotions:

> *I spent many long afternoons with people, the pictures fanning out across the table, then spilling out across the floor, a mingling of laughter and sadness ('That's my aunt, she insisted on carrying the potted plant because she wanted to hide how fat she was ...')*
>
> (Seabrook, 1991, p.173)

It may also be that, like Jo Stanley, although you may begin by thinking your photographs are simply a trigger for your work, they may end up being the major work:

> *The idea was that we'd just get hold of a few snapshots to act as triggers for the spoken and written memories we wanted. In fact the pictures became the cornerstone of the whole project, which included an exhibition.*
>
> (Stanley, 1991, p.60)

REFERENCES AND FURTHER READING (SECTION 4)

Hall, S. (1991) 'Reconstruction work: images of post-war black settlement', in Spence, J.O. and Holland, P. (eds) (1991).

Isherwood, S. (1988) *The family album,* Channel 4 Television.

Kuhn, A. (1991) 'Remembrance', in Spence, J.O. and Holland, P. (eds) (1991).

Martin, R. (1991) 'Unwind the ties that bind', in Spence, J.O. and Holland, P. (eds) (1991).

Seabrook, J. (1991) 'My life is in that box', in Spence, J.O. and Holland, P. (eds) (1991).

Spence, J.O. and Holland, P. (eds) (1991) *Family snaps: the meanings of domestic photography*, London, Virago Press.

Stanley, J. (1991) 'Well, who'd want an old picture of me at work?', in Spence, J.O. and Holland, P. (eds) (1991).

Warner, M. (1992) 'Women in the Victorian family album', *Creative Camera*, May.

5   USING ALREADY-RECORDED AUDIO SOURCES

by Joanna Bornat

Throughout the British Isles, collections of oral history tapes are preserved in local libraries, county and national archives, universities, museums, schools, local radio stations, and private collections. Oral history has enjoyed a boom since the early 1970s, with many locally funded projects making recordings for a variety of uses. For anyone embarking on a community history project, these are an invaluable and rich resource.

Already-existing recordings may cover topics you are interested in, they may include recordings with prominent individuals who have relevant experience, and they may also offer examples to you of interviewing and transcription styles.

You could start by contacting your local library, museum or city archive. Find out what tapes they have and whether they have listening or lending facilities. Nationally, a useful guide to collections is Lali Weerasinghe and Jeremy Silver's directory of sound collections (1989). Many of the collections they list include oral history material. They also include information on access and opening hours, related publications and a detailed subject index. Rob Perks's bibliography of oral history publications (1990) provides a valuable complement to the directory. Though it relates purely to printed sources, many of the publications cited are drawn from taped collections which are preserved and accessible to other researchers. In addition, some particularly useful resources are listed in Perks (1992) (see also the other catalogues and directories listed in the further reading at the end of this section).

Looking through past issues of the journal *Oral History*, particularly the section entitled 'Current British work', you will find references to collections made by a variety of organizations and individuals, including voluntary organizations, industry, community projects, local radio, town planning groups, campaigners and social care workers. Tracking down such collections may involve some detective work since some projects have lost funding and others have closed down. Fortunately, some still survive and many managed to deposit their collections in local libraries and archives.

You will find that tapes are kept under very different conditions depending on the size and budget of the organization or institution you approach. Some libraries and archives preserve their tapes under conditions which encourage use by the public, with playback and listening facilities, full transcriptions, subject indexing, and even opportunities for loan.

What is most likely is that you will be shown collections which are not transcribed but which may be accompanied by a brief description of the interviewee and the subjects covered.

An unedited and non-transcribed tape can have its advantages. In its unedited state you can listen to the way an interview develops and get an impression of some of the complexities of the interview relationship. You will be able to treat the recorded material as you would any other form of data. With a notebook to hand, you can jot down any points which are significant for you, note their position on the tape if the playback machine has a counter, and later rewind to transcribe in detail any part which you want to quote verbatim.

Of course, like any other set of historical data, already-recorded oral history has its drawbacks. You cannot be certain about the conditions under which the recording was made, who the interviewer was, how the interviewees were selected, or what was the interviewer's overall frame of reference for recording. You are subject to the interviewer's own choice of topic and line of questioning, and you may find that areas that interest you are not investigated in depth.

Another disadvantage of recorded oral history is the lengthy time it takes to work through a recording. Clearly it isn't as easy to skim through a tape as it is to skim a document. Of course, if the tape is fully transcribed then your task is a whole lot easier.

Individual tapes, and transcriptions, may be hard to manage in terms of quantifying evidence. You may need to invent your own system of coding or cross-referencing for someone else's collection.

Lesley Furlong, an Open University graduate, is an example of someone who used an already-recorded collection of transcribed audio tapes to augment her study of women workers at the Coalport China works, between 1850 and 1914. She was fortunate in finding full transcriptions of the tapes she listened to. Someone before her had spent more than a decade collecting interviews which she was able to sift through. Most of her evidence she drew from documentary sources, 'contemporary journals, newspapers, diaries, books, reports of Factory Inspectors and the census returns'. But the oral evidence added another dimension; it was:

> ... *the actual voice of the respondent which sets up a resonance which not only aids understanding but additionally empathises and recognises the common features shared by women across time and class. The excitement of hearing and seeing a respondent speaking the words which present us with confirmation of a particular feature or aspect is reproduced to some degree by the printed word on the page, but is no substitute for hearing the inflexion of the voice and seeing facial expression when someone is recalling their past. Mood and emotion can be flattened by presentation on the page and can lead to possible misinterpretation.*
>
> (Furlong, unpublished)

Nevertheless, Furlong admitted to frustration when the interviews went off in directions that did not interest her, and she felt that she had missed the excitement of the face-to-face interview.

In Chapter 7, we look at issues of access, clearance and copyright, particularly in relation to the Copyright, Designs and Patents Act of 1988. If you are thinking of using an excerpt in a publication, or to play to an audience, then you will have to seek clearance for use. The librarian or archivist in charge will be able to help you out with the necessary contact addresses. If the tapes you are using have no clearance details attached to them, then you will face more difficult problems in tracing the original interviewees or their next of kin.

Archived audio is a rich source, yet it is rarely consulted by researchers. The energies and commitment of interviewers over the years have left us with many hours of recorded history. Your own research and project work can only benefit from discriminating and appreciative use of this material.

REFERENCES AND FURTHER READING (SECTION 5)

British Words on Tape, 1991 (1991) London, Meckler. A directory of spoken word cassettes available in the UK, which includes lists of distributors, titles, and author and subject indexes.

Furlong, L. (unpublished) 'Reflections on methodology'.

Gramophone: spoken word catalogue, 1993 (1992) Harrow, General Gramophone Publications. This includes reminiscence and documentary items, as well as the usual drama, poetry and literature content.

Perks, R. (1990) *Oral history: an annotated bibliography,* London, The British Library.

Perks, R. (1992) 'Oral history resource list 1. Oral history and sound archive resources for history in the national curriculum', *Oral History,* 20, 1, pp.70–4.

Ward, A. (1990) *A manual of sound archive administration,* London, Gower. A guide to sound archives, their development, cataloguing, technology and copyright regulations.

Weerasinghe, L. and Silver, J. (1989) *Directory of recorded sound resources' in the United Kingdom,* London, The British Library.

6   FILM AND VIDEO AS SOURCES

by Angus Calder

When Thomas Alva Edison invented his 'kinetoscope' in 1889 and married it to the new celluloid film developed by George Eastman for his Kodak camera, a fearfully potent force was unleashed. A century later, the moving image, which in the form of the cinema has been an influential force in social life for decades, has achieved a dominant role in domestic life via TV and video. Vast quantities of film have been produced for innumerable purposes, ranging from 'home movies', latterly 'home videos', to Cecil B. De Mille epics and patiently made, expensive TV wildlife series. Now TV ransacks the archives for its own purposes, looking for everything from 'stock' film (a shot, *any* shot, of Tierra del Fuego) to 'rare' footage of, say, berry picking in Strathmore in the 1930s. Meanwhile, TV keeps on creating its own footage. A news item about redundancies in a factory will be tailored to make a point about 'hard times'. But it may contain unique and irreplaceable documentation of the physical features of a dying industry.

Recognizing this, the TV producer Peter Pagnamenta moved, with others, to set up the British Video History Trust (BVHT) in 1987. It is administered by the British Universities Film and Video Council (BUFVC), and supported by the BBC and, from 1992, by Central TV. Its aim is to assist local groups to record, on video, to an acceptable standard, aspects of life around them, through loaning equipment to them and teaching them how to use it. Now that so many people own rather impressive video cameras of their own, the emphasis has shifted towards instruction (as illustrated, for example, in the Open University programme *Shooting video history* (Calder and Lockwood, 1993)).

Projects submitted to a BVHT meeting early in 1992 included:

> *'Chocmas Noshim' – an Orthodox Jewish cultural group wants to record 'personal experiences and how they transmit to future generations traditional Jewish values'.*
> *'Life at the Lamb Inn' – three people want to record life at a pub in Oxfordshire 'which retains the local traditions of a tiny population ... soon to be lost due to the invasion of people from the ever expanding city of Oxford'.*

The aim in each case was to preserve for future generations very specific 'traditions'. Yet it is possible that people in 2042 will be as much, or more, fascinated by incidental details which, in 1992, were 'contemporary' rather than 'traditional', like clothes, hairstyles, and the aspect of changing streets. BVHT preserves all the film shot by its clients on the assumption that future TV programme researchers, and historians, may find anything and everything of use. (Did people really smoke in the streets then, Daddy?)

The moving picture archive is therefore richly diverse. And what film/video is available – perhaps shot by an amateur who just happened to be in the right place – can sometimes provide a unique visual source of information about some situation or event in the past.

But I have to stress that in this context you should not think 'Oh yes, I must check what that film or video archive might have about x' without first considering very carefully what your aim is and whether the time (and money) you might spend fiddling with film in the archive might not be equally well spent with a collection of photographs or plain printed sources.

There is a further complication. Like any source, film doesn't always deliver messages clearly, and it never provides them unambiguously. It is vitally important to bear in mind the key steps in evaluating a primary source emphasized in Chapter 2 (e.g. the question of origin: how and for what purpose was the source created?). Film has always taken money and effort to create. Where enough effort isn't made, the result can be 'illegible'. (I recall a TV producer showing me some virtually useless film of the aftermath of the Blitz in Sheffield: a man had driven through the town recording with his wobbling camera little more than a black and white blur.)

Careful interpretation is needed too, and, as in the case of family photographs (see section 4), some knowledge of the social conventions concerning accepted behaviour and how to film it.

Even the most elementary video of a wedding will surely involve 'posing': it is unlikely to show the best man being sick over the bridesmaid. Some charming 'home movie' footage exists of the exiled Russian composer Rachmaninov frolicking with his family in Switzerland: it wouldn't surprise me if a written document also existed recording that on that day the maestro felt particularly gloomy.

In short, you could spend a lot of time locating and viewing a promising patch of celluloid and get nothing 'solid' from it at all.

Despite all these caveats, don't let me stop you, if your research topic falls within this century, looking into the *Researcher's guide to British film and television collections* (Ballantyne, 1993), published by the British Universities Film and Video Council (BUFVC), and frequently updated. The fourth edition, published in 1993, besides containing valuable technical information, lists nearly 200 archives in the UK. These are subdivided as follows.

National, regional and local collections   Among the national collections are those at the Imperial War Museum and the National Film Archive: an archive with special responsibility for the national collection (not comprehensive). They do not lend prints, and like other archives are likely to charge for viewing. Many local record offices and libraries also hold 'archive footage'. Several archives are based at universities. The East Anglian Film Archive, based in Norwich at the University of East Anglia, is 'particularly strong on farming and rural activities', whereas the North East Film Archive located at the Metropolitan University, Manchester has a 'particular emphasis on industrial, urban life, illustrated in local cinema newsreels, advertising films, professional documentaries and amateur footage'. Kirklees Metropolitan Council hold, in Huddersfield Library, 'over 120 titles, relating to topics of local interest such as transport, industry, historic events, celebrations, etc.'. The Scottish Film Archive, based in Glasgow, specifies that it prefers 'consultations on the premises', but, 'if available, viewing copies may be sent out to enquirers. Some titles available as VHS viewing copies'.

TV companies   The rich archives of the BBC and the independent TV companies exist primarily for internal use, so there are barriers for outsiders wishing to use the material. For example, BBC Wales Film and Videotape Library (Cardiff) 'endeavours to deal with all enquiries but priority is given to BBC personnel ... making material available outside BBC premises can be technically and contractually difficult'.

Newsreel, production and stock shot libraries, etc.   These specialize, on a commercial basis, in locating footage on particular subjects, such as African warthogs or the British countryside. The British Movietones Film Library, for example, specializes in newsreel from 1929 to 1979. (Note also that copies of the issue sheets for British newsreels are held by the Slade History Register, c/o BUFVC.)

Specialized collections   Private individuals, industrial enterprises, museums, educational institutions and so on hold specialized collections. For instance, the Black Watch Archives in Perth could be where you might find a shot of your grandfather in a kilt: 'Applications to the Regimental Secretary.' The Film and Sound Resource Unit at the University of Ulster, Coleraine, finds and collects local archive film.

It may be that the BUFVC *Researcher's guide* will lead you directly to a helpful archive within a hour's journey of your home. But remember that archives have special rules of access, and have to charge realistically for viewing and for printing services.

Some regional archives make video material available commercially. The best source of information about both 'commercial' and non-commercial tapes is BUFVC, 55 Greek Street, London W1V 5LR. The Council will usually assist with enquiries, but it is a subscription-based organization and long or complicated searches may incur charges. Useful guides are *BUFVC distributors* (Grant and Sarmiento, 1990), updated in the form of the *BUFVC handbook for film and television in education 1991/2* (1991). *Videolog* (a fortnightly publication of video materials published in UK) is also useful, while the *British national film and video catalogue* (annual from 1963) lists all the commercial feature film and video distributed in the UK during the year. This listing is arranged by subject and may yield some material of interest to specific projects.

Please consider carefully whether time spent in locating and viewing archive footage will be prudently spent. If film is your special interest, you could work 'the other way round' – if you notice the availability on video of substantial footage on an aspect of the life of a community which interests you, you might consider putting a fairly minute, critical examination of this opportune evidence at the centre of your project.

REFERENCES AND FURTHER READING (SECTION 6)

Ballantyne, J. (ed.) (1993) *Researcher's guide to British film and television collections* (4th edition), London, British Universities Film and Video Council.

BUFVC handbook for film and television in education 1991/2 (1991) London, British Universities Film and Video Council. Includes a select list of distributors (and updates Grant and Sarmiento).

Calder, A. and Lockwood, V. (1993) *Shooting video history*, Milton Keynes, The Open University. A video 'workshop' on video recording for family and community historians.

Grant, C. and Sarmiento, M. (ed.) (1990) *BUFVC distributors: the guide to video and film sources in education and training,* London, British Universities Film and Video Council.

7   QUESTIONS AND INTERVIEWS

by Ruth Finnegan

So far this chapter has focused on sources that are already there. But researchers can also take a more active role, drawing their sources out from people's existing knowledge and experience.

Although asking questions is a basic human activity, their systematic research use has become a technical subject in its own right. So if you plan to use them as a *central* source in a large project, you would do well to consult some of the works listed at the end of this section. However since many family and community historians engage in *some* questioning – and appropriately so – some elementary practical guidelines may be useful. (Chapter 7 expands this in the context of oral history recordings; interviewing techniques are also demonstrated in Bornat and Kirkup, 1993 and Calder and Lockwood, 1993.)

A further reason for considering this topic is that some key written sources used by historians themselves ultimately arise from asking questions. Some understanding of this process is thus essential in evaluating such sources.

7.1   TYPES OF QUESTIONS AND INTERVIEWS

Several forms of interviewing or questioning are widely recognized in social and historical research. The most common context is face-to-face, but questioning also takes place through letters, written questionnaires, the telephone, or electronic mail.

Informal questioning   This form of question is *not* usually deliberately planned for a particular time or place, and can sometimes be quite accidental or opportunistic (e.g. meeting someone on a train; offhand queries over the telephone; long-term personal interaction; even perhaps probing your own memories); it is not always overtly defined as a 'research interview'. It can provide useful information, but this is usually about single and not necessarily commensurate cases (it is usually better, therefore, for a case study rather than for statistical analysis).

Open-ended interviews   These are more deliberate, usually specially set-up occasions, typical of many interviews in the oral history tradition (see Chapter 7, section 2). The speaker is allowed to range freely, with only minimal guidance by the interviewer: the primary object is usually to 'get the person talking'. Open-ended interviews are not necessarily effective for finding out specific facts or collecting statistics, but they are valuable for conveying personal experience and perceptions, and for opening up new dimensions.

Semi-structured interviews   These are more formalized than open-ended interviews, since the interviewer has a clearer agenda of topics or questions. (For examples, see Chapter 7; also Thompson, 1988, pp.296ff.) The interviewee still has some opportunity to shape the conversation, the interviewer's role being to guide discreetly rather than to check conspicuously through a list of topics. Such interviews can provide some scope for the interviewee's individual interpretations and also some comparability with others (see, for example, Jamieson's study (1987) of growing up in early twentieth-century Scotland).

Structured interviews and questionnaires   These are a common source in historical and social research, usually comprising pre-set questions to a substantial number of people, thus allowing comparison, generalization, and, if appropriate to the topic, statistical analysis. The questions are often on a proforma with spaces for the answers (which can be in pre-coded form). The format is often, but not always, multiple-choice, although more open-ended questions are sometimes included. The questions can be asked and their answers recorded by the researcher personally, by an assistant, or via a mailed questionnaire. Structured interviews/questionnaires can gather a great deal of factual, standardizable information in a relatively short time (the census does this, for example). But they have the disadvantage that, however carefully questions are formulated and pre-tested, some misunderstandings are almost unavoidable, and personal variations are squeezed into pre-set categories to give a possibly spurious impression of 'objectivity'.

7.2   ISSUES TO LOOK OUT FOR

Wording of questions   This is always important, above all in structured interviews where there is little opportunity for feedback about misleading or unintelligible wording. It is easy to introduce leading or loaded questions; and some terms are inherently ambiguous or emotive, or likely to carry different meanings to people in different situations, regions or age groups.

Rather than trying to memorize a list of possible mistakes, just be *actively* on the look out for potential misunderstandings, remembering that your own interpretations are neither authoritative nor universal. A quick way of increasing such sensitivity is to assess some actual questions.

_____ *EXERCISE 6.2* _____

(i)   Look at the list below. How many unsatisfactory questions can you spot, and why? (Despite its questionnaire format, many of the faults translate equally well into other forms of questioning.):

1   How old are you?: 1–20 / 20–30 / 30–40 / 40 and over

2   Do you work?: Yes / No

3   In your childhood, was it your mother or someone else who played with you, tended you when you were sick, and encouraged you at school?: Mother / Someone else

4   How important is the community you live in for your work and leisure?: Very / Fairly / Not at all / Don't know

5   What social class do you belong to?

6   When you went away as a domestic servant to your current employers, how impressed were you by their cultured way of life compared with the poor background in which you were brought up?

7

(a)   Do you belong to an ethnic minority group?: Yes / No

(b)   If yes, do you feel solidarity with other members of the group through your traditional ties and shared identity? Yes / No / Don't know

8   What was your mother's name?

(ii)   Having made your own assessment, match up each question with one or more of the (commonly-made) criticisms below:

A   Apparently separate categories not in fact (a) mutually exclusive or (b) comprehensive.

B   Categories not necessarily refined enough for useful analysis.

C   Double (or triple) question: needs *double* (triple) set of answers, not just one as assumed in question.

D   Complex question, *one* part of which is answerable, but includes subsidiary elements (e.g. ascribed reason) which are not necessarily acceptable but hard to challenge.

E   Ambiguous question:

(a)   central terms have a number of different possible meanings and/or are vague,

(b)   technical or academic language, not necessarily intelligible.

F   Apparently simple question which could present problems for some respondents (e.g. those from composite families – step, adopted, separated; or in part-time, home-based work; etc.); and is especially misleading if it demands a simple 'yes/no' answer.

G   Questions weighted towards a particular answer:

(a)   the 'Have you stopped beating your wife?' variety,

(b)   implicitly evaluative language which tends to push one viewpoint,

(c)   pushing respondents into pre-set or absolute categories where their preferred answer might have been 'it depends ... '.

H   Answer very likely to be affected by *who* asks the question, especially if the questioner is in a position of power over the respondent.

Answers/comments p.301

Personal relations during the interview   All questioning involves human interchange, not just objective information transfer. You therefore need to be aware of the expectations of both parties: are certain responses being given just to meet the questioner's perceived expectations; to further some hidden agenda; from tiredness, frustration or excitement; or from considering the likely reactions of other parties (present or not)? Where does power lie as between interviewer and interviewee and how does this affect the interchange? The setting of the interview may also be relevant here (relaxed rather than in a formal studio, say), as is its length – it is hard, especially for older people, to sustain an interview much beyond an hour. (For other comments on the dynamics and conduct of interviews, see Chapter 7, section 2; also Bornat and Kirkup, 1993.)

Memory, fallibility and hindsight   Memories are affected, of course, not only by plain forgetting but also by our own personal and social experience (for further comment see Chapter 7, section 2.2; also Volume 1, Chapter 4, section 3). It is true that what people remember or say they remember may itself be interesting, even if not actually accurate. But people also forget or re-interpret, so it can never just be assumed that because something is 'recorded in interview' it is necessarily 'the truth'.

Representativeness   The necessity for highly sophisticated sampling techniques to select interviewees is sometimes overemphasized. It is also arguably less relevant in questions and interviews relating to family and community history (where local or personal results may be sought rather than national trends) than in large-scale market research or public opinion polling.

Nevertheless, any selection of people for questioning should not be *un*representative of the 'population' to be covered. Asking men in their fifties about their work experiences or their childhood memories, for example, might cover the population of males from that age cohort at a particular place and time, who may also have a particular class status – but it will scarcely be representative of men of other ages or backgrounds, far less of the population as a whole (how about women?). Similarly, answers to questioning in Cardiff would probably not represent the population of southern Ireland; nor are interviews with farmers in Yorkshire necessarily representative of Pakistani settlers in Manchester; nor are interviews with Methodist lay preachers in London representative of Ulster building workers. This is obvious once stated, but it is sometimes forgotten. Taking just one or two examples is fine for starting a case study, or to illustrate local or personal diversities. But going on to generalize or to claim uniformity – as even established historians and social scientists, not just inexperienced researchers, sometimes do – is unjustifiable.

A further discussion of some forms of sampling can be found in Chapter 8, section 6. However, the most important practical prerequisites are applying cautious common sense in order to avoid *un*representative conclusions, and making the imaginative effort to see beyond one's own inevitably narrow horizons.

Recording interviews   There are various possibilities. Tape recording has the advantage of capturing the speaker's own words, and freeing the interviewer's hands and eyes from the task of writing. It can give rise to a more relaxed situation, therefore, once the speaker has got used to the tape recorder's presence. But setting up and testing the machine can cause problems if the interviewer is inexperienced, and transcribing and locating material on tape are both time-consuming activities. Writing more, or less, full notes at the time, preferably amplified and checked immediately afterwards, can be off-putting to the speaker, and gives a more limited and less direct record than tape; but it is convenient, widely used, and effective for certain purposes, giving an easily consulted record. Making no record at all at the time is sometimes unavoidable (particularly with opportunistic questioning), and can still be useful if notes are made soon afterwards, but it does leave more to the (inevitably fallible) memory of the researcher. Whichever form of recording is adopted, it is helpful to write an additional commentary afterwards on significant *un*spoken aspects of the interaction.

Courtesy and ethics   As in other human interactions, the usual courtesies apply, such as trying not to inconvenience or exploit those you are interviewing; expressing appreciation (a letter of thanks afterwards); and not misleading interviewees about the purposes or use of any interview. The issues of ownership and permission for use are also important (see Chapter 7, section 3.2).

EXERCISE 6.3

Of the various sources you have encountered (e.g. those discussed earlier in Part II), can you identify any that arose from questioning or interviewing? If so, are there any implications for their dependability as sources?

Answer/comment p.301

REFERENCES AND FURTHER READING (SECTION 7)

Adams, G R. and Schvaneveldt, J.D. (1985) *Understanding research methods,* New York, London, Longman. See especially Chapter 10.

Bell, J. (1989) *Doing your research project: a guide for first-time researchers in education and social science,* Milton Keynes, Open University Press. See especially Chapters 7 and 8.

Bornat, J. and Kirkup, G. (1993) 'Oral history interviews', audio-cassette 1B in Braham, P. (ed.) *Using the past: audio-cassettes on sources and methods for family and community historians,* Milton Keynes, The Open University.

Briggs, C.L. (1986) *Learning how to ask: a sociolinguistic appraisal of the role of the interview in social science research,* Cambridge, Cambridge University Press.

Calder, A. and Lockwood, V. (1993) *Shooting video history,* Milton Keynes, The Open University. A video 'workshop' on video recording for family and community historians.

Drake, M. (ed.) (1994) *Time, family and community: perspectives on family and community history,* Oxford, Blackwell in association with The Open University (Course Reader).

Jamieson, L. (1987) 'Theories of family development and the experience of being brought up', *Sociology,* 21, pp.591–607. Reprinted in Drake (1994).

Seidman, I.E. (1991) *Interviewing as qualitative research,* New York, Teachers College Press.

Seldon, A. (1988) 'Interviews', in Seldon, A. (ed.) *Contemporary history,* Oxford, Blackwell.

The Open University (1993) DEH313 *Principles of social and educational research,* Unit 12, *Asking questions,* Milton Keynes, The Open University.

Thompson, P. (1988) *The voice of the past: oral history* (2nd edn), Oxford, Oxford University Press. (For examples of outline interview guide, see pp.296ff.)

PART III

METHODS AND TECHNIQUES

✤ ✤ ✤

CHAPTER 7

RECORDING ORAL HISTORY

by Joanna Bornat

In his book *The voice of the past* (1988), Paul Thompson describes the shift towards an open acknowledgement of the value and validity of memories of the past, as a historical source. In response to those who query the validity of memory, he counterposes the subjectivity of documents which, as a product of human action, are just as likely to be affected by bias.

He argues that, although historians made generous use of the oral accounts of eye-witnesses throughout the nineteenth century, their training as decoders of written and printed material meant that they regarded documentary sources as having greater certainty and reliability. During the last twenty years, however, oral history has undergone something of a renaissance amongst certain historians. This chapter considers some of the implications of this and describes the methods by which you can engage in recording oral history yourself.

1 WHAT ORAL HISTORY CHANGES

Oral history makes two major contributions to family and community history. It provides access to areas of the past which may be undocumented; at the same time, it introduces changes in the practice of being a historian. Before I go on to discuss collecting and analysing oral history, I want to look at each of these contributions in turn.

1.1 BEHIND THE DOCUMENTS

In his research into fishing communities in East Anglia, Trevor Lummis discusses several examples where documentary sources are incomplete or lacking when set beside oral sources. For example, he shows that Norfolk and Suffolk fishermen were under-recorded because on census day they were away working from West Country ports (Lummis, 1987, p.76).

Oral evidence can also illuminate aspects of the past which were never documented. In 1990 I interviewed a group of women in Bute Town, Cardiff, for the Open University Course K259 *Community Care*. I wanted them to talk to me about their community between the two world wars, before the coming of the welfare state:

We were very sheltered really because everybody knew everybody so there wasn't much you could get up to without everybody seeing you or reporting you. Every female in the street was your auntie and every man was your uncle … And even when I was given permission to wear lipstick I use to hide my face when I went walking past Auntie Rosie's ... It's hard to keep a secret now. You'd got to be really clever to keep a secret. And I think the very nature of how we are and how we'd been brought up is how to keep a secret. And in a lot of cases you wouldn't want to. There's no need really for it the way we were brought up living. People knew who we were and what you were and where you came from. It was no good trying to be different.

(The Open University, 1993)

Memories of community life tell us something about how families worked as social groups, where power lay, how people experienced the closeness of community and the demands of family life. They are evidence of the subjectivity of experience, as well as the power of the social and economic controls that determined decisions about courtship, marriage, family size and life chances in general.

In 1975 I spent some time interviewing in the Colne Valley area of West Yorkshire. I was interested in finding out about the relationship between home and work and how this determined women's involvement in trade union activities. Existing documentary sources provided little evidence of women's presence as workers or activists. In talking to older women about their lives as millworkers in the first twenty years of this century, it soon became clear to me that family and community played a large part in determining women's wage-earning roles. A Miss Woodcock described how she had no choice but to go into the mill. Her wage was needed as part of the family income. She would have liked to have been a dressmaker, but she couldn't because: 'Well for the simple reason that you had to pay to learn and you'd no wages. You'd no wages. If you learned your trade you'd no wages' (Kirklees Sound Archive, 1975).

She started at the mill on four shillings a week and remained a wool textile worker all her life. Miss Woodcock was typical of a population growing up in a community dominated by one industry. The range of opportunity available to children was determined by individual family composition and history and by an education system which prepared children in her social class for what was seen as appropriate for their future needs as wage earners or mothers. My research indicated that women, though in a majority in the wool textile industry and its main union, were limited in the work and union roles they played by family and gender constraints (Bornat, 1986).

1.2   CHANGES FOR THE HISTORIAN

Oral history changes the practice of being a historian, through its espousal of a method which traditionally has been central to sociology: the collection of personal documents. Ken Plummer (1983) outlines the history of this method, beginning with the early social surveys of Mayhew, Booth and the Webbs (see Chapter 4, section 6), and following on through the impact of Thomas and Znaniecki's study *The Polish peasant* (1958) on the developing sociology of the 1920s and 1930s. He traces the way in which sociologists came to focus on the importance of soliciting accounts of life experience as a means to understanding how the individual makes sense of social situations and broader social forces.

The personal documents which sociologists and historians have drawn on include diaries, autobiographies, letters, and, of course, interviews. Oral historians have learned much about how to set up and conduct interviews from the practice of social scientists. Perhaps less well documented is the effect of the interview on the historian. Becoming an interviewer means being mindful of your interpersonal communication skills, respecting differences in perspective, understanding the influence of inequalities of class, age, gender and race on personal interactions, and acknowledging the interviewee's ownership and rights in the product of the interview, the oral history account.

2 COLLECTING ORAL HISTORY

In this section I shall look at the stages of collecting and analysing oral history. There is only space to cover the bare bones of this process. For a thorough grounding you should consult the references at the end of this chapter (especially Humphries, 1984; Perks, 1992; Thompson, 1988; and also, for further illustration, Bornat and Kirkup, 1993).

2.1 GETTING READY FOR THE INTERVIEWS

To begin with, you should have an outline idea of your research area and whom you might approach to interview.

2.1.1 CHOOSING A THEME

You need to start with some kind of theme. This will help you to frame your questions. Being able to describe your area of interest will also help your interviewees to prepare themselves when you come to talk to them about being interviewed. Your theme may be quite broad; for example, 'growing up', 'first jobs', 'family life between the wars'. Alternatively, it may be quite specific; for instance, it may relate to a particular local industry, an event or a personality.

EXERCISE 7.1

Pause for a while to think about a suitable theme for the ideas you might be interested in researching. Note down some headings which you might use if you were going to explain your topic to someone.

You will find this a helpful activity in preparing yourself for shaping up your research. Thinking your way into the theme helps you to set boundaries to what it is you really want to know about. It also helps you with the preliminary research you will need to do.

2.1.2 PRELIMINARY RESEARCH

Before you start your interviewing you need to spend some time on research into your chosen area or theme. You will need to familiarize yourself with general discussions around your theme: for example, changes in the demography of the family in early twentieth-century Britain, or the history of the coalmining industry. These may raise questions for you which help you to set boundaries for your research. There will be secondary sources, books already published, which will give you the background you need: local histories, autobiographies and biographies of people and personalities connected to the times and issues in which you are interested. There will be the primary sources: newspapers, minute books, photographs, street directories, maps and records. Your local studies library or record office will be a first stop. You will almost certainly find that there are audio and even video tapes which are relevant. Some of the tapes may be transcribed, but in most cases you will find that you have to spend some time listening and making notes.

   If your chosen theme relates to a well-known individual, you may be able to look at documents and accounts which tell you something of that person's life and times. You will be able to turn to *Who's Who*, newspaper reports, existing biographies, the histories of organizations like trade unions, companies, clubs or associations, or perhaps even a collection of personal papers deposited in a library or archive.

Allow yourself plenty of time for your preliminary research, but be prepared to come back to do some more once you have started on your interviews. You will find yourself learning from your interviewees, and new lines of enquiry will continue to suggest themselves as your project develops.

2.1.3   HOW MANY INTERVIEWS?

Depending on the nature of your project, you will need to decide how many interviews to carry out. If you are planning on researching a general theme rather than an individual person's history, then you should be thinking about making your project manageable in terms of your time, your budget and your future life! This means fixing on the number of interviews you think should be completed, at the same time bearing in mind the extent to which you will be able to find a representative number of voices.

Oral historians are not entirely in agreement over the issue of sampling in oral history research. Trevor Lummis is strongly in favour (Lummis, 1987, Chapter 4), arguing for a quota-based approach. He suggests that oral history projects should seek out a range of interviewees who are representative of different types of experience in relation to the topic under investigation. In his research into the fishing industry of East Anglia he spread his sixty interviews over men who had worked in steam drifting, sail trawling and inshore work, and interviewed both rural and urban fishing families.

Lummis argues that his approach helps to minimize the effect of bias in oral history interviewing, which is inevitable given different survival rates and patterns of mobility. Other oral historians, with smaller projects perhaps, or with different objectives, find that the construction of a representative sample is less relevant. For example, in her study of women's experience of wartime, Bridget Macey (1991) interviewed one woman, Mrs Weekes, in the company of her daughter. Her analysis of Mrs Weekes' recall provides insights into issues of separation and meaning. Like Lummis, she is interested in recording information, but she uses the interview data and the experience of carrying out the interview to bring out more interpretive issues. As a result, she is able to describe the hardships of women's wartime lives, in which work was combined with childcare, but she is also able to consider the way in which Mrs Weekes looks back on the war years.

The kind of interview which Bridget Macey carried out provides fascinatingly detailed data, allowing us to contrast public and private accounts of major historical epochs, but it also helps to create an understanding of how an older person remembers and reflects on the past. Mrs Weekes was certainly influenced, as we all are, by current interpretations of the war years, but she was also remembering from the perspective of a long life, as a mother, grandmother and older person.

2.1.4   MAKING CONTACT

Finding your interviewees may take some time. If you are thinking of approaching a group of people who already know each other, like members of a trade union, church or club, then you may find the process of contacting relatively straightforward. The first people you contact may suggest others and things will snowball. If you are embarking on a more obscure topic, or one which is outside your own experience, then you may have to try a variety of ways of contacting possible interviewees. You could try an appeal through local or national newspapers, local radio, magazines, or even an advert in a shop window.

If you are looking for older people to interview, you will need to familiarize yourself with the world of older people and make approaches to local residential homes, day centres, community centres and pensioners' associations. You may find that a social worker, religious leader or health visitor is prepared to help put you in touch with someone to interview.

2.1.5   ASKING THE QUESTIONS

Although it may feel more reassuring to have a carefully worked out list of questions, it isn't always a good idea to work questions out in too much detail beforehand. For one thing it can be offputting to the person you are interviewing if you keep looking down and checking through your papers. A list of detailed questions can also make your interview style rather too rigid. You need to be prepared for the unexpected, for new and interesting ideas, and to be flexible in your responses and questioning.

As an alternative to a schedule of questions, it is useful to have a structure prepared, perhaps jotted down on a single sheet of paper, so that you can remind yourself what you planned and where you have got to. The kind of structure you choose will depend on the subject of the interview. Whatever your focus, a chronological approach is usually most helpful to both you and your interviewee.

EXERCISE 7.2

As part of your preparation for your interview, find someone you can practise on. Ask them to interview you and then try asking them questions. Discuss what you found worked best, and also what felt difficult to ask or to answer. Being interviewed is perhaps the best preparation you can give yourself for an oral history interview.

If you have been interviewed you will probably realize that some questions lead to better responses than others do. You will want to avoid questions which only lead to a one-word answer – 'yes' or 'no'. Instead, think of ways of framing questions which will allow your respondent to answer as fully as possible without you suggesting the answer. Instead of asking, 'Was that an enjoyable experience?', ask, 'How did you feel about that?' Ask people to describe, comment and give their opinions. Make your questions open and uncomplicated.

Plan some basic questions which you can begin with, like name, date and place of birth, who the interviewee's parents were and what they did for a living. The interview will develop its own shape according to whether your topic is particularly specialized or focused on some place, issue or experience.

The following checklist is a slightly altered version of one that appears in an introduction to oral history prepared by Rob Perks (1992):

Family and early life

*Memories of **family background** and **grandparents** and their influence; **parents** – where they came from, their jobs, their characters, could you talk to them, were you close to them; **brothers and sisters** how you got on, what happened to them later; everyday life in **childhood**, describe the **house** you lived in, who did the **housework** and the garden, what were the tasks; describe **food** and mealtimes; parents' attitudes to **discipline**; parents' **ambitions**; children's **games** and family **leisure – sports, pubs, books, etc.; weekends and holidays; weddings** and **funerals**; attitudes to **money**; going **shopping**; describe the **street**, the **town** or **village**, the community, neighbours, who was important, interesting characters; did the family move house and if so where to; local **places of worship** and local **politics**; **education** – school and beyond; important friendships and influences; **youth** – going out to the cinema, or dances, or pubs, or sport; music, bikes, gangs, tensions with your parents; first boy and girlfriends; past attitudes to **sex**; **wartime experience** or national service.*

Work

***First job** – why you chose it, how you got it; describe the **workplace**, what exactly you did, who you worked with; other early jobs and then **main job** – why and how; did you plan a **career**, or find it by chance; **training**; describe a **typical working day** at different stages; chances for* *promotion; important **influences** at work, friends and enemies; professional **organizations** or unions; any part-time work; (for women) did you have any breaks from work; (for both sexes) how did you arrange childcare; social life connected with work; what you are most proud of.*

Later family life and leisure

*Whether single or married; while **single**, key friendships and leisure activities; if married, how you met your **husband or wife**, their background, character, jobs; wedding; setting up **house**, handling money together, dividing **decisions and chores**; **ideal of marriage** – what matters most, if it ended and why; describe **homes**; **children** – childbirth, childcare, ideals of parenting, affection and discipline, hopes and ambitions for children; family and own **leisure** and holidays; radio and television, games and sports, books and hobbies; **friends** and relationships; entertaining; **clubs** and societies; the **community** – neighbours, shopping, religion and politics; **later life** – retirement, any new activities, becoming grandparents; friendships in later life.*

In Thompson (1988, pp.296–306), you will find a more detailed list of 'model questions' which you may find helpful.

2.2   INCLUDING THE INTERVIEWEE IN THE PROCESS

It may seem strange to stress the importance of including the interviewee; after all, the interview isn't possible without one! However, there are good reasons for stressing the role and contribution of the people you will be interviewing. Interviewees may be willing, even keen, to contribute their account to building a picture of the past. They may be pleased and flattered to know that their story is important and will be valued by others. There are ways of making sure that these people, and others who may be less certain about their involvement, feel in control and have ownership in the process of recording and taping their memories.

Oral history making involves people talking about quite personal, sometimes private, aspects of their lives. You may appear as a younger, more powerful and assertive person. The interview may stir up powerful emotions, bring back forgotten incidents and experiences, not all of them pleasant. Before your interview *you must make clear to your interviewees what your purpose is and what you will be doing with the resulting data.* If you are planning to publish any of the interview material, then you will have to let them see this first. We'll be coming back to issues of access and clearance later. The copyright laws safeguard an interviewee's legal rights in terms of ownership and publication. You will need to make clear what this means.

The point of raising issues of ownership and control at this stage is simply to emphasize the rights which the interviewee has in the process. It is your responsibility as an interviewer to ensure that your respondents feel comfortable and reassured, as they begin. They should also be made aware that they can exercise control over the process if they wish.

EXERCISE 7.3

So far I have emphasized the positives. Look back through what you have read so far and try to think of any problematic issues which recording and interpreting oral evidence raise for you. Note down any that occur to you.

Some points you may have noted are:

o   the effect of the power and assertiveness of the interviewer on what interviewees remember, and the possibility that interviewees may try to say what they think is expected of them;

o   the possibility that an interview may stir up emotions, heighten awareness;

o   the extent to which memories can be inaccurate, selective, or suppressed;

o   the fact that you may be interviewing survivors, or a group selected by broader social forces or even by chance;

o   the fact that you can only record the living: a chronological barrier;

o   the extent to which each interview is a separate unique account.

Oral historians debate and discuss these issues as you will find from the literature. But as a well-known Italian oral historian argues: 'the task is to participate in different memories, to share their differences not in any way in an attempt to demonstrate their universality but rather to insist on the diversity and plurality of memory' (Passerini, 1992, p.18).

2.3   USING TECHNOLOGY

Oral history interviewing is usually understood to mean using some kind of machine for recording your dialogue. Taping has many advantages over note-taking. It is immediate and complete. You can hear all the emphases, the inflections, accents and emotions in a taped interview. Taping frees you up to be more personal as you speak. Though the machine may seem intrusive at first, it quickly fades out of sight as interviewer and interviewee both become involved in the interview process.

You can always use the machine to break down initial barriers between you and your interviewee. Discuss the best location for the machine and where you are both going to sit. Let the interviewee help you to set up the machine, test out the tape and play it back; and show them how to use the pause button if there is one so that they can decide what is to be included if they wish to do so.

Getting the right tape recording equipment and knowing how to use it is the most important first step to preserving people's life stories on tape. Your recordings will be unique and irreplaceable historical 'documents' which you may want to use in many different ways after-wards – perhaps on radio or television – so getting the best quality recording which reproduces the original as closely as possible is vital. (Please note that the quotations in the remainder of section 2.3 are all from Perks, 1992, pp.14–16.)

'There are many different makes and modes of portable tape recorders on the market, but only three basic types: digital, reel-to-reel (or open reel) and cassette recorders. The professional high quality digital and reel-to-reel machines, which are used by broadcasters, give the best results and reel-to-reel tapes are generally regarded as better for archiving. But few people can afford these machines. … For more modest budgets it is possible to buy an excellent portable cassette recorder at a very reasonable price which will give you "broadcast quality" results.' Then 'there are the many small personal stereo cassette recorders'. Many of these tend to have 'built-in microphones which give poor results, so it is best to find one with a socket into which an external microphone system can be plugged'. You should also look out for cassette recorders which have noise reduction systems such as Dolby. 'This reduces the levels of tape hiss during recording and in the case of Dbx prevents what is known as "print-through", a slight echoey effect.'

'Nowadays most portable tape recorders will run on batteries and using rechargeable batteries saves a lot of money.' Some recorders have built-in rechargeable batteries which can be plugged into the mains for overnight recharge.

Next you need a good microphone. If you are planning to do 'one-to-one interviews indoors then tie-clip or lapel microphones are best'. These are relatively inexpensive. If your machine 'records in stereo and has two microphone sockets, get two microphones – one for your interviewee and one for yourself. They can be attached discreetly to your clothing and give excellent results. … In many cases people forget they are wearing them completely.' This means the technology is minimized and 'you can concentrate on the interview itself. Lapel mikes operate using small hearing aid type batteries and should last for over 100 hours in normal use.'

Finally, if you want to record a 'group of people talking, say around a table', you should get 'two uni-directional hand-held microphones and place them back to back on stands. Or, if your recorder has only one microphone socket, there are some cheap flat or pressure zone microphones on the market which give adequate results.'

'Generally the more you spend the better the recording equipment you are likely to get.' It is worth investing in good equipment or 'looking out for second-hand or reconditioned tape recorders at reputable dealers'. You can often buy them for half their original price. Alternatively you may be able to borrow some from a local history group, a library or a museum.

When it comes to tape, the National Sound Archive recommend using 'Zonal or Ampex standard or long-play tape if you are using a reel-to-reel recorder and recording at a fast speed – either 7.5 or 3.75 inches per second (ips). Cassette recorders all run at the same speed and have the advantage of using cassette tapes which are compact, cheap and easy to load. They have the disadvantage that you cannot edit them without copying (dubbing) them on to reel-to-reel tape.' When buying cassettes go for a reputable make and preferably use C60s which last for one hour (thirty minutes per side). 'It is not necessary to buy the more expensive chromium or metal type cassette, the ordinary ferric (FE) type is perfectly adequate for oral history.' Whatever tape you buy, remember to 'set the controls on your recorder to match the type of tape you are using. If the original recording was carried out using Dolby B then set the machine to Dolby B when playing it back.'

'Once you have got all your equipment it is a good idea to familiarize yourself with how it all works, so that while you are interviewing someone the technology is kept to a minimum, leaving you to concentrate on the person not the machine. Read the instruction book carefully' and try out recording with someone else. 'This should iron out any technical problems and give you confidence both in using the equipment and in asking questions.'

2.4 THE INTERVIEW

You have made your contact, arranged a mutually convenient time and place, done your research, prepared your questions, tested your recording equipment. You are ready for your interview.

An interview is a social relationship, one that is usually played out on the territory of the person you are interviewing. You are their guest almost always, so you will want to be pleasant, friendly and relaxed. At the same time you will have needs, as an interviewer, which will require careful negotiation.

If you are interested in one particular person's memories you may want to make this a one-to-one experience. Try to make it clear beforehand that you prefer to be alone with your interviewee. A third person present may be a distraction or discourage someone from talking as freely as either of you would wish. Of course there are times when other people present can be a help, particularly if they end up sparking off new memories.

You will want to make sure that the room you record in is comfortable and quiet. Avoid a room with a lot of hard surfaces like a kitchen, otherwise your voices will be distorted by echo. Try for a room which is away from a busy main road. Then, check for loud ticking clocks, noisy budgerigars, automatic switches or roaring fires. If you can minimize the contributions of all these sources of noise, so much the better, but it may not be possible. After all, you are almost certainly going to be recording in someone's home and your aim is to find a relaxed and comforting environment, one where your interviewee feels at ease and in control.

Your interviewee should choose the chair they feel most comfortable in and you should aim to draw up to it so that you are as close as possible, with the recording equipment nearby. While you are arranging the tape-recorder and the microphone, keep up conversation, be friendly and encouraging. Place the microphone on something near to you both which is soft, like a cushion or an upholstered stool. A hard surface like a table will give you poor sound quality. A clip-on microphone should be about 23 cm. (9 in.) from someone's mouth. If it makes you both feel easier, let the interviewee clip it on to their own clothing. Arrange the recording equipment so that you can read any dials, but ensure that it is not placed intrusively between you. Test your sound levels before you begin properly, by asking something informal like, 'What did you have for breakfast?'; then listen, rewind and start your interview.

While you are interviewing, keep the questions short. Remember the aim is to hear someone else talk, not you. Try not to interrupt or talk over the other person and if there is a silence, don't worry. Sometimes people need time to think about what they are going to say. Just let the tape run on while they collect themselves. It's important that you let the interviewee know how valuable you think their memories are, so make sure you listen carefully and maintain eye contact. Be encouraging by nodding and smiling, where appropriate, and avoid saying 'yes yes' or 'really' just to keep things going.

You should avoid contradicting or giving your opinion, unless you are asked, and you should try to be tolerant of ideas and world views which you may find difficult to accept.

As you complete each tape, make sure that you label it immediately with the name of the interviewee and the day's date. There are two small safety lugs on the back edge of a cassette tape; break these off straightaway to protect the tape from being erased or over-recorded.

Make sure that your interviewees have your address and phone number so they can contact you afterwards. You may well have made an impact on their life which they may feel like reflecting on and talking about. Write to thank all interviewees for their time and remind them what their interview is contributing and how much you value their tape. Ultimately you will be sending them a copy of their tape and the transcription if you make one.

When you are back at home, copy your tape if you can; many hi-fi systems now have twin cassette decks. Make yourself an interview summary sheet (Table 7.1 shows an example of an interview sheet used by the British Library National Sound Archive). Your own version of an interview summary sheet should include a section for a summary of the main points covered in the interview (if you wish, you can use the reverse side of the sheet or a separate sheet for this

Table 7.1 Example of an interview summary sheet

Interview summary sheet	
Ref No: Collection Title:	Playback No:
Interviewee's Surname: Interviewee's Forenames: Date of Birth:	Title: Sex:
Date(s) of Recording: Location of Interview: Name of Interviewer: Type of Recorder: Total Number of Tapes: Mono or Stereo: Noise Reduction:	 Type of Tape: Speed: Original or Copy:
Additional Material:	
Copyright/Clearance:	
Interviewer's Comments:	

Source: adapted from an interview sheet used by the British Library National Sound Archive

purpose). Filling in the sheet means that you keep basic information about the tape and your interviewee, as well as a summary of the main topics covered in the interview. Finally, make sure your original tapes and the copies are stored securely and *separately* under cool, dry and dust-free conditions.

3   INTERPRETATION AND ANALYSIS

Your tapes contain unique recordings of individual experience, speech characteristics, imagery, dialect forms and cultural and historical references. They are a rich and vivid record.

3.1   TRANSCRIPTION AND INTERPRETATION

Transcribing tapes into a written form is essential if you are going to use them for research or for displays or publications. Of course, writing and speaking are not the same. We use different codes and grammatical forms for each. And however carefully you transcribe your tapes you will inevitably find inaccuracies as you check back. Transcription is always an inexact process.

Transcription means transferring into hand- or type-written form as much as you can of what you have recorded. Opinions differ as to whether you should record every hesitation, emphasis and repetition. But you should realize that you need to allow plenty of time. Even with a word processor and a recording machine activated by a remote control foot pedal, you will find that an hour of tape takes approximately five hours to transcribe. You can, however, save time by transcribing sections of your tapes, selecting these as you proceed.

The advantage of transcription is that you get to know the contents of the tapes really well. This means that when you come to select themes, look out for particular details and make comparisons, you are already familiar with the structure and pace of the interview, and can build these sensibly into your final analysis. Transcribing also helps you to evaluate your questioning style. Seeing an interview laid out as text, you can identify which questions are more sensitive to the needs of the interviewer and interviewee than others, and take account of this in your interpretation.

With your tapes transcribed, you can add information to your interview summary sheets, perhaps listing key words, subjects, and place names mentioned. Ultimately you could use such lists to form a computer database, storing and accessing the information through a coding system.

3.2   OUTCOMES

Your taped material isn't simply data of a particular type; it is someone's life experience. Interviewees have ownership in the material on tape and could restrict what you do with it afterwards. This is important for many interviewees who may be keen to see their account recognized as having value and worth in their community. It is also important for people who, while happy to be interviewed, do not want their account to be published. There are ethical issues to be aware of here.

One obvious way of making people's rights clear is by means of a recording consent form, which you will need to make for yourself (a sample form is shown in Table 7.2). You should use such a form whether or not you intend making public use of the material you have recorded. The form gives your interviewee an opportunity to stipulate whether or not they wish to place restrictions on how the interview is used (e.g. only after a number of years, or not for commercial purposes).

You need to be aware of your legal responsibilities too. The 1988 Copyright, Designs and Patents Act stipulates that copyright rests with the interviewee. So if you want to use any material you have recorded for broadcasting, publication or a public lecture, then you should request the copyright holder either to give you explicit permission to use it for that purpose (see Table 7.2), or, alternatively, to assign copyright to you or to your organization (see Table 7.3). If copyright is not assigned, then the material is not only owned by the individual, but will be passed on as part of their estate when they die. Remember you are only asking them to assign rights over that particular interview. You aren't preventing them from talking to anyone else about the same things.

There are a couple of exceptions to the Act. 'Fair dealing' provides for limited extracts from an interview to be used for purposes of criticism or review. In addition, it is possible to look at material in an archive for limited private research use (unless the owner has laid restrictions on access – see Table 7.3), provided you don't publish anything from it afterwards.

Table 7.2 Sample recording consent form

Recording consent form

Date(s) and location(s) of recording: ....

Details of contribution: ....
I hereby consent to the recording of my contribution. It may be used, in whole or in part, in any or all of the following ways *(NB please delete and initial any uses which you wish to exclude)*:

1 for purposes of education and research

2 in an edited, or abridged form

3 for public use or playback to an audience

4 broadcasting

5 publication

Please indicate any additional restriction which you wish to place on the use of your contribution:

....

Signed: .... Name: ....

Date: .... Address: ....

Table 7.3 Sample copyright assignment form

Copyright assignment form

I hereby assign the copyright in my contribution to ....
for public use in research, publication, education, lectures, local or national sound archives, or broadcasting.
If you wish to restrict access to your contribution for a period (up to 30 years), please specify here:

....

Signed: .... Date:...

Address: ....

You should consider seriously the possibility of offering your recordings to a local studies collection and/or the British Library National Sound Archive so that others can make use of them. (The address of the National Sound Archive is 29 Exhibition Road, London, SW7 2AS.) You will need to attach the necessary documentation (brief summary of contents and a copy of your interview sheet, as in Table 7.1). Archives are likely to wish copyright to be assigned to them (see Table 7.3).

Oral history evidence has been used in a wide variety of forms and in different settings. Academic publications are one outcome, but, in addition, booklets, tape/slide programmes, museum displays, drama, touring exhibitions, edited sound tapes, video, family history collections have all made use of oral history. Older people have contributed to the National Curriculum, to radio, to museum conservation, to work in hospital and residential care, and to local, county and national archives, such as the National Sound Archive in London.

With our recording machines and our multi-media uses of oral history we have moved a long way during the present century. But perhaps we start off with the same interests as earlier generations of oral historians: uncovering hidden history and valuing the memories of members of our families and communities.

REFERENCES

Bornat, J. (1986) '"What about that lass of yours being in the union?" Textile workers and their union in Yorkshire, 1888–1922', in Davidoff, L. and Westover, B. (eds) *Our work, our lives, our words*, London, Macmillan.

Bornat, J. and Kirkup, G. (1993) 'Oral history interviews', audio-cassette 1B in Braham, P. (ed.) *Using the past: audio-cassettes on sources and methods for family and community historians*, Milton Keynes, The Open University.

Humphries, S. (1984) *The handbook of oral history: recording life stories*, London, Inter-Action Inprint.

Kirklees Sound Archive (1975) recording deposited in Kirklees Sound Archive.

Lummis, T. (1987) *Listening to history: authenticity of oral evidence*, Hutchinson, London.

Macey, B. (1991) 'Social dynamics of oral history making: women's experience of wartime', *Oral History*, 19, 2, Autumn, pp.42–8.

Passerini, L. (1992) (ed.) *Memory and totalitarianism*, International Yearbook of Oral History, Volume 1, Oxford, Oxford University Press.

Perks, R. (1992) *Talking about the past: oral history*, The Historical Association in association with the Oral History Society.

Plummer, K. (1983) *Documents of life: an introduction to the problems and literature of a humanistic method*, London, Allen & Unwin.

The Open University (1993) K259 *Community Care*, audio-cassette 2, side 2: *Oral History, Band A: Bute Town*, Milton Keynes, The Open University.

Thomas, W.I. and Znaniecki, F. (1958) *The Polish peasant in Europe and America*, New York, Dover Publications (first published 1918–20).

Thompson, P. (1988) *The voice of the past: oral history* (2nd edn), Oxford, Oxford University Press.

CHAPTER 8

QUANTITATIVE TECHNIQUES

by Michael Drake (Introduction, sections 1–6 and 10), Deirdre Mageean and W.T.R. Pryce (section 7), and Roy Lewis (sections 8 and 9)

Before turning to the next chapter – which I'm sure many of you are tempted to do immediately! – can I invite you to linger, at least for a page or two? I make this plea because I know that many historians are put off by anything to do with numbers, statistics, quantitative methods, call them what you will. However, there are some historians who believe that 'if you can't count it, then it's not worth knowing'. Here I take an approach somewhere between the two. To begin with I want to show that numeracy in history is not so unusual as you might suppose. Then I want to present a handful of techniques, at least some of which I believe you will find useful. This will be neither a comprehensive nor a high-level treatment: lack of space forbids the former, and my own competence the latter. At the end of the chapter, however, you will find references to books and articles which will carry you further – as will Chapter 9.

1 STATISTICS IN HISTORY: THE CASE FOR AND AGAINST

The word 'statistics', like 'history', has a double meaning. On the one hand statistics are numbers that describe certain phenomena, e.g. prices, football results, imports and exports. On the other hand they are methods used to collect, describe and analyse such numbers. Again, as with history, the distinction is important, for in order to determine the value of statistics as numbers, we need to know something of statistics as methods.

All of us use statistics in the first of these two senses principally because they make things more precise and so enhance meaning. 'Ireland decisively beaten at Twickenham' makes a good headline, but no rugby enthusiast will rest until the precise score is ascertained. Nevertheless all of us, both in everyday speech and when writing history, do tend to draw a great deal on words which are *implicitly* quantitative rather than provide numbers, which are, of course, *explicitly* quantitative. It has been said that implicit measurement is 'usually … crude, uncontrolled and subject to serious misunderstanding and error' (Dollar and Jensen, 1970, p.8). By keeping an eye open for implicit quantification in your reading you will be able to decide whether those strictures are justified.

EXERCISE 8.1

Turn to Chapter 4 and read the first paragraph of the section on poll books and electoral registers (section 2). Pick out the words indicating *implicit* quantification. How, by replacing these with statements of explicit quantification – numbers, in other words – would the passage be improved?

Comments p.301.

Apart from giving precision to what we write, statistics can provide several other services. For instance, they can guide us to the questions we might ask of historical data. If we add up the burials in a parish register and discover a sharp increase in, say, July and August, we would then focus our attention on those causes of death that were especially prevalent in the summer. If when analysing a census enumerator's book (CEB) we find that 75 per cent of households consist of parents and their children only, we would seek out factors that could have brought about precisely this form of household structure.

A second reason for using statistics is that they help us express our ideas on the relations between sets of objects, i.e. correlation. A third justification for statistics is that they help us in our search for pattern and form. This is a goal we often set ourselves in family and community history. The range is wide: from establishing patterns on the ground (e.g. distribution of population, industries, settlements; migration flows) and family or household configurations, to examining the form taken by a picture or interview. Finally, statistics facilitate our search for abstraction. Some historians of the family and community do seek to generalize – to produce general propositions or theories that will explain phenomena in other situations and circumstances. Often this requires considerable amounts of empirical data expressed and manipulated numerically. Examples are to be found in demography (Malthusian theory, in its later development; the theory of the demographic transition); in historical geography (central place theory or theories of urban segregation); and in family and household formation (where such abstractions as the family cycle or the life cycle come into play).

There are drawbacks to statistical methods. The most obvious is that they require an effort to learn them, practice in order to gain proficiency in applying them, and skill in their correct use. Also, statistical techniques usually give us approximations, averages or probabilities. The apparent exactness of the numbers produced can easily lull us into a false sense of security: an average, as we shall see, can be quite meaningless. Furthermore, the products of statistical techniques are only as good as the material on which they rest. Source criticism has to be applied as rigorously as to literary sources (for the questions to be asked see Chapter 2). Finally, statistics do create problems of communication. If a piece of work is – to borrow the late Professor F.J. Fisher's comment on certain economic histories of the nineteenth century – 'full of every sort of figure except the human' (Harte, 1971, p.186) you should not be surprised if your readers are put off.

2   DESCRIBING DATA

Before the historian can manipulate the available quantitative data statistically, it is necessary to describe and categorize the types of data. Three categories are normally used:

1   *Nominal data* are, as the expression suggests, data categorized by their *name*. Men, women, teachers, carpenters, doctors, plumbers, shop assistants, makes of cars and types of housing: all are examples of nominal data. Statistically there is not much one can do with this kind of data, except to count it, i.e. so many men, so many women; 10 teachers, 15 carpenters, 42 shop assistants, so many Rovers, so many Hondas, etc. This can be informative: for example, the data can show the ratio of men to women in different jobs, and how this varies regionally or over time.

2   *Ordinal data* are a form of nominal data that can be ranked in some way. For instance, one could rank different occupations from those with the highest to those with the lowest social prestige. Preferences for food, leisure activities, etc. can be ranked in the same way.

3   *Interval* and *ratio data* are so named because they use standard units of measurement. The terms are often used interchangeably, though, in so far as you will come across either, *interval* is

the more commonly used term. This is rather paradoxical since most of the data you will actually come across will be ratio data. The distinction lies in the fact that you can add or subtract interval data, but not multiply or divide them. Temperatures are an example of interval data because, though standard units of measurement are used, they are not equidistant. In other words, $10°C$ is not twice as warm as $5°C$. Age, measured in years, months, etc. is ratio data because someone aged 4 years is twice as old as someone aged 2 years and half the age of someone aged 8.

The importance of this categorization is that the kind of statistical analysis you can carry out will depend upon whether the data at your disposal are nominative, ordinal or interval/ratio.

Schema A: Examples of types of data

Nominal: occupation

Ordinal: state of health

Interval: temperature in Celsius or Fahrenheit

Ratio: age

_____ *EXERCISE 8.2* _____

The above description is somewhat skeletal. To put flesh on it let us see if you can recognize the different types of data. Figure 8.1 shows a page from the Aylesbury Prison register of 1872. You will see that quite a lot of information is gathered about the prisoner, e.g. name, place of last residence, trade or occupation. Categorize the data given into nominal, ordinal, and interval/ratio data.

Answer/comments p.302.

---

3 AVERAGES

If our study concerned James Dewley only, we wouldn't need any of the skills being described here. But when we want to write about lots of James Dewleys who have one or more of his characteristics, i.e. prisoner, servant, age, physical characteristics, birthplace, education, etc. – in other words when we want to deal with *groups* of people – then we need some way of encapsulating, in one or two figures, their principal characteristics. One way of doing this is to produce an *average*, a measure of central tendency. When most of us use the word 'average', we are talking about the *mean*, and it is interval data that constitute the material for the calculation. For example, if we say 'the average age of the class was 15 years and 3 months', then we have added together the ages of all the members of the class and divided this total by the number of members. This is very useful if we wish to compare groups of different sizes in order to determine, say, the average age at marriage.

But what can we do with nominal and ordinal data? For the former we use the *mode,* i.e. the most frequently occurring observation.

_____ *EXERCISE 8.3* _____

Look at Table 8.1. What is the modal occupation shown in the table?

Answer/comment p.302.

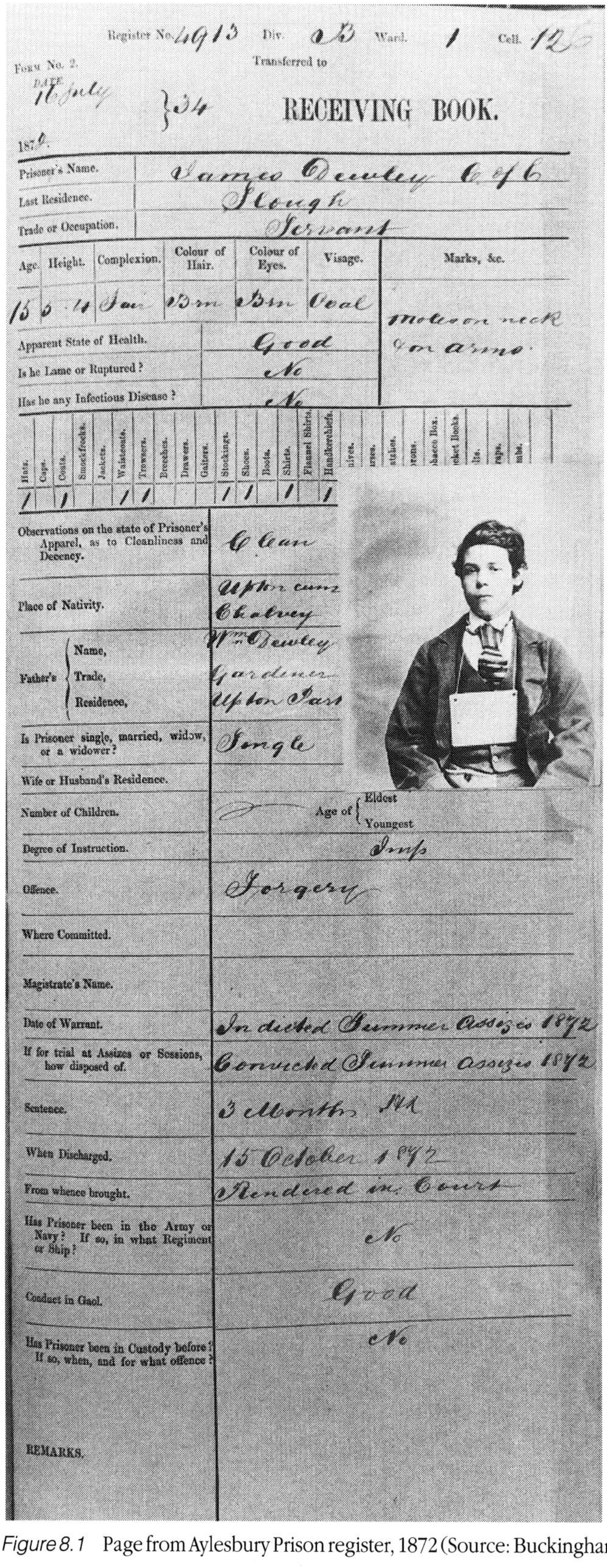

Register No. 4913 Div. B Ward. 1 Cell. 12

Transferred to

Form No. 2.

DATE 16 July } 34

RECEIVING BOOK.

1872.

Prisoner's Name.	James Dewley C of C
Last Residence.	Slough
Trade or Occupation.	Servant

Age.	Height.	Complexion.	Colour of Hair.	Colour of Eyes.	Visage.	Marks, &c.
15	5 · 4	Fair	Brn	Brn	Oval	moles on neck & on arms

Apparent State of Health.	Good
Is he Lame or Ruptured?	No
Has he any Infectious Disease?	No

Hats.	Caps.	Coats.	Smockfrocks.	Jackets.	Waistcoats.	Trowsers.	Breeches.	Drawers.	Gaiters.	Stockings.	Shoes.	Boots.	Shirts.	Flannel Shirts.	Handkerchiefs.
1		1			1	1				1	1		1		1

Observations on the state of Prisoner's Apparel, as to Cleanliness and Decency.	Clean
Place of Nativity.	Upton cum Chalvey
Father's Name,	Wm Dewley
Father's Trade,	Gardener
Father's Residence,	Upton Park
Is Prisoner single, married, widow, or a widower?	Single
Wife or Husband's Residence.	
Number of Children.	— Age of { Eldest / Youngest
Degree of Instruction.	Imp
Offence.	Forgery
Where Committed.	
Magistrate's Name.	
Date of Warrant.	Indicted Summer Assizes 1872
If for trial at Assizes or Sessions, how disposed of.	Convicted Summer Assizes 1872
Sentence.	3 Months HL
When Discharged.	15 October 1872
From whence brought.	Rendered in Court
Has Prisoner been in the Army or Navy? If so, in what Regiment or Ship?	No
Conduct in Gaol.	Good
Has Prisoner been in Custody before? If so, when, and for what offence?	No
REMARKS.	

Figure 8.1 Page from Aylesbury Prison register, 1872 (Source: Buckinghamshire County Record Office)

Table 8.1 Social classification of the thirty electors who supported Whateley's candidature (Bath election, 1855) and whose names began with the letter 'A'

Class		Number
I	Gentleman (10); Clergyman (2); Captain (1); General (1)	14
II	—	—
III	Confectioner (1); Florist (1); Shirtmaker (1); Builder (1); Tailor (1); Lodging house keeper (2); Pawnbroker (1); Sexton (1); Cabinet maker (1); Wine merchant (1); Baker (1); Livery stable keeper (1); Draper's assistant (1); Grocer (1)	15
IV	Gardener (1)	1
V	—	—
	Total	30

Source: *Bath poll book for 1855*, Bath Central Library

You will have noticed that in Table 8.1 I have arranged the voters in terms of their social class. I did this using a classification by occupation devised by Professor Alan Armstrong (see Chapter 3, section 2.1). In other words I have put the voters in a certain order – created, therefore, ordinal data. To get an average for this we use the *median*. This is the mid point of a distribution, i.e. the score of the middle case in a distribution. Here we have five social classes, ranked from the top (I) of the social scale to the bottom (V) with the median occupation in Class III – if only just. What this means is that whereas *only* the mode can be used on nominal data, both the mode and the median can be used on ordinal data. With interval data we can use the mode, the median and the mean, but not indiscriminately! This is because our data may well be distributed asymmetrically, i.e. skewed in one direction or another. Looking at Table 8.2, the rateable values of the properties enfranchising those electors who voted for Whateley are distributed more or less symmetrically, with the higher values (six of £80 or more) being counterbalanced by the lower ones (six of £20 or less). Hence the mode, median and mean are about the same. However, if the sample had shown two properties rated at £200 each, in place of two rated at £20 each, the mean would have been £66, the median £55, whilst the mode would have remained the same at £50. This is an example of how a small number of rogue or atypical values can have a disproportionate impact on the mean, and it shows why, in this case, the median gives us a better idea of the distribution's central value. Other examples of asymmetrical distributions are incomes, household or family size, age at death, and age at marriage.

Table 8.2 Rateable values of the properties enfranchising the thirty electors voting for Whateley whose surnames began with the letter 'A' (rounded to the nearest £10)

Rateable value (£)					
50	80	100	20	50	70
30	20	70	80	30	20
60	110	50	50	50	90
60	20	20	140	40	50
30	60	10	40	60	60

Source: *Bath poll book for 1855*, Bath Central Library

EXERCISE 8.4

What are (a) the modal, (b) the median and (c) the mean rateable values of the properties listed in Table 8.2?

Answers/comments p.302.

Figure 8.2 gives an idealized indication of the relationship between the three measures, depending upon the nature of the distribution (i.e. whether symmetrical or asymmetrical).

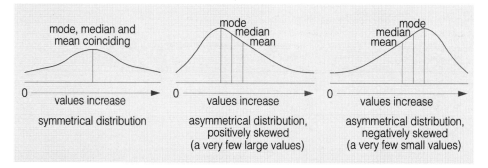

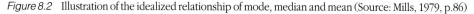

Figure 8.2 Illustration of the idealized relationship of mode, median and mean (Source: Mills, 1979, p.86)

Schema B: Averages

Mean = arithmetical average

Mode = the most frequently occurring observation

Median = the mid point in a ranked set of observations

4   THE SPREAD: OF WHICH 'MIDDLE AGED' IS AN EXAMPLE

It is often useful to say something about the dispersion of a distribution: in other words, to what extent it is bunched or spread around the middle. One way of doing this is simplicity itself: just take the highest and lowest value to give you the *range*.

EXERCISE 8.5

What is the range of the data given in Table 8.2?
Answer/comment p.302.

The answer to Exercise 8.5 is not particularly exciting! However, if I were to say that, in comparing the range of the rateable values of property enfranchising the supporters of three candidates at the election, I found that for one it was £10–£40, for another £10–£140 and for the third £80–£180, one might admit (grudgingly perhaps?) that here was something worth looking into. For if we assume that the rateable values tell us something about the respective wealth of the various electors, it would appear that the differences in the range suggest that the candidates found their support among different sectors of the electorate.

The problem with the range is that it can be dramatically affected by one outlier, i.e. a particularly high or low value. In Table 8.2 the elector with property rated at £140 is one such; so, to a lesser extent, are those rated at £90, £100 and £110. To overcome this problem it is usual to use a measure known as the *standard deviation*. Unlike the range, but like the mean, this takes into account *all* the values in the distribution, not just the two extreme ones. Given a normal distribution, we would expect about two-thirds of the values to be within ± 1 standard deviation from the mean; 95 per cent within ± 2 standard deviations; and 99 per cent within ± 3. The calculation of this measure is easy but tedious. Fortunately now, as with most of the calculations described in this chapter, pocket calculators, and increasingly pocket computers, take the grind out of doing them. Table 8.3 provides a guide to the calculation. I have tried to make this and the other guides as 'user-friendly' as possible. Don't be put off by the formulae and the Greek letters; you will soon get used to them. Because these measures encapsulate so much information in such a succinct manner, I hope you'll agree with me that the effort required to calculate them is worthwhile.

Table 8.3 The standard deviation: a guide to calculation

Stage	In symbols	In words	Examples
	S	The standard deviation for …	Rateable value of property held by eight Tite voters, Bath constituency
	$S = \sqrt{\dfrac{\Sigma(X-\bar{X})^2}{N}}$ $= \sqrt{\dfrac{N\Sigma X^2 - (\Sigma X)^2}{N}}$		William Abraham £40 Henry Adams £20 Thomas Adams £20 Hilar Aicher £20 Charles Ainsworth £30 James Aldous £40 Charles Allen £10 Francis Thomas Allen £20
A	X^2	Square each of the observations of rateable value of property held by Tite voters. That is, multiply each number by itself	$40 \times 40 = 1{,}600$ $20 \times 20 = 400$ $20 \times 20 = 400$ $20 \times 20 = 400$ $30 \times 30 = 900$ $40 \times 40 = 1{,}600$ $10 \times 10 = 100$ $20 \times 20 = 400$
B	ΣX^2	Add up or sum the squared values resulting from stage A. Σ is the Greek letter *sigma*, meaning 'the sum of …'	$1{,}600 + 400 + 400 + 400 + 900 +$ $1{,}600 + 100 + 400 = 5{,}800$
C	$N\Sigma X^2$	Multiply the number resulting from stage B by the total number of observations. The symbol used for this is 'N'. As we are looking at the rateable values of eight voters, our $N = 8$.	$8 \times 5{,}800 = 46{,}400$
D	ΣX	Sum the eight observations	$40 + 20 + 20 + 20 + 30 + 40 + 10 +$ $20 = 200$
E	$(\Sigma X)^2$	Square the number resulting from stage D	$(200)^2 = 200 \times 200 = 40{,}000$
F	$N\Sigma X^2 - (\Sigma X)^2$	We now subtract the number obtained in stage E($(\Sigma X)^2 =$ 40,000) from the number obtained at stage C ($N\Sigma X^2 =$ 46,400)	$46{,}400 - 40{,}000 = 6{,}400$
G	$\sqrt{N\Sigma X^2 - (\Sigma X)^2}$	Take the square root of the number resulting from stage F	
H	$\sqrt{\dfrac{N\Sigma X^2 - (\Sigma X)^2}{N}}$	Finally divide the result of stage G by the number of observations (N)	

The worked-out example in Table 8.3 shows that the standard deviation of the rateable values enfranchising this set of voters is £10. With a mean of £25 and a standard deviation of £10, some two-thirds of the values should lie between £15 and £35, i.e. within an interval of one standard deviation above and one below the mean.

_____ *EXERCISE 8.6* _____

Look at Table 8.4. Find (a) the standard deviation and (b) the mean of the distribution of rateable values.

Answers/comments p.302.

Table 8.4   The names of the first eight electors casting their votes for Whateley, in the *Bath poll book for 1855,* together with the rateable values of the properties that enfranchised them

Name	Rateable value (£)
William Abbott	50
George Abraham	30
Edward H. Acton	60
George Adams	60
Robert Alexander	30
William Alexander	80
John Allen	20
William Proctor Anderdon	110

5   RATES AND RATIOS

The percentage is perhaps the rate that most people are familiar with. Again, turning absolute numbers into percentages allows them to be compared. To demonstrate this let us go back to Table 8.2. Even with the relatively small number of cases given there, it is not easy to grasp their meaning. The mean, mode, median and standard deviation go some way. The percentage gives us an additional insight.

_____ *EXERCISE 8.7* _____

In Table 8.5 we see that one out of the thirty Whateley voters was enfranchised by property worth a value of £10. To express this as a percentage we do the following: $1 \div 30 \times 100 = 0.033 \times 100 = 3.3\%$. Five voters were enfranchised by property with a value of £20. Expressed as a percentage of the total number of voters this is $5 \div 30 \times 100 = 0.166 \times 100 = 16.7\%$. Note that in the former case I 'rounded down' from 3.33... to 3.3, as the last figure was less than 5; in the latter I rounded up to 16.7, because the last figure of 6 was more than 5. Now complete the table and comment on your findings.

Answers/comments p.303.

Table 8.5 Percentage distribution of rateable values of properties enfranchising the thirty Whateley voters whose surnames began with the letter 'A' (rounded to the nearest £10)

Rateable value (£)	Number of voters	Percentage of voters
10	1	3.3
20	5	16.7
30	3	
40	2	
50	6	
60	5	
70	2	
80	2	
90	1	
100+	3	
	30	

In population studies one often comes across crude rates – for example of births, deaths and marriages. To calculate these we take the number of births (deaths or marriages) occurring over a year, divide this by the population producing them and multiply by 1,000. Thus, if a population of 10,000 produces 200 births in the course of a year, the crude birth rate will be $200 \div 10,000 \times 1,000$ = 20 births per 1,000 *mean* population. Note the term *mean*. Though this is conventionally not included in the expression of a crude rate, it reminds us that we are relating the number of births (deaths or marriages) to the average population, usually taken as that at the mid point of the year for which the rate is being calculated. The rates described here are termed *crude* because the events (births, marriages, etc.) are related to the entire population, though it is only a part of that population that contributes to the majority of the events, e.g. women of child-bearing age in the case of births, the very young and the old in the case of deaths.

Demographers have devised other, more refined measures. For example, the *total fertility rate* (TFR) relates the number of births to the number of women in each group within the child-bearing period (see Table 8.6).

Table 8.6 The total fertility rate (TFR): a guide to calculation

(1) Women aged (years)	(2) Births per 1,000 women per year in each age group	(3) Births per woman per year in each group
15–19	15	0.0150
20–24	150	0.1500
25–29	250	0.2500
30–34	180	0.1800
35–39	110	0.1100
40–44	40	0.0400
45–49	25	0.0250
	770	$0.7700 \times 5 = 3.850$

The total arrived at in column 3 is multiplied by five because it is assumed that each woman spends five years in the age groups represented in column 1 and is, therefore, exposed five times to this particular level of fertility. The resulting number (3.85) indicates the *mean* number of children each woman in this population would have, were the fertility rate in each age group to remain the same throughout her fertile period.

Demographers use the TFR to calculate the *gross reproduction rate* (GRR), which is the TFR with respect to female births. To calculate this quickly, multiply the TFR by 0.49 (not by 0.5 as there are slightly fewer female births than male births). If the resulting figure is above one, the population is *possibly* able to reproduce itself; if below, it cannot. The word *possibly* is used here because the GRR does not take account of the fact that not all women entering the fertile age group will live all the way through it. The *net reproduction rate* (NRR) makes allowances for this (see Table 8.7).

Table 8.7 The net reproduction rate (NRR): a guide to calculation

(1) Women aged (years)	(2) Births per woman per year	(3) Female births per woman per year	(4) Estimated average number of years per woman	(5) Expected female births per woman (3) × (4)
15–19	0.0150	0.0074	4.2	0.0311
20–24	0.1500	0.0735	4.1	0.3014
25–29	0.2500	0.1225	4.0	0.4900
30–34	0.1800	0.0882	3.8	0.3352
35–39	0.1100	0.0539	3.7	0.1994
40–44	0.0400	0.0196	3.6	0.0706
45–49	0.0250	0.0123	3.5	0.0431
	0.7700	0.3774		1.4708

NRR = 1.4708

Even the NRR does not solve all the problems, since the calculation assumes no change in fertility levels between each age group. A recent example will make this clear. In the 1950s and 1960s women in the UK began to have their children earlier and within a shorter time span. Thus the age groups 20–24 and 25–29 experienced a change in fertility levels as compared with their forebears. These women did not, however, go on to have the same level of fertility as their contemporaries aged 30–50 when they in turn reached those ages. In other words, the NRR does not take account of changes in the timing of births over the fertile period. For that one needs to follow each cohort (age group) as it passes through the fertile period.

The TFR, GRR and NRR, together with cohort rates, can be calculated straightforwardly for the present day, but only with difficulty for the nineteenth century or earlier – especially at the local and regional levels. It is, however, useful to know of their existence, partly because this will enable you to understand the recent literature, and partly because this makes you aware of the crudity of the rates that you can calculate.

Is there any other way of overcoming the drawbacks inherent in the crude rates, given the sources available to family and community historians prior to this century? One is the *child/woman ratio* (CWR). This measure of fertility can be calculated using only the information provided in, say, the CEBs or census reports. It is usually expressed as so many children (*not* births) under 1 or under 5 years of age per 1,000 women aged 15–44 or 15–49 years (adopted, by convention, as the child-bearing years of most women). Thus, if you take the age column of the CEBs for the community or communities you are interested in, you can tot up the number of women aged, say, 15–44 years, divide this figure *into* the number of children aged, say, under 1 year, and multiply by 1,000. Obviously, the strengths of the measure are that it can be calculated from one source and it does relate the number of children to the women likely to have produced them. However, if comparisons are made over time or between one community and another, you can never be sure that differences in infant mortality are not affecting the result of the calculation. This can be overcome by calculating the *general fertility rate* (GFR). This relates the number of *births* to the number of women aged 15–44 or 15–49 years.

To show the kinds of problems of interpretation that can arise, I calculated the child/woman ratio and the GFR for Scotland and Ireland in 1871 and compared the results with the crude birth rate for each country (see Table 8.8).

Note that the CWR is virtually identical in Scotland and Ireland, but both the CBR and the GFR are higher in Scotland than in Ireland. Is the discrepancy here because the registration of births was less efficient in Ireland than in Scotland, or was infant mortality lower in Ireland than in Scotland?

Table 8.8 Crude birth rate (CBR), general fertility rate (GFR) and child/woman ratio (CWR) for Scotland and Ireland, 1871

	CBR	GFR[1]	CWR[2]
Scotland	34.5	148	583
Ireland	28.1	127	584

[1] *Births* per 1,000 women aged 15–44 years
[2] *Children* 0–4 years per 1,000 women aged 15–44 years

Source: derived from Mitchell (1992)

Another measure that family and community historians should find useful is the *singulate mean age at marriage*(SMAM; see Table 8.9), simply because it too can be calculated from a census that gives the proportions of people married and single in each age group. This measure is therefore particularly useful when you have this information but not actual ages at marriage – a very common occurrence. There are – naturally! – problems with SMAM, espcially if marriage or mortality patterns are changing rapidly, or if the area has experienced heavy in-migration of young people (this will inflate the proportions never married) or out-migration (see Schürer, 1989, p.69). Nevertheless, SMAM is a useful weapon to have in one's arsenal.

Table 8.9 Singulate mean age at marriage (SMAM): a guide to calculation
Example: SMAM for female population of Essex in 1851

Age	Female population	Percentage of female population who were single
15–19	15,497	97.5
20–24	14,694	64.8
25–29	13,205	35.8
30–34	11,705	21.3
35–39	9,970	15.3
40–44	8,812	12.6
45–49	7,412	11.3
50–54	6,746	10.0

Mean years of singleness per 100 women aged under 15 years Since 100% unmarried under age 15:	$15 \times 100 = 1,500$
Years of singleness per 100 women aged 15–49 years	$(97.5 + 64.8 + 35.8 + 21.3 + 15.3 + 12.6 + 11.3 + 10 = (268.6) \times 5 = 1,343$
Total number of years of singleness per 100 females up to age 50	$1,500 + 1,343 = 2,843$
Some women in this population will never marry. On the assumption that none do so after age 50, we estimate this by averaging the proportions aged 45–49 and 50–54 years	$(11.3 + 10) \div 2 = 10.65$
Estimated number of years of singleness experienced by those never married by age 50	$10.65 \times 50 = 532.5$
For the women who married, the total number of years of singleness per 100 women	$2,843 - 532.5 = 2,310.5$
Actual percentage of Essex women who married by age 50	$100 - 10.65 = 89.35\%$
Thus 89.35 females in Essex in 1851 had experienced 2,310.5 years of singleness before their marriage. Therefore the singulate mean age at marriage is	$2,310.5 \div 89.35 = 25.86$

Source: Schürer (1989) pp.67–9

Technique for relating actual to expected number of marriages per month   The time of year when people marry can be an important indicator of the social and economic pressures upon them. It is well attested that over time, and across space, people do marry at different times of the year, though more work needs to be done. As a measure of this, the crude totals of marriages per month suffer from two drawbacks. First, it is difficult to see any pattern in them, other than that one monthly total is greater or smaller than the next. Second, they are difficult to compare over time and between different communities, especially when the numbers involved vary, as they usually do, for instance between a community with a population of 10,000 and another with a population of 100,000. To overcome these drawbacks, it is useful initially to calculate the *expected* number of marriages across the year, on the assumption they are evenly distributed – account being taken of the differing numbers of days in a month; and then to calculate the *actual* number of marriages as a percentage of the *expected* number. Table 8.10 shows how this is done.

Table 8.10 Relating actual to 'expected' marriages per month: a guide to calculation
Example: Marriages in Orkney (Scotland) 1856-65

Jan	Feb	Mar	Apr	May	June	July	Aug	Sept	Oct	Nov	Dec	Total
104	151	103	49	74	89	43	32	34	58	81	167	985

A	Divide 985 by 365.25 (the 0.25 is to take account of leap years) = 2.7
B	Multiply 2.7 by 31 or 30 (for months with 31 and 30 days respectively) = 83.7 and 81.0
C	Multiply 2.7 by 28.25 (for February: again the extra 0.25 is for leap years) = 76.3
D	Divide each monthly 'actual' total by the appropriate 'expected' one (expected, that is, if all marriages were distributed equally across the year), e.g. January total = 104 ÷ 83.7 = 1.24
E	Multiply monthly proportions arrived at in stage D by 100 to get actual monthly marriages as percentage of expected ones, e.g. January expected marriages is 1.24 × 100 = 124%

_____ *EXERCISE 8.8* _____

Calculate the actual number of marriages as a percentage of expected ones for each month in Orkney, 1856–65. How do you interpret the distribution?

Answers/comments p.303.

6   SAMPLING

Sampling is very much a part of everyday life. One of my earliest memories is of my mother sampling the inside of a cake by sticking a darning needle into it when she took it out of the oven. If the needle emerged as clean as it went in, the cake was apparently done; if it had mixture sticking to its sides, it was not, so back in the oven it went. Experience had taught my mother that half a dozen or so pricks with a needle into different parts of the cake was sufficient to tell her the condition of the *whole* cake. To take another example, examiners believe they can test a student's knowledge about a course that has taken a year to study, by asking half a dozen questions. To examine *every* aspect would be clearly impossible. In both these instances what people are doing is gaining knowledge about the *whole* of whatever it is they are after, when, for a variety of reasons, they only have access to a *part*.

The advantages of sampling are considerable. It means that generalizations can be made, and judgements arrived at, about very large bodies of data through sampling just a small amount. More remarkably, if we select our sample correctly, so that it is truly representative of whatever body of data we are examining, then regardless of the size of that body of data (called the 'population', whether it be people, plastic bottles, or whatever), the sample size will be the *same*. For example, you may want to know the mean size of 5,000 families. A properly drawn sample numbering, say, 250 families, would do the trick. Even if you wanted to find the mean size of 100,000 families, you would not have to increase the size of the sample. However, if the sample is not properly drawn, it will not provide a true picture. Some examples from everyday life will make that clear. When we watch a television report of a football or cricket match we are often offered only a few minutes of a one-and-a-half hour game or a whole day's play. We get a sample right enough, but it is not representative of the game as a whole. In fact this is tacitly admitted by the title 'highlights' that is given to such samples. Even if we see the whole game or day's play, the TV producer selects what we see because several cameras are in use at the same time, from which one shot at a time is shown. This is, no doubt, a good thing, since a true sample would probably show more shots of footballers chewing gum or batsmen patting pitches than we could stomach!

The examples of samples given so far are *subjective*. My mother *knew* – from experience – into which parts of the cake she should stick her needle; similarly examiners *know* what questions are likely to test a student's knowledge of a course; and the television producer *knows* what his cricket- or football-loving public wants to see. Family and community historians must also operate in this way on many occasions. Convenience is often crucial, i.e. access to a source. Experience may often provide the means of drawing a sample of what seems to be typical or critical cases, e.g. for a study of a particular occupational group or a set of streets. In oral history work a *snowball* sample may be necessary. This is one whereby the initial contact suggests further ones; for example, you may want to study the life of miners or railwaymen, know only one or two, but get other names from them. Often one does a piece of work and then seeks to indicate the extent to which the findings are representative. Historical demographers often do this *after* they have studied a particular parish over a few years.

The problems with this kind of sampling are twofold. First, since the sample is subjective, you are dependent on the skill of the person drawing the sample, a skill that is often no more than intuition. Second, there is no way of proving that the sample is truly representative of the whole. That is only possible if you can draw a sample in which *all* members of the population have an *equal* chance of being drawn. To do that a *sampling frame* is needed. This is the complete body of evidence – or 'population' – to be sampled. It could be a CEB, the entries in a directory, the voters in a poll book, or the responses to a questionnaire. Having got a sampling frame (not always as easy as indicated here, especially when qualitative material – literature, for instance – is being handled), a sample is drawn. There are various ways of doing this.

One way is to draw a *systematic sample*. If we were, for example, to take a systematic sample of the names in *Who's Who 1993*, we could start at a page chosen at random to reduce the chance of bias entering into our selection procedure (e.g. by drawing a number out of a hat) and take, say, every 50th page from then on. Whether we choose every 50th, 30th, 37th page etc. depends on how big a sample we want, given that the book contains 2,093 pages. The problem with the systematic sample is that there is always a danger of introducing bias into the selection. For one reason or another your choice of every 5th, 10th, 20th case might just fall on the atypical. For an interesting illustration of the use of systematic sampling see Volume 2, Chapter 4. (For further information on sampling generally see Schofield, 1972; Henry, 1990.)

The best type of sample, and the one that should be adopted if the data and time permit, is the *random sample*. This does not mean 'any old sample' – quite the contrary. A truly random sample requires the use of a table of random sampling numbers. Such a table is produced so that at any point in the table any number, or sequence of numbers, has an equal chance of appearing next. These tables are readily available in libraries or can be bought relatively cheaply. Table 8.11 gives a part of one: just enough to complete Exercise 8.9.

Table 8.11 A table of random sampling numbers (part of)

20	17	45	04	03	64	27	56	08	72	67	28	64	00	52	49	64	17	90	08	42	28
74	49	44	91	62	49	49	05	95	97	85	86	50	94	74	98	18	43	53	82	04	49
94	70	16	23	61	00	49	74	37	99	40	10	66	98	50	26	65	58	98	17	49	31
22	15	04	50	89	03	20	26	05	79	94	55	66	91	49	46	79	90	08	91	78	15
93	29	32	70	01	72	48	87	55	85	11	63	33	58	19	65	07	23	37	21	12	18

Source: Lindley and Miller (1968) p.12

_____ **_EXERCISE 8.9_** _____

To show you how you can use a table of random numbers, let us draw on some real data. Suppose we wanted to know the *mean* age on 1 January 1993 of people who appeared in *Who's Who 1993*. (The choice of *Who's Who 1993* has been made because it will be available in many libraries for at least a few years to come.) Since we are talking of 2,093 pages of entries, the job would be pretty daunting, so let us take a sample of 50 (hardly likely to be big enough to be representative, but sufficient to demonstrate the technique). First, what is our sampling frame to be? It should be all the individuals appearing in the text, but this means numbering every single entry. Assuming you are using a library copy, you'll soon find yourself in trouble if you do that! So let us, instead, take the page numbers of the book and then the first *full* entry on each page. We won't take someone whose entry is already part-way through at the top of the page. On the other hand, if the first entry you come across is the name only with a reference to the full entry, then go to the latter. Thus, for example, if the random number table were to throw up page 29, you would work out the age for Sir David Alliance; if it gave you page 114 you would find that the first name given is 'Bass, see Hastings Bass, family name of Earl of Huntingdon', so you would go to the entry for him on page 951.

   We are now ready to select our fifty names. Let's begin at the top left of Table 8.11 (though we could begin anywhere if we had the complete table, say by the toss of a coin), working down each block of five entries. Our sampling frame is 2,093 pages, so we need to use the group of four numbers. Had it been 100 or less, we could have used the groups of two. The first number, therefore, is 2,017. We turn to page 2017 and find that the first entry is Sir (Kenneth) Michael Wilford, born on 31 January 1922 and therefore 70 years of age on 1 January 1993. Our next number is 7,449, which is outside the limits of our sampling frame. So are the next five numbers (9,470; 2,215; 9,329; 4,504; 4,491). If we are going to have to pass numbers like this, an already tedious task becomes more tedious still. We can get round this partially by rephrasing 'the numbers above 2,000 as repeats of the 1 to 2,000 series' (Gregory, 1971, p.102). This means that the numbers 2,000–3,999, 4,000–5,999 etc. can be retermed as 1–1,999 in each case. Going back to our random sampling number table, 7,449 now becomes 1,449. This is within our sampling frame, so we turn to page 1449 and find the first entry to be Parkyn, Brian (Stewart). He was born on 28 April 1923, and therefore on 1 January 1993 was 69 years of age. Now carry on like this until you have got your fifty names and ages and know whether they are men or women. If no age is given, move to the next random number.

   When you have got your fifty ages, you can work out the mean.

Answers/comments p.304.

_____ **_EXERCISE 8.10_** _____

From our sample of ages from *Who's Who 1993*, what is:

1 the age range;

2 the modal age;

3 the median age;

4 the standard deviation in years;

5 the overall picture of the distribution?

Answers/comments p.304.

Exercise 8.10 describes our sample of entries in *Who's Who 1993* in statistical terms: range, mode, median, and so on. Note that the mean was found in Exercise 8.9. But remember that we are dealing with a sample. How sure can we be that these attributes of our sample are those of the population as a whole (i.e. the entire number of entries in *Who's Who 1993*)? Table 8.12 shows how we go about answering this question for one attribute of the sample, namely the mean.

Table 8.12   Estimating the population mean from a sample: a guide to calculation (based on a sample of 50 entries in *Who's Who 1993*)

Stage	In symbols	In words	Examples
	$\dfrac{2S}{\sqrt{N-1}}$	The population mean from a sample	To find the mean age of the entries in *Who's Who 1993* at the 95% confidence level
A	$\bar{X}$	Calculate the mean of the sample	= 60.96
B	S	Calculate the standard deviation of the sample	= 12
C	$N-1$	Subtract 1 from the number (N) of observations in the sample	$50-1 = 49$
D	$\sqrt{N-1}$	Take the square root of ($N-1$)	$\sqrt{49} = 7$
E	$\dfrac{S}{\sqrt{N-1}}$	Divide the standard deviation (S) by the square root of ($N-1$)	$\dfrac{12}{7} = 1.7$
F	$\pm\dfrac{2S}{\sqrt{N-1}}$	Multiply the sum reached at the end of stage E by 2	$1.7 \times 2 = 3.4$

At the 95% confidence level the population mean was 60.96 ± 3.4. Put in everyday language, this means we can be 95% confident that however many random samples of 50 entries we take, the mean age of the entries will be in the range of 57.6 to 64.4 years, and that the mean age of *all* the entries in *Who's Who 1993* is *likely* to lie here. Note that we are dealing with probabilities. Nevertheless, given the saving in time and effort, you, like me, will probably find this acceptable.

Another calculation we can carry out is to estimate from a sample the proportion of items in a population with a given attribute. For instance, we noted that in our sample from *Who's Who 1993* there were 42 men and 8 women. How certain can we be that this *proportion* applies to all the entries? The calculation is made in Table 8.13 and is derived from what is called the standard error of a sample.

Our calculation of the standard error of a sample leads us to the $64,000 question: 'how big a sample should one draw?' This is not quite like asking 'how long is a piece of string?', but it is going in that direction. The answer depends on several factors:

o   How confident do we want to be in the result, e.g. 95% or 99% confident? (If the former, then out of 100 samples, five or fewer would give us an incorrect answer; if the latter, then one or fewer would do so.)

o   What confidence interval is acceptable? For instance, in the case illustrated in Table 8.13, is it to be $16\% \pm 10.4\%$ or $16\% \pm 4.2\%$?

o   The nature of the population being sampled. For example, going back to the entries in *Who's Who 1993*, the analysis showed that a minority – in fact quite a small minority – were women. Or, likewise, the mean age was relatively high and the range comparatively narrow, given that people live from 0 to 100 plus years. The situation could obviously have been different. At one end of the scale *all* the entries could have been of men, the mean age could have been higher or lower, the range wider or narrower. In other words, there could be a smaller or a greater amount of *variability* in the population, or *variance* as it is called. This will affect the chance of the sample being representative of it.

Table 8.13 Estimating from a sample the proportion of items in a population with a given attribute (e.g. being a woman): a guide to calculation (based on a sample of 50 entries in *Who's Who 1993*)

Stage	In symbols	In words	Examples
	$S(p)$ $S(p) = \sqrt{\dfrac{pq}{N-1}}$	The standard error of a sample	To find the proportion of women listed in *Who's Who 1993*, given the proportion in the sample is 16%
A	pq	p here stands for the proportion of sample items with the attribute, and q the proportion without. The two are multiplied	$p = 16\%$ $q = 84\%$ $pq = 1{,}344$
B	$N-1$	Subtract 1 from the number in the sample	The sample is 50 entries $50 - 1 = 49$
C	$\dfrac{pq}{N-1}$	Divide the figure reached at the end of stage A by that reached at the end of stage B	$\dfrac{1{,}344}{49} = 27.4$
D	$\sqrt{\dfrac{pq}{N-1}}$	Take the square root of the number reached at the end of stage C	$\sqrt{27.4} = 5.2$
	$S(p)$	The standard error of the sample is 5.2	

From this we can be certain that the proportion of women listed in *Who's Who 1993* is 16% ± 10.4% (i.e. twice the standard error of the sample). This is quite a considerable spread. Had our sample been larger we would have been able to narrow the spread. Thus if we had taken a sample of 300 and still got 16% women, our calculation would have been as follows (we start at stage B):

B	$N-1$	$300 - 1 = 299$
C	$\dfrac{pq}{N-1}$	$\dfrac{1{,}344}{299} = 4.49$
D	$\sqrt{\dfrac{pq}{N-1}}$	$\sqrt{4.49} = 2.1$
	$S(p)$	$= 2.1$

We could then be 95% certain that the proportion of women listed in *Who's Who 1993* was 16% ± 4.2% (i.e. 2 × standard error): that is, between 12% and 20%.

In deciding on our sample size, each of these factors must be taken into account. So here goes. Remembering that in sampling we are dealing with approximations and probabilities, let us suppose that we want to estimate the size of the sample (conventionally expressed as n_0) of the entries in *Who's Who 1993* that will allow us to calculate the percentage of women listed. We want to be 95 per cent certain that the percentage of women in our sample will be no more than ±2 per cent different to the percentage in the population as a whole. We make use of the following formula:

$$n_0 = \frac{pq}{V}$$

where p = the proportion of sample items with the attribute,

and q = the proportion of sample items without the attribute.

V, in this instance, is the variance of the sample. It is calculated using the following formula:

$$V = \frac{d^2}{t^2}$$

where d = half the desired confidence interval ($\pm\, d$ which in our example is $\pm\, 2$ per cent)

and t = the normal deviate corresponding to the confidence level chosen and is read off Table 8.14.

Table 8.14 Percentage of estimates of all possible samples of a given size falling within a range of values defined as the mean of the sample estimate ± normal deviate

	Range (mean ± normal deviate)					
Normal deviate	0.67	1.28	1.64	1.96	2.58	3.29
Percentage falling in range	50	80	90	95	99	99.9

Source: Schofield (1972) p.155

For our purposes we have chosen to be satisfied with a 95 per cent certainty that our sample estimate lies within a confidence interval of $\pm\, 2$ per cent. Our value of d is therefore 2, and t is 1.96, i.e. the normal deviate corresponding to 95 per cent certainty as given in Table 8.14.

EXERCISE 8.11

Suppose we had wanted to be 99 per cent certain, with a confidence interval of $\pm\, 1$ per cent. What would our values of d and t be?

Answers p.304.

For our illustration, $V = \dfrac{2 \times 2}{1.96 \times 1.96} = \dfrac{4}{3.84} = 1$

Had we been starting our calculations from scratch, we would have had no idea what proportion of the entries in *Who's Who 1993* were women, though we could well have guessed it would be less than 50 per cent. However, we have taken a small pilot sample which indicated that the percentage of women (at the 95 per cent confidence level) was $16 \pm 10.4\%$ (Table 8.13). So let us say that of the *Who's Who 1993* population as a whole we could expect no more than about 25 per cent to be women. If we wanted to play really safe we could estimate the population variability to be at its maximum, i.e. 50 per cent. But as this would increase our sample size unnecessarily we will stick with 25 per cent. Thus we say that p = 25% and q (the proportion of men in the population) = 75%. We now go back to our formula:

$$n_0 = \frac{pq}{V}$$

Therefore $n_0 = \dfrac{25 \times 75}{1} = 1{,}875$

This, then, is the size of the sample needed to determine the proportion of women among the entries in *Who's Who 1993*.

_____ **EXERCISE 8.12** _____

Just to make sure you've grasped the various elements of this calculation, have a go at the following. At a confidence level of 99 per cent and a confidence interval of ± 5 per cent, what size of sample would be required of women entries in *Who's Who 1993*, assuming maximum variability in the population (i.e. 50 per cent)?

Answer/comments p.304.

We now turn to calculating the sample size for an estimated mean value. The procedure is not dissimilar to that we've already gone through, since it involves putting actual numbers into simple equations. As with our estimate of the proportion of women among *Who's Who 1993* entries, an estimate of the mean age of all entries requires the desired sample variance (V) and the variance of the population (S^2), i.e. the standard deviation squared. As when we calculated pq, V is determined by how precise we want our estimate to be. Our procedure is as follows.

We want our estimate of the average entries in *Who's Who 1993* to be ± 2 years, with a 95 per cent confidence level:

$$n_0 = \frac{S^2}{V}$$

$$V = \frac{d^2}{t^2} = \frac{2^2}{1.96^2} = \frac{4}{3.84} = 1$$

$$n_0 = \frac{S^2}{1}$$

To calculate S^2 we have to take a small pilot sample. We will use the one already made. This gave us a value for S^2 of 144 (i.e. 12×12). Therefore

$$n_0 = \frac{S^2}{V}(1 + \frac{2}{n}) = \frac{144}{1}(1 + \frac{2}{50}) = 144 \times 1.04 = 150$$

Since we have already taken a sample of 50, all we need to do is to take another one of 100 and add the two together.

I hope that in spite of the somewhat tedious description of the nitty gritty of basic sampling technique, its possibilities have shone through. Community historians are faced with many sources containing hundreds, thousands, tens of thousands of items, such as households, families, individual ages, birthplaces, occupations and so on in the CEBs; names and addresses in electoral registers; rateable values in rate books; names in parish registers; wages in wage books. Sampling provides a wonderful tool to help explore these sources of information. Only the elementary sampling techniques have been described here; I hope you will be interested enough to go further (see Schofield, 1972).

_____ **EXERCISE 8.13** _____

In Tables 8.1 and 8.2 I drew a sample of Whateley's voters, namely those whose surnames began with the letter A. Quite apart from the size of the sample, can you see why a sample drawn in this way might not adequately represent the population as a whole?

Comments p.305.

7   STATISTICS OF MIGRATION

by Deirdre Mageean and W.T.R. Pryce

7.1   NET MIGRATION BALANCES AND NET MIGRATION RATES

Geographers were among the first social scientists to embrace the quantitative revolution, though their enthusiasm has waned somewhat in recent years. Nevertheless, the arguments for using statistics that have been put forward in this chapter still apply. Here, then, we present some statistical techniques for use in spatial analysis: an important technique for the community historian.

Table 8.15 Estimating net migration for a given area: a guide to calculation

Stage	In symbols	In words	Example
	Net M $= P_{t2} - [P_{t1} + (B - D)]$	Net migration	To find the net migration occurring in county X between 1861 and 1871 where: population in 1861 = 50,000 population in 1871 = 60,000 births, 1861–71 = 17,000 deaths, 1861–71 = 10,000
A	P_{t2}	P_{t2} stands for the enumerated population of county X at time *t2*, i.e. the later of the two dates, 1871	60,000
B	P_{t1}	P_{t1} stands for the enumerated population of county X at time *t1*, i.e. the first of the two dates, 1861	50,000
C	$B - D$	From the total number of births occurring in the interval, subtract the total number of deaths	17,000 – 10,000 = 7,000
D	$P_{t1} + (B - D)$	To the number at stage B add the number obtained at stage C	50,000 + 7,000 = 57,000
E	$(P_{t2}) - [P_{t1} + (B - D)]$	From the number at stage A subtract the number obtained at stage D	60,000 – 57,000 = 3,000
	Net $M =$	Net migration to county X between 1861 and 1871 was 3,000	

If the estimated population (as calculated in Table 8.15) is less than the enumerated population at the second census, then it can be assumed that the difference has been brought about by *net* in-migration; if the estimated population turns out to be greater, then it can be assumed that *net* out-migration has occurred. This calculation can be done for either males or females or total populations. This method is particularly useful for estimating net migration totals for towns and cities for which migration data are not tabulated separately. However, it is important to under-stand what *net* migration means. In the example, the net in-migration of 3,000 persons could conceal a gross or total outflow of 10,000 in the ten years balanced by an inflow of 13,000; moreover, those leaving and returning within the inter-censal period are not counted (see Volume 2, Chapter 1, section 1; also Chapter 4, section 2.3). Such an estimate is therefore described as 'net population change by migration'.

In the above example migration is expressed in absolute terms, but it can also be expressed as a *rate*, i.e. so many migrants per 1,000 of the underlying population. The calculation is a simple one, expressed by the formula

Net $M \div P_{f1} \times 1,000 = \dfrac{3,000}{50,000} \times 1,000 = 60$ migrants per 1,000 population for the years 1861–71, or 6 per 1,000 per year.

We could have made the rate a little more precise by using the 1865 population: we estimate this to have been 55,000, i.e. half-way between 50,000 and 60,000. Our calculation would then be

$\dfrac{3,000}{55,000} \times 1,000 = 54.5$ per 1,000 for the decade as a whole, or 5.5 per 1,000 per year.

7.2 STANDARDIZED STATISTICS IN MIGRATION STUDIES

The numbers of migrants leaving or entering an area can be misleading if just the raw, absolute numbers are used. To a large extent the volume of migrants is dependent on the population of the sending community or the size of the areas involved. To obtain meaningful comparisons the statistics need to be standardized. This is done quite simply by expressing the number of migrants as a proportion of the population of sending or receiving areas (as a percentage, or, when very small numbers are involved, per thousand). There are occasions when it may be more appropriate to standardize by area, e.g. migrants per thousand acres, per hectare or per square mile.

A good example of the need for standardization occurs when one relates the inward movement of migrants to a town or village in terms of distance bands around it, e.g. from 0–5 miles, 6–10 miles, and so on (rounding the mileages up or down to whole numbers). One problem associated with these measurements is that the area of each successive ring is greater than that of the previous ring. If people *are assumed to be evenly distributed through the area*, the population in the outer rings will be much larger. More migrants, therefore, will come from within the outer than from the inner zones (see Figure 8.3).

This method of measuring migration is widely used, but usually without full attention being directed to these inherent spatial statistical problems. Fortunately, by using a very simple calculation the migration figures can be standardized to take account of area and distances.

The number of migrants from each distance band is determined by the index number based on the area of a circle, πr^2. The calculation of these indices is straightforward, as is shown in Table 8.16. First, the radii of the migration bands are listed in miles or kilometres (column 1). The calculations then proceed step by step in the successive columns by following the instructions, until the index numbers are obtained (column 6). Using this method, the appropriate index number can be calculated for sets of concentric circles of any radius.

Table 8.16 Indices of differences between migration areas

(1)	(2)	(3)	(4)	(5)	(6)
r	r^2	πr^2	$\pi r^2 - \pi r^2$		Index
Radius of circle (miles/kilo-metres)	Radius of circle squared	Area of circle	Area of succeeding circle minus area of circle	Area of band	Ratios of areas of successive bands to first inner circle
5	25	25π	25π	25π	1
10	100	100π	$100\pi - 25\pi$	75π	3
15	225	225π	$225\pi - 100\pi$	125π	5
20	400	400π	$400\pi - 225\pi$	175π	7

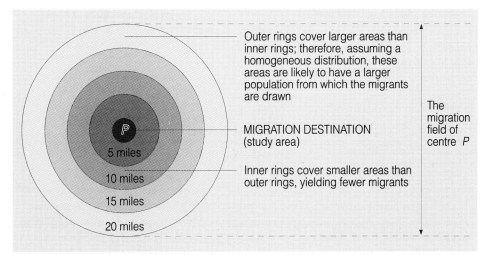

Figure 8.3 Hypothetical migration field and the areas within each concentric sending zone

Next, this index number is used to weight the numbers of migrants, as shown in Table 8.17. In this example the bulk of migration took place over a short distance (up to 5 miles). Inspection of the 'raw' statistics shown in column 4 of Table 8.17 suggests that with 102 migrants, the third distance band (11–15 miles) was the most important source of longer-distance movements. Now look at the standardized migration flows shown in column 5 of the table. After standardization by area it is clear that there were relatively fewer migrants from this third distance band than the raw figures first suggested.

Table 8.17 Calculation of a standardized migration flow: an example

(1) Distance band order	(2) Distance band (miles/kilometres)	(3) Weighting (index number from col. 6 of Table 8.16)	(4) Number of migrants (as counted by plotting on map)	(5) Standardized migration flows (col. 4 ÷ col. 3)
1	0–5	1	147	147
2	6–10	3	62	20.7
3	11–15	5	102	20.4
4	16–20	7	20	2.9

On this basis, the third distance band is no more important than the second, although *in absolute terms* greater numbers came from the more distant origins. On the other hand, in reality people are very rarely distributed evenly throughout an area, which is the underlying assumption of Table 8.17. In practice, population densities can usually be related closely to the distribution of towns, villages, land use and the physical characteristics of the land surface. This method of standardizing migration flows is of considerable value, however, in the study of migration and movements in rural communities (see, for example, Watson, 1978, and Millard, 1982).

7.3   TESTING THE SIGNIFICANCE OF THE DIFFERENCE BETWEEN TWO PROPORTIONS

Using this test we can compare, for example, the proportion of males in a parish with that for a larger area of which it forms a part, e.g. a county, region or country. The methods to be followed use the formula for the *standard error of a sample* (for a detailed guide to the calculation of this, see Table 8.13). All these calculations are easy to carry out using a pocket calculator, *providing you work carefully through the instructions step by step*. In the examples used here, all the data have been extracted from the 1801 published census returns (see Table 8.18).

Table 8.18 Sex ratios, 1801: England and Wales, and selected parishes in north-east Wales

(1)	(2) Males	(3) Population (N)	(4) Proportion of males in the population as a percentage of column (3) (p)
England and Wales, 1801	4,254,735	8,892,536	47.85
Examples Abergele, 1801 Northop, 1801	848 1,130	1,748 2,219	48.51 50.92

Source: *Census of Great Britain, 1851*, pp. 54–5, 58–9

We start with the *null hypothesis* that there is no difference between the proportions of males enumerated in these specific parishes and in England and Wales as a whole. We assume that the variation in proportions between parishes is due to random effects and that these will follow the normal distribution. In others words, we expect only 5 per cent of parishes to have proportions of males which deviate from the England and Wales 'average' by more than $\pm$ $2S(p)$ (i.e. by more than twice the standard error). If the proportion does fall *outside this range*, then we conclude that there is evidence (at the 5 per cent confidence level) that the parish in question is significantly different from 'average' ratios in England and Wales. Depending on local circumstances, these differences may have been brought about by selective migration (see Volume 2, Chapter 4, section 2.1). Table 8.19 presents details of the calculations, stage by stage, using the proportions shown in column 4 of Table 8.18.

Table 8.19 Significant differences between proportions: a guide to calculation

England and Wales

In 1801 for England and Wales, the proportion of males, p_{EW} = 47.85% (where p = proportion and EW = England and Wales)

Individual parishes

Example 1: Abergele

Stage **A** For Abergele parish in 1801, the proportion of males, p_A = 48.51%. If there is no significant difference between Abergele and the ratio for England and Wales, this can be used to estimate the overall proportion of males in England and Wales with the confidence interval given by $\pm 2S(p_A)$. To do so, the standard error of the sample must be calculated, using the formula

$$S(p) = \sqrt{\frac{pq}{N-1}}$$

In this example, p = 48.51, and thus q = 100 – 48.51 = 51.49

$$N = 1748$$

Stage **B** Now $S(p_A)$ $= \sqrt{\dfrac{48.51 \times 51.49}{1748-1}}$

                  $= \sqrt{\dfrac{2497.77}{1747}}$

                  $= \sqrt{1.4297}$

                  $= 1.196$

     and $2S(p_A)$ $= 2 \times 1.196$

                  $= 2.39\%$

Stage **C** Thus, the 95% confidence interval for the England and Wales proportion of males *based on Abergele parish* is 48.51 $\pm$ 2.39%, or 46.1–50.9%.

Table 8.19 Significant differences between proportions: a guide to calculation *(continued)*

Stage **D** The actual mean value of the proportion of males in England and Wales is 47.85%, and this lies within the confidence interval of stage C.

We conclude, therefore, that (at the 5 per cent confidence level) there is no evidence of significant differences between the proportions of males in Abergele parish and in England and Wales in 1801.

Example 2: Northop

Stage **A** For Northop parish in 1801 p_N = 50.92%

Stage **B** $S(p_N)$

$$= \sqrt{\frac{50.92 \times (100 - 50.92)}{2219 - 1}}$$

$$= \sqrt{\frac{50.92 \times 49.08}{2218}}$$

$$= \sqrt{\frac{2499.15}{2218}}$$

$$= \sqrt{1.1268}$$

$$= 1.06$$

and $2S(p_N)$ $= 2.12\%$

Stage **C** Thus, the 95% confidence interval for the England and Wales proportion of males *based on Northop parish* is 50.92 ± 2.12%, or 48.8–53.0%.

Stage **D** The actual mean value for England and Wales is 47.85%, but this lies outside the confidence interval calculated in stage C.

Therefore, at the 5 per cent confidence level, the null hypothesis of no difference in the proportions of males in Northop parish and in England and Wales generally is rejected. That is, there is evidence of a significant difference between the two proportions, which may be due to selective in-migration.

8   THE CALCULATION OF URBAN FUNCTIONAL INDICES

by Roy Lewis

All settlements have service functions of one sort or another (see Volume 2, Chapter 5). Depending on their size, location, economic base, etc., these can vary both in number and intensity. Geographers have developed a number of indices which allow us to measure these differences. Here are two of them.

The location coefficient (C)   The location coefficient is a measure of the centrality of an urban centre (see Volume 2, Chapter 5). It is calculated from the following formula:

$$C = \frac{t}{T} \times 100$$

where t = one trade outlet of function t

T = total number of outlets of function t within the study area (i.e. in all urban centres)

C = location coefficient of function t.

The functional index   The functional index is a measure of the facilities provided by different urban centres. The calculation procedures are quite straightforward and will be illustrated by reference to Tables 8.20 and 8.21.

Table 8.20 Raw data and location coefficients

(1)	(2)	(3)	(4)	(5)	(6)	(7)
			Centres		Total	Location coefficients
Functions	A	B	C	D		
Grocers	5	5	10	5	25	4
Butchers	2	2	4	2	10	10
Jewellers	1	0	1	0	2	50
Accountants	0	0	1	0	1	100

Source: Lewis (1975) p.53

1   First, notice the layout of the data matrix (Table 8.20, columns 2–5). The various urban centres could have been named, but here they are indicated by the letters A, B, C and D which occupy the *columns*. Conversely, the specific functions (obtained from entries in trade directories) have been classified into four functional categories – grocers, butchers, jewellers and accountants – and these occupy the *rows*. In short, this is a 4×4 data matrix, showing functions against centres.

2   The location coefficients shown in column 7 of Table 8.20 are produced by the application of the above formula to the data. Thus, for example:

$$\text{Grocers: } C = \frac{1}{25} \times 100 = 4$$

$$\text{Butchers: } C = \frac{1}{10} \times 100 = 10$$

$$\text{Jewellers: } C = \frac{1}{2} \times 100 = 50$$

3   Centrality values are calculated for each function and centre by multiplying the relevant location coefficients (Table 8.20, column 7) by the number of outlets present in the centres (Table 8.20, columns 2, 3, 4 or 5). Thus, for example:

Grocers in Centre A = $4 \times 5 = 20$

Grocers in Centre C = $4 \times 10 = 40$

Jewellers in Centre A = $50 \times 1 = 50$

The results of these calculations are then laid out as a second data matrix, as in Table 8.21.

Table 8.21 Centrality values and functional indices

(1)	(2)	(3)	(4)	(5)
			Centres	
Functions	A	B	C	D
Grocers	20	20	40	20
Butchers	20	20	40	20
Jewellers	50	0	50	0
Accountants	0	0	100	0
Functional index	90	40	230	40

Source: Lewis (1975) p.53

4   The functional index (Table 8.21, row 5) for each centre is then obtained by the summation of the centrality values for each function which relate to the various centres, i.e. the totals for each centre (Table 8.21, columns 2–5).

5   Once the functional index has been calculated, it can be used for further analyses in a number of ways. If comparisons are to be made of differences in functional status *between places*, then all the centres can be ranked, with those with the highest scores at the top and those with the lowest

scores at the bottom of the list. However, when changes in status *over time* are involved, the functional index should be expressed in relative terms by calculating the score for each centre as a percentage of the total scores at each date. This yields the *functional index percentage values*.

9 MEASURES OF RESIDENTIAL SEGREGATION

by Roy Lewis

Given the availability of social data for sub-areas of a town or city, such as census enumeration districts, grid squares or streets, a number of standard techniques can be used to measure the degree of residential segregation displayed by different sectors of the population (see Volume 2, Chapters 6 and 7, section 1).

At the simplest level, it is possible to plot the percentage distributions of single variables by sub-areas, such as the percentages in different social classes, or in overcrowded households, or sharing particular places of birth. Broad social contrasts can be revealed by this method, and perhaps certain spatial correlations will emerge by comparing maps, say between percentages in the lowest social classes and the extent of overcrowding.

Here are three more useful measures, using percentage distributions, to assess the degree of segregation of people with different birthplaces.

Index of dissimilarity (I_D) This is a measure of the similarities in the spatial patterns of two different birthplace groups in a town, city, etc. The derived index ranges between 0 and 100. A value close to 0 indicates that the two groups have similar spatial distributions; the closer the value is to 100, the greater the degree of segregation. The index is derived from the formula:

$$I_D = \frac{\Sigma(Xi - Yi)}{2}$$

where Σ means 'the sum of', Xi = the percentage of birthplace group X in each sub-area i, and Yi = the percentage of birthplace group Y in each sub-area i.

The hypothetical example in Table 8.22 shows the calculation of the index. In effect, the comparatively high I_D shown in the table indicates that 55 per cent of the Welsh would have to move in order to have a distribution similar to the Irish.

Table 8.22 Calculating the index of dissimilarity (I_D)

(1) Sub-areas of city *(i)*	(2) Percentage of persons from Ireland *(X)*	(3) Percentage of persons from Wales *(Y)*	(4) Percentage difference *(X – Y)*
1	35	5	30
2	25	5	20
3	15	10	5
4	15	35	20
5	10	45	35
Σ	100	100	110

$$I_D = \frac{\Sigma(Xi - Yi)}{2} = \frac{110}{2} = 55$$

Index of segregation (I_S)   This index compares the spatial distribution of one birthplace group with the total population. Again, the range of values is between 0 and 100, with higher values indicating a greater degree of residential segregation. The index is derived from the formula:

$$I_S = \frac{I_D}{1 - \dfrac{\sum Yi}{\sum Xi}}$$

where I_D = the index of dissimilarity between the total population X and birthplace group Y, $\sum Yi$ = the total number of birthplace group Y in the city, and $\sum Xi$ = the total population of the city.

Table 8.23 shows the calculation of the index. The high index shown in the table reveals that this particular group occupies segregated areas within the city.

Table 8.23 Calculating the index of segregation (I_S)

(1) Sub-areas of city (i)	(2) Birthplace group (Y)		(4) Total population (X)		(6) Difference in percentages (columns 4 and 2)
	%	Number	%	Number	
1	5	10	40	400	35
2	5	10	20	200	15
3	10	20	10	100	0
4	35	70	10	100	25
5	45	90	20	200	25
Σ	100	200	100	1000	100

$$I_D = \frac{\sum(Xi - Yi)}{2} = \frac{100}{2} = 50$$

$$I_S = \frac{I_D}{1 - \dfrac{\sum Yi}{\sum Xi}} = \frac{50}{1 - \dfrac{200}{1000}} = 62.5$$

Location quotient (LQ)   The location quotient is used to show those *areas* where, for example, birthplace groups are concentrated in the city. A location quotient can be calculated for each birthplace group in each sub-area. Values range around 1. If a sub-area has an *LQ* greater than 1 for any birthplace group, then that group is over-represented in that particular area. The index is calculated from the formula:

$$LQ = \frac{Yi}{Xi}$$

where Yi = the percentage of birthplace group Y in sub-area i, and Xi = the percentage of total population X in sub-area i.

Table 8.24 shows the calculation of this measure. In this example, birthplace group Y is over-represented in sub-areas 4 and 5, and under-represented in areas 1 and 2.

Table 8.24   Calculating the location quotient (*LQ*)

(1) Sub-areas of city (*i*)	(2) % of birthplace group (*Y*)	(3) % of population (*X*)	(4) $\dfrac{Y}{X}$	(5) *LQ*
1	5	40	5/40	0.125
2	5	20	5/20	0.25
3	10	10	10/10	1.00
4	35	10	35/10	3.50
5	45	20	45/20	2.25

It is necessary to sound a warning note over the use of all these measures of residential segregation. In part the index values reflect the size of the sub-areas within the town or city for which the data are compiled in the first instance. It is likely that large sub-areas will mask subtle differences that occur on a local scale within the city, say by street or block.

At more sophisticated levels of enquiry the use of multivariate statistical techniques is common, whereby social patterns in the city are defined on the basis of a much larger number of variables which are analysed simultaneously.

10   CONCLUSION

by Michael Drake

It would be far-fetched to suggest that quantification is the be-all and end-all for family and community historians. Nevertheless, some knowledge of its possibilities – and associated problems – is necessary in order (a) to be able to understand quite a large amount of the existing literature in the field and (b) to be able to contribute to it.

If you have found this introduction to quantitative methods of interest, you should seek out at least two other sets of techniques which, for lack of space, we have not been able to deal with. The first embraces various measures of correlation, or the association between different phenomena. You will find different measures (their technical name is correlation coefficients) suited for nominal, ordinal and interval data. The second set of techniques are the so-called tests of significance. As their name indicates, these enable you to decide whether or not – and to what degree – the results you arrive at could come about by chance. For both sets of techniques see Matthews and Foster (1989) and Haskins and Jeffrey (1990).

EXERCISE 8.14

If you have worked through this chapter, now is an appropriate moment to think back over its content. If your memory is good write down the advantages and the disadvantages of quantification that we have discussed. If, like mine, your memory isn't what it was, give it a nudge by quickly flicking through the chapter once again.

Comments p.305.

REFERENCES AND FURTHER READING

Note: entries marked with an asterisk are suggestions for further reading.

Census of Great Britain, 1851: Population Tables I (Numbers of inhabitants, 1801–1851), England and Wales, XI Welsh Division, London, HMSO, 1952.

Dollar, C.M. and Jensen, R.J. (1970) *Historian's guide to statistics: quantitative analysis and historical research*, New York, Holt, Rinehart and Winston.

Drake, M. (1974) *The quantitative analysis of historical data*, Units 1–4 of D301 *Historical data and the social sciences*, Milton Keynes, The Open University Press.

Floud, R. (1979) *An introduction to quantitative methods for historians*, 2nd edn, London, Methuen.*

Gregory, S. (1971) *Statistical methods for geographers*, 2nd edn, London, Longman.

Harte, N.B. (ed.) (1971) *The study of economic history: collected inaugural lectures 1893–1970*, London, Frank Cass.

Haskins, L. and Jeffrey, K. (1990) *Understanding quantitative history*, Cambridge, Mass. and London, MIT Press.*

Henry, G.T. (1990) *Practical sampling*, London, Sage.*

Lewis, C.R. (1975) 'The analysis of changes in urban status: a case study of mid-Wales and the middle Welsh borderland', *Transactions*, 64, pp.49–65.

Lindley, D.V. and Miller, J.C.P. (1968) *Cambridge elementary statistical tables*, Cambridge, Cambridge University Press.

Matthews, H. and Foster, I. (1989) *Geographical data: sources, presentation and analysis*, Oxford, Oxford University Press.

Millard, J. (1982) 'A new approach to the study of marriage horizons', *Local Population Studies*, 28. Reprinted in Drake, M. (ed.) *Population studies from parish registers*, Matlock, Local Population Studies.

Mills, D.R. (1979) 'An introduction to statistics', Unit 2, section 4 of *History in the social sciences*, Units 1–2 of D301 *Historical sources and the social scientist*, Milton Keynes, Open University Press.

Mitchell, B.R. (1992) *International historical statistics: Europe 1750–1988*, 3rd edn, Basingstoke, Macmillan.

Schofield, R.S. (1972) 'Sampling in historical research', in Wrigley, E.A. (ed.) *Nineteenth-century society: essays in the use of quantitative methods for the study of social data*, Cambridge, Cambridge University Press.*

Schürer, K. (1989) 'A note concerning the calculation of the singulate mean age at marriage', *Local Population Studies*, 43, pp.67–9.

Watson, R. (1978) 'Measuring migration', *Local Population Studies*, 21, p.61.

Who's Who 1993, London, A. and C. Black.

CHAPTER 9

COMPUTING

by Kevin Schürer (section 1) and Magnus John (section 2)

Computing offers additional possibilities for family and community historians. Not everyone will wish to get involved with computers, but, as this chapter illustrates, exploiting computers opens up further methods and opportunities in research – and sometimes shortcuts too. Though it is only sensible to consider the use of computers carefully rather than plunge in without thought, computers can aid historians both in storing and manipulating their own data, and in accessing the data built up by others

1   COMPUTING OPPORTUNITIES IN FAMILY AND COMMUNITY HISTORY

Probably a majority of historians nowadays use word-processors to create and edit the texts they write. However, since the mid-1970s the use of computers for the earlier stages of historical research has also increased at a dramatic rate. My aim is to give you some idea about the development of computing in history from its quantitative beginnings. I describe some early studies that drew on CEBs, parish registers and other nominal records. After some words on the use of computing in local history and genealogy, I end with some advice on how you can make a start.

What are computers most likely to be useful for?

When computers made their first impact in historical research in the 1960s they were very much the tool of historians with a leaning towards quantification. This is evident from the pioneering work of Fogel (1964) on American railways, Aydelotte (1954) on the composition of the House of Commons in the mid-nineteenth century, and Speck and Gray's (1970) investigation of eighteenth-century poll books. This emphasis was not too surprising. The machines available to historians then seem like dinosaurs compared with the sleek desk-top computers of the 1990s, in terms both of size and ability; while the skills required to work them, in many cases to perform the simplest of tasks, were those of a programmer, a vocation normally associated with an education in the mathematical sciences rather than the humanities. The personal computer revolution of the 1980s, and more important the growth and development of computer software packages which accompanied it, have swung the emphasis away from quantification to a more rounded approach. Yet, as with other research tools, an individual's perception of the computer's potential contribution to historical research and the reality of the situation may often be at odds.

1.1   THE CEBS AND COMPUTING

The census enumerators' books (CEBs) are a key source in family and community history. They also hold a special position in the interaction between history and computing. Of all the historical source materials available to us, the nineteenth-century census was not only one of the first to be computerized, but has proved to be by far the most popular historical source for conversion into machine-readable form.

For the census books of Camberwell, for example, Dyos and his team 'punched' the information on to five cards for every household recorded in the Camberwell CEBs, each card being seven by three inches in size with eighty columns for punching the necessary holes per card (Dyos and Baker, 1968). The details relating to the individuals recorded in the CEBs were transformed from the written word into a series of numeric codes, which in turn were entered on the cards in a fixed rigid pattern, the same information appearing in exactly the same position on the same card for each household. In the case of the Camberwell project, positions on the cards were allocated for information relating to the household head, spouse, up to twelve children, six relatives, ten lodgers, six servants and two visitors – a total of 38 persons per household. For each person, codes for age, occupation and birthplace were entered, marital status was coded for head's relatives, lodgers and servants, and a relationship code was assigned to relatives.

This form of data processing served as a model for others for much of the 1970s and even the early 1980s, and is still to some extent with us today. The perceived need to transform historical source materials into a predefined number of fields of information or variables, each usually coded or standardized in some fashion, was perhaps rather unfortunately perpetuated by the types of large software packages available to social scientists working on the mainframe computers of their universities. For example, earlier versions of the much used *Statistical package for social scientists* (SPSS) recommended that data be reduced to numeric codes and that fixed-column formats be used.

1.2 THE POPULATION OF ENGLAND 1541–1871: A RECONSTRUCTION

Although the Camberwell project may have been the model for many early computerized projects (Armstrong, 1974), there were also other innovative schemes, harnessing the latest technology to undertake work which simply would not have been feasible without the use of computers.

One such project, headed by Wrigley and Schofield of the Cambridge Group for the History of Population and Social Structure, attempted to reconstruct the population history of England from the mid-sixteenth to the mid-nineteenth century (Wrigley and Schofield, 1981). Based principally on parish register material, a key feature of this project was the sheer size of the data assembled and analysed. From the outset it was decided that the research should be national in scope. This, however, created an immediate problem, since no central repository of parish registers exists and the resources available to the Cambridge team did not allow for the enormous amount of staff hours which would have been needed to assemble the raw data. So the Cambridge team appealed to local historians, family historians and genealogists to abstract information from parish registers on their behalf, filling in *pro forma* tables detailing numbers of baptisms, marriages and burials for a given parish for each month, for every year from the start of the registration process (1538) to the establishment of the civil registration system in England (1837).

Somewhat to the surprise of the researchers in Cambridge, the response from people volunteering to help was tremendous. In all, information relating to over 500 parishes was transcribed and sent to Cambridge. Unfortunately, deficiencies in the registration material meant that not all could be used. Checks on the completeness of the registration reduced the sample to 404 parishes spread throughout the counties of England. Consequently, the analyses on which the reconstruction was based took the form of a large multidimensional data matrix of the dimension 404 (the number of parishes) × 300 (300 years) × 12 (number of months in a year) × 3 (baptisms, marriages, burials) – in all, some 4.363 million cells of data.

It was not just the scale of the project which made it special. Equally important were methodology and technique. Given the way the data were amassed, as well as the problem of using parish register material as a proxy measure for births and deaths, the data materials had to be thoroughly tested to ascertain their representativeness, then weighted and adjusted accordingly. Once this extensive range of checks had been satisfactorily carried out, the data were analysed using the path-breaking technique of *back projection*. Moving backwards through the series of births and deaths from a terminal census (in this case that of 1871), the specially written computer program estimated the population size, the age structure of the population, the net migration rate, and the general levels of mortality and fertility at quinquennial points. These characteristics gave the project, and with it historical demography itself, something of a pioneering role in the application of computing techniques to historical research, demonstrating that hypotheses could be tested and interpretations advanced on a scale which would be virtually unthinkable without the aid of a computer.

1.3   THE COMPUTER AND NOMINAL RECORD LINKAGE

At the same time, the team at the Cambridge Group were also developing a series of tailor-made computer programs to perform nominal record linkage (in other words, the linking of information relating to individuals across several different documents and sources – see Schürer, 1993) in order to carry out fully automated family reconstitutions. Although much progress has since been made, this is still a topic which preoccupies a large number of computer-using historians. It was also central to the project headed by Alan Macfarlane at the Department of Social Anthropology, Cambridge. Whereas the demographic reconstruction work of the Cambridge Group was very much at the macro level, the Macfarlane project was an intensive micro study, aiming to make machine-readable every surviving document relating to the north Essex village of Earls Colne between the fifteenth and eighteenth centuries. The basic assumption was that, for this village (as with most others), the collective worth of the various surviving documents was greater than the sum of the parts. A meaningful understanding of the development and social organization of the village could only be gained from viewing documents in the context of other documents. What was needed to understand the social and economic forces of Earls Colne was what Macfarlane termed a full 'community reconstitution'. Sheer volume of data played an important role in the Earls Colne project, but more important was the fact that the technical problems associated with computerizing essentially textual rather than quantitative sources were confronted head on. An ingenious but complicated system was devised to enable the document text and the structural context of the source material to be represented in machine-readable form, allowing linkages of people, places, circumstances and events to be drawn across documents (Macfarlane, 1977; Jardine and Macfarlane, 1978).

1.4   THE ADVENT OF THE 'USER FRIENDLY' COMPUTER AND ITS USES

The projects outlined above were undertaken on a large university mainframe computer running bespoke programs written in a low-level computer-programming language. This necessitated the close cooperation of computer scientists, statisticians and historians – not to mention numerous data-entry assistants, upon whose shoulders fell the laborious task of inputting and checking the data. With such human and capital requirements, it is not surprising that, irrespective of desire, the introduction of computing techniques into their research was impractical or impossible for a large number of historians.

Fortunately, the hardware and software revolutions of the 1980s have largely helped to overcome such problems. Both the real and relative costs of computing have fallen dramatically over the last decade, and, equally important, computers have become a great deal easier to use. The development of so-called 'user-friendly' software packages has eased the interchange between people and machines, making the trained computer programmer's skills less necessary.

As a result, the use of computers in historical research and teaching has mushroomed since the mid-1980s. This is true not only numerically, but also in terms of scope. Computers are no longer the preserve of quantitative-orientated historians, and those who continue to dismiss the use of computers in history as reducing Clio's craft to 'painting by numbers' are lamentably out of touch. A British Academy-funded survey carried out in the early 1990s bears testimony to the fact that a diverse range of historical interests is represented within the 'history and computing' community. Although the nineteenth century and the decennial census dominates, a wide range of sources covering a broad time frame has been computerized for the purposes of historical research.

What other sources might be computerized?

Medievalists have made machine-readable manorial court rolls (Williamson, 1984), clergy ordination records (Davis, 1990), and the text of the Domesday Books (Ayton and Davis, 1987); early-modernists have converted probate inventories (Groves, 1990; Currie and Alcock, 1989; Weatherill, 1987), wills (Groves, 1990), listings material, and parish registers (Wrigley and Schofield, 1981; Schürer, 1987); while modern historians have computerized charity records (Page, 1993), ownership information (Morgan and Moss, 1989), poll books (Drake, 1971; O'Gorman, 1989; Green, 1989; Hirst and Bowler, 1989), trade directories (Young, 1990), union records (Treble, 1987), and correspondence and diary evidence (Nenadic, 1990). For further details and examples, see the entries in Schürer and Anderson's (1992) *Guide to historical datafiles held in machine-readable form.* In addition, sources are being linked to provide multi-source (or meta) databases, facilitating prosopographical (i.e. biographical) and longitudinal-type investigations.

1.5   LOCAL HISTORY, GENEALOGY AND COMPUTING

Local historians and genealogists have long used computers to store and process the information they collect. Some local family history societies are avid computer-users, making machine-readable transcriptions, particularly of parish register and census material, often for an entire county (see the various issues of *Family History News and Digest*). This should come as no surprise, especially since those in search of their family ancestry are particularly keen to use indexes of sources, and to create indexes for others to use. What better than a computer to sort a list of individuals by name, by place of birth, by place of residence, or any other item of information which is defined in the source material? Indeed, the largest, most ambitious and painstaking project converting historical material into machine-readable form to date is probably the British 1881 Census Project, still currently in process and sponsored by the Genealogical Society of Utah. The project was initiated by the British Genealogical Record Users' Committee (an informal group including representatives from the Federation of Family History Societies, the Society of Genealogists, the Institute of Genealogical and Heraldic Studies, the Public Record Office, and the Genealogical Society of Utah) to index the national census of 1881 – not a sample, but rather the entire census for England, Wales and Scotland, all 29.71 million person records (for further details see Genealogical Society of Utah, 1991, and Schürer and Anderson, 1992, pp.168–9; see also section 2.1 below, and Chapter 12, section 5.4 for another example, the Irish Genealogical Project, which is intended to create a comprehensive genealogical database for all Ireland).

As well as large-scale data-gathering exercises, family historians and genealogists have been particularly active in two other areas of history and computing. The first of these is the development and recommendation of standards for the coding and interchange of data. Access to information and information exchange, whether computerized or not, has always been an important element in the pursuit of genealogy, yet when the information in question takes the form of computerized data, because of the maze created by the incompatibilities of computing hardware and software, a measure of common agreement is needed to maximize efficiency and minimize misunderstandings. In this regard, the family historians with their GEDCOM system (GEnealogical Data COMmunications – a standard developed by the genealogical section of The Church of Jesus Christ of Latter-day Saints) have slightly stolen a march on their computer-using cousins in academia (Hawgood, 1991). A similar development amongst academic historians is the application of SGML (Standard Generalized Markup Language) principles to the generation of machine-readable versions of historical source materials. SGML is an agreed international standard which, via the insertion of a series of pre-defined 'tags', indicates the structure of machine-readable texts (in this case transcripts of historical documents) in a hardware- and software-independent form, and consequently offers a convenient vehicle with which to exchange and disseminate data (Greenstein, 1991).

The second area where, unlike general historians, genealogists and family historians have been particularly active has been in the development, production and marketing of a large and growing range of software packages specially designed to address their own data-handling requirements: for example, the generation of personal biographies, the drawing of family trees, and the representation of lineages (see Hawgood, 1989, and also the up-to-date reviews in the Society of Genealogists' quarterly journal, *Computers in Genealogy*). The main reason for their lead in this regard is the more limited range of source materials used and the relative uniformity of the research goals in view. Since the computing demands of general historians are not so well defined, the majority tend to rely on software packages designed primarily for commercial or business applications rather than the specific needs of historians. One important exception is the Kleio project, headed by Manfred Thaller of the Max-Planck Institut für Geschichte, Göttingen, Germany, which seeks to produce and maintain a software package designed explicitly for the needs of computer-using historians (Thaller, 1987; an English version of this package is available from Dr P. Denley, Department of History, Queen Mary and Westfield College, University of London, Mile End Road, London).

1.6   MAKING A START

So how should the would-be computer-using historian proceed?

Do you need to use a computer for your research?

The first question to ask, and one which is sometimes overlooked, is whether or not the computer really is necessary. Clearly, a computer can process things quickly; it can sort and count far faster than any human (even a historian!). But in assessing the 'real' time of computing one has also to take into account the time taken to learn how to use the necessary hardware and software effectively, as well as the time taken for data entry and checking. So in the initial stages you may put a lot of time and effort into learning the new skill without getting much back in return – the real benefits (particularly in time-saving) tend to come in the long term. As a consequence, if the research in question requires only a small amount of sorting through data and counting observations, it may not be particularly efficient to employ a computer to do it. Just as no one would go to the time and expense of learning to use a word processor in order to leave a note for the milkman, it may not be worth entering a parish register into a computer simply to tabulate the number of baptisms, burials and marriages per decade. You should also ask whether your objectives might be met by simply taking a sample of your data (see Chapter 8, section 6).

Let us assume, however, that there are advantages to be gained from using computers in the particular piece of research you have in mind. How should you start? First, you should resist the temptation to rush in. Remember, the computer learning-curve is quite steep, so seek lots of advice before starting to climb up it. Do some background reading, speak to friends or neighbours who are already computer-users, and above all, if you have the opportunity, discuss your ideas with other historians who have already ventured down the computing path and can point to common pitfalls along the way.

One of the first mazes that you will enter involves the choice of hardware and software. This may be quite restricted if there is only one machine available and this houses just one or two software packages. But if you are looking to buy your own equipment, the choice is considerable. Fortunately, there is a large stock of magazine literature available in newsagents and public libraries which assesses and evaluates the current computer hardware (admittedly not usually with historians in mind), and this is often a good guide. Comprehensive guides to the software market are not so easy to come by, but a brief guide to software has been produced especially for historians by the Computers in Teaching Initiative Centre for History at the University of Glasgow, and this could be the starting point for most novices (Spaeth, 1991). It is impossible to make hard and fast recommendations, but a useful principle is to avoid both the very new and the very old.

In choosing software, one of the most important considerations is not so much the capabilities of the software *per se* but the form and structure of the information contained within the historical document to be computerized. All historical documents have a structure: some – family diaries or letters, for example – are very loosely structured; others, such as CEBs, are very highly structured. The more structured the document, the easier it is to process with a computer, and it is for this reason that census materials were among the first to be computerized.

Having said this, what is actually meant by structure? To answer this it is necessary to understand how information is stored and processed by computers. In general, most database-management software requires the information it processes to be organized in a certain way. First of all, the data are broken down into *units of observation* or *records*: these might be the individuals recorded in a baptism or burial register, or the couples recorded in a marriage register. Each record will then have one or more *variables* or *attributes*: for example, first name(s), surname, date of event, in the case of burials and baptisms; or bride's surname, groom's surname, bride's father's occupation, groom's father's occupation, and so on in the case of marriages. In turn, the variables will each be allocated a *value*. In most cases, this will be a character string (i.e. one or more words), such as 'John', 'Smith', or 'Master Carpenter'; alternatively, it may be a numeric value: 52, 67, or 9, as in the case of age. Consequently, given this form of organization, one can see how the pages of the CEBs appear to fit computerization so well (see Figures 3.3 to 3.5 in Chapter 3, section 2.1), because the lines running across and down the page, separating individuals and columns of information, mirror the kind of rectangular matrices which software packages create internally to organize their data. With this image in mind, you can see that it might be the case that not all records will contain information on the whole range of variables: to take the census example, only the minority of individuals (i.e. records) will have information recorded concerning disability, the final and often forgotten column of the census page. Thus, to rectangularize the data structure, those records with no information for a given variable will need to be allocated missing values, either implicitly or explicitly.

In addition to this basic 'flat' or rectangular form of database (see Figure 9.1(a)), it is also the case that, depending on the software chosen, it may be possible to define various record types within any single database, each with a different array of given variables. These differing record types may correspond to separate structural levels in the data, perhaps representing some hierarchy of information, or they may be related to one another in some other way. To return to the example of the census, one might conceive of one level of information where each record or

(a) A flat or rectangular database

nos	h	address	x-name	surname	age	occupation	occode
1	1	3 High St	John	Smith	45	Butcher	61
2	1	3 High St	Mary	Smith	43	Butcher's wife	93
3	1	3 High St	James	Smith	8	Scholar	11
4	1	3 High St	Mary	Green	17	Servant	43
5	2	Station Cottage	Henry	White	34	Railway lab.	21
6	2	Station Cottage	Eliza	White	30	–	–
7	2	Station Cottage	John	White	7	Scholar	11
8	2	Station Cottage	Alice	White	5	Scholar	11

C

A

B

(b) A relational or hierarchical database

h	address
1	3 High St
2	Station Cottage

A   C   B

occode	occupation
11	Scholar
21	Railway lab.
43	Servant
61	Butcher
93	Butcher's wife

C   A   B

nos	h	x-name	surname	age	occode
1	1	John	Smith	45	61
2	1	Mary	Smith	43	93
3	1	James	Smith	8	11
4	1	Mary	Green	17	43
5	2	Henry	White	34	21
6	2	Eliza	White	30	–
7	2	John	White	7	11
8	2	Alice	White	5	11

C   A   B

A = Columns, fields, variables or attributes

B = Rows, records or observations (for flat files)

C = Table, file or relation

——— One-to-one relationship

——€ One-to-many relationship

)—€ Many-to-many relationship

Note: This census example illustrates only one-to-many type relationships. For discussion of the alternatives, see section 1.7.

Figure 9.1 Two forms of representing a census document in the computer

observation equates to a new household, with variables providing details on address and size, for example, with a second level for individuals containing variables covering name, age, marital status and so on. These two record types would also share a common variable, say household number, through which information on the different levels could be matched and processed accordingly. Such bodies of data with multi-level record structures are often referred to as hierarchical or relational databases, and the various rectangular interlocking structures within them as tables (see Figure 9.1(b)).

Given this model, it is clear that it is easier to define a structural pattern for some documents than for others. Generally speaking, the more textual a source the more loosely structured it will be. Consequently, if such sources are being computerized, care needs to be taken to ensure that the software chosen allows an appropriate amount of textual analysis (such as concordance and word-proximity searches) and flexibility in the definition of record types. Above all, it is important not to allow the proposed analysis to be strait-jacketed by imposing too rigid a data structure on the source material. The structure of the data files which historians create should be defined by the documents themselves, not by the software used to analyse them.

Even when the necessary computing hardware and software are in place, you should resist the temptation to rush ahead with entering data into the machine. First, it may be the case that appropriate information for your needs already exists in machine-readable form. The History Data Unit at the ESRC Data Archive, University of Essex, has assembled a large collection of historical source materials in machine-readable form, most of which are available for dissemination to researchers according to the user's requirements (see Figure 9.2). In particular, a large collection of parish level census material is available, and in order to avoid unnecessary duplication of effort it is certainly worth checking what has been undertaken already (see section 2 below, and also the guide by Schürer and Anderson, 1992). Secondly, it is better to test the new techniques of computing on a little – a few chosen records with an appropriate range of variables – rather than a lot.

In preparing the machine-readable version of the document in question, a general principle is to collect the information in a source-oriented fashion; that is, to record the information as closely as possible to the original source, in terms of content as well as structure. Computer-using historians who practise data reduction (omitting various parts of the document) all too often come to regret the decision later on during the research process. If the fullest amount of information is stored in the computer, then all the questions which could be asked of the original document can also be asked of the machine-readable version. Anything short of this will be just a partial transcription and will be at risk of suffering from misinterpretation or incomplete examination.

Before too long you will face the problem of coding. In simple terms, this is a convenient method of standardizing or grouping together ranges of values for given variables. For example, in analysing occupational structure it is useful to have all of those undertaking similar jobs grouped together: carpenters, sawyers, joiners and turners, maybe. This is best done by allocating a single code, usually a straightforward number, to the values which you wish to analyse as a single group. Yet again there is a danger in being too hasty. Since most of the eventual analyses will be based on the coded rather than the actual values, it is worth spending some time on designing a robust scheme (i.e. one that can deal with most eventualities). Ideally, the tasks of data entry and coding should be split into two distinct phases, with codes allocated after the full range of original values has been safely stored in the computer. This means that you can allow for what might previously have been unexpected; and since the original values will always be stored in the machine, groupings can be updated and adjusted as your ideas develop, as interpretations change, and as the research progresses (for further comments on coding, see Morris, 1990; Schürer, 1990; Schürer and Diederiks, 1993).

1.7 ANALYSING THE BRISTOL BUSINESS COMMUNITY: AN EXAMPLE

These principles can be illustrated by a brief example. Irrespective of the specific aims, sources, hardware and software – which may be very different in any particular case you may be pursuing – one recurrent issue to note is the problem of interpreting the logical structure of the documents being used, and representing this in the automated processing. This important point was stressed in section 1.6.

STUDY: 22 *Trading Community of Shifnal, 1841-1861*

===

PURPOSE: To provide a database of information on trading families in Shifnal in the mid-nineteenth century.

CONTENT: Information on traders and trading families has been compiled into a database with the following information: surname; first names; personal identification; number; address; age; occupation; birthplace; sex; relationships.

SOURCE: Trade directories, census records, tithe records, rate books. [Shropshire County Record Office].

PERIOD: 1841 to 1861 (To be extended).

PLACE: Shifnal – Shropshire.

HARDWARE: Amstrad 1640 (MsDos).

SOFTWARE: dBase III+.

REFERENCE: Hill, Trevor, 'The Trading Community of Shifnal 1841-1861', (unpublished MA dissertation, Department of English Local History, Leicester University).

STUDY: 126 *Census Data for Oxfordshire, 1851*

===

PURPOSE: To provide a full transcript of the 1851 census for all Oxfordshire parishes. The information is held on disc and microfiche and the surname indices have been published as a series of twelve booklets.

CONTENT: All persons residing in Oxfordshire on the night of the census in 1851. Full transcript including details of name; age; sex; marital status; occupation; birthplace; relationship to head of household. A separate file of surname indexes has also been compiled.

SOURCE: Census enumerators' books. [Public Record Office: HO 107].

PERIOD: 1851.

PLACE: Abingdon, Banbury, Bicester, Chipping Norton, Headington, Henley, Oxford, Thame, Wallingford (Berks.), Witney, Woodstock – Oxfordshire.

HARDWARE: PC (MsDos).

SOFTWARE: Lotus 123.

REFERENCE: The Oxfordshire Family History Society have published the surname index in a series of twelve booklets.

Figure 9.2 Examples of computer-based studies taken from a recent guide to historical data files in machine-readable form (Schürer and Anderson, 1992, pp.23 and 87); many of these are available through the ESRC History Data Unit. This guide is a useful source of ideas about possible computer uses

The example is Harvey and Press's analysis of the business community of Bristol at the turn of the twentieth century (Harvey and Press, 1991). This faced the problem of being a multi-source study using a variety of materials, some having regular structures (such as registers of officers of the Chamber of Commerce), others being unstructured text (for example, obituaries and similar items found in newspapers). In describing the problems of representing an array of sources in a single integrated database, the authors provide a splendid account of database specification and design. They first distinguish between a source-based and a model-driven approach. In the former, the researcher captures a broad range of sources in machine-readable form, and then uses the computer to help discover the various connections between them. For the latter, the researcher starts with a predetermined set of well-defined objectives and has in place already a fairly clear idea of the data required and how the information in the various sources interrelates. Thus, items of information may be selected from within a wider-ranging document according to the specific research goals in view. The Bristol project, the authors claim, fell under the second heading; probably the majority of research projects include aspects of both approaches.

The focus of Harvey and Press's article is the use of the Bristol material to illustrate conceptual data modelling; in particular, entity-relationship modelling (ERM), one of the more widely used data-modelling techniques. The central key to ERM is the mapping of the various relationships between the variables of the component files (or tables) of the combined database being examined. The relationships fall into one of three categories: one-to-one, one-to-many, or many-to-many.

Using this approach, for CEBs, a network of relationships might be described as follows: within one enumeration district there are many streets; within each street there may be many houses; within each house many households; within each household many people, and so on (Schürer, 1991). As illustrated in Figure 9.1(b), most of the relationships in the census material are of the one-to-many kind, illustrating the hierarchical nature of the source, whilst in the Bristol case the pattern of relationships described by Harvey and Press are more complex. For example, a one-to-one relationship exists between a database holding information on MPs and another on constituencies, since by definition each constituency has only one MP and vice versa; whilst a database providing information on the board members of various companies will have a many-to-many relationship to a database of individuals giving company affiliation, since each person could be a member of several companies, and each company might have several board members. The specification of such relationship networks, argue the authors, is critical to understanding the structure of the planned database (and by implication the source materials being used), and in turn planning the computer system in which the data should be held and analysed. The software chosen by Harvey and Press was Oracle, a powerful relational database-management system integrating elaborate text interrogation facilities. This package is mainly used on midi or mainframe systems. It is, however, also available for PC computers, and similar examples of projects utilizing relational databases with PC-based software can be found in Allberry (1991) and Gutmann et al. (1989).

EXERCISE 9.1

1   Review this section by compiling a brief list of some uses to which computing has been put in family and community history, using:

(a)   mainframe computers;

(b)   modern, user-friendly, small-scale computers.

Also note any potential problems about such uses.

2   Consider how far any of these uses would be helpful for your own research.

Answers/comments p.305

Finally, it must be remembered that the computer not only offers speed in searching through, sorting, and counting data; as a result of this time-saving, it also offers flexibility – the ability, that is, to test out ideas and examine correlations within the data which would simply not be attempted if the research were undertaken manually. To sum up, in computerizing your data you must take care not to build in your own inflexibilities through the adoption of an oversimplistic data structure, excessive data reduction, or restrictive coding practices.

2   USING DATABASES

by Magnus John

Look at Chapter 13, section 5.2 ('Computerized local studies collections') for examples of the kinds of material from which computerized indexes and databases are produced.

What conclusions can you draw?

o   The sources are varied: books, newspapers, registers, photographs, films, prints, etc.

o   Sources may be from many different media: illustrations, printed records or books, tapes (audio, video, films).

o   Different forms of computerized data have been produced: indexes (to photographs, films, audio tapes, illustrations); databases: on-line or on CD-ROM.

o   There is a large (and increasing) number of databases.

So while you may not wish to use computers for creating your own computerized records on the lines indicated in section 1 above, you may well want or need to explore some of the many existing databases. Indeed, the use of databases generally is spreading (see, for example, Schürer and Anderson, 1992), reflecting the growing interest in computer applications more generally. In the workplace, commerce, libraries, research organizations, institutions of higher learning, schools, and in the home, users' varied needs are being met by database systems of all sizes.

In the context of family and community history, however, the application of database systems cannot be isolated from the structure of the sources from which the data has been extracted (see section 1.6 above). The variety of sources, types of data, their physical appearance, appeal, content, and size are all relevant for the form in which the user ultimately has access to the materials.

2.1   RELEVANT SOURCES OF INFORMATION

So let us briefly look at some of the sources commonly consulted by researchers studying family and community history: parish registers, census data, immigration lists, poll books, photographs, journal articles, audio tapes, films, and newspapers. Examples of most of these are available in local studies collections. However, given the all-encompassing nature of the subject, reflecting the patterns of life of individuals, families and communities, these sources are often fragmentary and scattered (migration and changing economic and social circumstances affect people as well as towns and cities).

These diverse records have appealed to a number of interest groups. Consequently, decisions about them are bound up with political and economic considerations, particularly in the case of local studies collections. Because their content is often localized, they remain relatively specific or small-scale, even if some of the data eventually become computerized. At the extreme end are standard sources – census data, for example – collected, coordinated and made available on a national basis, and thus more amenable to commercial exploitation than purely personal or local data. So also are parliamentary papers in the House of Commons Library, where an on-line computer-based index for recent material has been introduced (POLIS: Parliamentary On-Line Information System). In between are materials/collections with direct educational or research appeal which may attract funding from an autonomous educational institution – the ESRC, for example – to meet national research interests; or the massive Irish Genealogical Project, supported by governmental and European development funding, which is gathering together computerized indexes of such sources as parish registers, tithe books, civil registers and census returns (see Grenham, 1992, pp.272ff.) At the other extreme are the private associations and commercial ventures where membership entitles individuals to access to, for example, computerized directories to the genealogical research being undertaken by members.

The interests of the various groups involved – commercial or educational, societies, public service institutions, etc. – do not always overlap, although they impinge upon each other. The 'protective' element within each group tends to inhibit the development of joint database systems – though the political and financial advantages of collaboration might eventually prevail (a few collaborative exercises are already under way, such as the 1881 British census transcription project or the Irish Genealogical Project). That would in no way preclude the continued use of 'old technology' (Seton, 1991) such as films, audio-tapes, photographs, diaries. As entrenched and valid forms, these are simply irreplaceable, although computerized indexing is becoming a popular method of identifying and retrieving information from films, photographs and audio material.

2.2 DATABASE SYSTEMS: THEIR RELEVANCE AND USE

Why use databases?

Is a computer search necessary when there are so many printed documents and other sources available for research? How do these printed sources compare with computerized indexes or databases? The checklist in Schema A summarizes the advantages and disadvantages of using a database as against printed sources.

Schema A: Features of printed sources as against databases

Printed sources	Databases
Printed indexes and abstracts have a limited number of access points, e.g. author and/or subject.	More malleable than text in responding to search strategies.
May need to search through a variety of sources and several indexes compiled by several hands.	Even where more than one computerized index is involved, search time is faster and results more comprehensive.
May need to travel if sources are located in different libraries.	Access to a computer terminal may be all that is necessary to retrieve the data on-line. (This is not true of all databases or computerized indexes, however.)
Printed indexes and abstracts are not as expensive to produce as databases.	Databases are expensive to produce and to use.
User-friendliness: many people are more accustomed to printed sources.	Required knowledge of special languages etc. to conduct searches may inhibit use by some (but attract others). Also, computers can go wrong!
Portability	Databases are not generally widely accessible

The two types of information system are, therefore, complementary and both have their uses. The most common types of database are:

o   *Bibliographic*: a database whose records comprise bibliographic citations, with details of author, title, publisher, date, etc., and sometimes also abstracts of the documents cited. (A typical example is DIALOG.)

o   *Numeric*: a database of statistical and numeric data. Such data can be extracted or calculated and transferred to a spreadsheet or statistical compilation as a secondary operation.

o   *Full-text*: contains full text of the source or reference cited. This form lends itself readily to CD-ROM as a medium, since it can store vast quantities of text and is generally manipulable to keyword searching.

o   *Mixed numeric and text:* there is a growing tendency to separate out this fourth category of database, which contains both statistical and/or numeric data as well as textual information. An example would be computerized records containing categorized information on particular topics or sources, such as CEBs (see section 1.1 above).

Looking back at Schema A, you will recall that one advantage of databases is that they are more malleable to search strategies – rather than having to search all through the (sometimes massive) data, you can often search for particular points through keywords or other indexed categories.

First, however, you have to get access to the database. Databases come in various forms. A small database (e.g. a machine-readable series of CEBs) may be available on floppy disc or similar. For larger ones, you are likely to need access to a CD-ROM or a computer network using a terminal. Where there is a CD-ROM version of the database you need, use it. You pay no connection charges and many libraries now acquire databases on CD-ROM. The scope for using computer networks, especially in institutions of higher learning, is enormous and constantly expanding (especially but not only for bibliographic databases, including catalogues of libraries in Britain and overseas).

For both CD-ROM and network use, find out what service exists locally, and ask for any printed guides. For network searches in particular, there is often an intermediary who can help with the special commands needed (for further comments on on-line information retrieval, see Hartner, 1986).

2.3   HOW A DATABASE SEARCH WORKS: AN EXAMPLE

To use technical language, the basic search techniques in many database systems adopt variants of a Boolean logic system. Descriptors defining concepts pertaining to the search topic are used in conjunction with operators, such as '*and*', '*or*', '*not*', to express logical processes that are to take place on searches for the defined categories.

Let us turn this into a practical example. You might have access to a suitably organized computerized version of the 1851 Census data for Buckinghamshire, and wish to identify the number of *farmers* who were *heads of household* in a *particular town* (Winslow).

To do that, we need to initiate a search strategy combining the relevant operators ('*and*' etc.), with the search descriptors (i.e. the categories: farmer; household head; Winslow). So our search command will combine FARMER *and* WINSLOW *and* HEAD to isolate those records of farmers who are heads of household in Winslow from those listed under other descriptors, such as 'farmers' wives' and 'farm labourers'. We could also isolate all farmers in Winslow, through the search command FARMER *and* WINSLOW – which would also find 'farmers' wives' and 'farm labourers'. The index will reveal figures for each category that are combined at the next search stage, which only selects those records where the three categories occur. (Fewer references are

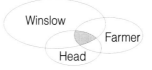

Figure 9.3 Searching for farming household heads in Winslow

likely to be retrieved after the *'and'* operator has been used in this way to combine the concepts.) Graphically, the result of the search is represented in Figure 9.3.

On-line searching thus has its own methodology. As well as the necessary command language to direct the processes, the categories used as search terms need to be consonant with the terms and concepts used to index the data stored in the database.

The same principle applies when on-line search systems allow 'free-text' searching. In this case, *all* words in the database act as index words as well as the controlled index terms specified or added by the database producer. A 'free-text' database gives users greater flexibility, while at the same time transferring from the indexer to the user the need for more thought about what is to be retrieved. The value of 'free-text' searching to the researcher has been enhanced in some systems by the use of 'proximity operators' to link terms in a search enquiry.

2.4 TRENDS FOR THE FUTURE?

In some ways, database systems are not as yet very developed in family and community history. This may partly be because of the great variety of printed and other 'hard copy' material available. Besides, other technological media – such as microfilms, microfiche and audio-tapes – are already too well established and recognized for changes to overtake current practice for some time (Hollerton, 1986). Furthermore, though the opportunities offered by on-line searches are growing, the cost of producing suitable databases from variable and scattered information cannot be ignored. Apart from efforts made in computerizing local studies collections and the extensive genealogical projects, the development of databases generally tends to focus upon current information (Nicholas and Connoly, 1987, p.530).

But there are also some hopeful trends. Various primary sources are being transcribed and entered into databases, such as The Cheshire Parish Register Project, 1538–1971 (Walker, 1983; see also the references in Schürer and Anderson, 1992, and in section 1.4 above). Organizations like the Federation of Family History Societies, the Society of Genealogists, the Irish Genealogical Project, and local family history societies are making more sources available, both printed and in the form of databases. It is true that only a small proportion of the material within the local studies collections has been computerized: the task is massive, given the huge spread of materials, such as local newspapers, journals, photographs, etc. in local libraries throughout Britain. But increasingly, however slowly, these sources are being opened up for researchers. Examples include: computerized indexing of over 25,000 illustrations in the Kent Local Studies Illustration Collection (Dunn, 1986); a bibliography of local studies material in the East Yorkshire region available on-line to public access from the Brynmor Jones Library at the University of Hull (English, 1989); computerized information on the 1881 Census for Shropshire and on local newspapers, in the Shropshire County Library (Carr, 1987, pp.13–14).

Dewe has charted the rise in importance of local studies collections in libraries (Dewe, 1987). In parallel with the growth of interest in tracing ancestral links and the advent of new technology, the level of interest in computerized records since the 1980s has been phenomenal. It is becoming important to researchers to exploit resources from several access points, not just the printed page. Computerized search methods and techniques open up 'hidden' sources in local studies collections by indexing keywords which can be utilized in search enquiries. The increase in computerized data archive collections (such as the Centre for Research in Ethnic Relations, University of Warwick, and the ESRC Data Archive at the University of Essex – see ESRC, 1992), in creating new research databases (such as the British nineteenth-century labour markets database – see Southall, 1990), and in computerized bibliographic data relating to specific geographical areas (as at the University of York – see English, 1989) is a trend which can only continue.

However, the fact remains that the effort to computerize data in local studies collections has been confined to pockets around the country (see Chapter 13, section 5). Researchers in family, social and community history may know about developments in other parts of the country because of their research interests, but there is no national index of local studies research interests. Perhaps the constantly changing pattern of local studies research has something to do with this. Also, lack of money probably holds local studies collections back from becoming computerized and more widely available.

Thus, in the short term at least, influence may remain with larger organizations, including the commercial producers of on-line databases and CD-ROMs. The largest computerized index of family records worldwide is the International Genealogical Index (see Chapter 4, section 3.5). The scale of the enterprise is impressive by any standards, given the effort required to coordinate it. Is that level of coordination impossible in Britain? Public libraries could certainly learn from this initiative (most have invested in the local or national records from the Index on fiche).

Large organizations holding records with wide appeal are becoming aware of the possibility of providing greater access to their material through the production of CD-ROMs and/or on-line facilities. Organizations such as ESRC, HMSO, PRO, and The British Library are all introducing or sponsoring services which exploit new technology. It may be that over time organizations such as the Federation of Family History Societies and other local history societies will mount joint enterprises to create databases produced through the collaboration of their members.

At the moment, university and research libraries have greater access than public libraries to computer network facilities. Higher education institutions provide networking facilities to their staff (and students) via JANET (the Joint Academic NETwork). This allows files and mail to be transferred electronically between users in different universities, and facilitates on-line searching of catalogues and bulletin boards held at remote sites; for example, the BIRON (Bibliographic Information Retreival On-line) guide to holdings at the ESRC Data Archive, and BIDS (Bath Information and Data Service) which includes a number of citation indexes. JANET also provides a gateway to other computer networks, such as EARN (European Academic Research Network) and the American network BITNET (Because It's Time NETwork), thus enabling communications and searches to be undertaken at an international scale. Is this the trend for the future?

REFERENCES AND FURTHER READING

Allberry, S. (1991) 'HYPERTEXT using Hypercard on Apple Macintosh for family historians and one-name studies', *Computers in Genealogy,* 4, 2, pp.60–3.

Armstrong, A. (1974) *Stability and change in an English county town. A social study of York 1801–51,* Cambridge, Cambridge University Press.

Aydelotte, W.O. (1954) 'The House of Commons in the 1840s', *History,* New Series, XXXIX, 137, pp.249–62.

Ayton, A. and Davis, V. (1987) 'The Hull Domesday Project', in Denley, P. and Hopkins, D. (eds) (1987).

Bagg, J. (1992) 'Introduction to database systems for anthropologists', *Bulletin of Information on Computing and Anthropology*, 8, pp.2–9.

Carr, A.M. (1987) 'The MSC and Local Studies – the Shropshire programme', *The Local Studies Librarian*, 6, 2, pp.13–14.

Currie, C.R.J. and Alcock, N.W. (1989) *Vernacular Architecture*, 20.

Davis, V. (1990) 'Medieval English clergy database', *History and Computing*, 2, 2, pp.75–87.

Denley, P. and Hopkins, D. (eds) (1987) *History and computing*, Manchester, Manchester University Press.

Denley, P. et al. (eds) (1989) *History and computing*, II, Manchester, Manchester University Press.

Dewe, M. (1987) 'Local studies and the new technology: the British experience', *Information Development: The International Journal for Librarians, Archivists and Information Specialists*, 3, 1, January, pp.23–9.

Drake, M. (1971) 'The mid-Victorian voter', *Journal of Interdisciplinary History*, 1, 3, pp.473–90.

Dunn, C. (1986) 'Computer indexing the Kent Local Studies Illustration Collection', *Local Studies Librarian*, 5, 1, Summer, pp.11–15.

Dyos, H.J. and Baker, A.B.M. (1968) 'The possibilities of computerizing census data', in Dyos, H.J. (ed.) *The study of urban history*, London, Edward Arnold.

English, B. (1989) 'Electronic bibliography: an example from East Yorkshire', *The Local Historian*, 19, 3, August, pp.117–19.

ESRC (1992) 'National ethnic minority data archive launched', *News from the ESRC*, February, p.6.

Family History News and Digest (1992), 8, 4, pp.115–24.

Fielding, N. and Lee, R. (eds) (1991) *Using computers in qualitative research,* London, Sage.

Fogel, R.W. (1964) *Railroads and American economic growth: essays in econometric history,* Baltimore, Johns Hopkins Press.

Genealogical Society of Utah (1991) 'Computerization of the 1881 census', *Computers in Genealogy*, 4, 2, pp.53–6.

Gilmour-Bryson, A. (ed.) (1984) *Computer application to medieval studies*, Kalamazoo, Western Michigan University Press.

Green, E.M. (1989) 'Social structure and political behaviour in Westminster, 1784–1788', in Denley, P. et al. (eds) (1989).

Greenstein, D.I. (ed.) (1991) *Modelling historical data: towards a standard for encoding and exchanging machine-readable texts*, St. Katherinen, Scripta Mercaturae Verlag.

Grenham, J. (1992) *Tracing your Irish ancestors,* Dublin, Gill and Macmillan.

Groves, J. (1990) 'Housing in North East Cheshire in the age of rebuilding 1600–1760', *Cheshire History*, 25, pp.30–9.

Gutmann, M.P. et al. (1989) 'Keeping track of our treasures: managing historical data with relational database software', *Historical Methods*, 22, 4, pp.128–43.

Harter, S.P. (1986) *On-line information retrieval: concepts, principles and techniques*, Orlando, Florida, Academic Press.

Harvey, C. and Press, P. (1991) 'The business elite of Bristol: a case study in database design', *History and Computing, 3,* 1, pp.1–11.

Hawgood, D. (1989) *Computers for family history: an introduction* (3rd edn), London, Hawgood Computing Ltd.

Hawgood, D. (1991) *GEDCOM data transfer: moving your family tree*, London, Hawgood Computing Ltd.

Hirst, D. and Bowler, S. (1989) 'Voting in Hertford 1679–1721', *History and Computing,* 1, 1, pp.1–13.

Hodges, M. and Pryce, W.T.R. (1993) 'The personal computer: a useful research tool', audio-cassette 3B in Braham, P. (ed.) *Using the past: audio-cassettes on sources and methods for family and community historians*, Milton Keynes, The Open University.

Hollerton, E. (1986) 'Modern techniques and media in local studies; a weekend school at Loughborough University, 19th–21st September 1986', *Local Studies Librarian*, 5, 2, Winter, pp.6–8.

Jardine, C.J. and Macfarlane, A.D.J. (1978) 'Computer input of historical records for multi-source record linkage', in Flinn, M.W. (ed.) *Proceedings of the 7th International Economic History Congress*, Edinburgh, 2, pp. 71–8.

Kibley, F. (ed.) *Selected proceedings from the CAL '89 Symposium*, Oxford, Pergamon.

Macfarlane, A. (1977) *Reconstructing historical communities*, Cambridge, Cambridge University Press.

Morgan, N. and Moss, M. (1989) 'Urban wealthholding and the computer', in Denley, P. et al. (eds) (1989).

Morris, R.J. (1990) 'Occupational coding: principles and examples', *Historical Social Research*, 15, 1, pp.3–29.

Nenadic, S. (1990) 'Identifying social networks with a computer aided analysis of personal diaries', in Mawdsley, E., Morgan, N.J., Richmond, L.R. and Trainor, R.H. (eds) *Historians, computers and data. Applications in research and teaching*, Manchester, Manchester University Press.

Nicholas, D. and Connoly, K. (1987) 'Information technology developments in the newspaper industry and the future of the librarian', *Library Association Record*, 89, 10, October, pp.530–1.

O'Gorman, F. (1989) 'Electoral behaviour in England, 1700–1872', in Denley, P. et al. (eds) (1989).

Page, S.J. (1993) 'Research methods and techniques – researching local history: methodological issues and computer-assisted analysis', *The Local Historian*, 23, 1, pp.20–30.

Ryan, N.S. (1985) 'Gtree: a system for the interactive display and editing of kinship information', *Bulletin of Information on Computers in Anthropology* (University of Kent), 3, pp.6–15.

Schürer, K. (1987) 'Historical demography, social structure and the computer', in Denley, P. and Hopkins, D. (eds) (1987).

Schürer, K. (1990) 'The historical researcher and codes: master and slave or slave and master?', in Mawdsley, E., Morgan, N.J., Richmond, L.R. and Trainor, R.H. (eds) *Historians, computers and data. Applications in research and teaching*, Manchester, Manchester University Press.

Schürer, K. (1991) 'Standards or model solutions? The case of census-type documents', in Greenstein, D.I. (ed.) (1991).

Schürer, K. (1993) 'Nominal lists and nominal record linkage', audio-cassette 2B in Braham, P. (ed.) *Using the past: audio-cassettes on sources and methods for family and community historians*, Milton Keynes, The Open University.

Schürer, K. and Anderson, S.J. (eds) (1992) *A guide to historical datafiles held in machine-readable form*, London, Association for History and Computing.

Schürer, K. and Diederiks, H. (eds) (1993) *The use of occupations in historical analysis*, St Katherinen, Scripta Mercaturae Verlag.

Seton, M. (1991) 'Information technology', in Dewe, M. (ed.) *Local studies collections: a manual*, vol.2, London, Gower.

Southall, H. (1990) 'The British nineteenth-century labour markets database at Queen Mary and Westfield College, University of London', *Local Population Studies*, 45, pp.74–6.

Spaeth, D.A. (1991) *A guide to software for historians*, Computers in Teaching Initiative Centre for History with Archaeology and Art History, Glasgow.

Speck, W.A. and Gray, W.A. (1970) 'Computer analysis of poll books: an initial report', *Bulletin of the Institute of Historical Research*, XLIII, 107, pp.105–12.

SPSS–X user's guide (3rd edn) (1988) Chicago, SPSS Inc.

Thaller, M. (1987) 'Methods and techniques of historical computation', in Denley, P. and Hopkins, D. (eds) (1987).

Treble, J.G. (1987) *Sliding scales and conciliation boards*, Oxford, Oxford Economic Papers.

Walker, G. (1983) 'Local studies and the new technology: report of the LSG Weekend School', *Local Studies Librarian*, 2, 1, Spring, pp.11–13.

Weatherill, L. (1987) 'Using data retrieve to analyse data from a sample of probate inventories', in Denley, P. and Hopkins, D. (eds) (1987).

Williamson, J. (1984) 'One use of the computer in historical studies: demographic, social and economic history from medieval English manor court rolls', in Gilmour-Bryson, A. (ed.) (1984).

Wrigley, E.A. and Schofield, R.S. (1981) *The population of England: a reconstruction*, London, Edward Arnold.

Young, C. (1990) 'Computer assisted mapping of the credit fields of nineteenth century rural tradesmen', *History and Computing*, 1, 2, pp.105–11.

PART IV

PRESENTATION, DISSEMINATION AND PUBLICATION

❖ ❖ ❖

CHAPTER 10

WRITING AND PUBLISHING YOUR WORK

by David Wilson

When you started your family or community history research, you may have had no particular aim of writing it up in mind. But, even if you were not initially very sure about what you would do with your findings, you probably had some intention of telling other people about them – members of your family, neighbours, fellow researchers, or perhaps a wider public.

This chapter will outline some of the ways in which you can write up and present your work to others. The subject and extent of your research will probably suggest its own readership. It may be, for example, that you only want to write a summary family history for members of your own family; or perhaps you are preparing a project as part of your studies. Alternatively, you may think your work will interest a range of people in your wider local community, in your town, city or district. The chapter does not aim to set out fixed rules of writing and presentation. However, whatever outside audience your work may have – and even if you just want to summarize your findings for yourself – there are a number of general points which you will find it helpful to bear in mind as you write up your research. Such 'principles of presentation' apply whether you decide to write a final report and just make a handful of photocopies of it, or whether you want to publish your research in a booklet or newspaper article.

Whatever your intentions, it is likely that at some point you will want to *write* your findings out in some final form, if only as a record of your work which is more accessible than the notes and other summaries you have produced during your research. And, with the advent of computer word-processing and graphics software – commonly called 'desktop publishing' packages – it is easy to produce an account of your work which will look good and provide a basis for preparing different versions of it for presentation to others. It is also easy, and not too expensive, to publish your work, and sections 2 and 3 set out some basic information to help you prepare your research for publication, taking account not just of design, layout and printing, but also of marketing and distribution.

Even if you don't want to publish your work, the principles of presentation and publication considered here will help you plan an effective way of writing up your research. The refinements of professional editing and design, outlined in section 3, might seem more detailed than you require, but an understanding of them will help you achieve a more polished end result, whether it be a project report or a book. This chapter is inevitably only a brief introduction to writing and publishing. The books listed at the end of the chapter – most of which should be available from your local library – will provide further information, and you should consult them if you want to follow up the advice given here.

1   EFFECTIVE PRESENTATION

Whatever your subject and whatever your intended form of presentation, there are a number of aspects to consider to help you prepare your work effectively. They might seem obvious, but it is easy to forget them if you are particularly close to your project. The author and critic Arthur Quiller-Couch once gave the advice to writers: 'Murder your darlings'. By this he meant that the writer should be wary of what he or she feels too close an affection towards; others are unlikely to feel the same affection for these 'darlings', so they should be struck out. This is overly poetic and dramatic advice (perhaps I should have been wary of keeping it in here!), but it makes a point of great importance: when preparing your work for presentation, it is essential to try to step aside from it and view it dispassionately.

This is not easy, but rereading your work *a few weeks after* completing it can be effective. Asking someone else to read it can also help. If you do this, beware of two dangers. First, beware of reacting defensively to comments, criticism and advice; it is easy to be over-sensitive and protective about your work. But secondly, beware of taking every criticism seriously and exhaustively revising your work. Even if you see room for improvement each time you look at it, repeated revision can become self-defeating perfectionism.

So how can a workable balance be struck? The essential point is to remember that your writing must *communicate*. And good communication is not just a matter of writing clearly. More than anything else, good communication means having a sure sense of your readership and presenting your work in a way which is appropriate for that audience.

1.1   AUDIENCE AND READERSHIP – WRITING TO BE READ

Your research studies will probably suggest a potential audience, and it may be one with which you are quite familiar. You may also feel that there is a wider public which might be interested in your work, but it might be hard to imagine that audience. Either way, assessing and trying to meet your potential readers' interests, expectations and likely requirements is the single most important principle of writing and presentation. You will not be able to write up your research successfully with a vague notion that *anyone* (or even that anyone with an interest in your subject) will find it interesting and enjoyable. It must be 'pitched' right for an imagined, intended 'market'. But this is easier to acknowledge than to achieve.

To start with, you need to choose an effective vehicle for presenting your research and ideas. There is little point in trying to cram complex, very personal or localized, detailed research into a newspaper article, or attempting to write about a subject requiring extensive illustration in a small booklet which cannot do justice to the pictures. And you should not expect a publisher to find a lengthy study of your family as inevitably interesting or marketable as you do. On the other hand, you may be able to adapt parts of your work to suit a wider audience. There will almost certainly be something in your research, however personal, which could be written up for a local newspaper or a local history association journal.

Whatever audience you aim for, even if it is just your family or neighbours, it is worth thinking carefully about how you present your work. Table 10.1 provides a checklist of questions about presentation. Considering your own work in terms of these questions should help you avoid a lot of potential pitfalls.

Table 10.1   Checklist of questions about presentation

Focus	What is the focus of your study? What exactly are you setting out to show?
Selection	What is relevant to the subject and focus of your study? It is easy to include too much detailed information or too little. What might your prospective readers be expecting to find out?
Background	What can you expect your readers to know already? What will they need to know by way of background and historical context to make sense of your study and its significance?
Explanation	How much explanation do you need to give of technical terms, difficult concepts or foreign words?
Signposting	How can your subject be expressed concisely and attractively to grab attention and to signal what you will be presenting? An informative and appealing title is essential; in longer works, a preface or introduction, and a clear contents list help readers to grasp the scope of the work and follow its argument.
Argument	How can your argument or theme be effectively supported? Explain your argument clearly, ensure sufficient evidence is included and that the significance of the evidence is explained. Draw explicit conclusions where appropriate rather than leaving the reader to make sense of your argument.
Execution	Do you do what you say you are going to do? It can be extremely confusing to a reader to expect one thing and find the author has wandered off in a different direction.
Structure	How can the material be best organized? A typical structure has chapters, containing headings and sub-headings; appendices can be used for less central or supporting material.
Style	What style is appropriate? Newspapers print in narrow columns, and long, complex sentences are difficult to follow in this format. Should the style be formal or chatty?
Illustrations	Are photographs necessary, helpful (and practicable; see sections 3.2.2 and 3.4), and drawings (e.g. maps, family trees)?
Tables	Can statistical data be most effectively presented in table form? Is there other information which could be presented in a table; chronological sequences of events, for example?
Special features	Is there anything in your study which could benefit from being presented in a different and distinctive form? For example: colour photographs or facsimiles of material which is only really useful if in colour; and recorded interview material which may need careful transcription and presentation to appear in print, or may be worth providing on audio-cassette.
References	Are references to other material important or necessary? How might they be best presented – in endnotes or footnotes or in the text?

_____ *EXERCISE 10.1* _____

To see how some of the questions in Table 10.1 might apply in practice for your own research studies, try writing one (or both) of the following:

1   A plan and an opening paragraph for a 700-word article for a local newspaper. Think about an appropriate focus (headline and subject) and style; outline how much information you think you will be able to include. Would an illustration or a sketch map be helpful?

2   A preface, of about 250 words, for a book (or booklet). A preface is an author's address to the reader explaining briefly: what the book is about and what it covers; why it has been written and its purpose; who it is for; and what is significant, different and distinctive about it. (This could be covered in an 'introduction' rather than a separate preface, but in a longer book the introduction will be a more extended account of the background to the subject and the book's argument.)

If you found Exercise 10.1 difficult, you may have found yourself wondering how other writers have tackled newspaper articles or prefaces. You may even have looked at some for comparison and for clues as to how to approach the tasks. If you did, you were taking a step towards doing some market research.

1.2   MARKET RESEARCH

Looking at how you can market your work will help you get your presentation right, because you will become better aware of what markets exist, and what your readership might expect. Thinking about and investigating potential markets is instructive in various ways, providing models for you to follow, and perhaps to avoid.

Market research is not as daunting as it sounds. There are some straightforward steps you can take to gain an understanding of market opportunities and publishing options. Finding out how other local family and community history researchers have published and presented their work, and comparing your studies with theirs, is a useful start. Alternatively, enquire at your local library, especially if it has a local studies archive. Even if it is small, the librarians could advise you about finding out about local publications and local newspapers, and they will have access to reference books of publishers and periodicals. At the very least, you could compare publications on subjects similar to your own. Bookshops are also good places for research. Most booksellers stock some work of local interest. Large chain booksellers often give their local managers scope to purchase limited stock locally, so they are worth a visit as well.

What should you be looking for? To begin with, see what is available: whether there is a local newspaper which has a regular or occasional local history column; whether there is a market for local studies booklets – ask booksellers how well individual titles sell and who buys them (there will be a tourist market in some areas); what has been published recently covering similar sorts of subject to your own. There are a lot of small publishers who specialize in local publications, so ask whether there are any in your area.

Your own ideas will become clearer the more you find out, and then you can focus on particular books and consider different publishing options. Look carefully at the journals, booklets or books which impress you as being especially effective and appropriate vehicles for your work; for example, if your work includes a lot of photographs, look at the quality of reproduction in other books. Note the publishers of such books, or the printers of booklets which have been published by the author. (All publications should carry the names and addresses of the printer and publisher, usually near the beginning or at the end.) Also note the prices, and examine the books for style, approach and design; read the back cover blurb, and look at the preface and introduction. This will help you develop experience of how authors and publishers set about presenting their material, and this awareness will aid your own writing, whether you want to publish it or not. Finally, this sort of market research provides the basis for selling your work if you do publish it. You can go back to the bookseller and the library to promote it with a clearer sense of what its appeal will be.

2   GETTING YOUR WORK PUBLISHED

When attempting to get your work published, the most important thing to bear in mind is that you must 'sell' it to the publisher. By this I do not mean that you have to make wild claims about it, but rather that you must present a clear, realistic and convincing case for its merit. You cannot assume that its virtues are self-evident.

2.1   JOURNALS, MAGAZINES AND NEWSPAPERS

Writing an article for a local family or history association journal or magazine may be the first publishing option you think of (see Chapter 13, sections 2.1 and 3.1). Even if you have greater publishing ambitions, getting an article published in such a forum will provide useful practice and be a good basis for more ambitious projects.

Most journals, whether local or national, have instructions about submitting articles. These specify the maximum number of words required, how the manuscript should be typed, how many copies should be submitted, how illustrations should be provided, that all third-party copyright permissions should be obtained by you, and other details of presentation and style. Such instructions for contributors are sometimes printed in the journal, though not always in every issue. However, the preliminary pages of the journal should state the name of the person to contact about submitting articles, usually the editor. You can also form some idea of the journal's requirements by looking at recent issues.

If you have not had any dealings with the publication before, and if it is not clear how to submit your work, write to ask for advice. Give the proposed title of your article, say a little about it, and ask whether it is the sort of article which would be considered for publication. Unless you are very uncertain about the journal's requirements, it might be better to prepare a nearly final version of your article before contacting the editor. Then your letter will be more definite and purposeful, and you will be in a position to submit quickly.

Having ascertained the submission requirements, you should follow them very carefully. It is important to ensure that what you submit is complete, correct and final. Although you will probably be expected to check page proofs, you will not be expected to change anything but only correct errors introduced when the text was typeset or laid out. (At the time of writing, many, if not most, journals and books are still conventionally typeset, but this is changing as computer word-processing makes rekeying unnecessary.) You may have to pay for any changes you make. Keep a copy of what you have submitted, and, if you want your manuscript returned, include the cost of return postage.

If you have an article accepted for publication in a journal you should not expect payment, but you should be sent at least one copy of the issue or copies of offprints of your piece. Publication may take some time, but you should be advised of this when your work is accepted. The editor will also advise you of any editorial amendments, and you should be consulted if these are substantial. Also check at this point what restrictions, if any, there may be on reprinting the article elsewhere, in case you wish to use the article in another context.

2.1.1   NEWSPAPERS

The idea of publishing a newspaper article focusing on some exciting and newsworthy aspect of family or community history research is attractive. Such an article might also help you in your research if you want to appeal to some group to come forward with relevant information.

From looking in local newspapers you will have found whether such articles already feature. If you would like to contribute, contact the editor or author in charge of the slot. A phone call to the newspaper should give you a name, if this is not already clear. You can then find out how you might contribute. If there are no such articles, you could write to the newspaper's editor with a clear proposal for one or more pieces.

In either case, you must be able to convey a strong sense of the interest of what you can provide, so you will need to think carefully about possible topics and why they will appeal to the newspaper's readers. It would be best to have a succinct, clearly argued proposal written out before contacting anyone. Evidence of your ability to write in an appropriate style and to an appropriate length will also help. The success of your proposal will depend on how effectively you sell it and yourself. A one-off article will be accepted or rejected quite quickly, but you may not have much control over how it appears – it may be cut and edited to fit. Getting agreement for a series of articles may take longer, and you will be required to adhere to tight deadlines, but you should have more control, and get some remuneration.

2.2   BOOK PUBLISHERS

It may seem over-ambitious to think about getting a book published, but if your work would be of interest locally, there may be a small publisher who would take it on. In areas with a significant tourist industry, there is considerable market potential for books on subjects of local interest. An increasing number of small-scale publishers cater for this market in the form of short books and booklets as well as full-length books. It may also be that your work has a wider national appeal to a small but specific market and could be published, probably at a high price, by a specialist publisher.

The market research outlined in section 1.2 should allow you to find out which publishers would suit your work. Many authors contact publishers indiscriminately, and it cannot be stressed enough how important it is to contact only those publishers who are experienced in publishing similar sorts of books – proposals for books which do not fit in with a publisher's other titles will be rejected immediately, not because such proposals are bad ones, but because the publisher could not do them justice.

When you have made a selection of potential publishers, you can explore your options for publication further by contacting them for advice. It is not necessarily an advantage to have written your book before approaching a publisher. An appropriate, interested publisher will be able to help you develop and improve the publication, and advice at an early stage can ensure that you are not wasting your time. However, you do need to approach a publisher with a specific written proposal in the first place. It is worth taking some time over your proposal, because you must communicate what it is you want to write effectively enough to convince a busy publisher that it is worth investing time and money in. What form should the proposal take and what should it cover?

_____ **EXERCISE 10.2** _____

Imagine you are a publisher, or an adviser to a publisher. An author's proposal for a book is sent to you to decide whether it is worth publishing. List the kinds of information you would need the author to provide to enable you to form a clear picture of the proposed book. Remember, you know nothing about it except what the author tells you.

(This activity is not asking you to make publishing judgements, but to think about what you need to be told by the author before you can begin to make a publishing judgement.)

Preparing a publishing proposal is a little like writing a preface (Exercise 10.1), in that you need to show what the book will be about and why it should be written to convince a publisher that it is worth publishing, just as a preface aims to convince a reader that a book is worth reading. But you should provide more information as well; see Table 10.2. Also, ensure that your proposal is laid out clearly; you would be surprised how difficult it is to find out, from some authors' proposals, what their book is about.

Your proposal, with a brief covering letter, should be addressed to the editorial director or an appropriate commissioning editor. You might be able to find the name of the editor from a directory of publishers, or you could phone the company to ask for an appropriate name.

The commissioning editor who receives your proposal will, if interested, send it to an adviser for assessment, or contact you for more information. This process can drag on, and you should write or phone to find out what is happening if you have heard nothing after a month. The

Table 10.2 Types of information required in a publishing proposal

1   A brief (1–2 page) statement of what the book is about, why it has been written, who it is for, and why it is distinctive and interesting. You might include some details about yourself, your research and any other work you have published.

2   A table of contents with sufficient description to convey what each chapter covers.

3   An indication of intended length in words (of each chapter as well as the book as a whole), together with an indication of the number and type of illustrations. Also indicate which chapters (if any) are already written, and how long it will take to complete the book.

4   If possible, brief comment about any other books on the subject, and how your book will be better.

5   A sample chapter to provide a 'flavour' of the book and your style. (This is not essential but an interested publisher may ask for one.)

outcome could be rejection, acceptance, or advice about how the proposal should be amended to make it suitable for publication. If you feel that you are being asked to change more than you wish, without any certainty of publication, say so. Most editors will be keen to develop a project if they think it has potential, but they will be reluctant to enter into a commitment to publish until they are sure.

Working with a publisher can be a harrowing or a rewarding process (sometimes both). Just as the publisher assesses you and your book, you should assess the publisher. Does it seem to be the right company to publish your work? You can form some opinion by looking at the company's other publications, by asking other authors published by the company, and by enquiring carefully about the ways the publisher will enhance your work and what efforts will be put into marketing it. If all seems well, ask for a contract as soon as possible and be wary of doing too much extra work without one.

There is not scope here to consider the range of publishing contracts or author–publisher relations, but a good relationship should be stimulating and productive. The publisher's investment of time and money will be considerable, but you should gain some financial return from the book if it sells well. Although you will lose some control over the presentation of your work, the result should be one with which you are both pleased.

You may feel, though, that the attractions – and restrictions – of being published by a commercial publisher are inappropriate, or you may be looking for something more modest. One option to consider is publishing your work yourself.

3   PUBLISHING YOUR WORK YOURSELF

It has always been possible to publish your own work, but it is a lot easier today to produce good-quality books or booklets at a reasonable cost. With the advent during the 1980s of desktop publishing software for home computers, it is no longer necessary to use, and pay for, a typesetter to key and lay out text ready for printing. Anyone with good word-processing and page layout facilities on a computer can do this work, leaving only the printing and binding of multiple copies for a third-party printer. Even if you do not have access to a computer, print technology is such that clean typescript produced from a carbon-ribbon typewriter can be used to print from.

This section will outline the stages of publishing and book production, so that whatever you are able to use – whether a typewriter, a high-quality software package, or even whether you employ a typesetter – you will have a clearer idea of the tasks which need to be done and what they involve.

Publishing may seem a mysterious business. As with any industry or craft, it has its own specialist terminology which adds to the mystique, and publishing is a complex subject because

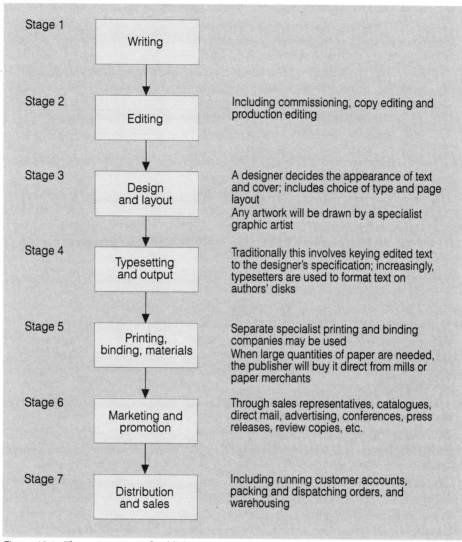

Figure 10.1   The major stages of publishing

it encompasses a range of activities which are complicated in their own right. There is not space here to explore all these complexities, but the aim is to provide you with a basic understanding sufficient for you to prepare a polished version of your research and embark on publishing it.

Figure 10.1 shows the stages any publication must pass through, and indicates the tasks a commercial publisher carries out at each stage. Some of these activities run in parallel. For example, a publisher will market and promote a book at the same time as it is being edited, designed and printed, and even for the small-scale publisher, early marketing can help determine how many copies to print. In a large publishing house, the tasks involved at each stage will be carried out by different people – author, editor, designer, typesetter, etc. – whereas, when publishing your own work, most of the work can be undertaken by one person – you – especially if you are using a computer publishing package.

The tasks of publishing are essentially the same for large and small publishers, and anyone who produces and makes available a book can be called a 'publisher'. However, if you think that there is a market for your work, there are advantages in making this role 'formal'. To do this, choose a name for yourself as publisher and write to the Standard Book Numbering Agency (address and details are in the *Writers' and Artists' Yearbook*). You will be given a publisher number and a list of numbers for each book you publish; these are ISBNs (International Standard Book Numbers) which uniquely identify every book published throughout the world. The process is quite straightforward and having an ISBN for your book makes bookshop ordering easier.

3.1   EDITING

Commercial publishers employ different types of editor for different tasks. For self-publication, the editorial tasks can be divided into three; these are outlined below.

3.1.1   PUBLISHING DECISIONS AND PRODUCTION PLANNING

It is important to start with an overview of the publishing process because decisions made at the earliest stage affect the other stages and have cost and quality implications. In commercial publishers these 'publishing management decisions' are usually made by senior editors. These editors will have built up experience of the consequences of such decisions. You may not have this experience, but don't be concerned if Table 10.3, which indicates what they cover, is unsettling because you don't know the answers or don't understand the terminology. It is a

Table 10.3 Checklist of publishing and production decisions

What size should the book be?	One of the following standard book sizes is likely to be appropriate (although other standard sizes are available): A5 (210 × 148mm) Metric demy octavo (216 × 138mm) Metric royal octavo (234 × 156mm)
How many printed pages will it make? (Estimating a book's extent is known as 'casting off'.)	This depends on: (a) the total number of words (b) the design (type size and text area) (c) the number and size of illustrations (d) front matter (prelims) and end matter (index) Casting off is a skilful art, but if you are preparing your work on computer to final output stage you will know the number of pages when you have laid the text out. If you try to cast off earlier, base your calculation on the average number of words per typical printed page, but allow for extra space at the start and end of chapters, and around headings or other features.
How many copies?	You should have some idea of how many you want for family, friends and neighbours and how many you might sell to local bookshops. There are print economies of scale, so print more than this minimum quantity, but beware of printing a lot and ending up with a garage full of books!
What will the book cost to produce?	You will not know until you have obtained quotations from printers (and other suppliers if you are using them), but you will not be able to get prices until you can provide a complete print specification, including an estimate of the number of pages (see section 3.4).
Is it cost-effective?	Some aspects of the specification may lead to disproportionate extra costs. For example, printing presses print 8, 16 or 32 pages at a time. So if a book of 64 pages, to be printed in two 32-page sections, turns out to be 68 pages, the extra cost would be disproportionately greater. Also, one printer may have better prices for one size or extent of book than another, so get quotations from more than one printer.
How long will it take?	Printing should take 4–6 weeks. If you are editing, designing and laying out the book yourself, the schedule is up to you, but a commercial publisher would do this work over a period of about 6–9 months.
What price should it be sold at?	See section 3.5.1

question of registering now that these are decisions which have to be made. All publishers, however experienced, will reassess their plans and decisions during the production cycle, and you should find them less daunting by the time you have finished reading this chapter.

3.1.2   COPY-EDITING

Copy-editing means preparing the matter which is to be printed (the 'copy') for the printer, and it can involve a wide range of tasks, including rewriting. But as author as well as editor, you should have ensured that your work is clearly written and sensibly structured (see Table 10.1). So what work remains to be carried out when copy-editing?

In broad terms, copy-editing means checking the text and amending spelling, grammar, punctuation, style and presentation to ensure correctness, clarity, consistency and completeness. It also involves making sure that all the elements of the publication are complete; for example, title page, bibliographic information (on the back or verso of the title page), and page numbers.

Checking the text   When copy-editing you must pay attention to all the details of the work, so it must be read extremely carefully. As author, your 'final' read through is likely to concentrate on sense, intelligibility and readability. A professional copy-editor would initially read a manuscript with the same concerns, but would then reread it focusing on its minutiae. As editor, you should submit your work to a similar detailed scrutiny. And, however careful you think you were as author, you will almost certainly spot details which are inconsistent or which have been inadvertently omitted.

In the space available, it is impossible to provide a complete list of features to which you should be alert when copy-editing, but Table 10.4 gives some indication of the sort of details to

Table 10.4   Examples of details to attend to when copy-editing

Abbreviations	Is it clear what an abbreviation stands for? It is always helpful to spell out abbreviations when they first appear. Avoid inconsistency (e.g. UK and U.K., or UK and U.S.A., or UK alternating frequently with United Kingdom).
Capitalization	Capitals can easily proliferate, though the trend now is to use few initial capitals. It is important to be consistent (e.g. in respect of people's titles), but be aware of different meanings (e.g. conservative and Conservative).
Dates	Are dates presented in a consistent style (e.g. March 16, 1954 or 16 March 1954; 19th Century or nineteenth century)? Use the minimum number of numerals when indicating a span of years: 1862–6 rather than 1862–66, but there are exceptions: 1914–18.
Headings	Do the headings of sections and sub-sections reflect the structure of the text? Are they consistent with each other and in comparison with each other so as to reveal to the reader the significance or subordination of different parts of the text?
Hyphenation	A common kind of inconsistency because use varies (e.g. is 'common sense' two words, or hyphenated, or one word?). And note distinctions in grammatical role: 'this is common sense' and 'a commonsense (or common-sense) attitude'.
Illustrations	Illustrations need labelling in a numbered sequence (Figure 1 etc.) for ease of reference in the text.
Notes	Footnotes or endnotes (notes collected at the end of the book), or possibly both, for different purposes?
Numbers	Often tricky: 10 or ten? Usually spell out smaller numbers and be consistent; but note advantages of 'five 10-day periods' even if 'ten' is used elsewhere.
Quotations	Single or double quotation marks? The former are usually preferred. Displayed quotations (see section 3.2.1) do not need quotation marks.
References	Consistent? Complete? Which system is to be followed? (This book uses the author–date system.)
Spellings	There are acceptable alternative spellings for many words but it is incorrect to be inconsistent. Follow an established alternative throughout: one basic alternative is *ise* and *ize* (e.g. 'organise' and 'organize').

look out for. In each instance, it is a question of checking for correctness, clarity, consistency or completeness, or a combination of these.

Copy-editing might seem an unnecessarily 'nit-picking' chore, but if you are preparing your work using a reasonably sophisticated word-processing package, you will have some useful software tools to help (e.g. spelling and syntax checkers and automatic footnote and renumbering facilities). Relying on the computer is no substitute for reading hard copy carefully, however, and until you have developed copy-editing skills you may wonder whether taking such trouble is worthwhile. So, to put it in perspective, bear in mind the following:

o   Any single inaccuracy, inconsistency or omission may not be noticed by readers, but cumulatively they can build up and become an increasing obstacle to clarity. Good copy-editing should be transparent; that is, it should allow the meaning of the text to communicate with the reader without any distraction.

o   'Correctness' is important, but there are alternative styles of 'correctness' – for example, 'ise' or 'ize' spellings. What matters is *consistency,* because inconsistency can be more distracting than anything else.

Completing the book   A book consists of more than just the author's text. It also contains different sorts of apparatus to aid the reader. An obvious example is a list of contents. Checking the list and adding page numbers is a copy-editing responsibility. This is one aspect of ensuring that all the elements of the book are complete. Other elements to check are listed in Table 10.5.

Table 10.5 The elements in a complete book

Preliminary pages (prelims)	Title page	– Title, author and publisher
	Title page verso	– Publisher's address, copyright line, ISBN
	Contents list	– Contents of book and page numbers
	Preface	– Perhaps not necessary in short booklets
	Acknowledgements	– Help acknowledged *and* third-party permissions (see section 3.1.3); sometimes included with end matter
Page numbers	Arabic throughout or roman for prelims? Top or bottom of page?	All pages should be numbered, but the numeral need not appear on prelim pages; left-hand (verso) pages carry even numbers, right-hand (recto) odd numbers.
Running heads	Book or Part title on verso, chapter title on recto	This line at the top of the page (separate from the text) is most useful in longer books; may be combined with the page number.
Captions list	Figure or plate captions	A separate list of these is needed if the illustrations are to be positioned by a typesetter or printer.
Cover	Front cover, spine, back cover	Title, author and publisher's name for the front of the cover and the spine (if there is one); blurb, ISBN, publisher's name for the back.
End matter	Index	An index is always useful. It should be prepared last, when the contents and page layout are finalized.

EXERCISE 10.3

Look at how the items in Table 10.5 are presented in this book. In particular, examine the prelims and list the various kinds of bibliographic information included on the title page verso.

3.1.3 COPYRIGHT

You will want to protect your work and should include a copyright line on the title page verso which claims it as your own (e.g. 'Copyright © 1994' and your name). Other people's work is similarly protected. So if you use anyone else's work you must get permission to do so, and this applies to text, tables, drawings, photographs and maps. The questions to consider and the actions to take in the case of material which is not your own are listed in Table 10.6.

It is unlikely that you will meet serious objections or incur significant cost when applying for the use of third-party copyright material in a small-scale, local publication. And if a high permissions charge is quoted, negotiate with the copyright holder. What is most important is that you take all reasonable steps to get permission, that you acknowledge properly the use of material which is not your own, and that you do not use anything where permission has been explicitly refused.

Table 10.6 Copyrights checklist

What is protected by copyright?	In the UK, the published and unpublished work of a living author is protected; it remains protected for 50 years from the end of the year in which the author died. If the author died before publication, it is protected for 50 years from the end of the year in which the work was first published. Photographs and illustrations are 'works' which are similarly protected.
Who owns it?	The originator of the work is usually the owner; if the originator is dead, his or her descendants or assignees are the owner.
	Commissioned photographs or illustrations are owned by the person who commissioned them; the originator may have some rights, and photographs taken after 1989 also accord rights of permission to a person/persons photographed.
Must permission be obtained?	The law provides for limited use of copyright material without seeking the permission of the owner (e.g. short quotations). There is no specified number of words allowed; rather, the law says that use must not be made of a 'substantial' part of the work without permission.
	Thus, a picture requires permission as a complete work; a verse from a short poem is a 'substantial' part of the work; short quotations from longer, prose works are usually not 'substantial'.
	You should seek permission to use any material which is of a personal nature.
	Full source references to *all* quoted material must be given.
How can permission be obtained?	Write to the owner stating what you want to reproduce and the kind of publication the extract or picture will appear in (e.g. book or limited circulation booklet).
	In the case of published material you should write to the publisher to ask for permission.
What will permission cost?	For reproduction in a small-scale publication, probably nothing; but a fee may be requested in the case of a poem, especially if the author is well-known.
	In the case of photographs, there may be a search fee and a print fee if the picture is obtained from a library.
What if permission is refused?	Find out why. You may be able to agree more limited use or meet particular conditions.
What if you get no reply?	Repeat your original enquiry, twice, keeping copies of your correspondence.
What if the owner can't be traced?	If you have taken all reasonable steps to trace and contact the owner you may use the item in question, but it would be unwise to use material if it is of a sensitive or controversial nature, or if you think the owner might refuse.
What happens if an untraced owner complains after your book has been published?	In your acknowledgements (see Table 10.5), make it clear that you have attempted to contact all relevant copyright holders. This, combined with supporting correspondence, should protect you from any unreasonable claim.

3.2   DESIGN AND LAYOUT

Good design, like good editing, should be transparent. Rather than drawing attention to itself, its role is to allow the sense of a book to communicate clearly with its readers. A good design can enhance a book in many ways, reflecting the structure of the text and allowing particular features, such as illustrations, to be shown to best effect.

If you are using a word-processing package you will be able to look at how different typefaces work and experiment with different page layouts. Alternatively, you could examine other publications to analyse what you like and what you think works. If you are employing someone else to typeset and lay out your book, you should find out what typefaces and design features are available. Typesetters will be able to show you sample typesetting in different sizes and styles.

3.2.1   TEXT DESIGN

There is a lot of specialist typographic and design terminology. You do not need to master this, but some awareness of it will help you design your own work or discuss a design with a typesetter. Figures 10.2, 10.3 and 10.4 show examples of type and layout. Look at the figures carefully to see the descriptive terminology used.

Figures 10.2 and 10.3 show four different typefaces in a limited number of different sizes. There are many different faces and sizes to choose from, but when selecting a design it is worth keeping to the principles of legibility, structural clarity, consistency and simplicity.

The name of the first typeface is 'Bookman'; the one below, 'Avant Garde'. Most typefaces fall into one of two broad categories called 'serif' and 'sans serif'. As you can see, Bookman is a serif face, Avant Garde a sans serif face. Typefaces differ from one another in many other subtle ways: compare the variations above in letter shape, weight and thickness of line, x-height, set, size of counter, and length of ascender and descender. Avant Garde looks the larger typeface of the two, but both are the same size when measured by the traditional printer's scale. This measurement is in 'points' and 72 points are roughly equal to one inch. What is measured is the type body; usually, but not always, this is equal to the distance from the top of an ascender to the foot of a descender. Both examples above are 72 point.

Figure 10.2   Describing type

Type is measured in points (pt
72 points = 1 inch
12 points = 1 pica

Example: Times

The heading above is set in 14pt bold. The space below the heading is 6pt. The heading is ranged left; that is, in line with the left-hand side of the text area.

Each notch =
12 points

This paragraph is indented one pica. The text is 11 on 12pt Times roman, which means that the letters are 11pts in size with 1pt between each line. Such interlinear spacing is called 'leading'. It is not easy to measure the size of type, but the 12pt space taken up by each line is easily measured with a points ruler. The text is justified, meaning that each full line extends across the full width of the text area. This is achieved by fine adjustments to the spaces between words and letters.

Depth scale
rulers can be
purchased – the
best allow you
to measure lines
between 6pt
and 14pt deep,
in gradations of
half points

> This text is 9 on 10 pt roman, and this is one way of presenting longer quotations. When separated from the main text in a separate paragraph they are called 'displayed quotations'. The quotation is indented 2 picas and separated from the preceding main text by a 6pt space. The text is unjustified. The source line following the quotation is ranged right.
>
> (Source line)

Serif faces, like
Times, are
usually
preferred for
continuous text
because it is
generally
believed that
they are easier
to read

This is 11 on 12pt Times italic. Most typefaces are available in roman, bold and italic versions. Other versions exist for some of the more popular faces; for example, bold italic, semi bold, light, small capitals. Both Times and Helvetica are widely available. Times is probably the most commonly used text typeface, partly because it is fairly economical on space and because a full range of alphabetic, numeric and mathematical characters are available.

Example: Helvetica

The heading above is set in 14pt bold. The space below the heading is 6pt. The heading is ranged left; that is, in line with the left-hand side of the text area.

Each notch =
13 points

The set of Helvetica is wider than that of Times, which means that the type takes up more room, even though this text is 11pt, like the Times example above. Helvetica also looks bigger because of its large x-height. The leading used here is 2pt, so the text would be described as 11 on 13pt Helvetica roman.

The width or
length of line is
called its
'measure'. Text
measure is
described in
picas. The text
measure here is
23 picas

Each notch = 12 points/1 pica

Figure 10.3 (above)   Type samples
Figure 10.4 (opposite)   A simple layout grid for a metric demy octavo page

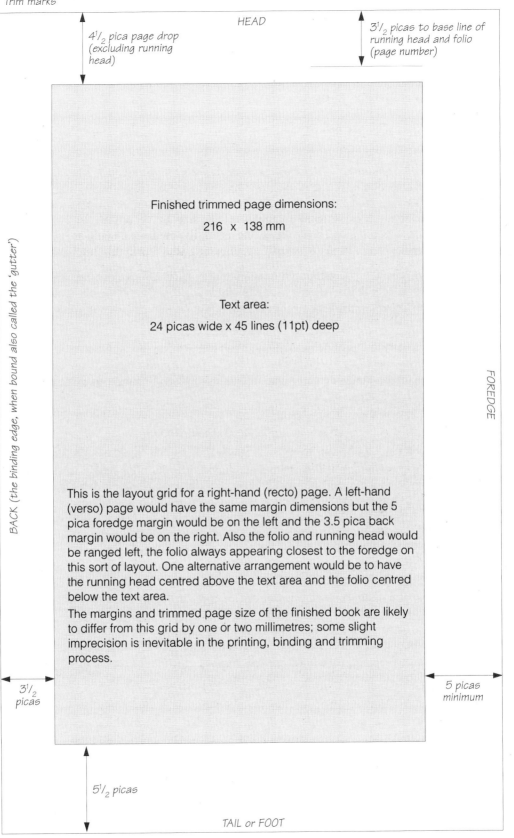

Trim marks

$4^{1}/_{2}$ pica page drop
(excluding running
head)

$3^{1}/_{2}$ picas to base line of
running head and folio
(page number)

BACK (the binding edge, when bound also called the 'gutter')

FOREDGE

Finished trimmed page dimensions:

216 x 138 mm

Text area:

24 picas wide x 45 lines (11pt) deep

This is the layout grid for a right-hand (recto) page. A left-hand
(verso) page would have the same margin dimensions but the 5
pica foredge margin would be on the left and the 3.5 pica back
margin would be on the right. Also the folio and running head would
be ranged left, the folio always appearing closest to the foredge on
this sort of layout. One alternative arrangement would be to have
the running head centred above the text area and the folio centred
below the text area.

The margins and trimmed page size of the finished book are likely
to differ from this grid by one or two millimetres; some slight
imprecision is inevitable in the printing, binding and trimming
process.

$3^{1}/_{2}$
picas

5 picas
minimum

$5^{1}/_{2}$ picas

TAIL or FOOT

Legibility   The most important requirement is a design which presents no legibility problems for the majority of readers, but legibility also means 'good readability'. Legible design cannot be prescribed categorically because it is achieved by combining various features effectively. Decisions which affect legibility include choice of typeface, type size, measure and number of words per line, interlinear spacing and number of lines per page. The typeface should be suited for continuous text, there should not be too many words in each line (or too few, causing a lot of word breaks), and lines should not be too close together.

Structural clarity   The different structural elements of the text should be distinguished from each other by size, by use of italics or bold, and by space. Any hierarchy of headings (chapter, section, sub-section) should be reflected in the design. Other structural elements include displayed quotations, figure captions, lists and sub-lists (to name a few), and their design appearance should be varied, usually very slightly, to show their distinction. Style sheets in word-processing software are useful aids to achieving this structural categorization.

Consistency   Structural clarity can only be achieved if all instances of each structural element look the same (e.g. all chapter headings must look alike). Overall consistency is important too; for example, avoid having varying numbers of lines on each page as this produces uneven page depth.

Simplicity   A lot of different typefaces and type sizes can easily clutter the text, so keep your choices simple. One typeface is often sufficient – bold and italic versions of the main text (roman) typeface providing different weights for headings and sub-headings – though a different face for main headings can be useful.

3.2.2   ILLUSTRATIONS

Any illustrations in your work must, obviously, fit on the page; they should also fit in the designated type area. If illustrations are an important feature of the book, you will have chosen a page size to accommodate them effectively, but whatever the page size it is likely that you will have to spend some time assessing and indicating how they should appear.

Artwork (that is, drawn illustrations like maps) can be drawn to fit, and well-executed drawings enhance a publication, but they can be expensive if you have to pay an artist to produce them. Usually, if artwork is to be drawn for a particular book, it is drawn larger than it will ultimately appear, because the quality will improve when it is reduced photographically to the 'right' size (a common reduction is to 66 per cent of drawn size). The critical dimension is width – the final drawing should fit within the text measure – but depth is also important if the illustration is large.

Photographs and any pre-existing artwork you use are likely to be of different sizes, so they need sizing individually. For example, if a photograph is 160mm wide and it has to fit within a 27 pica measure (114mm), it will need to be reduced to 70 per cent of its original size. Use a calculator to gauge reductions, and remember to check that the reduced depth also fits neatly within the text area. Always be careful not to mark photographs – even an impression caused by writing on paper resting on a picture may show up when printed. The printer will carry out the work of reducing the photographs to size, so discuss how you should present the sizing instructions. If you are supplying the printer with output to print from, when laying out the text you will need to leave an appropriate amount of space for each picture and indicate exactly where it should be placed.

3.2.3   COVERS

Cover design is important, and one of the advantages of being published by a commercial publisher is that the publisher should bring considerable expertise to the creation of an effective cover design. But simple typographic covers are easily created on a word-processor and a photograph can be incorporated without great difficulty. You will need to discuss what is technically feasible and appropriate with your printer, who will be able to advise you of colour options and their cost implications.

3.3   OUTPUT – WHAT YOU SUPPLY TO THE PRINTER

When your book is in final page form on your computer or your typesetter's computer (if you employed one), you need to determine what you should supply to the printer – that is, what the final output should be.

You should discuss this with your printer, but the most likely requirement will be that you should supply some form of camera-ready copy (CRC). CRC from a typesetter is likely to be what is called bromide output; from your desktop computer it may be laser printer output; and it could even be carbon-ribbon typewriter output, if that is how you have chosen to produce your work up to this stage. All can be used to print from, but the quality will vary. Bromide output provides a high resolution, sharp image of the text, producing a crisp finished print appearance; typewriter output leads to a low quality print finish which will lack crispness and perhaps blackness. Computer printer output from a laser printer is between these extremes, but it is good enough to produce a finished quality which only experts are likely to notice is any different from bromide output. To achieve this, the output must be of even blackness and fairly sharp (technically, at least 300 dots-per-inch (dpi)); the image from dot-matrix printers is not sharp enough. What you should be careful to ensure, however, is that you agree in advance with your printer exactly what you will be supplying.

3.4   PAPER, PRINTING AND BINDING

You will almost certainly want a printer to supply paper and cover material, and to bind the book, as well as print it, so the printer is the last stage in the production process. But, as suggested above, it is worth establishing contact with printers before the printing stage is reached. A printer's strengths, limitations and advice could influence how you plan your publication.

How do you find an appropriate printer? If anyone you know can recommend one, that is a good start, and if the printer specializes in handling the kind of book you want to produce, then you may not need to look any further. If there is a quick-print shop locally, this may be suitable. Alternatively, look in *Yellow Pages*; phone calls to a few printers, to ask what sorts of work they handle with an indication of what you want printing, should give you a short list. Selecting a printer from your short list is more difficult; ask for quotations to help you decide. If a printer is well equipped to produce the kind of work you want efficiently, this should be reflected in a competitive price. Check that cheapness is not at the expense of quality by looking at samples of the printer's work. Comparing printers' prices and quality will give you a broader understanding of your options.

You will want some idea of what the book's production will cost, but in the early stages of planning you may not be sure about about its specification. Some printers can provide lists of standard prices. Others will be vague about price until you provide a print specification. You could either create a specification close to what you think you will produce, or you could send a copy of a book or booklet and ask what it would cost to print something exactly like it. Table 10.7 lists the information you need to give and the choices you need to make in asking for a specific price.

Table 10.7 The information needed in a print specification

What is supplied	Probably 'camera-ready copy' (CRC); or give details about the length of the manuscript if the printer is to typeset it. Also state the number of photographs (if any).
Number of copies	State the quantity you think you will want plus a 'run-on' quantity (i.e. the price of a smaller number of copies run on after the initial quantity): e.g. '500 copies plus 100 run on'.
Size of book	State a standard size (see Table 10.3).
Number of pages	State the total number of pages. Plan in terms of 16-page sections.
	Smaller printers and quick-print shops can produce booklets in 4-page or 8-page sections economically; the longer the book the cheaper it should be, pro rata, to print in 16- or 32-page sections, if the printer has large printing presses.
	(Count both sides and include blanks; all pages count. A book with prelims numbered i–iv, followed by pages numbered 1–58, and ending with 2 blank pages, makes a book of 64 pages.)
Text printing	Usually one colour – black; full colour work is expensive.
Type of paper	Ask the printer to recommend and specify. If photographs need to be reproduced to a high quality, this will affect the choice of paper. Ask for samples.
	(Paper is a major subject in itself; all you need to be sure of is that the print quality will be good and suit your material.)
Binding	Paperback: saddle-stitched, perfect or sewn? Hardback (cased) with jacket or printed boards?
	Saddle-stitching (i.e. stapling in the spine) is cheap and suitable for short books (up to 64 pages); but note that the spine is too rounded to print on. Perfect binding (gluing the pages into the spine without sewing them together) is a cheap alternative. Sewn paperback binding is stronger but more expensive.
Cover printing	Two colours are likely to be appropriate, unless you want a full colour photograph on the front.
Cover material	Printer to recommend and specify.
Delivery	State where copies are to be delivered.

There are other details printers may want to know, and any quotation is likely to say something like 'subject to sight of copy'. A specification covering the categories listed above should, though, provide a good idea of the likely cost. When you have chosen a printer, you should check whether there are any further points of detail which need clarification. You may, for example, want to check how well the photographs you want to use will reproduce; old prints can be of very variable quality.

When you are satisfied, confirm in writing your acceptance of the quotation, agree payment terms (a deposit or even full payment may be required in advance), and confirm a schedule and delivery instructions. Note that the quantity a printer delivers may be more or less than you ordered. There are agreed trade tolerance percentages which cover this; the percentage allowed varies according to print run.

3.5   PROMOTION AND DISTRIBUTION

Your publication arrives; what do you do with it? After checking that it has been produced to the standard you expected, and that the invoice and quantity delivered are correct, you will want to send copies to family and friends. Even if you had no intention of promoting your book, there may be other individuals and organizations which might be sent a copy: for example, the local library, local family or community history associations, and local schools. You may receive enquiries about its availability, even without any active promotion on your part.

If you embarked on this venture with a view to selling copies, you should undertake some promotion. To start with, you must send a gratis copy of the book to the British Library (and there are other copyright deposit libraries which are entitled to request a free copy). It may also be worth sending other free copies out for review; the local press may be interested in an interview or a feature. In addition, you could prepare word-processed leaflets to pin up in libraries or to circulate to local booksellers. Visit local bookshops to ask if the booksellers will stock some copies, perhaps for a trial period, and return to see if the book has sold and take repeat orders.

3.5.1 PRICE AND SELLING TO BOOKSELLERS

It is a good idea to set a price for the publication, whether you want to sell copies or not. You will probably not address this issue exactly like a commercial publisher, but there are lessons to be learned from commercial practice.

A commercial publisher will work on the basis that a book which has a unit production cost of, for example, £2 (i.e. the cost per copy of setting, printing, binding, etc.) must have a retail price of at least £10 or £12. Booksellers will buy copies at a discount of 30–35 per cent, so the publisher will receive £7 or £8 for each copy sold. From this amount, the publisher has to pay the cost of production, a royalty to the author, a promotions cost, internal editorial, production and marketing costs, and the cost of distribution (which includes the cost of postage to most bookshops in the UK); what is left is profit. However, a commercial publisher will also adjust the retail price to suit the market. So, if the example given above had to be priced competitively to sell well, the publisher would set the price at £9.95; but if it was a specialist book with a limited potential market the price would be £15 or more.

When setting a price for your book, you should attempt to recover some costs, as long as the price is realistic. Your market research will have given you an idea of the prices of other, similar publications, and you should set a price in line with these. The main cost you will want to recover is what you paid the printer (and the typesetter, if you used one). This may be difficult because the shorter the print-run, the higher the unit cost, but if you did produce the CRC yourself, you will have saved a considerable cost which was unavoidable a few years ago.

The other cost you will need to allow for when setting a price is the discount to booksellers. If a 'good' cover price for selling to the public is £6, you should be looking to sell copies to the bookseller at £4, thereby giving the bookseller an income of £2 on each copy sold. You will need to negotiate an appropriate agreement and discount, but it will be likely to be in the order of 25–35 per cent. You may be asked to accept trade on a sale or return basis, which protects the bookseller if the book does not sell, in which case a lower discount may be appropriate. Conversely, a bookseller who places a firm order for ten or twenty copies should be rewarded with better terms. It will be in your interest to sell in bulk in this way rather than one or two copies at a time.

Though there may be variations in discounts according to quantity ordered, you must make sure that your terms of sale are reasonably consistently applied to all bookshops. You will also need to be clear about payment. Booksellers usually expect thirty days credit from publishers (sometimes longer in the case of major retail chains). As a small-scale publisher, your cash-flow may not be critical, but you will want to avoid having to chase for payment, so try to ensure that workable payment arrangements are agreed in advance. In the case of one or two copy orders, for example, it may be best to request cash with the order.

To end this section on publishing your own work, look back at Table 10.3. If you had to prepare part of your research for publication, how would you address the questions posed in Table 10.3? You may not know precise answers, but you should now be able to outline a publishing and production plan.

4   CONCLUSION

This chapter has covered a range of different ways of writing up your work for presentation or publication. Some parts may have interested you more than others. But, underlying the details about approaching newspapers or printers, there has been the same theme: effective presentation. Whether you want to present your work to a general, public audience or to a more intimate audience, the same principles apply. Better understanding of the disciplines of copy-editing and of design, for example, should help you to structure and set out your research more effectively and more clearly. Similarly, market research in examining and comparing other publications should give you ideas about how to present your work. Ultimately, the choice of presentation is yours, but whatever you decide, I hope that this chapter has helped you think about the options available in such a way as to prove useful in writing up and presenting your research.

FURTHER READING

If you want to follow up any of the subjects discussed in this chapter, a selection of books to consult is listed below. Many of them are classics in their field and invaluable aids to writers and publishers.

Blackwell (1991) *Guide for authors*, Oxford, Basil Blackwell. A friendly, readable account of how to approach publishers and the service you should expect from them.

Baverstock, A. (1990) *How to market books*, London, Kogan Page. A general introduction.

Butcher, J. (1992) *Copy-editing: the Cambridge handbook*, 3rd edition, Cambridge, Cambridge University Press. Comprehensive and thorough, this is the best, most authoritative guide to good editorial practice.

The Chicago manual of style, 14th edition (1993) Chicago, The University of Chicago Press. Full of excellent editorial advice and examples of appropriate style and usage; and eminently practical guide to the would-be publisher.

Clark, C. (1988) *Publishing agreements*, 3rd edition, London, Unwin Hyman. Examples of all kinds of publishing contracts, with comments on standard and typical practice.

Clark, G. N. (1988) *Inside book publishing*, London, Blueprint/Chapman and Hall. A clear introduction to what publishers and publishing staff do.

Directory of publishing: United Kingdom, Commonwealth and overseas (annual) London, Cassell and The Publishers Association. This directory lists the names and addresses of publishing companies, gives details of their specializations and provides contact names.

Hart's rules for compositors and readers, 39th edition (1983) Oxford, Oxford University Press. A standard guide to all the finer points of style, spelling and presentation.

McLean, R. (1980) *Manual of typography*, London, Thames and Hudson. An introduction to typography and book design.

The Oxford dictionary for writers and editors (1981) Oxford, Clarendon Press. With Butcher and *Hart's Rules*, an essential reference book which answers common problems of spelling and appropriate usage.

Riden, P. (1983) *Local history: a handbook for beginners*, London, Batsford. Chapter 7 contains excellent advice about writing local history journal articles and books.

Society of Authors, 'Quick Guides', London. The Society publishes brief guides about a variety of relevant subjects, including copyright, permissions and contracts.

Williamson, H. (1983) *Methods of book design*, London, Yale University Press. The standard work on book design, including coverage of paper, printing and binding.

Ward, A.J. and Ward, P. (1979) *The small publisher*, Cambridge, Oleander Press. An enjoyable, practical account of starting up as a small publisher.

Writers' and artists' yearbook (annual) London, A. & C. Black. This is full of useful addresses and information covering ISBNs, publishers' contracts (usually called 'Publishers' Agreements'), and copyright law; it also includes advice about self-publishing.

CHAPTER 11

OTHER FORMS OF PRESENTATION AND DISSEMINATION

Additional forms of presentation can often usefully supplement, even replace, the written word. You may not so far have considered the practical possibilities of using these, as large or elaborate presentations, whether in writing or any other medium, may not be an immediate outcome of research undertaken within tight time constraints. But even in the shortest report you can benefit by knowing something about alternative forms of presentation (the use of diagrams, for instance), so you will find glancing through this chapter useful. At a later stage you may well want to disseminate your findings more widely (indeed, you might justifiably feel under some obligation not just to keep them to yourself), and may wish to explore the kinds of channels discussed here.

Although the details differ, the guiding principles described in Chapter 10 are relevant here too. They include the importance of organizing your material, and the need to think about the audience you are addressing and how you can communicate with it – which, in turn, means being clear in your own mind as to what you want to convey. You also need to know something about how to exploit your chosen medium effectively (or your selection of media: they can often profitably be combined).

Once again, the material you wish to use will sometimes be protected by copyright, so you may need to take account of this (for general guidance on copyright see Chapter 10, section 3.1.3).

1   USING PHOTOGRAPHS AND PICTORIAL MATERIAL

by W.T.R. Pryce

Photographs, picture postcards, maps – indeed any pictorial materials – are of considerable use to the researcher, either as illustrative material, or as sources: the former being the more usual. In this television age, we live in a world of ever-changing images. Indeed, many now prefer information in a pictorial rather than in a textual form. Old photographs can, therefore, bring an additional dimension to most family and community histories. And, by adopting a few relatively simple techniques, pictorial materials can be made to reveal much new information.

A single photograph of a particular group of ancestors or locality is of considerable interest in itself, showing, for instance, family resemblances, the clothes worn, the nature of house fronts, specific items in a shop window, the former layout of a familiar street. The value of photographs is enhanced considerably when they are analysed as part of a *series* of changing images associated with a particular theme. For example, *The Edwardians in photographs*, by Paul Thompson and Gina Harkell (1979), draws on a large number of old photographs to portray aspects of social life, poverty, town life and the countryside, and related themes, including the 'moral order'. Like many a written record, photographs constitute a small, highly selective sample of the real world. To what extent, therefore, do they provide insights that are always valid

– especially when picture-taking in past times was restricted to special occasions? Such questions are worth pondering when you use photographs and other pictorial material (for further discussion, see Thompson and Harkell, 1979; Becker, 1979).

1.1   COMPILING A PHOTOGRAPHIC ARCHIVE

If not already assembled in family archives, local museums or record offices, an appropriate clutch of old pictures will have to be brought together from different sources (for useful suggestions, see Taylor, 1984). Creating a representative picture archive requires considerable dedication and much time – sometimes several years. For example, collecting the material for my book *The photographer in rural Wales* (Pryce, 1991) took twelve years of part-time work and involved considerable travel. Over 300 original photographs were copied and 244 (from 33 different sources) have been included in the book. Some of the photographs are used in this section to illustrate presentational techniques.

In using old pictures we need to ensure that the presentation is organized so as to enhance our understanding of particular topics. Thus, short interpretative captions, based on contemporary reports in local newspapers, local or family records, oral tradition, interviews and surveys, must accompany each picture.

Preparing family histories that make a real contribution to community history requires our photographs to be presented in a structured framework. Since the late 1960s, when 'heritage' became fashionable, increasing numbers of studies have appeared, intended mainly for a local readership, under such titles as *Burgerville in old pictures, Burgerville then and now,* or *The changing face of Burgerville* – all fictitious titles to illustrate the point! Compiled mainly from reproductions of old photographs, maps or picture postcards, such studies rarely offer readers clear commentaries, interpretative captions, or the context in which the material came into being. Usually, the pictures are presented in an arbitrary fashion with, at best, some sort of assumed date order.

In assembling a collection of old photographs as sources in their own right, what principles should be followed?

Clear objectives need to be adopted. Don't copy *all* the photographs in a collection. Be selective. If the project is on a specific family, then pictures of its members, their friends, offspring, homes, etc. will figure prominently. The same principles apply for research into the history of an institution such as a local school, church, women's society, trade union, or welfare club. If the primary concern is with a particular community, town, village, suburb or street, the focus will probably be broader, with the emphasis less on individuals – unless prominent in community life – and more on the ways individual streets have changed, on particular shop fronts and other premises, or on various cultural pursuits – religious, educational, literary, musical, or sporting. Table 11.1 indicates the range of topics covered in *The photographer in rural Wales* (Pryce, 1991; for a further example see Thompson and Harkell, 1979).

One must, then, identify specific needs: the sudden discovery of an 'interesting' picture or topic tangential to the main theme often results in much time and effort being wasted going up blind alleys. Therefore, once a source of pictures has been found, make a preliminary survey, evaluating them in terms of your research objectives, *before* doing any copying (see Chapter 6, section 3.3 for copying techniques). Time also needs to be set aside for checking the date and authenticity of each picture.

Table 11.1   Contents list from *The photographer in rural Wales*

CONTENTS
Forward
List of Figures
Preface
CHAPTER 1: INTRODUCTION
CHAPTER 2: LANDSCAPE ARTISTS AND PHOTOGRAPHERS
CHAPTER 3: PICTURE POST CARDS AND THEIR PUBLISHERS
CHAPTER 4: SOURCE COLLECTIONS AND ACKNOWLEDGEMENTS

THE ARCHIVE:
1 LLANFAIR CAEREINION IN ITS SETTING
2 THE TOWN AND ITS MAKEUP
2.1 The mid-nineteenth century town plan
2.2 Urban morphology and layout
2.3 Market Hall and the old Market Square
2.4 Broad Street
2.5 High Street and Top Llan
2.6 Watergate Street
2.7 Bridge Street
2.8 Llanfair bridge, Dolgoch and Pool Road
3 AFON BANW AND THE COUNTRYSIDE[1]
4 VILLAGES AND HAMLETS
4.1 Llanerfyl
4.2 Llangadfan and Y Foel
4.3 Llanllugan and Cefn Coch
4.4 Llwydiarth
4.5 Manafon and New Mills
4.6 Meifod
4.7 Melin-y-ddôl
4.8 Pont Robert
4.9 Tregynon
5 CULTURAL INSTITUTIONS
5.1 Religion
5.2 Welfare societies
5.3 Brass bands
5.4 Education
5.5 Eisteddfodau[2]
5.6 Llanfair Public Hall and Institute
5.7 Llanfair Electric Light Society, 1914–1950
5.8 Argricultural Society
5.9 Sports activities
5.10 Commemorations[3]
6 WAR-TIME SCENES
6.1 World War I
6.2 World War II
7 TRANSPORT AND LINKS WITH THE OUTSIDE WORLD
7.1 Horse-drawn vehicles
7.2 Llanfair Railway
7.3 Bicycles
7.4 The first motor cars
8 LLANFAIR TOWN IN MORE RECENT TIMES
8.1 Photographic survey, April 1977
8.2 Aerial views, October 1986
SELECT BIBLIOGRAPHY
Index

[1] That is, 'The River Banw and the countryside'.
[2] Local festive gatherings for musical, literary and craft competitions.
[3] Parades to celebrate Empire and Coronation Days.

(Source: Pryce, 1991, pp.v–vi)

1.2   KEEPING ACCURATE RECORDS

Once appropriate photographs have been identified and copies made, it is important to compile an accurate record of each one. In practice, this is best done when selecting the photographs, *after* the evaluation but *before* copying. Many details can be lost through a hurried session of note taking towards the end, perhaps, of a lengthy visit to inspect available pictures. You should record the actual date shown on the picture (or make an estimate) and its subject matter, including details of individuals and features shown in the photograph.

As far as possible, aim to track down original pictures rather than making copies from copies. Usually, this produces a higher quality of reproduction. Also, the name and address of the photographer may be on the picture, especially if it has been preserved on its original mount. Scenes on picture postcards have to be regarded as originals unless you can locate the original negatives or a higher-quality photographic print. Last, but not least, note the format of the original: is it a daguerreotype (rare), an ambrotype (not so rare but still unusual), a carte-de-visite, a cabinet print, a lantern slide, a picture postcard, a mounted half-plate bromide print with sepia toning, a tintype print, a print from a negative made by a snapshot camera, or what? This will help date the picture (see Chapter 6, section 3.2).

1.3   LAYOUT AND PRESENTATION

The time will come when the 'history' has to be written, the project completed. What are the best ways of doing this? The answer rests mainly on whether the study is text-led or picture-led. In the former you use old pictures to illustrate matters discussed in the text; in the latter the pictures are central, each having its own caption and interpretative text. In larger studies you may use both methods. For example, in preparing *The photographer in rural Wales* (1991) I had two objectives: (1) to present a photographic survey of life in a small country town; and (2) to provide an account of the various *ways* in which life in a relatively remote rural community was *recorded* photographically over 130 years from *c*.1860. It soon became clear that these twin aims could not be met effectively in a single mode of presentation. I therefore decided to separate the material into two parts. The main one (referred to as the 'photographic archive') was picture led, with just sufficient text for interpretative purposes. The other part, dealing with the historical context and the ways in which the photographic records had come into existence, required a more detailed analytical narrative – in fact, four lengthy chapters. Here the text was supported by only a few photographs, one or two tables, and illustrations. Finally, just prior to publication, I realized that the order of presentation needed changing, so that the four background chapters preceded the eight picture-led ones (Table 11.1).

1.4   SUGGESTIONS FOR USING OLD PHOTOGRAPHS

Finally, here are some practical suggestions as to how information in specific pictures can be enhanced. The focus is squarely on *presentation*. (For techniques – for example, how to improve the clarity of a faded photograph – see relevant further reading cited in Chapter 6, section 3.)

There are many different ways of presenting old photographs. You are limited only by the nature of the source material, your own ingenuity, and, if publication is intended, printing techniques and cost. You can adopt one or more of five methods of presentation, whether for slides for a lecture, a one-off research report, an article, or a book.

Reproductions showing original format   On occasion it is appropriate to reproduce old photographs to reveal their original format; for example, when information on this helps our understanding of the subject matter or indicates the date (see Chapter 6, section 3, and Plates 1 to 5 in the plates section).

'Then and now' photographs   One widely used technique is to present an old photograph alongside a modern one taken from the same spot. (Differences in camera optics can result in the later photograph not recording exactly the same perspective as the earlier one.) In Figure 11.1, for example, although the rebuilt church is shown in the bottom photograph (Figure 11.1(b)), the nineteenth-century layout of the town of Llanfair Caereinion still remained in 1977. Moreover, although several new and substantial buildings have been erected in the town centre (Figure 11.1(b), lower right corner), a comparison of rooftops, chimneys, etc. indicates that many of the smaller houses and shops still form part of the urban fabric. As noted in Chapter 6, section 3.4, photographic comparisons like this can help us plot a built-up area in former times, and can add detail to our maps.

(a) Llanfair Caereinion, c.1860

(b) Llanfair Caereinion, 15 April, 1977

Figure 11.1 'Then and now' photographs: both pictures were taken from the same spot (Source: Pryce, 1991, pp.28 and 200)

Selective enlargements   Another technique is to make selective enlargements of just one part of an old photograph. This can reveal interesting details that otherwise may not be noticed. Figure 11.2(b) is a selective enlargement of Figure 11.2(a). The enlarged section shows two labourers repairing the pavement, and reveals much more of their attire, together with details of the buildings and shop fronts. It shows more clearly the two well-dressed women posing for the photographer, and the late-Victorian high-wheeled pram. Also revealed is a tell-tale indicator of those quiet years before the coming of the motor car: patches of horse droppings extending from the immediate foreground into the middle distance! This selective enlargement, then, tells us much more than the original photograph with its relatively uninteresting foreground.

(a) Original picture postcard, c.1903

(b) Selective enlargement of the central area in (a)

Figure 11.2   Bridge Street, Llanfair Caereinion, *c*.1903 (Source: Pryce, 1991, p.77)

247

Identifying people You may want to identify individuals in group photographs. Depending on the size and arrangement of the group, this can be done either by listing people in an extended caption or by using annotated diagrams. In Figure 11.3, which shows a small church choir, the names of individuals are listed row by row, left to right. As all the individuals shown are dead, the identifications were made by elderly residents who were their contemporaries. No other source could supply such information.

Figure 11.3 Group photograph with individuals identified in the caption

Llanfair Caereinion parish church choir, *c.*1936. The parish church has maintained a mixed-voice choir for several generations

Row 1 (boys, left to right): Russel Jones (son of police officer), Arthur Thomas (Factory House, Bridge St.), Dennis Hughes (Wynnstay Hotel), Alcuin Jehu (Bryn Llys, Bridge St., killed in World War II D-Day landings in France), Stanley Jones (Market Sq., son of grocer), Teddy Jones (Bryn Banwy, Top Llan, killed in World War II)

Row 2 (men): Evan Richards (Mount Rd., postman), Llew Jehu (Brynllys, garage owner, father of Alcuin Jehu), Rev. J.E. Rowlands (Vicar), Thomas Richards (tailor, father of Evan Richards), Richie Evans (Bryn Banwy), W. Metcalfe, MPS (photographic chemist, Bridge St.)

Row 3 (men and women): R.D. Hughes (Beehive Bakery, Mount Rd.), Miss Maggie Madley (Sylfaen Farm, Castell Caereinion; organist), Maurice Jehu (Conservative Party Agent, Bridge St.), Billy Roberts (Star Shop, Bridge St., Pearl Assurance Agent), Fred Pool (Einion Cottages, off Bridge St., painter and decorator), Jim Samuel (Watergate St., painter and decorator), John Willy Evans (Bryn Banwy, garage mechanic), Miss Megan Jehu (Bryn Meurig, Top Llan), George Haynes (Pool Road Cottages, baker)

Row 4 (women): Miss Edith Evans (Bryn Banwy, shop assistant), Miss Mary Griffiths (Black Lion Inn, maid servant), unidentified (probably a maid in one of the banks or at Bodeinion, not originally a native of Llanfair), Miss Annie Williams (Einion Villa, sister of Llew Williams, blacksmith), Mrs E.M. Breese (Arfryn, Wesley St.), Miss Agnes Pain (teacher at Llanerfyl, married Billy Roberts, Star Shop, Bridge St.), Miss Lottie Batterby (Chapel House, Watergate St.), Miss Doris Breese (Arfyn, Wesley St.), Miss Winny Jones (Bryn Banwy, sister of Teddy Jones (Row 1))

(Source: Pryce, 1991, p.117)

When larger groups are involved, or the individuals are not arranged systematically, a row by row listing is inappropriate. In this case, you should make an outline cartoon, with identifying numbers or letters, initially in black ink, on tracing paper or film laid over the photograph. The cartoon picks up only key features from the photograph – a lady's hat, the hairline of one person, the body outline of another. You can then reduce the cartoon, as required, on a photocopier and place it alongside the photograph with explanatory text (see Figure 11.4).

Figure 11.4   Group photograph with identification cartoon and extended caption

Llanfair Caereinion County Intermediate School: reunion of old pupils, *c.*1909. The following have been identified by elderly natives of Llanfair (numbers refer to the key diagram):

1. Dr Arthur Watkins (son of Watkins, Registrar of Births, Marriages and Deaths, Brynmair); 2. Winnie Watkins, Penarth Farm (became missionary in China, retired to live in Deganwy); 3. Miss Dot Morgan (teacher of history); 4. Ethel Wynn Humphreys (sister to Percy Lloyd Humphreys); 5. unknown; 6. Gweno Humphreys (daughter of Dr Humphreys, Mount Einion); 7. Mrs C. Heber Humphreys (formerly Miss Theodore, here shown in her early 20s); 8. Miss Williams (teacher, daughter of the Vicar of Llanllugan); 9. Ella Morris, Red Lion Hotel; 10. Miss Ethel Watkins (former pupil, then assistant mistress; daughter of Watkins, Brynmair (see 1)); 11. Grey Evans, sister of Ifor Annwyl Evans (died early of TB); 12 and 13. unknown; 14 Ifor Annwyl Evans (son of draper); 15 and 16. unknown; 17. Percy Lloyd Humphreys, Tylisa, manager of Midland Bank (killed in World War I); 18. Mrs Bessie Peate; 19. a daughter of Corner Shop, Watergate St.; 20. unknown; 21. Miss Annie Hughes, Bon Marché; 22. unknown; 23. Mary Pugh, Y Fron, Penarth; 24–26. unknown; 27. Miss Sarah Ann Jones, Newbridge Farm, Meifod; 28. ?Mrs Jones, Brynpistill, Eithnog; 29 and 30 unknown; 31. Susie Davies (later Mrs George Hughes of Dolgoch Cottages); 32–48. unknown

(Source: Pryce, 1991, p.143)

Annotated photographs   You can improve the presentation of rural or urban scenes by annotation. For example, each of the premises shown in Figure 11.1 can be identified and named, either by directly annotating the photograph itself (involving overprinting), or by creating a cartoon with identifying letters or numbers.

We have dealt with only a few possibilities here. Do not feel restricted to just these. Be ever on the lookout for new methods of presenting information pictorially. Traditionally, there has been a general reluctance to accord photographs the status of an original source. I have tried to dispel those misgivings. You should do your bit by including, as you would in a report based on documentary or statistical sources, full details of the original photograph's format, its origin, date and where it can be consulted. And, if you are publishing, don't forget about the question of copyright clearance (see Society of Authors, 1990, and also Chapter 10, section 3.1.3).

REFERENCES AND FURTHER READING (SECTION 1)

Becker, H.S. (1979) 'Do photographs tell the truth?', in Cook, T.D. and Reichardt C.S. (eds) *Qualitative and quantitative methods in evaluation research*, London, Sage.

Pryce, W.T.R. (1991) *The photographer in rural Wales: a photographic archive of Llanfair Caereinion and its region, c.1865–1986*, Llanfair Caereinion and Welshpool, The Powysland Club.

Society of Authors (1990) *Copyright in artistic works including photographs* (Quick Guide 11), London, Society of Authors.

Taylor, L. (1984) 'The photograph as a social document' and 'Picture researching', in Steel, D. and Taylor, L. (eds) (1984) *Family history in focus*, Guildford, Lutterworth Press.

Thompson, P. and Harkell, G. (1979) *The Edwardians in photographs*, London, Batsford.

2   THE PRESENTATION OF DATA THROUGH TABLES, CHARTS AND MAPS

by John Hunt

Data can usefully be assembled as tables, charts and maps. The key issue is the relevance of data to an argument, and making that data relevant requires *selection*. Quantitative data have to be presented meaningfully. Large amounts of unordered information are difficult to work with, and even more difficult to understand. So the first thing you need to do is to select and organize your evidence. Data may need to be amalgamated, but be consistent in the method used and make your groupings appropriate so that you do not lose any significant information.

2.1   TABLES

Tables should be laid out neatly with columns of figures set directly under one another. The title should be positioned above the table and prefaced by a number. Within the columns of a table, text is best ranged left, whole numbers should range right, and numbers with decimals should be centred on the decimal point. Column and row headings should be concise and clear and should indicate the units of measurement involved. If you are thinking of drawing up one 'jumbo' table of data, consider whether it would be better subdivided into a number of smaller and more specific ones. Good word-processor software will enable you to achieve many of the above layout features. A table can be descriptive in itself and does not necessarily need to be explained by great chunks of text. One common error, however, is to use overly brief titles which neither explain what the table is about nor indicate, when relevant, the period covered. In the text, always refer to tables by the numbers you have assigned to them – there is no need to repeat the titles (for some examples, look at the tables in Chapter 3, section 1).

2.2   CHARTS

The aim of a chart is to assist in the *comprehension* of an idea or set of data. A chart should not be overdesigned and overelaborate, nor should too many be used (tempting with computer software!). Charts should relate directly to the most evident and significant message you wish to convey. Often this is achieved by making *comparisons* (e.g. by ranking data; by comparing data over time; by plotting frequency of occurrence; by showing a relationship; or by showing relative importance).

Pie charts   Because a circle gives such a clear impression of representing a total unit, a pie chart is ideal for showing the relative sizes of four or five components of some whole. Because the eye is used to moving in a clockwise direction, the most important segment should start against the 12 o'clock line (see Figure 11.5(a)). If no segment is more important than another,

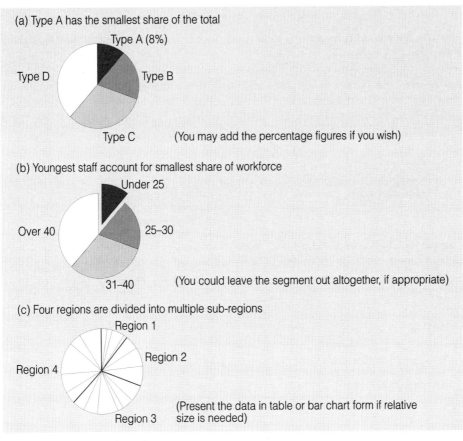

Figure 11.5   A variety of pie chart presentations

consider starting with the smallest, followed by the next smallest, etc. To focus attention on a component, use either darker shading or separate that segment from the pie (see Figure 11.5(b)). (You can obtain 100 per cent divided templates which make plotting pie charts easier.)

There are always exceptions to any rule; if the objective is to show the multitude of subdivisions within, say, Regions 1 to 4, then a pie can still be constructed but no useful measurement can take place (see Figure 11.5(c)). In such a case, it is probably better to present the data in the form of a table or bar chart, so that the relative sizes of the subdivisions can be distinguished more easily.

Figure 11.6 demonstrates how components which are similar can be shown on different pies emphasizing, perhaps, performance in each region, variation between regions, or (if arranged 'spatially') an effective geographic relationship

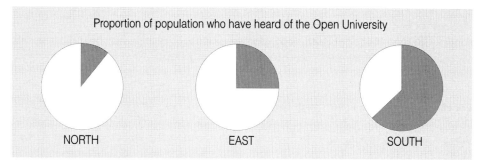

Figure 11.6   Spatial presentation through pie charts

The data in Figure 11.6 are 'made up'. Why not plot some real data and consider the spatial implications?

Bar charts   Bar charts can be constructed for varying purposes. For example, a simple bar chart could show size distribution over a number of years. In Figure 11.7(a), the vertical axis is scaled and the horizontal axis is simply marked off in years. In Figure 11.7(b), a simple bar is combined with a pie to arrive at a rather more sophisticated chart.

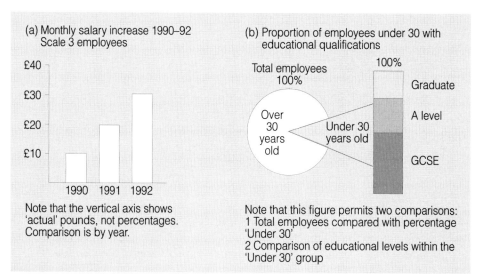

Figure 11.7   Using bar charts

Bar charts are good at showing item comparison (e.g. between Persons A, B, C, etc.). Figure 11.8 shows bars arranged horizontally. The bars may be ordered so as to emphasize a name or value, or the sequence can be haphazard (to emphasize unevenness). Shading can help separate out a specific item – perhaps the one the others are being compared to (see Figure 11.8(a)). A deviation bar chart, where bars extend left or right (or above and below) a zero line can suggest unfavourable or negative conditions (see Figure 11.8(b)). Although optional, it is usually helpful to show numeric values, either by adding these at the ends of the bars or by incorporating a scale on which the values can be read. Overlapping and grouping the bars can also be used as a technique to save space whilst at the same time bringing in another variable (e.g. two different time periods) (see Figure 11.8(c))

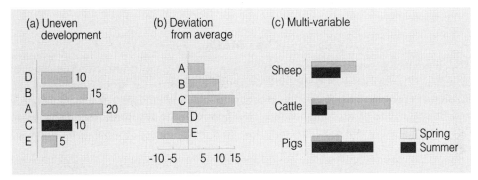

Figure 11.8   Horizontal bar charts

Histograms   Histograms (see Figure 11.9) are used to display grouped data and frequency. Grouped data simply refers to the selection of a series of numbers in a range, or class; for example, age groups. Frequency is a measure of 'occurrence' – that is, how many times a number occurs within a range or class. The important feature to remember about histograms is that the horizontal (x) axis is used to plot the range/classes whilst the vertical (y) axis is used to plot the frequency. The technique of drawing a histogram is reserved for non-continuous (discrete) data (i.e. the grouped data upon which a histogram is based must be non-continuous).

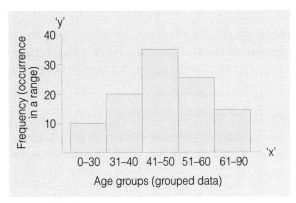

Figure 11.9   Sample histogram presentation

To construct a histogram you will need to determine the groups of data that are appropriate and meaningful to the *range* of data. This can be done by plotting the number of times a particular figure occurs (y axis) and observing how these are distributed along their range (x axis). Once all the values are plotted, look out for any obvious groupings and natural breaks on which to base your grouped data.

2.3   GRAPHS

Graphs use exactly the same data found in histograms, but present the 'picture' in a different way. With a graph, data are condensed to just a set of points which are then joined up to make a line or curve. This 'trend' line can help determine values left by gaps in the original data. You should take some care in constructing a graph and even more care in its interpretation! To help others understand the message or emphasis, use different thicknesses of solid and dashed lines or a combination of dots and dashes. Do make sure you 'key' or identify the different categories of data and do not use more than four or five altogether. Show average values to help compare your data. Axes should be labelled and data ranges identified clearly. (For an example of a graph, see Volume 1, Figure 3.2.)

2.4   MAPS

A well-produced, neat and relevant map can be a major asset to research. The essential ingredient of a map is the relationship between data and space – i.e. spatial connectivity and location. For presentation purposes it is important to show a linear scale, orientation (if north is away from the vertical), main location points and features, and a key. Three distinctive types of map can be identified, based on the concepts of data shown at a point, by a line, or encompassed in an area.

Point and proportional symbol maps   One of the simplest and most widely used types of point distribution map is the dot map – where data are represented at points by dots. Dots, which are of uniform size, are placed locationally (see, for example, Volume 2, Figure 6.7). Graduated or proportional symbol maps are an excellent method of representing quantitative data distribution. The symbols should be sufficiently different to enable the map user to distinguish value differences (see, for example, Volume 2, Figure 6.5). It is possible to construct proportional symbols mathematically so that symbol size corresponds exactly to data value, but this can make perceiving small differences between values difficult.

Line maps   Isopleth maps show statistical data by joining points of equal value with a line (isoline). Contour maps (showing lines of equal height) are a well-known example. Lines can be interpolated between data points and a series plotted to show a regular increase or progression. Remember that isolines may not cross and that colouring or shading between isolines can assist in interpretation. Lines should be numbered or identified by width or style. (See Volume 2, Figure 6.6 for an example of an isopleth map.)

Area maps   Shaded area (or choropleth) maps are defined on the basis of their relationship between quantities and area. Although the commonest choropleth map is one showing density (of population, cattle, etc.), this form of map can also be used for other aspects, such as ratios, averages and percentages. However, a choropleth map must *not* be used to show absolute values. The first stage of construction would be to depict the boundaries of the relevant statistical unit (i.e parish, district, county); the second to calculate density; and the third to construct a series of distinguishing data ranges. Values may be divided arithmetically, geometrically, equally, or into quartiles. Too few ranges may give an impression of comparative uniformity whilst too many might confuse. To help you decide how many, plot your data as a scattergram and look out for about five 'natural' breaks. When drawing up an area map, you may leave your lowest range white but your other shadings should *not* simply be lines at different angles – a shading density *must* be apparent. (See Volume 2, Figure 8.3 for an example of a shaded area map.)

Flow maps   Flow maps do not strictly fall into the preceding three categories. They are concerned with movement from place to place and their main purpose is to represent movement as well as volume. For example, in the last century, Harness used shaded lines to symbolize the volume of traffic and freight along Irish railways, making the width of line proportional to amount of goods carried (see Chapter 6, section 2.4, Figure 6.6). The width of the flow-line is the important factor, the length simply shows direction and connectivity.

Handy hints on presentation   When you prepare maps, remember to leave 3–4 cm. (about

required, bind in an A3 piece of paper (but trim an inch or so off so that it folds in easily). Use more than one colour. If several copies of a map are required, you should consider using a colour photocopier to obtain these. Use overlays on tracing paper firmly attached by tape. Use consistency in identification. When constructing a map, generalize main physical features, such as rivers, coastline and roads – a smooth indication is all that is required. Use graph paper to help with layout, lettering, key and scale. Differentiate feature types by changing lettering characteristics, such as capital letters only, upper and lower case, or different colour and size. Use density to focus attention. A neat edge (rectangle) around your work helps to give it a finished look!

Note that if you wish to reproduce – or even photocopy – maps, there may be copyright restrictions; your local librarian will be able to advise you (see Chapter 10, section 3.1.3).

FURTHER READING AND REFERENCE MATERIAL (SECTION 2)

Hindle, P. (1988) *Maps for local history*, London, Batsford.

Matthews, H. and Foster, I. (1989) *Geographic data: sources, presentation and analysis*, Oxford, Oxford University Press.

Mills, D. and Pryce, W.T.R. (1993) 'Preparation and use of maps', audio-cassette 3A in Braham, P. (ed.) *Using the past: audio-cassettes on sources and methods for family and community historians*, Milton Keynes, The Open University.

Northedge, A. (1990) *The good study guide,* Milton Keynes, The Open University.

3 TALK AND AUDIO

by Ruth Finnegan

Do not underestimate the value of *talking* as a mode of presenting and disseminating your results. Lectures, talks, seminars, and other forms of oral presentation are among the most effective and widely practised modes of communication at every level.

Their scope and context obviously vary. It could be an informal progress report to a small group of friends, a talk at a local school, a presentation to a local family or local history society, a formal lecture for a large audience, or a talk on local radio. All these can be effective channels for both communicating and getting feedback on your findings.

There are no foolproof ways of delivering a good talk, if only because different audiences expect different things. Some common-sense points might seem too obvious to mention (see Schema A) – except that even experienced speakers sometimes forget them.

Schema A: Some practical points to consider when speaking

o *Prepare* beforehand (remembering *who* and *what* it is for).

o Be *audible.*

o Be *interested* in your subject.

o If possible, *speak from notes rather than reading a manuscript* word for word; or, if you *have* to read, look at the audience as well (professional academics are sometimes the worst sinners: don't emulate them!).

o Think about the *audience's reactions.*

o *Don't go on too long.*

Additional material to support or complement your speaking is worth considering. Depending on practicality and circumstances, this could include:

o Handouts – either for people to keep or to be passed round and returned (e.g. written documents or summaries; photographs; maps; material objects).

o Slides.

o Overhead transparencies etc.

o Film/video.

o Audio recordings (including sound effects or specific excerpts as part of a spoken talk).

o Computer demonstrations.

All need planning beforehand, the details depending not only on your own purposes and constraints but also on the expected audience. Some presentations demand complex preparation and some technical expertise: for example, a spoken commentary and/or music linked to a slide presentation, or a special display (see also section 5); but simple ones can be effective too.

Another possibility is a presentation through an audio-recording based on your own recordings (see Chapter 7; also Bornat and Kirkup, 1993) and/or on a selection of already-recorded or archive tapes. Either way, you may need permission to reproduce the material (see Chapter 7, section 3.2). Rob Perks's recent booklet (1992) gives some practical advice:

Producing a slide-tape pack is not as daunting as it sounds. When copying photographs or documents on to slides, put them flat under some glass, light them well, and re-photograph them onto black and white film. One way of rough editing a tape together is by copying the chosen extracts from the master tape on to another tape. This can be done with cassette tape, but to get a more finished product you will need to copy on to an open-reel tape, then edit it using an editing block, a sharp blade and splicing tape. You can buy tape editing kits quite cheaply.

(Perks, 1992, p.30; see also Smith and Wilkinson, 1989)

Further advice and suggestions can be found in the further reading and reference material listed at the end of this section (especially Kirkup and Clegg, 1993).

Broadcast talks or presentations may also be feasible, the best way to start probably being local radio. Vic Lockwood (Senior Producer at the BBC Open University Production Centre) gives the following advice:

One way of passing on an oral archive to a local community is by persuading a local radio station (which you could track down via the local telephone book) to broadcast the material. If you choose this route of publication, then you need to take account of the following points:

1   The quality and level of sound recording must be exemplary.

2   The material presented must be of sufficient interest to a significant number of the station's audience.

3   You should have in writing copyright clearances from the speakers that you have the right to offer the material to the station.

FURTHER READING AND REFERENCE MATERIAL (SECTION 3)

Bailey, E.P. (1992) *A practical guide for business speaking*, New York and Oxford, Oxford University Press. Despite its title, this is full of practical advice on speaking on any subject, with special emphasis on visual aids.

Bornat, J. and Kirkup, G. (1993) 'Oral, history interviews', audio-cassette 1B in Braham, P. (ed.) (1993) *Using the past: audio-cassettes on sources and methods for family and community historians*, Milton Keynes, The Open University.

Calder, A. and Lockwood, V. (1993) *Shooting video history*, Milton Keynes, The Open University. Although dealing with video, much of the advice (e.g. on planning, interviewing, obtaining clearance, etc.) is equally applicable to audio.

Green, H. (1979) *Projecting family history: a short guide to audio/visual construction*, Plymouth, Federation of Family History Societies.

Kirkup, G. and Clegg, J. (1993) 'Presenting your findings through audio-vision', audio-cassette 6B in Braham, P. (ed.) (1993) *Using the past: audio-cassettes on sources and methods for family and community historians*, Milton Keynes, The Open University.

Perks, R. (1992) *Oral history: talking about the past*, London, The Historical Association/Oral History Society.

Smith, T. and Wilkinson, R. (1989) 'Setting up a local recall pack', *Oral History*, 17, pp.43–8.

4   USING VIDEO AS A MEANS OF PRESENTATION

by Angus Calder

Making your own video of family or community history can be an exciting challenge. It requires careful planning at the outset and considerable patience at the editing stage.

Crucial questions

1 What is this video for? If its purpose is 'scholarly', your aim must be to present evidence as fully and neutrally as you can. This could conflict with the perfectly valid alternative aim of producing an *entertaining* and *evocative* video for showing to family or community.

2 How long should it be? There are many Hollywood stories of wildly expensive films which got completely out of hand, but you won't have time to complete an epic. Nevertheless, you must consider whether a carefully edited 30- or even 15-minute film, emphasizing essential points, may be more telling, and usable, than an hour-long one which preserves 'ums' and 'ers' in interviews, and, incidentally, pleasing shots of the environment. Conversely, you might feel that keeping hesitations and self-contradictions by interviewees is essential to the honesty of your presentation, and that the environment filmed (e.g. a living room with family heirlooms, photographs and souvenirs) is eloquent in itself.

Further details can be found in the further reading and reference material listed below, including treatment of both technical aspects (e.g. the importance of considering *sound* as well as visual aspects, and the process of editing) and 'human' issues such as conducting interviews and obtaining clearances.

FURTHER READING AND REFERENCE MATERIAL (SECTION 4)

Calder, A. and Lockwood, V. (1993) *Shooting video history,* Milton Keynes, The Open University. A video 'workshop' on good video-producing, which presents a local history group's experience of producing a video so as to demonstrate and teach the basic principles, both technical and social, of high quality video production in family and community history. Produced for the Open University course DA301 and supported by written notes by Angus Calder and Vic Lockwood.

Humphries, S. and Gordon, P. (1993) *Video memories: recording your family history,* London, BBC Education. A guide to recording family history on tape or video.

5 EXHIBITIONS

by John Hunt

The Great Exhibition of 1851 must have been the ultimate place to show off the results of research, knowledge and skills. Perhaps the millennium celebrations in the year 2000 will provide such an opportunity for some of us! The reality for an academic researcher is slightly more mundane – a journal article perhaps; a chapter in a book; maybe even a whole book! A most useful means of 'showing off' would be a small exhibition of highlights using tables, figures, maps, photographs, sounds and objects. An exhibition should focus attention on excellence through an assembly of variations on a theme. It should not simply be a collection of things or facsimiles but should structure a set of ideas around a theme and communicate these, as research aims and achievements, clearly to the viewer.

5.1 SCALE AND LAYOUT

The scale of an exhibition is related to size of display area, location and number of prospective viewers. An effective display can be mounted on simple A1-size (594 × 841 mm.) cardboard panels. Because of the relative smallness of such a display, presentation has to be highly selective: each photo, graphic and piece of text has to be dramatic, meaningful and sufficiently large to be seen. All displays should be linked in some way by design and content. For example, if a display is mounted along a corridor wall, not an uncommon setting, it is essential to use brilliant colours, have the most important and detailed work at eye-level, and incorporate features intended to catch the attention of those on the move.

Scales of presentation vary: a display in an informal home setting; a display in a small public area (e.g. the foyer of a bank); a display for a small group of historians, perhaps in a tutorial/classroom setting; an exhibition in a public lecture theatre or arena. Each presentation scale has its own set of 'rules', but some of these are common to all. The first 'rule' is to make a sketch plan on which the learning objectives of the exhibition are made clear. Learning is based on attention, concentration, absorption and evaluation. Your sketch plan should include a 'route' along which the viewer travels, indicate the physical properties of the equipment to be used, and highlight features to be included such as lighting, texture and colour. The exhibition can include tactile objects, movement, sound and places for handout leaflets. If possible, let your viewer participate, ask a question. Have a graphic that 'shouts' *compare me to that*.

5.2 CONTENT AND CONTACT

The content of an exhibition will be based on the culmination of many months' work. Don't try to tell the whole story – pick one particular year, one particular family, one particular activity. Use simple summary tables, charts and maps to emphasize your main findings. Many square metres of empty display panels can be a daunting challenge to fill – the larger the space, the larger the images you have to present. Don't forget to use a blackboard, tables and existing shelves to help make your exhibition multidimensional. What must be clear is the *relationship* between objects, pictures and text. Enlarge text on a photocopier to make characters at least 6 mm. ($\frac{1}{2}$ in.) high. Use short summary paragraphs; don't expect viewers to read whole pages. Leave a contact name, address, phone number (or better still get viewers to leave theirs) so that contact can be made later for 'fuller' information.

5.3   PURPOSE AND PARTICIPATION

Whenever you set up a display or exhibition you do it with a particular purpose in mind. You need to display information to viewers so that they will fit it in with what they already believe as well as attach new meanings to their knowledge. For an exhibition to be successful, viewers must be attracted and their attention concentrated. When they become interested, they will want to participate and challenge, and will become receptive to new thoughts and concepts. You want your research to become part of the viewer's consciousness.

Don't call it a single theme exhibition – call it an exposé; that will pull them in!

PART V

LOCATING SOURCES AND REFERENCES

❖ ❖ ❖

CHAPTER 12

A GUIDE TO RECORD OFFICES, LIBRARIES AND OTHER COLLECTIONS

The most common sources for family and community history include original records, printed works, paintings, photographs, audio and video archives, artefacts and the products of the human memory. This chapter provides an outline guide to the main locations where such sources tend to be collected. This will give you some idea of what you are likely to be able to find locally (and nationally – though national archives are unlikely to be your first port of call). You will still need to check precisely what is available within your reach, and this is worth doing as early as possible in your researches.

Section 1 lists some general finding aids to help you track down the repositories near you: record offices, local studies collections, reference libraries, museums, and collections of other material such as sound recordings, film or photographs. This is followed in section 2 by some practical advice about using archives. Section 3 describes some of the repositories in England and Wales – including some information on national libraries which may be of wider interest – while similar accounts are given for Scotland and Ireland in sections 4 and 5 respectively. In each case an annotated list of finding aids is followed by a general description of the main repositories and their likely holdings.

As will become clear, the organization of records varies in the different countries. For example, the English county record office tradition is not found in Ireland or in Scotland, both these countries having centralized their records more than England and Wales. However, regional councils in Ireland and Scotland are now building up archives. The differences in organization are related to the differing histories and thus differing political and administrative structures of these countries. Similarly, the 1921 partition of Ireland inevitably led to the shuffling of some categories of records between London, Dublin and Belfast.

Administrative developments continue to be relevant for the storing and financing of records. Thus the current local government review in England is likely to have implications for archive provision, and the situation described in this chapter will not necessarily be permanent.

It is also possible that current distinctions between locally and centrally held records will become less rigid through new technological opportunities for duplicating or retrieving material: this includes not just photocopying, but also microfilm or microfiche and, more recently, computer databases and networks.

Finally, although this chapter provides guidance on the general situation, repositories are not uniform. Records you expect to find may not be there or may not be complete. Equally, you may sometimes light on some quite unforeseen treasure, and have the good fortune to use it.

1 CHECKLIST OF GENERAL FINDING AIDS

by Paul Smith

At the most basic level you need to be able to discover what record offices, libraries and other collections exist, and find their addresses and telephone numbers. Here first, therefore, are references to some useful guides. Each has its advantages and disadvantages. Some can only be found in libraries, being available only in hardback and/or expensive; others are (at the time of writing) available as user-friendly paperbacks. Those produced annually will obviously be the most up-to-date (you should consult the most recent edition available), and no doubt new guides will appear in the future. But all are liable to date, so always check the latest situation by telephone or letter.

Section 1.1 lists guides with a wide geographical coverage, i.e. Great Britain or the United Kingdom as a whole, and sometimes also Ireland (guides confined just to England and Wales, Scotland or Ireland are listed later in the appropriate sections). The guides are presented under four headings (record repositories, libraries, museums, and audio-visual collections), but since these can overlap, you should look through the whole list.

1.1 RECORD OFFICES AND ARCHIVES

Cole, J. and Church, R. (comps), Cross, A. (ed.) (1992) *In and around record repositories in Great Britain and Ireland*, Huntingdon, Family Tree Magazine. Includes the Channel Islands. Informative paperback which succeeds admirably in its aims and is brimful of facts.

Foster, J. and Sheppard, J. (eds) (1989) *British archives: a guide to archive resources in the United Kingdom*, London, HMSO. Available in reference libraries. The most comprehensive official guide, clearly arranged with good indexes.

Gibson, J.S.W. and Peskett, P. (1993) *Record offices: how to find them*, 6th edn, Birmingham, Federation of Family History Societies. Not as comprehensive as Foster and Sheppard, but portable and regularly updated

Royal Commission on Historical Manuscripts (1991) *Record repositories in Great Britain. A geographical directory*, 9th edn, London, HMSO. Lists national and local record offices, together with university and special libraries or archives open to the public. Gives addresses, telephone numbers and opening hours.

1.2 LIBRARIES

Libraries range in size from local branch libraries to the British Library in London. A useful list is:

Libraries in the United Kingdom and the Republic of Ireland, London, Library Association Publishing Ltd. Published annually and arranged by type of library, e.g. public, academic, with addresses, telephone and fax numbers. Includes Channel Islands and Isle of Man.

To find out what is in libraries you need guides to their holdings. Two useful national ones are:

The libraries directory 1991–93 (1992) Cambridge, James Clarke. In three sections: public libraries in the UK, special libraries, and public and special libraries in the Republic of Ireland (special libraries include record offices and collections of photographs). Includes a good subject index.

The Aslib directory of information sources in the United Kingdom (1992) 7th edn, London, Aslib. New editions of this excellent aid appear every few years. Currently in two volumes, the second being the essential subject index.

NORTHAMPTONSHIRE

Northamptonshire Record Office,
Wootton Hall Park, Northampton NN4 9BQ
(0604 762129)

Northampton Central Library,
Abington Street, Northampton NN1 2BA
(0604 26774)

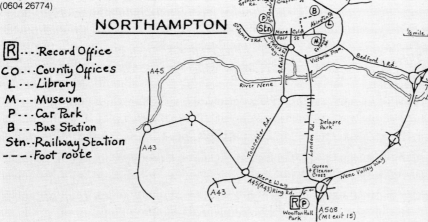

NORTHAMPTON

R...Record Office
CO...County Offices
L...Library
M...Museum
P...Car Park
B...Bus Station
Stn..Railway Station
----.Foot route

JERSEY

Judicial Greffe
States Building
Royal Square
ST HELIER
Telephone: (0534) 77111

Opening Hours: Monday to Friday enquiries in writing in first instance Signing
in Fee charged
Records: Civil Registration of births, marriages and deaths; wills and administrations; Royal Court; deeds.
Places of Interest: St Peter's Bunker Museum; Elizabeth Castle; Jersey Museum; La
Hougue Museum; Sir Francis Cook Gallery.
Tourist Office: Liberation Square, St Helier JE1 1BB. Tel: (0534)78000.
Remarks: Original records of baptisms,
marriages and burials held by local incum-
bents. For Roman Catholic records apply
to the Bishop of Portsmouth, Hampshire,
England (see entry). Census returns for the
Channel Islands from 1841 are in the PRO
Census Search Room, London. Further
reading: *Genealogical Research in the Channel
Islands* (*Society of Genealogists' Magazine* Vol
19 No 5, March 1978). *Family History in
Jersey* by Marie Louise Backhurst (1991).
No reply was received from the Judicial
Greffe and therefore the information re-
mains the same as in the previous edition.

4270
MANCHESTER LOCAL STUDIES
UNIT
Central Library, St Peters Square, Manchester
M2 5PD
Tel: 061 234 1979/1980
Telex: 667149 INFMAN G Fax: 061 234 1963
Local government library service
Enquiries to the Local Studies Officer
Subject coverage:
political, economic, religious, educational and
historical development of Manchester and the
region

Special collections:
Archives (approx. 10,000 linear feet) of
 churches, businesses and local government
Print Collection (approx. 142,000 items, prints,
 photographs, postcards, etc.)
Map Collection (approximately 10,500 items)
Broadside Collection (large collection - total
 unknown)
Local Newspapers from early 18th century
Parish Registers (large collection, Manchester,
 Cheshire and Lancashire)
Census Returns (Manchester)
Directories of Manchester, 1772-1969
Miscellaneous Collection (ephemera and three-
 dimensional objects)
Publications:
Peterloo: a bibliography (1969)
Peterloo 1819: a portfolio of contemporary
 documents (1975)
Municipal Palace: a bibliography on the
 construction and opening of Manchester
 Town Hall, 1877 (1977)
Selection of reproduction posters, mainly 18th
 century
Selection of reproduction maps, 800-1876

Figure 12.1 Sample entries from some key finding
aids: Gibson and Peskett (1993) (*top*), Cole and Church
(1992) (*above left*), and the *Aslib directory of information sources in the United Kingdom* (1992) (*right*)

Over the years local branches or national groups of the Library Association have published guides to library resources in a local area (many are out of print, but the relevant sections might be available locally). For example, a library in Penrith might have acquired the 1988 guide to *Library resources in Cumbria*. The Library Association's Reference Special and Information Section has published *Library resources in South-West England and the Channel Islands* (1978); *… the West Midlands* (1977); *… East Anglia* (1984); *… Yorkshire and Humberside* (1980); *… the North East* (1977); *… the North West* (1980); and *… the East Midlands* (1979). In 1984 the Scottish Library Association published *Scottish library and information resources 1984–1985*. Guides to local resources can sometimes be generated extremely 'locally': for example, 1981 saw the second edition of a *Directory of resources* published by Staffordshire County Library Headquarters, which focused on that county and the Black Country. It is always worth enquiring in your local reference library about any guide to resources for your area.

1.3   MUSEUMS

Of the many useful guides to locating museums, the most relevant for family and community historians in the UK and Ireland are:

Woodfield, P. and Stansfield, G. (1989) *Keyguide to information sources in museum studies*, London, Mansell. Part 2 has some 329 annotated entries.

Hudson, K. and Nicholls, A. (1989) *The Cambridge guide to the museums of Britain and Ireland*, revised edn, Cambridge, Cambridge University Press. Aims to be complete and has entries for over 2,000 historic houses, art galleries and museums arranged alphabetically by place.

Museums and galleries in Great Britain and Ireland, East Grinstead, Reed Information Services Limited. Published annually since 1955. Lists over 1,500 museums and galleries open to the public with a good indication of their scope.

Museums yearbook; including a directory of museums and galleries of the British Isles, London, Museums Association/Rhinegold Publishing Ltd. Published annually since 1955. Museums are listed alphabetically by town with details of admission charges, facilities, opening hours, reports and catalogues.

Shipley, D. and Peplow, M. (1988) *The other museum guide*, London, Grafton. Leisure oriented, it covers approximately 300 specialist and regional museums. Arranged by region with name and subject indexes.

Roulstone, M. (ed.) (1980) *Bibliography of museum and art gallery publications and audio-visual aids in Great Britain and Ireland*, 2nd edn, Cambridge, Chadwyck-Healey. Lists publications of 955 institutions. The audio-visual coverage ranges over slides, films, recordings and sound recordings, photographs and postcards.

1.4   AUDIO-VISUAL COLLECTIONS

Weerasinghe, L. (ed.) (1989) *Directory of recorded sound resources in the United Kingdom*, London, British Library, National Sound Archive. Hardback, available in some libraries, now starting to date but still enormously useful. (Further details in Chapter 6, section 5.)

British Universities Film and Video Council, *Researcher's guide to British film and television collections*, London, British Universities Film and Video Council. Regularly updated. (Further details in Chapter 6, section 6.)

See also Roulstone (1980) in section 1.3 above.

2   ADVICE ON USING ARCHIVES: SOME PRACTICAL POINTS

by Jane Cox

2.1   RECORD OFFICE PROCEDURE

Most people are more familiar with libraries and museums than with record offices, and it is advisable to know something about them before making a visit. Because their holdings are irreplaceable, record offices generally have more rules and regulations than libraries. The actual records are never let out on loan, and they must be handled with extreme care; nearly all offices insist that only pencils or typewriters be used for note taking, to avoid ink damage to the records. I suggest that you go armed with paper and pencils as there is not always anywhere to buy them. Cassette recorders, typewriters or laptop computers are sometimes permitted. A magnifying glass can be handy for deciphering manuscript details or small print.

Photocopying is only permissible for documents which are considered to be tough enough to withstand the process, and in accordance with the copyright laws (which normally allow copying for private study). Copies may not be ready the same day, or may need to be mailed (you commonly have to pay for the copying and the postage).

Some records have to be read on microfiche or microfilm. This may be an advantage, as difficult passages can be magnified by adjusting the machine. If a document is considered too frail for handling, the archivist may have the right to withhold it from the public altogether or only allow it to be inspected in certain controlled conditions.

Manuscript records are not normally kept on open access, and various procedures have to be gone through: finding the correct reference, filling in an application, giving it to the staff and waiting for the document to be delivered to a collection point. This all takes time, which should be allowed for. If the records are on film, the process will be quicker.

There are restrictions on access to the preserved records of central government. Records generally become available after thirty years. However, certain records may be closed for longer, for example medical records, the personal details on CEBs (see Chapter 3), and those containing information which may cause distress or damage to individuals and families. Other records from government departments may still be held in the departments (rather than by the Public Record Office) and such files may or may not be made available to individuals requesting to see them.

Many offices have a restricted number of seats or of microfilm or microfiche readers, and so have introduced booking systems or other limitations. It is as well to check before visiting on such things as: do you need to book a seat or reader; is there a charge; what are the opening hours (some, but not all, have a late evening and/or Saturday opening); and what guides to the holdings are available?

Unlike reference libraries, admission is usually regulated, so check in advance. Some record offices issue a reader's ticket on production of some positive means of identification, like a bank card or driving licence; others require a letter of recommendation or a photograph; some belong to the County Archive Research Network (CARN) scheme and issue a ticket that is valid for all participating offices. For security reasons, briefcases and handbags may have to be put in lockers (often requiring a returnable pound coin) and coats deposited in a cloakroom. You should be prepared to be separated from your belongings.

Old documents can be dirty, and some buildings are extremely cold in winter, so dress accordingly!

2.2   FINDING WHAT YOU WANT

Archivists are busy people, and the more you are able to work the system for yourself, the better you will be appreciated. That does not mean you should stumble about for hours without asking for information.

Most record offices have finding aids at several different levels. There may be a guide in leaflet form (this is worth asking for, in advance if feasible); an extract from the guide to the Gloucestershire Record Office is shown in Figure 12.2 (see also Figure 1.1 in Chapter 1). There should also be a more comprehensive catalogue, either printed on cards or held on a computer database. Local offices usually have an index arranged by place, which can be a useful starting point for a local study, and a subject card index with headings such as 'industries', 'schools', etc.

Means of reference are as variable as the documents they service. Unlike books which have a comprehensive alphabetical index, most records are unindexed. If they have an index at all (perhaps made by a contemporary as a working tool, or later by someone who realized the material's research potential) it may be physically separated from the records themselves. It is always a good idea to ask if there is an index to what you are consulting, as this may be kept in a separate section. An example is the Exeter Record Office, where many of the parish register indexes are in published form in the adjoining local history library.

3   RECORD OFFICES, LIBRARIES, AND OTHER COLLECTIONS IN ENGLAND AND WALES

by Jane Cox

In England and Wales you will probably find that the most useful places for consulting written sources are local record offices and local studies collections, so these are treated first (after a list of useful finding aids). This is followed by some references to regional or national collections that may be particularly useful.

3.1   FINDING AIDS: ENGLAND AND WALES

See also the guides listed in section 1.

Guy, S. (ed.) (1992) *English local studies handbook: a guide to resources for each county including libraries, record offices, societies, journals and museums*, Exeter, University of Exeter Press. The title is self-explanatory. Detailed and (mostly) up-to-date guide, paperback, arranged by county and giving full information on local studies libraries and collections, record offices, local history societies, local history journals, and museums with local studies collections. Contains addresses and telephone numbers. Includes Isle of Man.

Moulton, J.W. (1988) *Genealogical resources in English repositories*, Columbus, Ohio, Hampton House (*Supplement* published in 1992). Includes genealogical information of a general nature. Available in specialized reference libraries. 'Basically a "where to find" reference guide' (p.xx) and truly invaluable. Arranged sequentially: Greater London; counties; London boroughs, with each area entry concluding with a list of relevant genealogical and family history societies, plus journals or magazines. Gives addresses of the libraries of the Church of Jesus Christ of Latter-Day Saints (see section 3.7 below).

Cox, J. and Padfield, T. (revised Bevan and Duncan) (1990) *Tracing your ancestors in the Public Record Office*, London, HMSO. Although focused on the PRO in London, contains much useful general information, including a list of government bodies with useful archives.

SEARCH ROOMS

The main search room is for historical and genealogical records.

wills
1851 census
poor law records
parish registers
diocesan records
nonconformist
manorial
business
societies

maps
deeds
estate papers
borough records
quarter sessions
petty sessions
estate agents
solicitors
architects

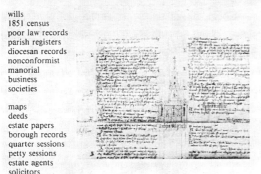

The Shire Hall search room is for other public and local government records, including local boards and district councils, county council, hospitals and schools. This search room is open by appointment only.

A *Handlist to the contents of the Record Office* is available (*see* list of publications).

ENQUIRIES

The staff can answer brief enquiries about availability of records by post or telephone, and research can be undertaken by the genealogist and record agent for a fee (please ask for details).

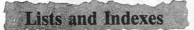

About half the contents of the Record Office have been listed in detail, and these documents can be quickly fetched for you from the strongrooms. Where only a draft list is available, written permission from the County Archivist is required and you *must* make an appointment to see them.

There are indexes of places, subjects and personal names, and specialist indexes to genealogical sources, maps and photographs. A guide to finding aids can be obtained from the Search Room counter.

EDUCATIONAL

School and college groups can be accommodated by prior arrangement. Teachers planning courses which involve local history studies should consult the Archives Education Officer at an early stage.

An extensive photocopy bank of documents specially selected for use in schools is available for consultation at the Record Office, and for loan or recopying at all Gloucestershire Teachers' Centres. Published packs on particular themes are available for purchase (*see* list of publications).

LECTURES

Talks are given to local history and other societies.

EXHIBITIONS

Public exhibitions are mounted periodically. Advice and assistance are offered to others wishing to display documents in this way.

Car park: the car park may be used free of charge by visitors to the Record Office. Please record your car registration number in the Search Room register and make sure your vehicle is removed at closing time.

Toilets: these are entered from the exhibition area.

Refreshments: a lounge, with drinks vending machine, is open Monday — Friday 8.45 am — 4.30 pm.

Disabled: access for wheelchairs is at the rear of the building, and there is easy access to all public areas (toilets excepted).

PHOTOCOPIES of most documents can be made on the coin-operated machine in the main search room. Copies ordered by post can usually be supplied within a few days. Microfilming and other photographic work takes longer.

MICROFICHE copies of most parish registers are now available self-service in the microfilm room. Other parish registers, 1851 census returns and other documents are on microfilm. No booking of readers is necessary. There is a coin-operated fiche printer, and prints from roll film can be ordered.

Figure 12.2 Extract from a Gloucestershire Record Office leaflet (Source: Gloucestershire Record Office)

3.2 LOCAL RECORD OFFICES

For research on family or community history the local record office is often the most useful repository; it is usually, though not always, combined with the diocesan record office. County record offices (CROs) exist for most counties in the county town (or county administrative centre if different), often within the council offices. The metropolitan boroughs and some others may have their own separate record offices (BROs).

Holdings in CROs and BROs typically include: parish registers of baptisms, marriages and burials, and bishops' transcripts of these; post-1837 registers of baptisms and burials for some nonconformist chapels; wills proved in local courts from about the fifteenth century to 1858; various parish records (e.g. churchwardens' accounts and vestry minutes); maps; marriage bonds and licences (often with some sort of index); municipal government and corporation records; local government records; council minutes; Medical Officer of Health reports; manorial records to 1922; poll books; electoral registers; rate books; records of some schools and hospitals; records of livery companies, some trade unions, local insurance companies, and other deposited business records; Poor Law records (pre-1834 in the parish records, thereafter arranged by Poor Law union); parish apprenticeship records; parish transportation records; deeds; filmed copies of CEBs relating to the locality (also sometimes locally compiled name indexes for the 1851 CEBs and – eventually – the nationally organized 1881 index, and relevant local street indexes); the International Genealogical Index (IGI) on microfiche arranged by county (entries for local counties); records of Quarter Sessions and Petty Sessions (i.e. crimes dealt with in local courts, often with calendars or abstracts in print); tithe maps and apportionments; transcriptions of monumental inscriptions; main local newspapers; and sometimes a photographic collection and local history library (see below).

3.3   LOCAL HISTORY LIBRARIES AND REFERENCE LIBRARIES

In many areas local history libraries are attached to the county or borough record offices, or to the area reference library. Some are quite separate. Some hold collections of printed material of local interest, books, maps, photographs, directories, etc., while others have manuscript collections such as rate books and vestry accounts, or oral recordings. As they vary so much it is essential to find out for yourself exactly what they have which might be of use. (For local studies collections which are partly computerized, see Chapter 13, section 5.)

The precise division of contents between local history libraries and record offices varies from area to area, but typically local studies collections include: local histories, published and unpublished, ranging from large-scale printed works like the Victoria County Histories (where available) to local memoirs or compilations made by schools or women's institutes); printed maps; photographs; local newspapers (not normally indexed, but sometimes with indexes to obituaries and/or birth, marriage and death entries); directories (sometimes these are kept in the local record office); parish magazines; electoral registers; CEBs on microfilm; microfiches of the local county (or counties) index from the International Genealogical Index; parliamentary papers and published government reports; published census material, e.g. printed material, or (from 1961) Small Area Statistics on microfiche; the *Return of Owners of Land, 1873–6*; reports of local social surveys, etc.; peerages; proceedings of local historical or archaeological societies; audio tapes from oral history recordings, etc.; and possibly some special collection, perhaps relating to something distinctive in the history of the town.

3.4   MUSEUMS

Local museums, whether general, regimental or industrial, may be a gold mine of information about the community, and curators are often prepared to share their sometimes considerable knowledge. Remember, though, that they are busy people and cannot do your work for you. (For guides, see section 1.3 above.)

3.5   LOCAL AUDIO AND VIDEO ARCHIVES

Sound archives can be particularly useful. These may be either separate or integrated with the repositories listed above, and contain the results of the many oral history projects conducted from the 1970s onwards. (For guides, see section 1.4 above.)

3.6   OTHER LOCAL RESOURCES

Institutions which may be worth a visit include:

Churches and chapels   The parish church, or sometimes the chapel, is still very much the repository for local history. It is worth a visit to look at memorials in the church, lists of local men lost in various wars, or any records that still remain there. You may also be able to see unpublished local histories and pick the brains of the vicar, minister, church warden or church secretary (who may suggest further contacts).

Churchyards and cemeteries   Although the traditional first port of call for the ancestor hunter is the graveyard, there are considerable difficulties in reading monumental inscriptions. Often the writing has been eroded by the weather, and it may be a long task finding particular families. It is best to ascertain first whether there are transcriptions in the CRO or local history library. Most cemeteries hold their own records which can be readily consulted. Lists should be in the CRO.

Schools and hospitals   Some hold their own records which they may be willing to make available by appointment (you might need to show that you have a legitimate interest, e.g. as next of kin).

Local firms   These sometimes have an archive of earlier records, though much has been destroyed in recent years, especially after take-overs.

Family and local history societies, etc.   There are hundreds of such organizations, most of which publish journals or news sheets. The members may have a great deal of local knowledge. Details are available from local libraries, the Federation of Family History Societies and the Association for Local History (for addresses see Chapter 13, section 2.1).

Personal and home-based collections and memories   Finally,   don't   neglect   the resource of personal archives and photograph albums, etc., or talking to older people.

3.7   REGIONAL AND OTHER MAJOR REPOSITORIES

There are too many of these to list individually, but it is worth investigating whether such a repository is within reach (for further details see the guides listed in section 1). Examples include major reference libraries covering a large area, such as the Birmingham Reference Library or Guildhall Library in London, and special collections such as the National Museum of Labour History in Manchester, or the North West Sound Archives in Clitheroe, Lancashire. University libraries sometimes have special collections of relevant material. There are also a number of family history libraries of the Church of Jesus Christ of Latter-Day Saints (LDS) throughout the country (open to non-LDS members); these contain genealogical material, such as microfiche copies of the International Genealogical Index (see Chapter 4, section 3.5) and the LDS Family Register (the index of names being researched and by whom), and sometimes copies of the British indexes of births, marriages and deaths, and some microfilmed American and Australian records. They can also order films from the genealogical source material microfilmed from all parts of the world and stored at Salt Lake City (including film of census returns and parish registers).

3.8   NATIONAL COLLECTIONS (ENGLAND AND WALES)

Although a fairly comprehensive story of a community and its members can be put together from local archives and printed sources, national and institutional collections can augment that story. The most significant for family and community historians are listed below (for the many others see the guides listed in sections 1 and 3.1).

Public Record Office (PRO), located on two sites: Chancery Lane, London, WC2A 1LR (CL); and Ruskin Avenue, Kew, Richmond, Surrey, TW9 4DU (K). The national state archive for

England and Wales, it holds some 90 shelf miles of records. The more obvious sources which cannot be consulted elsewhere include: records of service in the armed forces (K); wills (CL) (i.e. wills proved in the Prerogative Court of Canterbury, the senior probate court for the southern province, to 1858); nonconformist registers (CL); records of criminal and civil law (CL and K); records of immigration, emigration and the British overseas (including passenger lists, naturalization papers and registers of births, etc. from British embassies and consulates) (K and CL); records of dissolved companies and bankrupts (K and CL); and records of Poor Law Commissioners (K). Microfilm copies of the CEBs 1841–1891 and supporting material are in the Census Room (CL site). For further details on the PRO see Cox and Padfield (1990 – see section 3.1 above) and the very helpful series of PRO leaflets.

General Register Office (GRO), St Catherine's House, 10 Kingsway, London, WC2B 6JP (the Office of Population Censuses and Surveys). The address of the postal application section is: OPCS General Register Office, Smedley Hydro, Trafalgar Road, Birkdale, Southport, Merseyside, PR8 2HH. The GRO holds the records resulting from the compulsory state registration of births, marriages and deaths that started in 1837. The indexes are available at the GRO (with filmed copies sometimes held in LDS libraries, record offices and family history societies), but the records themselves can only be consulted through personal or postal purchase of copies of the certificates.

Principal Probate Registry (Principal Registry of the Family Division), Somerset House, Strand, London, WC2R 1LA. The Registry holds all wills proved in England and Wales since January 1858; also annual indexes on open access.

Borthwick Institute of Historical Research (York University), St. Anthony's Hall, Peasholme Green, York, YO1 2PW. Holds wills proved in the senior probate court for the Province of York to 1858; also records of the 1930s Rowntree Poverty Survey.

National Register of Archives, Royal Commission on Historical Manuscripts, Quality House, Quality Court, Chancery Lane, London, WC2A 1HP. Collects and disseminates information about manuscript sources (including private family papers) outside the public records; also holds manorial documents register.

National Library of Wales, Aberystwyth, Dyfed, SY23 3BU. Holds many Welsh parish registers, wills, tithe and estate records.

British Library (BL) is the UK national library, with several locations and specialisms. Its central site at Bloomsbury (Great Russell Street, London, WC1B 3DG, but due to move to St. Pancras) holds, among other material, humanities and social science books and various special collections (including manuscripts); access to the Bloomsbury reading rooms is limited, however. The most relevant three sites are listed below:

National Newspaper Library (BL), Colindale Avenue, London, NW9 5HE. Holds large collection of national and local newspapers.

Oriental and India Office Collections (BL), 197 Blackfriars Road, London, SE1 8NG. Besides general material on the various regions of Asia and North Africa, holds official British records relating to the Indian sub-continent up to 1947.

National Sound Archive (BL), 29 Exhibition Rd, London SW7 2AS. The national repository for recordings of all kinds, with an extensive oral history collection including the important National Life Story Collection.

Other useful collections and archives include:

Economic and Social Research Council (ESRC) Data Archive, University of Essex, Wivenhoe House, Colchester, Essex, CO4 3SQ. The national repository for social science machine-readable data, including many historical data files (for example Michael Anderson's sample of the 1851 CEBs, which can be obtained at near-cost price from the Archive in hard copy or machine-readable form). The Archive has recently established a History Data Unit, which it encourages researchers to exploit.

Society of Genealogists Library, 14 Charterhouse Buildings, Goswell Road, London, EC1M 7BA. Large genealogical collection including parish register and other local indexes not available elsewhere. The Society charges a daily search fee, or an annual or life membership fee.

BT Archives and Historical Information Centre, Room G09, Telephone House, 2–4 Temple Avenue, London, EC4Y 0HL. Responsible on behalf of PRO for historical telecommunications records. Holdings include near-complete set of telephone directories for the whole country back to 1879. Also has photographic library and local histories. Prior appointment advisable.

National Museum of Photography, **Film and Television**, Prince's View, Bradford, West Yorks, BD5 0TR.

For addresses of repositories for business archives etc. see the details in Chapter 4, section 5.4.

4 SCOTTISH ARCHIVES, LIBRARIES AND RESOURCES

by Ian Donnachie

The Scottish administrative state has been highly centralized for three hundred years, so many of the country's records have found their way into national collections, notably those of the General Register House (housing vital registers like parish and census records) and the Scottish Record Office (SRO) in Edinburgh (a major repository for most other archival categories). The National Library of Scotland, also in Edinburgh, houses the largest collection of historical books, has a substantial manuscript collection, and the most comprehensive map library in Scotland. The university libraries, the Mitchell Library in Glasgow, and others in major cities and towns also have extensive archival and book holdings of national significance.

This centralization has advantages and disadvantages: an enormous range of information about almost every aspect of Scottish family and community history from Wigtownshire to Shetland can be obtained in one place, but it is often far removed from the actual locality. For example, working in the SRO one is likely to find as much (if not more) about the history of, say, Orkney or Dumfries, than in the actual locations.

These two locations, however, are among many which do have well-developed archives and libraries, providing access to collections of the kind described for England and Wales, as well as local history reference libraries with holdings such as the Statistical Accounts (see Chapter 4, section 6), local and regional newspapers (dating back to the nineteenth century, and sometimes indexed), directories, maps, plans, prints and photographs. Indeed, regional and local archives are well-established almost everywhere, and have received much local material from the SRO and other central archives – either originals or microfilm copies. Further reform of local government in Scotland, which is high on the agenda at the time of writing (1993), may modify the present network of regional and district archives.

Start by contacting your nearest local history library (see section 4.1 for directories etc.). In all cases it makes sense to 'phone or write with any enquiry in advance of a visit. This can save a great deal of time and effort and get your project off to a good start.

4.1 SELECT LIST OF FINDING AIDS FOR SCOTLAND

The following focus on Scotland, but see also section 1.

Cox, M. (ed.) (1992) *Exploring Scottish history: a directory of resource centres for Scottish local and national history in Scotland*, Motherwell, Scottish Library Association/Scottish Local History Forum. A comprehensive listing of archives and local history libraries, including addresses, telephone numbers and holdings.

Dunsire, G. and Osborne, B.D. (eds) (1991) *Scottish library and information resources*, Motherwell, Scottish Library Association. A full list with addresses and telephone numbers.

Scottish Museums Council (1990) *Scottish museums and galleries: the guide*, Aberdeen, Aberdeen University Press and Scottish Museums Council. Lists about 400 museums, arranged by area; gives addresses, telephone numbers, opening hours and a short description.

The Scottish Records Association, c/o the Scottish Record Office (SRO), publishes datasheets on the record holdings of local repositories throughout Scotland; and the National Register of Archives (Scotland), a branch of the SRO, produces reports (available at the SRO, the National Library and other research libraries) on privately held records, and assists researchers in gaining access.

4.2 NATIONAL COLLECTIONS

General Register Office for Scotland, New Register House, Princes Street, Edinburgh, EH1 3YY. Main records include: Old Parish (or Parochial) Records (OPRs) covering births, deaths and marriages prior to 1855; post-1855 registers of births, deaths and marriages; marine, air and war registers; CEBs 1841–1891 (microfilm). Search rooms are always busy. Fees for searches and extracts are listed in a leaflet.

Scottish Record Office (SRO), General Register House, Princes Street, Edinburgh, EH1 3YY. Contains the widest ranging archive holdings; government and legal records; church records (such as Kirk Session and Presbytery records); many private and local records; and a large collection of maps and estate plans. There are extensive catalogues and guides to the various record groups, and a useful library of historical, biographical, legal and topographical works. Since there are two search rooms (Register House and the West Search Room in Charlotte Square) you should 'phone to check the location of the records you wish to consult. Admission by reader's ticket. Written enquiries to the Keeper of the Records at the address above.

National Library of Scotland, George IV Bridge, Edinburgh, EH1 1EW. Scotland's largest library, with special emphasis on Scottish history, life and culture. The reading rooms are for reference and research that cannot easily be carried out elsewhere (application form for reader's ticket available from the Superintendent of Readers' Services). The Manuscripts Division holds papers of individuals, families, estates and organizations; legal, financial and estate papers; maps; plans; photographs; and journals. A catalogue of manuscripts and inventories of other holdings can be consulted.

The Map Library, Causewayside Building, 33 Salisbury Place, Edinburgh. Provides comprehensive coverage of Scotland in topographical maps of all periods, and Ordnance Survey maps at all scales from 1801 onwards. Reference books include the Statistical Accounts to aid interpretation of maps and plans.

4.3   REGIONAL COLLECTIONS

Most regional councils maintain an archive, though the holdings are not standard. There are exceptions such as Fife, where records remain largely with originating authorities, mainly former burghs, or are housed in district archives or at St Andrews University Library. This situation exists elsewhere: for example, the impressive Strathclyde Regional Archives (Mitchell Library, North Street, Glasgow, G3 7DN) excludes records from some former burgh and district councils and Argyll county. It is therefore wise to check with your nearest local history library to establish the exact location of specific records or other sources to be consulted.

A good example of a regional archive is the Central Regional Archives Department, Unit 6, Burghmuir Industrial Estate, Stirling, FK7 7PY. Holdings cover a wide range of local authority and related records, including: school board minutes; school log-books; Kirk Session records; burial registers; pre-1855 monumental inscriptions for Stirlingshire, Clackmannanshire and parts of Perthshire; Registers of Testaments and Sasine Abridgements, indexed by person and place; trade, commercial and county directories; OPRs; CEBs (on microfilm); and local newspapers from 1836 onwards. *The Stirling Observer* is partly indexed (by persons and topics) from 1836 to the mid 1860s.

4.4   DISTRICT AND LOCAL COLLECTIONS

There is an excellent network of local history collections incorporating both primary and secondary sources in their holdings. Although by far the largest, the Glasgow Collection at the Mitchell Library has a typical range of holdings (Glasgow City Libraries, Mitchell Library, North Street, Glasgow, G3 7DN). This comprises over 20,000 books, along with periodicals, maps, plans, newspapers, illustrations, and photographs covering a wide range of topics on the history of the city. Useful sources include: voters' rolls; valuation rolls; OPRs; census returns; cemetery registers; Glasgow Post Office directories; 1,000 volumes of newspapers; illustrations and photographs; maps, including OS maps; and plans. The manuscripts include large collections of family and business papers.

4.5   MUSEUMS

Apart from artefacts, local and national museums have significant archive resources. The National Museums of Scotland have five libraries, including the Scottish Ethnological Archive (York Buildings, Queen Street, Edinburgh, EH2 1JD) and the library of the Scottish United Services Museum (The Castle, Edinburgh, EH1 2NG), whose holdings, like those of the others, can be consulted by appointment. Specialist museums are also of national significance, for example the Scottish Mining Museum (Lady Victoria Colliery, Newtowngrange, EH22 4QN) or the Scottish Fisheries Museum (Harbourhead, Anstruther, KY10 3AB), both of which house libraries specializing in the social and economic history of these sectors in communities throughout the country.

At the local level, Springburn Museum Trust (Atlas Square, Ayr Street, Glasgow, G21 4BW) is a good example of a small resource centre with a social history and photographic collection documenting this once-important railway engineering community. It has an active outreach and oral history programme. Many other local or folk museums also act as heritage centres, so that apart from the nearest library with a decent local history collection this is often a good place to start your research (for addresses and telephone numbers see the *Scottish Museums Council guide* (1990); for archival holdings see Cox (1992 – full reference given in section 4.1).

4.6 OTHER COLLECTIONS

There are so many other archival collections holding potentially useful material that it is invidious to select one example. But undoubtedly the Scottish Film Archive (74 Victoria Crescent, Glasgow, G12 9JN) is unique in its collection of non-fiction film covering many aspects of social, cultural and industrial history from 1897 to the 1980s. It includes local cinema newsreels, educational films, documentaries, advertising and promotional films, and amateur films. Much of the collection is catalogued. Visiting is by appointment, and charges are made for the use of material. For other audio and film collections see the directories listed in section 1.4 above.

5 RECORD REPOSITORIES IN IRELAND

by Brenda Collins

Two historic events govern the availability of historical records in modern Ireland. These are, first, the partition of Ireland in 1921 when the six counties of north-east Ireland remained as part of the United Kingdom, and the Irish Free State (now the Republic of Ireland) was created. The administrative centre for Northern Ireland became Belfast (and ultimately London), while Dublin continued as the administrative centre for the 26 counties which form the Republic of Ireland. Secondly, in 1922 there was a fire in the Public Record Office of Ireland in Dublin which destroyed much of the source material relating to the centralized government administration of Ireland prior to partition.

Although the National Archives in Dublin and the Public Record Office of Northern Ireland remain the most important national repositories, it is worth noting that in Ireland, as perhaps elsewhere, technological advances in duplicating records by photocopying, microfilm and microfiche have led to the dissemination of copies of centrally held records beyond their original repositories – already an advantage to the local researcher.

5.1 GUIDES TO IRISH SOURCES

There are no systematic finding guides to Irish repositories of the kind listed for Scotland or for England and Wales, but the following give useful information about sources and their location (see also section 1 above).

Crozier, M. and Sanders, N. (eds) (1992) *A cultural traditions directory for Northern Ireland,* Belfast, Institute of Irish Studies and Cultural Traditions Group of the Community Relations Council. Very useful list of locations and producers of relevant material, e.g. societies, museums, publishers, resources.

Grenham, J. (1992) *Tracing your Irish ancestors: the complete guide,* Dublin, Gill and Macmillan. Very well organized and contains really useful information on sources for local historians.

Helferty, S. and Refaussé, R. (eds) (1993) *Directory of Irish archives,* 2nd edn, Dublin, Irish Academic Press. Does not pretend to be comprehensive but rather aims to introduce the 'locations where primary source material for the study of Irish history can be found' (p.9). Record categories deliberately excluded are trade unions and business organizations. Arranged by institution, the entries note the major collections.

Kinealy, C. (1991) *Tracing your Irish roots,* Belfast, The Appletree Press Ltd. An authoritative, cheap, pocket-sized book written by a former genealogist and historian, covering all types of sources and repositories (also deals with sources on the Irish outside Ireland).

Macafee, W. (1976) 'Local historical studies of rural areas: methods and sources', *Irish Archives Bulletin*, 6, pp.4–31. Combines practical ideas with descriptions of sources suitable for their application, within the context of general Irish history (this last is now its weakest point because of the amount of new writing since 1976).

Nolan, W. (1982) *Tracing the past: sources for local studies in the Republic of Ireland*, Dublin. Excellent, the only book-length general study. Privately printed but available in many libraries throughout Ireland.

O'Sullivan, J.C. and Aylward, J. (1984) *Directory of Irish museums*, Dublin, Irish Museums Association and the Irish National Committee of ICOM. A bare listing of 126 museums throughout Ireland.

The Irish museums guide (1983) Dublin, Ward River Press in association with the Irish Museums Trust. Dated but, unlike O'Sullivan and Aylward, gives short descriptions of contents.

5.2   NATIONAL RECORD REPOSITORIES IN IRELAND

Repositories in this category hold many types of source material covering a large part of the country. Although records collected after 1921 tend, by and large, to be held in their respective national repositories, some are duplicated between locations in Dublin and Belfast, as also are many of those for the six counties of Northern Ireland in the pre-1921 period.

5.2.1   REPUBLIC OF IRELAND

National Archives (NA), Bishop Street, Dublin 8 (until 1988 known as the Public Record Office of Ireland or PROI). This holds the original enumerators' returns of the 1901 and 1911 censuses of all Ireland and the surviving fragments of earlier censuses; land records such as the Tithe Applotment Books, land valuation and Griffith's Valuation material (see Chapter 3, section 1.1), some landed estate records and those of the Encumbered Estates Court; some original Church of Ireland parish registers, and others as transcripts and on microfilm (see Grenham, 1992, for a list of all C of I registers and copies available in Dublin, i.e. at the National Archives, the National Library of Ireland and the Representative Church Body (RCB) Library); wills probated between 1858 and 1900 for all Ireland, and for the Republic of Ireland for the period after that date (many wills prior to 1858 are located in private or solicitors' collections of papers).

National Library of Ireland (NLI), Kildare Street, Dublin 2. This includes a large collection of estate records, microfilm copies of nearly all Roman Catholic parish registers to 1880 (some require local permission for access); a newspaper collection and some newspaper indexes (but the National Newspaper Library, Colindale, London, is the best single repository for Irish newspapers); a comprehensive collection of directories; Ordnance Survey memoirs (see Chapter 3, section 1.1); maps (a complete collection of the 6 inches to the mile OS maps 1833–42 and subsequent revised editions, and other scales; maps also in estate records); photographs (amongst others the Lawrence Collection, 1870s–1910, indexed alphabetically); emigration records (microfilm of passenger lists, letters and secondary material). Grenham (1992 – see section 5.1) gives a county-by-county source list which includes relevant National Library call-numbers, i.e. catalogue or press-mark numbers.

5.2.2 NORTHERN IRELAND

Public Record Office of Northern Ireland (PRONI), 66 Balmoral Avenue, Belfast BT9 6NY. This holds:

(a) *Public records pre-1922.* As the official repository for public records in Northern Ireland, PRONI has obtained copies of many pre-1922 public records originally held in Dublin repositories which relate to the six counties of Northern Ireland, including the 1901 and earlier fragmentary census returns, Tithe Applotment Books (1823–38), OS maps (from the 1830s first edition), Griffith's Valuation material (from 1858) and associated maps.

(b) *Private pre-1922 records.* These include (i) church registers: microfilm copies of Roman Catholic parish registers for parishes in the province of Ulster 1830–1888; Church of Ireland parish registers (many C of I registers were lost in the fire at PROI in 1922; copies of most of those surviving for the nine counties – i.e. the province of Ulster – are in PRONI, with originals in the library of the RCB); registers of Presbyterians (mostly from the early nineteenth century), Methodists, Society of Friends and Moravians. (ii) Landed estates: PRONI holds the largest collection of estate records in Northern Ireland (very well indexed and catalogued); also solicitors' records, business records, and abstracts, calendars and copies of wills. (iii) Emigration records: a large amount of material is held on emigration from Ulster (letters to and from emigrants, ships' passenger lists, sponsored schemes, government reports, papers of benefactors, etc.).

(c) *Public records of Northern Ireland.* These are records of the government departments of Northern Ireland since the early 1920s. In addition they include nineteenth-century adminstrative records where these have been superseded by twentieth-century successors. One example is Poor Law records (i.e. the archives of the Boards of Guardians administering the Poor Law from 1838 to 1923 in the Republic of Ireland and to 1948 in Northern Ireland. PRONI has records of all 28 Poor Law unions which operated in the area now covered by Northern Ireland, comprising workhouse admission registers, minute books and lists of those on outdoor relief, and the public dispensary records run by the Poor Law unions). Another example is school records, including grant aid applications of national schools 1831–89, giving information on each school, and registers of national and public elementary schools, generally from the 1860s, giving information on each pupil.

Linen Hall Library, 17 Donegall Square North, Belfast, BT1 5GD. Founded in 1788, this is a subscription library of material on Irish and local history, including a large collection of Irish newspapers, directories and ephemera (holds the *Belfast Newsletter* virtually complete from 1737, with computerized keyword index/database).

5.3 OTHER RECORD REPOSITORIES IN IRELAND

Some repositories hold more specialized source material or cover more restricted geographical areas than the national boundaries. Often source material has been duplicated between national and specialized/local repositories.

Department of Irish Folklore, University College, Belfield, Dublin 4. Sound, video and written archives of cultural heritage collected since the 1930s by independent researchers and by the Irish Folklore Commission.

Representative Church Body Library (RCB), Braemor Park, Rathgar, Dublin 14. The Library of the Church of Ireland, which has gathered together the surviving C of I registers and other associated material. Its holdings are listed in Grenham (1992 – see section 5.1).

Ulster Folk and Transport Museum, Cultra, Holywood, Co. Down, BT18 0EU. As well as a centre for the study of artefacts in their cultural setting, the museum library holds photographic collections. It also has an audio archive which contains recordings on aspects of cultural heritage and the BBC (Northern Ireland) radio archive relating to broadcasting, mainly from the 1960s. The museum greatly facilitates those researchers interested in 'doing' oral history.

Ulster-American Folk Park, Camphill, Omagh, Co. Tyrone, BT78 5QY. An emigration database which has keyword access to a wide range of material (mainly nineteenth-century), including letters, newspaper references and passenger lists from both sides of the Atlantic relating to emigration from Ulster and Ireland to the United States and Canada. The library also has copies of source material relating to the west of Northern Ireland.

5.4   GENERAL INFORMATION

Although the widest range of records is to be found in the national repositories, local libraries usually have photocopies or microfilm of some of the sources relating to their particular catchment area. In the Republic of Ireland, such library material is organized on a county basis, while in Northern Ireland libraries come under five Education and Library Boards, each of whose headquarters has a local history department. The Belfast Central Library has a very wide range of material, including parliamentary papers. The university libraries also have large Irish collections which can include some primary material.

The Ulster Museum in Belfast, the National Museum of Ireland in Dublin, and the county museums throughout Ireland also have libraries of relevant source material, particularly photographs and newspapers.

In addition, the family history centres of the Church of Jesus Christ of Latter-Day Saints in Belfast and Dublin have libraries containing indexes of family names and microfilm copies of some census and parish register material.

Family history and local history societies can also be extremely helpful resources (for details see Grenham, 1992 – full reference given in section 5.1; see also Chapter 13, section 2.1).

A further means of increasing the availability of source material at local level is the Irish Genealogical Project, which is intended to create a comprehensive genealogical database for all Ireland. Thirty-one IGP centres have been established in county libraries and heritage centres throughout the Irish Republic and Northern Ireland, where relevant records will be processed to provide a commercial genealogical service.

CHAPTER 13

SELECTED REFERENCE AND BIBLIOGRAPHICAL RESOURCES: SOME WAYS TO FIND OUT MORE

by Paul Smith (sections 1 to 4) and Magnus John (section 5)

To develop your research on a particular topic, you may need to locate further sources, both primary and secondary. This chapter suggests some of the ways in which you can do this. It maps out some important bibliographical and other resources for family and community historians, cross-refers you, where appropriate, to the relevant sections in this volume, and provides the information you will need to track down useful societies, journals, articles and books. Table 13.1 shows how the chapter is structured.

Table 13.1   The structure of Chapter 13

1	**Guides and handbooks**
1.1	General guides to sources
1.1.1	The 'Gibson guides': location guides for family and local historians
1.1.2	Other general surveys of sources
1.2	Guides to sources for specific localities
1.2.1	England and Wales
1.2.2	Scotland
1.2.3	Ireland
1.2.4	Overseas and migration sources
1.3	Some useful resource works: atlases and historical statistics
1.4	Dictionaries and encyclopaedias
2	**Societies and their publications**
2.1	Some important societies for family and community history
2.1.1	Federations and wider groupings of local history, family history and similar societies
2.1.2	Special interest groups and societies
2.2	How to track down further societies
2.2.1	General aids
2.2.2	Subject-specific aids
2.2.3	Local society publications
3	**Journals**
3.1	Some relevant journals for family and community historians
3.2	Finding aids to additional journals and their contents
4	**Searching further: bibliographies**
4.1	Bibliographies of bibliographies
4.2	Historical bibliographies
4.3	Bibliographies appearing in series
5	**Databases**
5.1	Directories, catalogues and services
5.2	Computerized local studies collections

1   GUIDES AND HANDBOOKS

Many of the sources you are most likely to exploit are discussed in Chapters 3–6 of this volume: for further information on them, you should consult the discussion and references given in those earlier chapters. You may already have used some of these sources in record offices etc. (tracing them, perhaps, through the various finding aids and other advice given in Chapter 12).

However, there are additional sources that you may wish to refer to. The works listed in this chapter can be consulted to find information about these other sources, as well as about the nature and range of sources more generally.

1.1   GENERAL GUIDES TO SOURCES

1.1.1   THE 'GIBSON GUIDES': LOCATION GUIDES FOR FAMILY AND LOCAL HISTORIANS

This series is so useful for giving both the location of and general information about certain key sources that they are worth listing separately (even if mentioned elsewhere too). They can be bought relatively inexpensively from family history and record office bookstalls, or by post from the Federation of Family History Societies (FFHS) (since they are regularly updated, look for the most recent edition). Relevant guides published (or due out) by 1993 are listed below by alphabetical order of title. All are published by the FHSS, Birmingham:

Gibson, J. (1992) *Bishops' transcripts and marriage licences, bonds and allegations: a guide to their location and indexes,* 3rd edn.

Gibson, J. (1990) *Census returns 1841–1881 on microfilm: a directory to local holdings in Great Britain,* 5th edn.

Gibson, J. and Rogers, C. (1992) *Coroners' records in England and Wales.*

Gibson, J. and Rogers, C. (1993) *Electoral registers since 1832; and Burgess Rolls: a directory to holdings in Great Britain,* 5th edn.

Gibson, J. and Mills, D. (1993) *Land tax assessments 1690–1950,* 2nd edn.

Gibson, J. and Creaton, H. (1992) *Lists of Londoners.*

Gibson, J. and Medlycott, M. (1992) *Local census listings, 1522–1930: holdings in the British Isles.*

Gibson, J. (1989) *Local newspapers, 1750–1920: a select location list.*

Gibson, J. and Hampson, E. (1992) *Marriage, census and other indexes for family historians,* 4th edn.

Gibson, J. and Medlycott, M. (1990) *Militia lists and musters 1757–1876,* 2nd edn.

Gibson, J. and Rogers, C. (1990) *Poll books, c.1695–1872: a directory to holdings in Great Britain,* 2nd edn.

Gibson, J. et al. (1993) *Poor Law Union records,* 4 parts: (1) *South East England and East Anglia* (Gibson, J., Rogers, C. and Webb, C.); (2) *The Midlands and Northern England* (Gibson, J. and Rogers, C.); (3) *South-West England, the Marches and Wales* (Gibson, J. and Rogers, C.); (4) *Gazeteer of England and Wales* (Gibson, J. and Youngs, F.A.).

Gibson, J. (1993) *Probate jurisdictions: where to look for wills*, 4th edn.

Gibson, J. (1992) *Quarter session records for family historians: a select list*, 3rd edn.

Gibson, J. and Peskett, P. (1993) *Record offices: how to find them*, 6th edn.

Darlington [14] (partly Yorkshire N.R.).
Durham County Record Office, Durham:
A. Valuation lists 1863-1929; rate books 1840-1910; adm. and discharge reg's 1912-58; creed reg's c.1900-50; births reg. 1911-39; deaths reg's 1877-1974; misc. records re. inmates 1871-95.
B. Min's 1837-1930; C'tee min's: SAC 1877-1904, Visiting 1887-1925, Boarding-out 1889-97, Children 1910-30, Institutions 1925-30, Assessment 1862-1930; rough reports 1919-30; letter books etc. 1852, 1915-28; ledgers 1837, 1904-30; reg. of securities 1869-1930; financial statements 1879-1928; statements of ac's 1889-1915; staff service reg. c.1897-1928; salaries 1905-30; Guardians' declarations of acceptance 1908-28; weekly returns outdoor relief (Northern) 1927-29; newspaper cuttings 1891-1902; list of assistant nurses c.1928; photo of Board 1930; overseers' balance books 1903-27; names and addresses of overseers 1919-27; w'h. ac's and day books 1895-1935; weekly and half-yearly reports 1927-48; wages ac's books 1918-37; stock etc. reg. 1910-43; out letters 1871-95; photos, soldiers and nurses c.1914-19; letters etc. re. examinations and removal orders 1842-1939 (incl. child emigration to Canada 1882-98); half-yearly statements on pauperism 1907-12.
Darlington Branch Library:
Notes on PL in Darlington from 1929 (typescript, 6pp.); 'Resolutions... re. PLUs of Darlington and Teesdale.'

Census Indexes

Derbyshire, 1851 (Derbyshire FHS). Full transcript of county under way. Index published for the following S.Ds., giving name, age, PRO ref (* = also on mfche.):
1: (1) Brailsford, Mayfield, Ashbourne; (2)* Calton, Hartington, Brassington. 5: (1) Duffield; (2)* Horsley; (6)* Wirksworth; 6: (1) Tutbury, Repton; 12: (1) Carburton, Pleasley, Blackwell; 13: (1)* Tamworth, Uttoxeter, Sudbury; 14: (1)* Shardlow; 14: (2)* Melbourne, Stapleford; (4) Spondon.
Enquiries re. publications, SAE, or searches of Master Name Index, SAE + £1 for up to max. of 10 folio numbers, estimate given for the number of remaining names (at same rate), or £1 per family for full transcript if folio no. is provided (no blanket searches), to Mrs I. Salt, 9 Moulton Close, Swanwick, Derbys. DE55 1ES.

Census of Child Population 1892. Entries in 8 volumes by district and street. Shows head of family, with children under school leaving age, with age and name of school attended (Mrs M. Pearce, Chesterfield & Dist. FHS. 10 Burgess Close, Hasland, Chesterfield, Derbyshire S41 0NP).

The 1832 Reform Act (2 & 3 Will.IV c.45) extended the county franchise by giving the vote to:
a) anyone having a life interest in, and occupation of, lands or tenements worth over £2 and under £5 per annum;
b) all other holders of real property worth at least £10, a figure reduced to £5 by the 1867 Reform Act (30 7 31 V. c.102); 1867 also gave the vote to occupiers (owners or tenants) of lands or tenements paying rent of £50 *per annum* or more.

In *boroughs* before 1832, the franchise varied widely according to local custom, an extensive electorate in Preston, for example, contrasting with that in the 'pocket boroughs' such as Old Sarum, Wiltshire, where the M.P. was elected by only eleven voters in 1802-3. Such limited franchise applied too to many more populous seeming places, the 'rotten boroughs', where it might be confined to members of the Corporation. The eighteen aldermen and burgesses at Banbury returned Lord North unopposed throughout his parliamentary career, whilst ensuring regular charitable contributions for the town (and, no doubt, themselves) from his father the Earl of Guilford, who lived nearby (see Jupp 1973; and for the earlier history of borough franchises, see Oldfield 1792).

Figure 13.1   Extracts from three 'Gibson guides': (top left) *Poor Law Union records* (1993) Part 2, p.21; (top right) *Marriage, census and other indexes for family historians* (1992) p.11; (bottom) *Poll books, c.1695–1872* (1990) p.5

1.1.2   OTHER GENERAL SURVEYS OF SOURCES

Edwards, P. (1993) *Rural life: guide to the local records*, London, Batsford. Takes various aspects of rural life, such as population and earning a living, and introduces the relevant sources. There is also a chapter on family and neighbourhood and a short bibliography. This book has to be read – one cannot just refer to it or look up a source.

Porter, S. (1990) *Exploring urban history: sources for local historians*, London, Batsford. Critical guide to relevant primary sources and secondary works.

Raymond, S. and Gibson, J. (1991) *English genealogy; an introductory bibliography* (2nd edn), Birmingham, FFHS. Extremely useful booklet containing: guides to sources; bibliographies; archives; directories; biography; births, marriages and deaths; memorial inscriptions; probate records; names; trade directories; religious records; occupations; local administrative and legal records; migration; local history; newspapers; genealogical journals and societies. It also has subject and author indexes.

Riden, P. (1987) *Record sources for local history*, London, Batsford. A guide to public records which can be searched 'reasonably expeditiously and profitably for local studies' (p.7).

Todd, A. (1987) *Basic sources for family history: 1: back to the early 1800s* (2nd edn), Ramsbottom, Allen & Todd. Covers the basics of family history research, and such sources as the census, rate books, newspapers, civil registration, etc.

West, J. (1983) *Town records,* Chichester, Phillimore. Chapters include: town maps and plans *c.*1600–1900; commercial directories 1763–1900; provincial newspapers from 1690; the national censuses 1801–1901; photographs as evidence 1840–1983. Also included are lists of further reading and a gazetteer of locations.

West, J. (1982) *Village records* (2nd edn), Chichester, Phillimore. '… a series of practical exercises in documentary study' (p.ix) with a 'set' of documents which are used to investigate four periods. Based on one community, but the careful reader will be able to apply its lessons to any part of village England.

Several of the societies listed in section 2.1.1 also produce useful guides to particular sources (especially the Society of Genealogists, the British Association for Local History, and the Historical Geography Research Group).

1.2   GUIDES TO SOURCES FOR SPECIFIC LOCALITIES

There is some overlap with items in the previous section (some of which focus more on certain areas – usually England and Wales – while also giving an overview). The following are more specifically focused (further information can also be tracked down via the relevant finding aids listed in Chapter 12).

1.2.1   ENGLAND AND WALES

Bevan, A. and Duncan, A. (1990) *Tracing your ancestors in the Public Record Office* (4th edn), London, HMSO (*PRO handbooks,* no.19). (Previous authors: Jane Cox and Timothy Padfield.) Ranges widely and relevantly – much more than a trace-your-ancestors book. Each chapter ends with a 'bibliography and sources' section.

Colwell, S. (1991) *Family roots: discovering the past in the Public Record Office,* London, Weidenfeld and Nicolson. Especially strong on sources relating to the law, land and taxation. See also her companion volume *Dictionary of genealogical sources in the Public Record Office*

(1992), London, Weidenfeld and Nicolson: a subject-based defining key to PRO documents with explanatory entries and PRO references.

Harvey, R. (ed.) (1988) *A guide to genealogical sources in Guildhall Library* (3rd edn), London, Guildhall Library (*Guildhall Library research guide*, no.1). Useful first chapter on preliminary work and printed sources.

Moore, J.S. (ed.) (1979) *Avon local history handbook*, Chichester, Phillimore. An example of a useful local publication (look out for others in your area).

Riden, P. (1989) *Local history: a handbook for beginners*, London, Batsford. A good basic beginner's book.

Rogers, C.D. (1986) *Tracing missing persons: an introduction to agencies, methods and sources in England and Wales*, Manchester, Manchester University Press. An excellent survey of possible sources, with special emphasis on twentieth-century sources and methods, such as NHS and other medical records, adoption records, and National Insurance records.

Rogers, C.D. and Smith, J.H. (1991) *Local family history in England*, Manchester, Manchester University Press. Examines the history of the family from 1538 to 1914; the exploitation of source material; and a family history research agenda, which aims to enthuse the user into actually getting material on paper, and succeeds.

Rowlands, J. et al. (1993) *Welsh family history – a guide to research*, Aberystwyth, Association of Family History Societies of Wales. Ranges over all aspects of the subject, with an excellent subject-arranged guide to further reading.

Stephens, W.B. (1981) *Sources for English local history*, Cambridge, Cambridge University Press. A good introductory chapter ranges over general sources and further chapters examine such areas as education, population, and poor relief.

1.2.2 SCOTLAND

Cory, K.B. (1990) *Tracing your Scottish ancestry*, Edinburgh, Polygon. A comprehensive book, which mainly covers General Register House-based material but looks more widely than census and registers and presents a user's-eye view of the offices. Lists useful addresses of Scottish archive centres, libraries, and family history societies, and obscure useful books.

Moody, D. (1986) *Scottish local history – an introductory guide*, London, Batsford. A good survey.

1.2.3 IRELAND

Begley, D.F. (1984) *Handbook on Irish genealogy; how to trace your ancestors and relatives in Ireland* (6th edn), Dublin, Genealogy Bookshop. Aimed very much at the 'diaspora' market. Includes a lengthy and interesting chapter on county maps and a helpful chapter on emigrant passenger lists to America. A revision is in progress.

Begley, D. F. (ed.) (1987) *Irish genealogy; a record finder*, Dublin, Heraldic Artists Ltd. An excellent survey of the sources.

Grenham, J. (1992) *Tracing your Irish ancestors – the complete guide*, Dublin, Gill and Macmillan: '... complete guide' is not an overstatement.

Kinealy, C. (1991) *Tracing your Irish roots*, Belfast, The Appletree Press Ltd. An authoritative short book which examines all types of sources including those for the Irish diaspora.

Moody, T.W. et al. (eds) (1984) *Maps, genealogies, lists; a companion to Irish history, Part II,* Oxford, Clarendon Press (*A new history of Ireland,* vol.IX). A useful range of summarizing maps.

Nolan, W. (1982) *Tracing the past; sources for local studies in the Republic of Ireland,* Dublin, W. Nolan. Has a useful bibliography on sources and their uses.

Prochaska, A. (1986) *Irish history from 1700: a guide to sources in the Public Record Office,* London, British Records Association (British Records Association Series, *Archives and the user,* no.6). Lists and briefly describes the classes of records relating to British government activities.

Ryan, J.G. (1988) *Irish records: sources for family and local history,* Dublin, Flyleaf Press. Lists available records for each Irish county separately, with a slight bias towards those in national repositories.

Ryan, J.G. (1992) *Irish church records: their history, availability and use in family and local history,* Dublin, Flyleaf Press.

Yurdan, M. (1990) *Irish family history,* London, Batsford. Emphasizes the sources for the study of Irish migration.

1.2.4   OVERSEAS AND MIGRATION SOURCES

Baxter, A. (1986) *In search of your European roots: a complete guide to tracing your ancestors in every country in Europe,* Baltimore, Genealogical Publishing Co. Lists types of records, country by country, with addresses and useful background information.

Currer-Briggs, N. (1982) *Worldwide family history,* London, Routledge and Kegan Paul. Covers European migration to the Americas, South Africa, Australia and New Zealand. Appendix 2 examines the chief sources of information.

Yeo, G. (ed.) (1988) *The British overseas; a guide to records of their births baptisms, marriages, deaths and burials, available in the United Kingdom* (2nd edn), London, Guildhall Library (*Guildhall Library research guide,* no.2).

Whyte, D. (1988) *The Scots overseas; a selected bibliography,* Birmingham, FFHS.

Given the focus of this volume, other overseas and migration sources are not listed here, but many countries produce guides to their records, often in association with family history societies etc. (see also selected references under 1.2.3 above).

1.3   SOME USEFUL RESOURCE WORKS: ATLASES AND HISTORICAL STATISTICS

The following can be useful for filling out your own research, or comparing your results with wider trends. (There are further relevant references in Chapter 4, section 6 (on social surveys), Chapter 6, section 2 (on maps and plans), and Chapter 3, section 1 (on the printed census materials).)

Langton, J. and Morris, R.J. (1986) *Atlas of industrializing Britain 1780–1914,* London, Methuen.

Mitchell, B.R. (1988) *British historical statistics,* Cambridge, Cambridge University Press. Replaces the author's previous *Abstract of British historical statistics* and *Second abstract of British historical statistics.* It contains the main economic and social statistical series for the

British Isles from early days to 1980–81. Material is grouped in subject areas and there is a subject index.

Mitchell, B.R. (1992) *International historical statistics: Europe 1750–1988*, London, Macmillan.

The statistical atlas of England, Scotland and Ireland (1882) Edinburgh and London, W. and A.K. Johnston. The compiler was G.P. Bevan. The maps, each one followed by several pages of listings of appropriate data, range over such areas as religion, education, crime, poverty, etc.

Vaughan, W.E. and Fitzpatrick, A.J. (1978) *Irish historical statistics: population 1821–1971*, Dublin, Royal Irish Academy.

Williams, J. (ed.) (1985) *Digest of Welsh historical statistics*, Cardiff, The Welsh Office. Contains tables of demographic, economic and social data, at local government level, from 1801 to the 1970s.

1.4   DICTIONARIES AND ENCYCLOPAEDIAS

In addition to general-purpose encyclopedias (often worth consulting when starting on a specific topic), the following specialist volumes are worth noting:

Fitzhugh, T.V.H. (1991) *The dictionary of genealogy* (3rd edn), London, A. & C. Black. A useful mini-encyclopaedia.

Friar, S. (1991) *The Batsford companion to local history*, London, Batsford. Arranged alphabetically with cross-references from 'primary entries' to a larger number of secondary entries, often ending with suggestions for further reading. Also a useful list of societies and organizations.

Markwell, F.C. and Saul, P. (1991) *The family historian's 'enquire within'* (4th edn), Birmingham, FFHS. Arranged alphabetically; contains definitions, explanations, dates, maps, bibliographies, and addresses. Regularly updated.

Richardson, J. (1986) *The local historian's encyclopaedia* (2nd edn), New Barnet, Historical Publications Ltd. Includes sections on: the local community and its administration; archives, documents and printed records; social welfare; law and order; trade, commerce and industry. Has a bibliography and a useful index.

2   SOCIETIES AND THEIR PUBLICATIONS

You will often find it helpful to contact other like-minded researchers to share mutual interests or exchange information. There is a large network of local societies to facilitate this contact, many with expertise on particular topics or localities, or with their own resources and publications. This section gives some useful addresses to start from, followed by advice on how to search out others.

2.1   SOME IMPORTANT SOCIETIES FOR FAMILY AND COMMUNITY HISTORY

In almost every area of the United Kingdom and Ireland there are family history and/or local history societies under some label or another (sometimes, for example, called 'archaeological societies'). Some are also organized at a regional level, or cooperate in federal or other groupings. Each is likely to issue some publication, if only a local newsletter. These societies cannot all be listed separately but can be tracked down through the federations listed below and through the sources in section 2.2 below, together with some of the finding aids in Chapter 12.

2.1.1   FEDERATIONS AND WIDER GROUPINGS OF LOCAL HISTORY, FAMILY HISTORY AND SIMILAR SOCIETIES

(Addresses given are those applicable in early 1993.)

Association of Family History Societies of Wales, c/o John Rowlands, 18 Marine Terrace, Aberystwyth, Dyfed, SY23 2AZ.

Birmingham and District Association of Local History Societies, c/o The Local Studies Department, Central Library, Chamberlain Square, Birmingham, B3 3HQ. Covers nearly 100 local societies concerned with local history, family history, etc. Publishes *The Birmingham Historian.*

British Association for Local History, Shopwyke Hall, Chichester, West Sussex, PO20 6BQ. Promotes the study of local history, including courses and other activities. Produces a range of useful inexpensive publications, including the quarterly *The Local Historian,* and *Local History News* (an excellent updating service for the world of local history).

Federation for Ulster Local Studies, Institute for Ulster Local Studies, Institute of Irish Studies, 8 Fitzwilliam Street, Belfast, BT9 6AW. A federation of more than 70 member societies from all nine counties; publishes *Ulster Local Studies* booklets.

Federation of Family History Societies (FFHS), c/o Benson Room, Birmingham and Midland Institute, Margaret Street, Birmingham B3 3BS. Aims to act as a unifying force among members and as a clearing-house for information. Sponsors and distributes a range of excellent (and cheap) publications, including the biannual *Family History News and Digest (FHND)* with a bibliographical section listing local publications by subject and the names and addresses of over 100 constituent societies (including link groups like The Anglo-German Family History Society).

Federation of Local History Societies (Republic of Ireland), c/o Mrs Sally Fitzmaurice, Laurel Lodge, Carlow, County Carlow, Ireland. Analogous, for the Republic of Ireland, to the Federation for Ulster Local Studies. Publishes *Local History Review* (annually).

Irish Family History Society, PO Box 36, Naas, County Kildare, Ireland. Publishes *Irish Family History* (a genealogical quarterly).

Scottish Association of Family History Societies, c/o Mrs I. Barnett, 5 Ochil Gardens, Dunning, Perthshire, PH2 0SR. Includes most family history societies in Scotland.

Scottish Local History Forum, c/o National Museums of Scotland, York Buildings, Queen Street, Edinburgh EH2 1JD. Organizes conferences; publishes occasional reference works, also *Scottish Local History* (three times yearly).

2.1.2   SPECIAL INTEREST GROUPS AND SOCIETIES

These are, of course, endless and their relevance depends on your interest. A small selection is listed below.

Association for the Study of African, Caribbean and Asian Culture and History in Britain, Institute of Commonwealth Studies, 28 Russell Square, London WC1B 5DS. Publishes a newsletter.

Association for Industrial Archaeology, The Wharfage, Ironbridge, Telford, Shropshire TF8 7AW. Publishes *Industrial Archaeology Review.*

The Cambridge Group for the History of Population and Social Structure, 27 Trumpington Street, Cambridge CB2 1QA. Established by Peter Laslett and Tony Wrigley in 1964, and a leading group in population and social research. Services and gives access to a database updating Mills and Pearce's bibliography (1989) of CEB-based research (see Chapter 3, section 2.2). Plays a role in the journals *Local Population Studies* and *Continuity and Change* (see section 3.1 below).

The Historical Association, 59a Kennington Park Road, London, SE11 4JH. National network with local branches and events, conferences, school activities. Publishes *The Historian*, pamphlets, journals.

Historical Geography Research Group, c/o Institute of British Geographers, 1 Kensington Gore, London SW7 2AR. Useful publications series.

Institute of Heraldic and Genealogical Studies, Northgate, Canterbury, CT1 1BA. Organizes conferences, seminars, courses; produces a range of useful publications, including the quarterly *Family History.*

Llafur: the Welsh Labour History Society, c/o Dr C. Williams, University of Wales College of Cardiff, PO Box 909, Cardiff, CF1 3XU. The Welsh national society for the study of social history and the ordinary person. Yearly conferences. Publishes *Llafur: the Journal of Welsh Labour History.*

Local Population Studies Society, c/o Sir David Cooke Bt, 8 Royal Crescent, Harrogate, North Yorkshire, HG2 8AB. Organizes conferences, brings together amateur and professional researchers, sponsors publications. Members receive *Local Population Studies* (LPS – see section 3.1) and book club.

Oral History Society, c/o Department of Sociology, University of Essex, Colchester, CO4 3SQ. Promotes oral history work through conferences, regional network and publications, including the twice-yearly journal *Oral History* (articles, reviews, extensive news section on local activities).

Social History Society of the United Kingdom, Centre for Social History, Lancaster University, Bailrigg, Lancaster, LA1 4YG. Yearly theme conference. Newsletter twice yearly.

Society of Genealogists, 14 Charterhouse Buildings, Goswell Road, London, EC1M 7BA. Issues many useful publications including the quarterly *Genealogists' Magazine* (with extensive index of recent library additions entered by subject); their computer group publishes the quarterly *Computers in Genealogy.*

Ulster Historical Foundation, 12 College Square East, Belfast, BT1 6DD. Publishes and/or distributes material on family and local history and their sources, including *Familia: Ulster Genealogical Review.*

Voluntary Action History Society, c/o Justin Davis Smith, VAHS, 29 Lower King's Road, Berkhamsted, Herts HP4 2AB. Formed in 1991 to further the historical analysis of voluntary action and support the preservation of voluntary sector archives.

2.2   HOW TO TRACK DOWN FURTHER SOCIETIES

2.2.1   GENERAL AIDS

Directory of British associations and associations in Ireland, Beckenham, CBD Research Ltd. This will probably be in your reference library. Use the latest edition available – the most recent at the time of writing is no.11, published in 1992. Use the subject index to check the topic you are interested in.

The 1990 British club year book and directory (1990) (7th edn), London, Eagle Commercial Publications Ltd. Another useful reference book of national scope, mostly leisure-oriented but deserves to be known better.

2.2.2   SUBJECT-SPECIFIC AIDS

Pinhorn, M. (1986) *Historical, archaeological and kindred societies in the United Kingdom: a list*, Hulverstone Manor, Isle of Wight, Pinhorns. Societies are listed alphabetically and topographically. There is a list of national societies (i.e. national in the scope of their interests – they could be local in name), and of those covering more than one county; also a list of 'useful addresses' which could still be useful.

Percival, A. (ed.) (1977) *English Association handbook of societies and collections*, published for the English Association by the Library Association. Though elderly, an extremely useful collection with some real nuggets. Use the 'Notes on the handbook' (pp.ix–xii) and the good index.

National Council of Social Service Standing Conference for Local History (1978) *Local history societies in England and Wales: a list,* London, SCLH (*Information for Local Historians*, no.3). Elderly but worth being aware of its existence. It lists under counties.

2.2.3   LOCAL SOCIETY PUBLICATIONS

Journals, magazines and other publications of local societies can be traced through Pinhorn (1986) (above) and:

Perkins, J. P. (1992) *Current publications by member societies* (7th edn), Birmingham, FFHS.

Perkins, J. P. (1992) *Current publications on microfiche by member societies*, Birmingham, FFHS.

Many are also listed in *Ullrich* (see section 3.2 below) and in *Family History News and Digest* (see under FFHS in Section 2.1.1). Your interest may have been instigated by something local to yourself – check with the main reference library for the area as it will probably maintain a list of local societies, groups too small to be picked up by printed aids, and it may also file their publications.

3   JOURNALS

I have called this section 'journals', but this is just one possible label for a category of publication which you might be happier calling 'periodical', or even 'magazine'. *Society publications* are dealt with in section 2 above.

It is impossible to list (let alone read) all potentially relevant journals. You may, however, find it useful to know about a few key ones – to browse through in a library, to see what the latest ideas are, consult for a particular topic, or (sometimes) consider as a possible publishing outlet. So this section provides a very selective list of some important journals, with information about how to trace others.

3.1   SOME RELEVANT JOURNALS FOR FAMILY AND COMMUNITY HISTORIANS

Note that many important journals are listed under the relevant organizations in section 2.1.1 above, and that many regional and local societies have their own journals or newsletters (often effective outlets for publishing). The list below provides a small selection of *additional* journals.

Continuity and Change (1986–) Cambridge, Cambridge University Press. Interdisciplinary and comparative journal on social structure, law and demography in past societies, directed to both specialists and non-specialists. Three issues a year.

East Midland Historian (1991–) Nottingham, University of Nottingham, Adult Education Department. Annual.

Family Tree Magazine (1984–) Huntington, Family Tree Magazine. Monthly. 'The British magazine with the international flavour.' Popular magazine with a very large circulation and wide range of readable and practical articles and comments directed to tracing British ancestry.

Irish Economic and Social History (1974–) Department of Modern History, Trinity College, Dublin. Annual.

Journal of Family History: Studies in Family, Kinship and Demography (1976–) Greenwich, CT, JAI Press Inc. Quarterly. American-based, the leading interdisciplinary academic journal on the history of the family.

Journal of Historical Geography (1975–) International quarterly (UK and North America). Substantial reviews of recent publications.

Journal of Regional and Local Studies (1980–) Hull, University of Humberside. Twice yearly. Publishes material of historical and contemporary interest with a regional and/or local focus, covering history, geography, sociology and urban studies.

Local Population Studies (LPS) (1968–) Twice yearly. Extremely useful and accessible interdisciplinary journal associated with (but not published by) the Local Population Studies Society and the Cambridge Group for the History of Population and Social Structure. Contains articles, news, comment.

Midland History (1971–) University of Birmingham, School of History. Annual. All aspects of history relating to the Midlands.

New Community (1971/72–) Centre for Research in Ethnic Relations, University of Warwick and Commission for Racial Equality. Quarterly. Includes articles on immigrant communities.

Northern History; A Review of the History of the North of England and the Borders (1966–) University of Leeds, School of History. Annual. Includes useful review of recent periodical literature.

Rural History: Economy, Society, Culture (1990–) Cambridge University Press. Twice yearly.

Scottish Economic and Social History (1981–) Glasgow. Annual.

Southern History: A Review of the History of Southern England (1979–) University of Brighton, Department of Humanities (Southern History Society). Annual.

Ulster Folklife (1955–) Cultra, Hollywood, County Down, Ulster Folk and Transport Museum. Annual. Covers Ulster's cultural, artistic, economic and domestic heritage.

Urban History Yearbook (1976–) Leicester University Press. Not strictly a journal but performs a similar function. Includes research articles, appraisals of source material and surveys of urban development; each issue includes detailed bibliographical references to around 1,000 classified and indexed items from periodicals and books.

Welsh History Review (1960–) Cardiff, University of Wales Press. Twice yearly. Reviews contents of all local history society journals published in Wales or connected with the country.

3.2   FINDING AIDS TO ADDITIONAL JOURNALS AND THEIR CONTENTS

You may want to trace other journals. If so, the major bibliographical aid in the tracing of current journals is:

Ullrich's international periodicals directory, New Providence, NJ, R.R. Bowker. The latest edition is the 31st for 1992/93. Available for consultation in most reference libraries although they may not have the latest edition as it is very expensive.

Should Ullrich not be available a substitute is:

Willings press guide, East Grinstead, Reed Information Services Ltd. Annual. Of its two volumes, (1) deals with United Kingdom titles and (2) with overseas titles.

Prior to this century, much valuable material appeared in general interest magazines. An eclectic range is covered by:

Poole's index to periodical literature (reprinted: Gloucester, Mass., Peter Smith, 1963) which in six volumes covers the years 1802–1906. From *Poole* turn to:

The Wellesley index to Victorian periodicals 1824–1900 (1966–1989) Toronto, University of Toronto Press; London, Routledge and Kegan Paul. The first four volumes give the tables of contents of a range of journals, identify contributors and give bibliographies of their articles and stories. The fifth volume gathers together the bibliographical material and has a separate bibliography of identified pseudonyms and initials.

Moving into this century, indispensable aids in searching for society publications in England and Wales are:

Mullins, E.L.C. (1968) *A guide to the historical and archaeological publications of societies in England and Wales, 1901–1933*, London, The Athlone Press. 'This volume lists and indexes the titles and authors of books and articles bearing upon the history and archaeology of England and Wales … issued to their members between the years 1901 and 1933 inclusive by more than four hundred local and national societies' (Foreword, p.v). *Mullins* (1968) complements the principal historical bibliography (see section 4.2 below).

Mullins, E.L.C. (1958, reprinted with corrections 1978) *Texts and calendars; an analytical guide to serial publications*, London, Offices of the Royal Historical Society (*Royal Historical Society guides and handbooks*, no.7), and (1983) *Texts and calendars II; an analytical guide to serial publications 1957–1982*, London, Offices of the Royal Historical Society (*Royal Historical Society guides and handbooks*, no.12). *Mullins* (1958, 1978, 1983) lists 'the publications issued in general collections or in series by official bodies and private societies wholly or partly devoted to the printing – in transcript or calendar form – of sources for the history of England and Wales' (Preface, 1983, p.v). The volumes cover the years 1802–1982 and are similarly arranged: official bodies; national societies; English local societies; Welsh societies.

Stevenson, D. and Stevenson, W.B. (1987) *Scottish texts and calendars; an analytical guide to serial publications*, London, Royal Historical Society; Edinburgh, Scottish History Society (*Royal Historical Society guides and handbooks*, no.14; *Scottish History Society*, 4th series, vol.23).

The *Mullins* volumes included Scottish material, but limited themselves to England and Wales for the publications of private societies. As *Stevenson* is designed as a Scottish supplement to *Mullins*, it limits itself to private societies. The only exceptions are some *Mullins* omissions placed in the Appendix (pages 189ff.). *Stevenson* was intended 'to update and partly replace two older Scottish reference works' (Preface, p.v): Terry, C.S. (1909) *A catalogue of the publications of Scottish historical and kindred clubs and societies, and of the volumes relative to Scottish history issued by His Majesty's Stationary Office, 1780–1908*, Glasgow, James MacLehose; and Matheson, C. (1928) *A catalogue of the publications of Scottish historical and kindred clubs and societies ... 1908–1927*, Aberdeen, Milne & Hutchison), but does not wholly do so.

Approaching the present day, the best way to track down useful material published in society and/or local magazines is via the *British humanities index* (BHI), a quarterly first published in 1962 (but first appearing in 1915 under the title *Subject index to periodicals*). The annual cumulated BHI volumes have an author index, but the best approach is through the subject index. Check such headings as 'History: Local' – or any other topic you wish to pursue (see Figure 13.2). BHI cannot be searched via computer. The beauty of BHI for our purposes is that until the end of 1991 it had good coverage of society publications in the local history field (unfortunately it deleted its coverage of such local journals with effect from 1992 but is still useful for other journals).

Similar to BHI in their indexing of journal literature are *Social sciences index* and *Humanities index* (both are published quarterly by H.W. Wilson, New York). The latter was founded in 1974, the former in 1907 as *International index to periodicals*, becoming *International index – a guide to periodical literature in the social sciences and humanities* in 1955, and *Social sciences and humanities index* in 1965. In 1974 this was divided to create the two services cited above.

Another extremely useful bibliographical tool is *Geographical abstracts*. This was born in 1972 and, after a history of name and arrangement changes, now appears monthly in two parts, of which we are concerned with *Geographical abstracts: human geography*. Use the contents page and check especially the sections: historical, population, people, and regions. The annual cumulated volume has a good index. *Geographical abstracts* is available as a computer searchable database (GEOBASE).

More specialist indexes are:

Genealogical periodical annual index; key to the genealogical literature (1962–) Annual.

Greater London local history directory and bibliography (1988–) Triennial.

Local studies index (1981–) Gateshead, Blackthorn Publications. Three issues a year. 'References are listed within county under the most specific heading ascertainable.' There are subject, topographical, personal, and company name indexes.

Raymond, S.A. (1991) *British genealogical periodicals: a bibliography of their contents*, 2 vols, Birmingham, FFHS. Volume 2 is particularly useful for family and community historians, dealing with sources (e.g. monumental inscriptions, probate records) and with family histories (i.e. family histories, biographical notes, and selected obituaries).

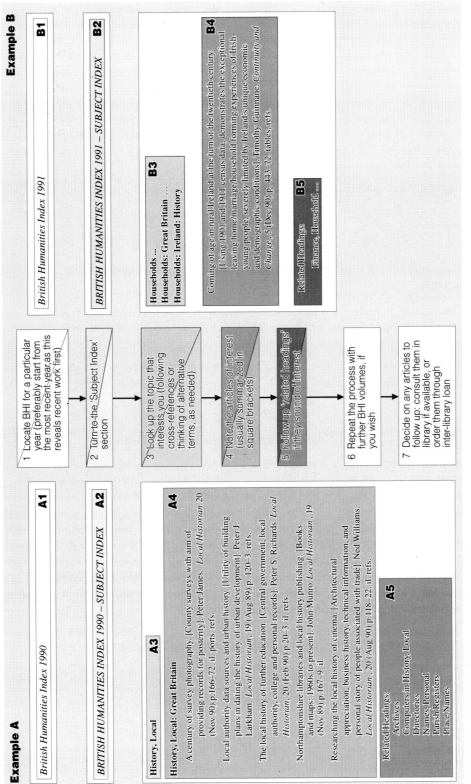

Figure 13.2 How to find articles on your topic in the annual *British humanities index* (BHI): two examples

4 SEARCHING FURTHER: BIBLIOGRAPHIES

If you want to find further references to a topic that you are researching, you have various options. Some you will no doubt already have thought of: following up relevant references at the end of books or articles you have read (not least in Volumes 1–3 of this series); looking up subject indexes/catalogues in libraries; looking at relevant shelves in local studies collections (haphazard, perhaps, but sometimes effective); scanning likely journals; or contacting possible co-researchers through the relevant societies.

But you can also take a more organized route, using the systematic bibliographies and indexes that are available – resources not always fully exploited by family and community historians. Using indexes to track down articles was described in section 3.2 (Figure 13.2 gave an example). But you can also turn to bibliographies: that is, to lists of books and/or journal articles and/or other material (for example, audio-visual), the common bond of which is the subject matter, which are arranged according to a classification scheme of the compiler's choice or devising.

4.1 BIBLIOGRAPHIES OF BIBLIOGRAPHIES

Bibliographic index: a world bibliography of bibliographies (1937–) New York, H.W. Wilson. This has three issues per year and an annual cumulation. It lists bibliographies containing more than fifty citations, no matter whether they are free-standing or part of a larger work. This can be useful for discovering if there is a recent bibliography on your topic of interest.

British national bibliography (1950–) London, The British Library. A very good means of tracking down non-journal publications in the UK. All items submitted to the Copyright Receipt Office of the British Library appear, many in advance of publication.

4.2 HISTORICAL BIBLIOGRAPHIES

Writings on British history 1901–33 (1968–70), 5 vols. London, Jonathan Cape for the Royal Historical Society. The most relevant sections are those on: bibliography and indexes; archives and collections; and English local history and topography. These volumes had strict inclusion criteria. Further volumes bring coverage down to 1945 (Jonathan Cape for the Royal Historical Society, 1937–60). A new publisher, London University's Institute of Historical Research brought coverage down to 1973/74 (1986). With the volume for 1975, the title changed to *Annual bibliography of British and Irish history*, with publication taken over by Harvester Press (Harvester Wheatsheaf in 1987), and from 1989 by Oxford University Press. Keeping up to date was clearly a problem, but this has greatly improved in recent years. This very informative bibliography is well worth consulting.

4.3 BIBLIOGRAPHIES APPEARING IN SERIES

The Federation of Family Histories Societies in association with S.A. and M.J. Raymond is publishing a valuable series of county-based *British Genealogical Bibliographies*, including volumes for: Dorset (1991); Somerset (1991); Gloucestershire and Bristol (1992); Suffolk (1992); Wiltshire (1993); Norfolk (1993); Cumberland and Westmorland (1993); Oxfordshire (1993); Buckinghamshire (due September 1993); and Hampshire (forthcoming). Also within the series, but published originally only by the Raymonds, are: Cornwall (1989); Devon (2 vols) (1990). Volumes in the series share the same internal arrangement of an introductory list of relevant libraries and record offices, followed by chapters on history, bibliography and archives, journals and newspapers, and so on.

Useful on-going bibliographies appear annually in several of the journals mentioned in Sections 2.1.1 or 3.1, notably in *Urban History Yearbook.*

5   DATABASES

by Magnus John

This section suggests directories and services you might consult if you are interested in undertaking a database search, whether searching for further references to work on particular topics, discovering the location or availability of particular works, or checking how far catalogues or materials in particular local collections have been computerized.

5.1   DIRECTORIES, CATALOGUES AND SERVICES

One or two databases were mentioned in the previous sections (for example, the *Geographical abstracts* database called GEOBASE), but you may want to search for others. The list below suggests where you can trace further databases.

On-line databases – general directories include:

ASLIB (1990) *UK online search services* (4th edn), London, Aslib. Provides details of organizations offering an online brokerage service.

Brit-Line: directory of British databases, vol.4 (1989) London, New York, McGraw Hill Book Company.

CD-ROM – catalogues of available CD-ROMs include:

CD-ROMs in print 1992: an international guide (1992), London, Meckler Ltd. Provides access to information via eight indexes.

The CD-ROM directory 1991 (5th edn) (1991) London, TFPL Publishing.

CD-ROM market place 1991: an international guide (1991) Westport, Connecticutt; London, Meckler Publishing.

Microinfo Limited (1992) *Scientific, medical, technical, business, educational and other reference services on CD-ROM*, Alton, Hampshire, Microinfo Ltd – CD-ROM Division. A catalogue listing with subscription rates of CD-ROM databases by subject, with title and publisher details also provided. A brief summary accompanying each title offers information about coverage, frequency, and size of records.

Silver Platter Information (1992) *Directory of CD-ROM databases 1992*, Norwood, MA, Silver Platter Information Inc.

Chadwyck-Healey (1992) *UK OP: the catalogue of United Kingdom official publications on CD-ROM*, Oxford, Chadwyck-Healey. Amalgamates HMSO publications catalogues on a CD-ROM with those published by international organizations but available from HMSO.

Machine-readable data generally – the following are particularly useful:

Schürer, K. and Anderson, S.J. (eds) (1992) *A guide to historical datafiles held in machine-readable form*, London, Association of History and Computing. Information on data holdings within the UK and a summary of data collections held overseas. Index by subject, source and place. The only printed source of its kind covering the United Kingdom. Invaluable.

ESRC Data Archive (1991) *Historical data to 1939,* Colchester, ESRC Data Archive. Data catalogue and index. Includes details of datasets which can be provided by the archive in machine-readable form.

Networked services – the main network in the United Kingdom is:

JANET: the UK Joint Academic Network established 1984. This links users to the facilities of over 2,000 registered computers on more than 150 sites within the UK. All universities and institutes funded by research councils are connected, as are many other educational institutions. JANET provides network services for collaboration and communication, including electronic mail, file transfer, interactive terminal-to-host access (remote login), and remote job submission. Facilities for links to computer users worldwide are also available through JANET.

The following may also be networked via JANET:

OPACS (Online Public Access Catalogues): comprises over 60 on-line UK library catalogues which can be searched over networks; details in JANET-OPACS (printed copies from the University of Sussex Library, Brighton, BN1 9QL).

BIDS is an on-line bibliographic database service, launched in 1991, free to anyone from a subscribing institution in UK higher education and research. It provides access to journal data going back to 1981, and to a variety of databases, including the 1981 Census. Contact *chest@uk.ac.bath* on JANET, or write to Bath University Computing Services, Bath, BA2 7AY.

Since new on-line services and increasing access are probably the trend for the future, it is worth enquiring locally – for instance, at your public library – as to what is available.

Networked services – for international networks, the best source is:

Laquey, T.L (1990) *The user's directory of computer networks,* Bedford, MA, Digital Press. Provides information about size, scope, access rules, and clientele of specific networks, including JANET. Provides details about networks to which each organization subscribes and their respective identity codes.

5.2 COMPUTERIZED LOCAL STUDIES COLLECTIONS

This final section reports a survey of computerized local history collections held in libraries in the UK and Ireland, indicating the patchiness of computerization. Large databases such as the International Genealogical Index (IGI) and the Irish Genealogical Project (see Chapter 12, section 5.4) have been excluded (as also has the local studies information database SCOTLOC maintained by the Scottish Library Association, Motherwell Business Centre, Coarsington Road, Motherwell, ML1 1PW). The exercise is not exhaustive, since record offices and some public libraries were not contacted and the overall picture can therefore only indicate the trend. We would, therefore, welcome corrections and updates for revised editions of the text. (For the address to write to, see page ii in this volume.)

From the total of 150 letters, replies were received to just over 50 per cent (76). Among these, 37 (24.6 per cent of the 150 total) library systems had computerized local studies collections of some kind, 18 (12 per cent) had projects likely to take off soon, while 21 (14 per cent) had no plans to establish computerized systems.

Library	Computerized section/material	Format of source material	Comments
ENGLAND:			
Avon County, Bristol	Oral history	Audio- and video-cassettes	Access to staff only, although viewing facilities exist upon request
Barnsley Libraries	Local studies collection	Printed books	No public access to computer files
Cheshire County Council, Chester	Local studies collection	Books, maps, census data	Computerized information service in fifteen branch libraries. Searches by staff only
Cornwall County Council, Redruth	Cornwall studies library	All printed material	Access to main catalogue is through branch libraries, although only larger branch libraries currently have the key-word retrieval facility
Devon County Council, Exeter	Local studies collection	Books, pamphlets, periodicals, manuscripts, negatives, art works	Several databases with varied index format. Applications by letter advisable
Doncaster Borough Council	Local studies collection	Printed material	Since 1986, only printed material added to stock has been included on the database
Hertfordshire County Council, Hertford	Local studies collection	Books and pamphlets	Journals, photographs and maps will be added later
Hull University: East Yorkshire Bibliography	Printed materials on East Yorkshire	Books, pamphlets, periodicals theses, manuscripts	Public access available to database from terminals in Hull University Library, via JANET or by any computer with a modem dialling one of two numbers
Kent County Council, Maidstone	Local studies collection	Illustration collection, mainly: prints, photographs, postcards, drawings, etc.	An index of over 25,000 illustrations depicting scenes and social life of over 400 towns and villages
Lancashire County Council, Preston	Local studies collection	Printed books only	On-line union catalogue of local studies material available to, and including material belonging to, the fourteen district libraries. Access is at present almost exclusively by library staff
Leicestershire County Council, Leicester	Local studies collection	Printed books only	Access to public currently on microfiche. Access through terminals will become available when new computer system is installed
Lincolnshire County Council, Lincoln	Local studies collection	Printed books, illustrations	Main libraries are now 'on-line' with smaller branches to follow soon. Indexing entries on illustrations now 14,000 (for over 40,000 items)
London:			
Bromley	Local studies collection	Printed books	Very small amount of books has so far been computerized. By April 1993, all books purchased will be recorded centrally on the computer

Library	Computerized section/material	Format of source material	Comments
Hillingdon, Uxbridge	Local studies collection	Books and pamphlets. Photographs to follow	On-line system directly available to all seventeen branch libraries in the borough and to the public via access terminals in all branches
Kensington and Chelsea	Local studies collection	Printed books	Local history book collection will eventually be included in the book stock of the library services which is already computerized
Sutton	Local studies collection	Printed books	Plans to incorporate the rest of the collection soon, including photographs, prints and drawings
Northamptonshire Record Office, Northampton	Records: business parish, local government, family and estate collections	Prints, photographs	On-line catalogues of various kinds of records: business, parish, local government, family and estate collections. Photos and prints are indexed, but access is through terminals operated by staff
Rochdale Metropolitan Borough Council, Rochdale	Local studies collection	Printed books and pamphlets	When completed, searches will be undertaken by staff only. Plans for photograph and map collections to be computerized when current operation is completed
Sandwell Metropolitan Borough Council, Smethwick	Local studies collection	Printed books and pamphlets	Work has only just begun and access to the public is a long-term prospect
Shropshire County Council, Shrewsbury	Local studies collection	Manuscripts, 1881 Census data, local newspapers 1892–1974	Databases are publicly accessible, but as they require experienced users to make the best use of them, members of staff usually undertake initial searches on behalf of readers. The Local Studies Library has been amalgamated with the County Record Office
Surrey County Council, Guildford	Local studies collection	Periodicals, 1841–91, census data, illustrations, parish registers	A variety of computerized indexes have been produced to facilitate searches, either in identification of sources or in physical location of material. Access to computer facilities not available to the public
(West) Sussex County Council, Worthing	Local studies collection	Printed books	Plan to link all 35 of the static service points by the end of 1992
Wakefield Metropolitan District Council	Local studies collection	Printed books and some periodicals	Access to public available via terminals in most branch libraries within the district
Warwickshire County Council, Warwick	Local studies collection	Printed books	In addition, a computerized index to map and theatre collections has been developed for material in the Leamington Library
Wolverhampton Metropolitan Borough Council	Local studies collection	Printed books, photographs, newspaper cuttings	Computerization of the collection in progress (April, 1992). Most searching will be done by staff

Library	Computerized section/material	Format of source material	Comments
(North) Yorkshire County Council, Northallerton	Local studies collection	Newspapers	Available on CD-ROM and is accessible to the public
IRELAND:			
Belfast	Linenhall Library	Newspapers	Computer index of *Belfast Newsletter* from 1737
North-Eastern Education and Library Board, Ballymena, Co. Antrim	Local studies collection	Printed books	Since October 1990, all newly-acquired books have been catalogued on the BLCMP Ltd database, as will the Library of Queen's University, Belfast, both of which have large local studies collections
South-Eastern Education and Library Board, Ballynahinch, Co. Down	Local studies collection	Printed books	Local newspapers will eventually be transferred to computerized indexing
Western Education and Library Board, Omagh, Co. Tyrone	Local studies collection	Printed books	Access by staff only
SCOTLAND:			
City of Aberdeen	Local studies collection	Newspaper cuttings	Recently began experimenting with computer storage and retrieval of newspaper cuttings. At a very early stage of development
Angus District Council, Forfar	Local studies collection	Printed books	Local history collection has been computerized and soon to follow will be indexes of newspaper and illustration collections
Bearsden and Milngavie District Council, Bearsden, Glasgow	Local studies collection	Printed books (and other materials)	From October 1992, public access will be via OPACs in each library
Edinburgh City Council	Local studies collection	Printed books	Possibility of developing computer-generated indexes for newspaper cuttings, photographs, prints and other items is being discussed
WALES:			
Clwyd County Council, Mold, Clwyd	Local studies collection	Printed books, maps, newspapers, photographs	Local history holdings of books and pamphlets is on-line on a free-text database and searches are carried out by staff on behalf of the public. Also held are computerized indexes to theses, local history journals, photographic collections and oral history cassette holdings

EXERCISES: ANSWERS AND COMMENTS

Exercise 3.1

Calculation of percentage increases can be set out as follows:

```
1911        19,678
1871         2,413
           ───────
Increase    17,265
```

Percentage increase 1871–1911 = $\dfrac{17265 \times 100}{2413}$ = 715.5%

```
1961        67,324
1918        25,100
           ───────
Increase    42,224
```

Percentage increase 1918–1961 = $\dfrac{42224 \times 100}{25100}$ = 168.2%

The calculation of these percentages brings the absolute or raw figures down to a common basis so that comparisons can be made: clearly Scunthorpe was growing over four times as quickly in the earlier period than in the later period. However, rapid increases on a small base can be achieved by relatively small absolute numbers; thus the actual increase in the earlier period was less than half the absolute increase in the later period. It is therefore necessary to keep both percentages and absolute numbers in mind.

Exercise 3.2

The number of persons normally resident in the private households of Scopwick and Kirkby Green was 353 and 135 respectively, a total of 488. The number of rooms available to them in 1921 was 431 plus 134 = 565. Divide the number of persons by the number of rooms:

$$\frac{488}{565} = 0.86 \text{ persons per room.}$$

Exercise 3.3

You could link the following:

1   Birthplace and occupation: to see whether there is any indication that, say, labourers came from different areas (or were more likely to be born in the place in which they were enumerated) than craftsmen or professional people.

2   Relation to head of family and age: to see what differences there were in family composition according to the age of the head of the family.

3   Infirmity (blind, deaf-and-dumb, etc.) and occupation: to see whether or not there is a difference in the incidence (or the reporting) of a particular infirmity, and the occupation of the father or mother etc. of the handicapped person. The 'etc.' hides some tricky decisions about the 'significant' relationship in this context and what meaningful comparisons can be made.

If you are fortunate enough to be working with the richer Scottish CEBs or the Irish householder schedules of 1901 or 1911, then your choice of correlation exercises will be that much greater, and could include religion and occupation; education and age or occupation or place; rooms with windows and occupation or place; and so on.

Exercise 3.4

1   You will be developing your own conclusions but here are some preliminary comments:

(a)   *Authenticity:* no real problems, except that the entries in the CEBs ultimately depend, of course, on the answers given at the household level, and the processing by the enumerators (thus they are subject to possible inaccuracy or misunderstanding); see Figure 3.2, and also the constraints and procedures explained at the beginning of the chapter and in section 2.1.

(b)   *Provenance:* see the descriptions at the start of the chapter and in section 2.

(c)   *Dating:* unambiguous, unlike some sources.

(d)   *Type:* official and standardized through set categories (but dependent ultimately on household heads and enumerators throughout the country).

(e)   *Origin:* see the start of the chapter and the beginning of section 2.

(f)   *Relevance:* this will depend on your topic and investigation.

(g)   *'Meaning':* note the meaning of the various categories and marks on the forms; see especially the annotations to Figures 3.3–3.8.

(h)   *Context:* note the need to supplement CEBs by the use of other sources, and by an understanding of the historical context.

2   Some ideas will be suggested by your own interests and research to date, while others might be stimulated by looking at the sources suggested here (particularly the review and bibliography by Mills and Pearce, 1989, and the guide by Schürer and Anderson, 1992), or by the many examples that draw on the CEBs in Volumes 1–3.

Exercise 4.1

1   Problems arise from several persons with the same name (e.g. John Jones, Evan Jones). Further evidence from independent sources (e.g. local rate/rental records, census enumerators' books) and the linking of a name with a specific house or street will be useful for the precise identification of individuals. In other words, clarification may be possible through techniques of nominal record linkage.

2   Multiple entries occur in the following lists:

Grocers, drapers and dealers in sundries

o   Hugh Ellis is also listed under 'joiners and carpenters';

o   Maurice Evans is listed as 'Morris Evans' under 'corn and flour dealers', and also under 'inns and public houses';

o   Evan Jones is listed as 'corn and flour dealer';

o   Richard Price is listed under 'butchers' as well as 'corn and flour dealers';

o   William Watkin is also listed under 'gentry and clergy' – as the Rev William Watkin (not at all unusual amongst non-conformist preachers who needed a bread-and-butter occupation).

Joiners and carpenters

o   John Ellis also appears under 'wheelwrights';

o   John Jones is also included under 'surgeons'. (Mercifully, in this case two persons may have shared a common name! But in the past some 'surgeons' did provide services as barbers and shavers.) The same name also appears as 'tanner' under 'miscellaneous'!

Miscellaneous

o Charles Humphreys, 'registrar of births, deaths and marriages', is also listed under 'Poor Law Union' as 'Relieving Officer'. Humphreys had his fingers in many pies. It is known from other sources that it was Charles Humphreys, not his wife Jane (as listed in directory), who owned the grocery and druggist shop shown in Figure 4.2 (see Pryce, 1991, pp.63–5).

o 'Richard Jones & Son, bookbinders' also appears under 'plumbers and glaziers'. Is this another instance of two individuals sharing a common name?

3 In general, despite the double entries, the list of trades seems to be fairly comprehensive and offers an adequate basis for the analysis of service functions (see Volume 2, Chapter 4).

4 Details are provided on road connections, mileages, on post office facilities, carriers, and the then nearest railway station at Shrewsbury (over the border in England!).

5 Retail traders, dealers and the names of individuals involved in public and professional services are listed. But, as we saw in answer (2) above, the incidence of double entries and ambiguous names does have to be taken into account. Depending on the research topic under investigation, double counting may, or may not, be appropriate. Joint occupations can be counted as separate *functions*, even if these are carried out by the same individual. On the other hand, joint occupations should not be counted as separate businesses or undertakings.

6 Slater's listing is based on specific crafts, trades and services. Undoubtedly, the great majority of these would have been workshop-based or conducted from retail premises. Unlike entries for Llanfair town in later directories, shopkeepers are not identified in Figure 4.1 as a separate group. This probably reflects the fact that, in the late 1850s, many items were still made locally.

7 Apart from the general description of the town at the beginning of the entry, not as much information is given on business addresses as in the later directories. Nevertheless, the names of residences occupied by the gentry and clergy, inns and public houses are given, together with the fact that the Poor Law Union Workhouse was then located in the distant town of Llanfyllin. In addition, the directory provides locational information on traders living outside the town (e.g. John Evans, miller, of Heniarth). Exact locations have to be worked out using local rental lists, estate records, original maps, and nominal record linkage techniques.

Exercise 4.3

The advantages of the 'extensive' method – characterized today by, say, the *Family Expenditure Survey* are:

1 Comprehensive coverage.

2 Provides national or regional data which can be used as a yardstick for more detailed investigation.

3 Sampling permits frequent surveys to be conducted at relatively low cost, so facilitating longitudinal and comparative studies.

Its disadvantages are:

1 Only as good as the sampling, and as its questions and answers.

2 Lacks the sense of reality obtained from studies of particular places, streets, people, etc.

The advantages and disadvantages of the 'intensive' method are the converse of the 'extensive' one, namely:

1 Limited coverage – but gives a sense of place, and of 'real' life.

2 Difficult to generalize from (the 'typicality' of York has often been questioned) – but provides data for detailed work on a particular locality.

3 If carried out in the comprehensive fashion of the Booth and Rowntree surveys, it is expensive (Rowntree sought information on 'housing, occupation and earnings of *every* wage-earning family in York' – Moser and Kalton, 1971, p.8), thus a regular series over time is difficult (although Rowntree did follow up his 1901 survey with later ones in 1936 and 1951).

Exercise 6.1

1 London House, Llanfair, Welshpool, Montgomeryshire.

2 River scene, Llanfair Caereinion (originally 'view').

3 No.1 (originally No.4).

4 Bromide chrom.

5 Full to edge.

6 1,000.

7 Four. See crossed out order/invoice numbers. If 1,000 copies were ordered each time, this suggests that 5,000 postcards were produced between *c*.1898 and 1921 when Mr Jones retired.

The inscription 'Miss Elsie Jones Collection' has been added recently for identification purposes (see Chapter 11, section 1.2 for the importance of this). The print was once owned by Miss Jones – the daughter of Levi.

Exercise 6.2

Here is my own list. You may have found more:

1 A

2 E, B

3 C

4 E, H, C

5 E

6 G, H, D

7 (a) E, F, G, H

(b) E, F, H, D and (especially) G

8 F

Exercise 6.3

Here are some examples: CEBs and other census reports; electoral registers; civil registers; social surveys like those of Booth and Rowntree. In assessing these or comparable sources based partly or wholly on interviews, remember that they are ultimately only as valid as the original interviews.

Exercise 8.1

o 'Most manuscript poll books': this could mean somewhere between 51 per cent and 99 per cent; to know precisely would be more satisfactory.

o 'not unusual for a local printer': again, one asks, 'how unusual': 30 per cent, 40 per cent, 75 per cent? And how local is local?

- o 'Some, however, contain much more': do we mean that 10 per cent, 20 per cent, 30 per cent, etc. do? And is 'much more' two, three, four or more items?

- o 'Most also give': see above for my comment on 'most'.

- o 'some go further': at least *two* illustrations are given in amplification of this. For anyone contemplating a project based on poll books, a precise, quantitative statement would be more helpful.

Exercise 8.2

Nominal data: church membership; last residence; trade or occupation; complexion; colour of hair; colour of eyes; visage; marks; lame or ruptured; infectious diseases; type of apparel; place of nativity; father's trade and residence; marital status; wife or husband's residence; offence; where committed; result of trial; 'from whence brought'; whether in army or navy; name of regiment or ship; previous record.

Ordinal data: state of health (if one presumes this was given as, say, very bad, bad, poor, fair, very fair, good, excellent); state of apparel; cleanliness; degree of instruction; conduct in gaol (if the same kind of description is given as presumed for 'state of health', i.e. a ranking that is a logical progression).

Interval/ratio data: age; height; number and age of children; length of sentence (if this had been hanging it would have been nominal).

Exercise 8.3

Gentleman – and by a long chalk! Had there been five gentlemen and five tailors, with no other occupation reaching this number, then we would have said the distribution was *bimodal*. Had three occupations shared the lead we would say the distribution was *trimodal*, and so on.

Exercise 8.4

(a) The distribution is *unimodal*, i.e. the single value of £50 occurs most frequently.

(b) The *median* is £50 too. Because there is an even number of values in the distribution, the mid point is somewhere between the 15th and 16th observation (had there been 31 observations the median would have been the 16th). To resolve the problem we take the 15th and 16th values and divide by two, i.e. $(50 + 50) \div 2 = £50$.

(c) The *mean* is the sum of all the observations (£1,620) divided by the number of observations (30), i.e. £54.00. Thus our three averages all come out at about the same value, but not quite. This is shown when we graph the distribution (Figure 8.A) or, more properly, put it in the form of a bar chart (Figure 8.B). The distribution is, in fact, somewhat asymmetrical; in this case it is skewed positively, i.e. with a few large values. Note that the one elector whose property was rated at £140 put more into the equation than the six electors (20 per cent of the total) with the lowest valuations.

Exercise 8.5

£10–£140. There is then a very wide distribution around the mean of £54.

Exercise 8.6

The standard deviation is £27.8. The mean is £55. We would expect that two-thirds of rateable values would lie ± 1 standard deviation from it, i.e. between £82.8 and £27.2, and that virtually all (99 per cent) would lie between ± 3 standard deviations of the mean, i.e. 0 to £138.4 – as indeed they do.

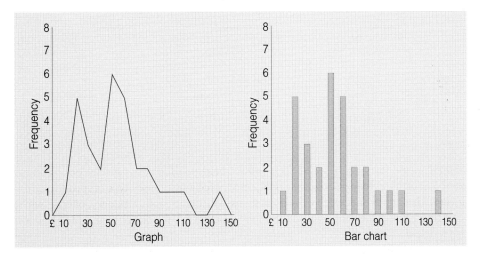

Figures 8.A (left) and 8.B (right) Distribution of the rateable values enfranchising the thirty Whateley voters whose surnames began with the letter 'A' (rounded to the nearest £10)

Exercise 8.7

Column 3 of the table should read (from top to bottom) 3.3, 16.7, 10.0, 6.7, 20.0, 16.7, 6.7, 6.7, 3.3, 10.0 to make a total of 100.1. That our total is not exactly 100 is because of the rounding up or down exercise. From our table we learn that 30 per cent of the values are £30 or less, and 20 per cent are £80 or more. Of course, these figures have no historical significance: the exercise is not designed for that purpose. However, it shouldn't need much imagination to realize that, given appropriate data, the percentage, like the other measures discussed, can be a powerful tool.

Exercise 8.8

Jan	Feb	March	April	May	June	July	Aug	Sept	Oct	Nov	Dec
124	198	123	60	88	110	51	38	42	69	100	200

There is a very strong concentration within the winter months (with 43 per cent of annual marriages taking place in the December to February quarter). Of the summer months only June has more than the expected number of marriages, and then not many more. For a fishing and grazing area one could well imagine that the winter months would be a relatively dead time in terms of economic activity. Getting to weddings might be difficult in winter, but if most marriages were between fellow Orcadians this may not have been a problem, Orkney being an archipelago of relatively contiguous islands. Did the Scottish propensity to marry on New Year's Eve apply here? And was the upturn in June due to a relative reduction in agricultural activity – just after lambing etc. – as it was across the sea in Norway? All these are hypotheses to be tested. I don't know the answers.

Exercise 8.9

Wilford	70	Brown	62	Stewart	66	Garrett	68	Goldberg	45
Parkyn	69	Barlow	56	Ellis	62	Muller	54	*Jones	57
Pendered	71	Holford	83	Richards	41	Maples	76	Newburgh	50
Bradley	46	Blackwell	54	*Goodchild	44	Pitt	76	Stronge	59
Moore	56	Green	53	*Emery	—	*Karn	53	Hitchings	87
		*Holland-		Adamson-					
Deva	44	Martin	78	Macedo	70	Humphries	58	*Sills	63
*Deech	49	Jackson	48	Patience	51	Warr	65	Briggs	71
*Rogers	—	*Allen	60	*Lowrey	87	Cousins	48	Cummings	49
Cunningham	68	Hilton	66	Cooke	75	Taverne	64	Howe	48
Matheson	80	Hewes	47	Lappert	64	Ealing	49		
Clarkson	63	*Rink	—	Gent	57	West	68		

* women

My list comprised 42 men and 8 women, so women accounted for 16 per cent of the sample (8 ÷ 50 × 100). I had to ignore three people because the age was not given. All were women. The mean age of my sample of 50 was 60.96 years (3,048 ÷ 50).

Exercise 8.10

1   41–87.

2   48, 49, 68: the distribution is trimodal.

3   61 (i.e. (60 + 62) ÷ 2).

4   12 years.

5   The age range is relatively confined, not unexpectedly given the sort of people who find themselves in *Who's Who*. Given that the mean and the median are virtually identical, the distribution appears comparatively symmetrical. The trimodal distribution, given it is based on only nine observations, is a bit of a red herring. That the standard deviation is as high as 12 years suggests a wide distribution around the mean. But remember our sample is small and may well not represent the precise distribution (or variance) of the population as a whole.

Exercise 8.11

$$d = 1$$

$$t = 2.58$$

Exercise 8.12

$$n_0 = \frac{pq}{V}$$

$$n_0 = \frac{50 \times 50}{V} = \frac{2500}{V}$$

$$V = \frac{d^2}{t^2} = \frac{5 \times 5}{2.58 \times 2.58} = \frac{25}{6.7} = 3.7$$

$$n_0 = \frac{2500}{V} = \frac{2500}{3.7} = 676$$

We would require a sample of around one-third of that required in our earlier exercise (676 rather than 1,875) because we have been prepared to accept a wider confidence interval (± 5 per cent rather than ± 2 per cent). This is despite the fact that we have raised our confidence level from 95 per cent to 99 per cent.

Exercise 8.13

Had we chosen the letter 'M' we might have got an over-representation of Scotsmen (i.e. all the 'Macs') or the letter 'O' might have over-represented the Irish.

Exercise 8.14

Advantages

o An economical way of describing and analysing a large amount of data, e.g. averages, sampling.

o An aid to precise thinking and expression (remember the problems of implicit quantification).

o A guide to interesting questions.

o A tool for getting at the relationship between human phenomena, e.g. correlation.

o A way of showing us patterns of behaviour, distribution, change, etc. using, for example, rates and indices.

Drawbacks

o Yet another skill to be learned and not only learned but maintained through constant practice.

o Does not provide the precision the unequivocal nature of a number would suggest, i.e. deals in probabilities, approximations.

o Demands even greater care in source criticism than for literary or oral sources, since numbers provide no clues – of themselves – as to their rightness or wrongness. An analogy: if you can spell, a spelling mistake jumps out at you. A list of numbers does not provide this check.

o Communication problems, as innumeracy is more widespread than illiteracy. Thus the demands on your powers of expression are greater than if a purely literary mode is adopted.

Exercise 9.1

1 (a) For examples, see sections 1.1–1.3. Besides time and cost constraints, problems related to the high level of technical computing expertise needed.

 (b) For examples, see sections 1.4–1.5. Note the possibility of sorting, analysing and linking a wide range of sources (e.g. those listed in Section 1.4; see also Schürer and Anderson, 1992; Hodges and Pryce, 1993). Less technical expertise is needed for modern, small, user-friendly computers, but there are still 'costs' in terms of time (a steep learning curve). There are also always the risks of taking on too ambitious a project and the potential dangers of oversimplifying or twisting the data by unwise decisions on data structure, 'data reduction', or coding (see section 1.6).

2 Hopefully the section will have stimulated you both (1) to think of possible uses to which you could put computing (most likely the user-friendly kind), and (2) to consider carefully the potential problems (and possible ways of dealing with them).

APPENDIX: SOME KEY DATES FOR FAMILY AND COMMUNITY HISTORY

by John Golby

This chronology is included in the volume for two main reasons. First, it contains the dates of some key events which are relevant to the study of family and community history. Secondly, it enables you to see at a glance many of the changes and developments that have taken place from 1800 to the present day.

The chronology is divided into five sections which are central to the themes running throughout the volumes, but there is no way any chronology can be comprehensive. During your studies you will be sure to find gaps. There is nothing to prevent you from adding to this chronology. Indeed, you will probably find it helpful to add important dates relating to *your* particular family and community research. You will then be able to relate your key dates to national events.

	Political	Economic	Communications and technology	Religion and education	Demographic and source related
1800-1	Act of Union, Britain and Ireland				First census
1805-65					
1811			Publication of first-edition one-inch Ordnance Survey maps for England and Wales	Founding of the National (Schools) Society Calvinist Methodists of Wales leave established Church of England	
1813					Introduction of printed baptismal and burial registers
1814				Founding of British and Foreign School Society	
1814-15	End of Napoleonic Wars				
1815			Stamp Duty on newspapers raised from 3d to 4d		
1816		Income Tax abolished			
1817			The *Scotsman* established		
1818			First steamship to cross Atlantic		
1822	Irish Constabulary compulsory in all counties				
1823	Catholic Association formed				
1825			First passenger steam train		
1828				Repeal of Test and Corporations Act	
1829	Metropolitan Police Act			Catholic Emancipation Act	
1831-2					Cholera epidemic
1832	First Reform Bill				Main collections of land tax assessments cease

Year	Political	Economic	Communications and technology	Religion and education	Demographic and source related
1833	Burgh Reform Act (Scotland) Police Act (enabling Scottish Burghs to establish police)	Failure of potato crop in Highlands; Abolition of slavery in the British Empire	Start of publication of one-inch to mile map of Ireland		
1834	Poor Law Amendment Act				
1835	Municipal Corporations Act		Highway Act begins modernization of roads (non-turnpike)		
1836			Reduction of Stamp Duty on newspapers to 1d	Commutation of Tithes Act	Marriages permitted in Registry Offices
1837					Civil registration of births, deaths and marriages in England and Wales
1838	Irish Poor Law Act	Irish Tithes Commutation Act	First electric telegraph		
1838–55					Main period for England and Wales Tithe Awards
1839	Rural Police Act (England and Wales forces permissible)				Registrar General publishes first annual report of births, marriages and deaths
1840	Irish Municipal Corporations Act		Penny postage introduced		Records of smallpox vaccinations begin
1841					Census Reports and CEBs, England, Scotland, Wales, Ireland (few CEBs, Ireland)
1842		Reintroduction of Income Tax			
1843				Establishment of the Free Church in Scotland	
1845	Poor Law (Scotland) Amendment Act	Potato blight in Ireland			Start of Irish famine followed by wholesale emigration; Registration of Irish Protestant marriages
1846		Repeal of the Corn Laws			Famine in Highlands
1847				Reports on the state of education in Wales (blue books); United Presbyterian Church of Scotland established	
1848	Last Chartist demonstration; Public Health Act		W.H. Smith starts railway bookstalls		Cholera epidemic
1849–52		Major evictions from agriculture holdings in Ireland			
1850				Restoration of Roman Catholic hierarchy in England	
1851			Cross Channel telegraph cable laid; First news agency, Reuters, formed in London	Census of Religious Worship in England and Wales	Census Reports and CEBs, England, Scotland, Wales, Ireland (few CEBs, Ireland); England and Wales more than 50 per cent urban
1852–3					Burial Acts, created Burial Boards

	Political	Economic	Communications and technology	Religion and education	Demographic and source related
1854–56	Crimean War				
1855	Metropolitan Board of Works set up for whole of London	Limited Liability Act	Abolition of stamp duty on newspapers		Civil registration of births, deaths and marriages in Scotland
1856	County and Borough Police Act completed the creation of English and Welsh police forces				
1856–87			Publication of first-edition one-inch Ordnance Survey maps for Scotland		
1857					Matrimonial Causes Act (transfers jurisdiction over divorces to courts)
1858	Property qualification for MPs removed			Jews admitted to Parliament	Divorces about 150 p.a. (England) Wills proved at Principal Probate registry
1861–65	American Civil War				
1861		Post Office Savings Bank set up		Newcastle Commission on elementary education	Census Reports, England, Scotland, Wales, Ireland (CEBs, England, Scotland, Wales)
1862	General Police Act (Scotland)				
1863			First London Underground Railway opened	School log books necessary for voluntary schools to get grants	
1864					Civil registration of births, deaths and marriages in Ireland
1865				William Booth's Christian Mission started	
1866			Transatlantic telegraph cable laid		Last major cholera epidemic Age of death appears in GRO death indexes
1867	Second Reform Bill (England and Wales.)				
1868	Reform Act (Scotland)				
1869	Artisan and Labourers Dwelling Act		*Western Mail*, first daily newspaper in Wales, published	Disestablishment and disendowment of the Irish Church	
1870		First Irish Land Act		Dr Barnado opens first home to destitute children Forster's Education Act	Married Women's Property Act (earnings of married woman legally her own)
1871	Local government boards set up to supervise public health and poor law Bank Holiday Act	Trade Unions legalized and given protection in the courts		Anglican tests abolished at Oxford and Cambridge	Census Reports, England, Scotland, Wales, Ireland (CEBS, England, Scotland, Wales) Irish-born population of England and Wales tops 0.5 million
1872	Secret Ballot Act			Education (Scotland) Act	
1873	Home Rule League founded in Dublin				
1874			Telephone patented by Bell		

Year	Political	Economic	Communications and technology	Religion and education	Demographic and source related
1875	Public Health Act Second Bank Holiday Act	Peaceful picketing legalized Artisans Dwelling Improvement Act			
1876				Primary education made compulsory	
1878				Christian Mission renamed Salvation Army Roman Catholic hierarchy restored in Scotland	Inward passenger lists of those arriving by sea from outside Europe available
1881	Householders of Scotland Act (giving some women local vote) Sunday Closing Act (Wales)	Second Irish Land Act			Census Reports, England, Scotland, Wales, Ireland (CEBs, England, Scotland, Wales). Gaelic speakers first recorded in census in Scotland Population of Glasgow tops 0.5 million
1882		Crofters' War		Formation of Church Army	Married Women's Property Act (property brought into marriage by wife 'her separate property')
1883		Napier's Commission on Highlands			
1884	Third Reform Bill				First cremations
1885	Secretary for Scotland established		Safety bicycle invented		
1886	Crofter's Holdings (Scotland Act)				
1888	County Councils Act		Pneumatic tyre invented		
1889	Establishment of London County Council Local Government (Scotland) Act	Charles Booth publishes *Life and labour of the people in London*		Intermediate Education Act (Wales) (establishes secondary schools throughout Wales)	
1890		Housing of the Working Classes Act			Outward passenger lists of those leaving by sea to areas outside Europe available
1891					Census Reports, England, Scotland, Wales, Ireland (last currently available CEBs for England, Scotland and Wales) 101,000 Jews living in the UK Welsh speakers first recorded by census in Wales and Monmouthshire
1893	Independent Labour Party founded	Publication of Royal Commission Report on land in Wales and Monmouthshire			
1894	Local Government Act (creation of elected parish, urban district and rural councils – women eligible to vote for parochial councils)	Death duties introduced			

Year	Political	Economic	Communications and technology	Religion and education	Demographic and source related
1896			Glasgow Underground opened		
1898	Irish Local Government Act				
1899–1902	Boer War				
1900			562 motoring convictions in England and Wales	Free Church of Scotland and United Presbyterian Church of Scotland merge	Approximately 500 divorces pa (England)
1901			First transatlantic radio message	Education (Scotland) Act	Census Reports, England, Scotland, Wales, Ireland (full returns, Ireland)
1902	Sinn Fein founded			Balfour's Education Act	
1903	Women's Social and Political Union founded	Irish Land Purchase Act	First successful flight of petrol powered aircraft		
1907	Women allowed to become borough and county councillors				
1908		Old Age Pensions Bill			
1909		Surtax on incomes over £2,000 introduced	National Library of Wales opened Bleriot flies the channel		
1910					Valuation Office Records
1911	Parliament Act Payment of MPs	First National Insurance Act			Census Reports, England, Scotland, Wales, Ireland (full returns, Ireland) Maiden name of mother appears in GRO birth indexes Surname of spouse appears in GRO marriage indexes
1914	Irish Home Rule crisis				
1914–1818	First World War				
1916	Easter Rising in Dublin				
1917	Russian Revolution	Report of Royal Commission on Scottish Housing			
1918	Representation of the People Act (all men over 21 and women over 30 enfranchised) Ministry of Health established			Education (Scotland) Act Fisher's Education Act	
1919	Provisional government and parliament of Irish Republic set up Sex Disqualification Removal Act (opens all professions to women except the Church)				Flu epidemic in Europe

Year	Political	Economic	Communications and technology	Religion and education	Demographic and source related
1920			First general radio broadcast	Disestablishment in Wales of Anglican church to form Church of Wales	
1921	Partition of Ireland and establishment of Irish Free State				Census Reports, England, Scotland, Wales Jewish population in UK rises to 300,000
1922			Radio broadcasting begins		
1923					Women allowed to obtain divorce on grounds of adultery alone
1925	Formation of Plaid Cymru				
1926		General Strike	British Broadcasting Corporation set up		Census Reports, N. Ireland and Irish Free State Registration of still births in England and Wales begins
1927		Trades Disputes and Trade Union Act	Opening of the National Museum of Wales		Registration of adoptions in England and Wales begins
1928	Women over 21 enfranchised		Combine harvesters first used in UK		
1929	Local Government Act (abolishes poor law guardians – responsibility transferred to county councils)	Start of Great Depression		Church of Scotland and United Free Church merge	Minimum age of marriage with parental consent raised to 16 from 12 (girls) and 14 (boys)
1930	Scottish National Development Council established		170,963 motoring offences in England and Wales		
1931					Census Reports, England, Scotland, Wales, N. Ireland (returns for England and Wales destroyed, summary statistical tables available)
1934	Scottish National Party founded				
1936			First regular TV broadcasts		Census Report, Irish Free State
1937			BBC Welsh Region started		Census Report, N. Ireland Divorce Act makes desertion and cruelty grounds for divorce
1938	Anglo-Irish agreement. Irish Free State becomes Eire or Ireland	Holidays with Pay Act			
1939-45	Second World War				
1939					National Registration Evacuation scheme – 3.3 million evacuated 43,000 women in armed forces and nursing
1941	Registration of Employment Act				No Census taken 1,370,000 official billeted evacuees 100,000 women in armed services

	Political	Economic	Communications and technology	Religion and education	Demographic and source related
1942	Publication of Beveridge Report				First US troops arrive in UK
1944				Education Act	4.5 million men in forces, 450,000 women
1946	New Towns Act		TV transmissions resumed		Census Report, Eire
1947	Independence of India				
1948		National Health Service starts			
1949	Ireland becomes a Republic Scottish Covenant attracts 2.5 million signatures supporting Home Rule	End of clothing rationing			
1951					Census Reports, England, Scotland, Wales, N. Ireland, Republic of Ireland Jewish population in UK 450,000
1951–53	Korean War				
1954		All food rationing ends	Commercial TV established		
1956	Suez crisis Hungarian uprising				Census Report, Republic of Ireland
1957	Treaties establishing EEC and Euratom Independence of Ghana				
1960	National Service ends Independence of Nigeria				
1961		Sunday opening of public houses in parts of Wales after local referendums			Census Reports, England, Scotland, Wales, N. Ireland, Republic of Ireland
1962	Commonwealth Immigrants Act Independence of Jamaica, Trinidad and Tobago	Scottish Development Department established			
1963	Independence of Kenya				
1964	Government Welsh Office established in Cardiff		Establishment of BBC2		
1965	Death Penalty abolished				
1966			Colour TV introduced		Census Report, Republic of Ireland
1967		Oil exploration begins			
1968					Abortion Act Commonwealth Immigrants Act Right of entry to UK of British Passport holders removed unless they had a parent or grandparent born in the UK
1969	Voting age reduced to 18			Open University established	Divorce Act ('irretrievable breakdown' as grounds for divorce) Asian citizenship withdrawn in Kenya and Uganda

	Political	Economic	Communications and technology	Religion and education	Demographic and source related
1971					Census Reports, England, Scotland, Wales, N. Ireland, Republic of Ireland / Quarter Sessions and Assize Courts abolished
1972	Ireland and Britain sign EEC Treaty / Local Government reorganization in England and Wales and Scotland / Ulster referendum. 'Direct rule' established in N. Ireland		Monopoly of BBC sound broadcasting ends		
1973				School leaving age raised to 16	
1975	Referendum in favour of staying in EEC	Sex discrimination and Equal Pay Act comes into force		Adult church attendances in England, Scotland and Wales 4.9 million	
1979	Devolution referendums in Scotland and Wales / First direct elections to European Parliament				Census Report, Republic of Ireland
1980		Council tenants permitted to buy their homes	2,238,000 motoring offences in England and Wales		150,000 divorces p.a. (England) / Daily average prison population in England and Wales 43,760
1981	British Nationality Act				Census Reports, England, Scotland, Wales, N. Ireland, Republic of Ireland
1982	Falklands War				
1984		Trade Union Act			
1985	Local Government Act (abolition of Greater London Council and five Metropolitan Councils)			Adult church attendances England, Scotland and Wales 4.6 million	
1986		Social Security Act			Census Report, Republic of Ireland
1988		Employment Act (end of closed shop)		Education Reform Act	
1991	Gulf War				Census Reports, England, Scotland, Wales, N. Ireland, Republic of Ireland

INDEX

adoption records 282
age
at death 79, 101; at marriage 77, 185
agricultural labourers, in CEBs 47
Anglican registers 111, 117
baptisms **72–6**
Annual bibliography of British and Irish history 292
archaeological societies 284
area maps 254–5
Armstrong's social classification scheme 47, 48–9
army records 270
Association of Family History Societies of Wales 285
Association for Industrial Archaeology 285
Association for Local History 269
associational records 117
atlases 124–5, 283–4
audio sources **154–6**
local archives 268; presentation of material by 256–7
audio-visual collections, finding aids **264**; *see also* libraries; museums; record offices
autobiographies 19, **103–8**, 115, 117, 164
evaluating 105–6; locally published 104; location 107; working-class 103–4, 105, 115; written by women 104
averages **177–80**

BAC (Business Archives Council) 85, 87
back projection 205
banking, sources on history of 86
baptism registers 4, **72–6**, 267
and choice of name 76; and timing of baptisms 76
bar charts 252–3
Bath poll book 63, 64, 65
BBN (*Bibliography of British newspapers*) 102
Benn's media directory 100, 102
BHI (*British humanities index*) 290, 291
bias, in oral history interviewing 166
bibliographies **292–3**
Bibliography of British newspapers (BBN) 102
biographies 19; *see also* autobiographies
Birmingham and District Association of Local History Societies 285
Birstall, religious affiliation in 72
birth rates 79, **183–5**
births
and baptism registers **72–6**; civil registration of 109–12; illegitimate 111
bishops' transcripts 279
BL *see* British Library
book publishers 226–7
booksellers, and publication of works 224, **239**

Booth, Charles 90, 105, 164
economic grouping scheme 47, 50; *Life and labour of the people in London* 47, 91–3, 95
Industry Series 91; Poverty Series 91; Religious Influences Series 93
Borough Record Offices (BROs) 267
Borthwick Institute of Historical Research 270
BPP *see* British Parliamentary Papers
Bradshaw, George 131
Bristol Business Community, analysis of 210–13
British 1881 Census Project 53, 206, 214
British Association for Local History 281, 285
British humanities index (BHI) 290, 291
British Library (BL) 270
depositing copies of published works 239; National Newspaper Library 101, 270, 275; National Sound Archive 173, 264, 270; NEWSPLAN programme 101–2; Oriental and India Office Collections 270
British Parliamentary Papers (BPP) 28, 57, 113–14
availability 114
British Telecom Archives 58, 271
British Universities Film and Video Council (BUFVC) 156, 158, 264
British Video History Trust (BVHT) 156
BROs (Borough Record Offices) 267
BUFVC (British Universities Film and Video Council) 156, 158
buildings 115, **121–3**
Burgess Rolls 279
burial grounds 123, 269, 273
burial registers 4, **78–9**, 267, 273
Business Archives Council (BAC) 85, 87
business records 4, 5, **84–6**, 115, 117, 268, 276
BVHT (British Video History Trust) 156

C of I *see* Church of Ireland
Camberwell project 204
Cambridge Group for the History of Population and Social Structure 13, 51, 204–5, 285
camera-ready copy (CRC) 237, 238, 239
cameras 136, 138, 139, 141, 142, 152
CD-ROM 215, 293
CEBs *see* census enumerators' books
census enumerators' books (CEBs) 4, 25, **35–53**, 113, 117, 273
and the 100-year rule 25; area descriptions on 37; availability of 25; British 1881 Census Project 53, 206, 214; and computing **203–4**, 212; contents 37–47; defining households 38–42; defining marital status 42; definition of 35; and fertility rates 184; Gibson

guide to 279; Irish records 275; locating 53, 268, 270; research exercise on 51–2; in Scottish regional archives 273; socio-economic grouping in 47–50; structure of 38; survival of 25; and valuation rolls 113; work of enumerators 35–7
census reports 25, **26–35**, 109, 117
and domestic servants 87; key information in 29–30; and occupations 86; small area statistics 35
central government records/sources 57
Chadwyck-Healey microfiche edition of BPPs 28, 114
Channel Islands 262
chapel registers *see* church/chapel registers
Charity Organization Society (COS) records 112
charts, presentation of data through **251–4**
child/woman ratio (CWR) 184, 185
chromolithographic process 146
Church of England
baptism registers **72–6**; visitation returns 79
Church of Ireland parish registers 275, 276
Church of Jesus Christ of Latter-Day Saints 53, 79, 207, 269, 277
churches/chapels
Anglican registers **72–6**, 111, 117; Irish records 276; as local resources 268–9; nonconformist registers 117, 267; registers 4, **72–81**, 267; Scottish records 272
churchyards *see* burial grounds
civil registers (of births, marriages and deaths) **109–12**, 117
access to 111, 270; and deaths 79–80; strengths and weaknesses of 109–10
class
and occupational status 47, 48–9; and photographs 152
cliometric view of history 12
club records 4, 115
colour photographs 141
commerce
changing world of 85; *see also* business records
commercial directories *see* directories
communities
choosing and defining 26; and landscape 122; local and newspapers 101; people's standing in 115; scattered 116; territorially defined 116; tracing movement within 67
community history projects, and census reports 26
community reconstruction 205
companies
archives 84, 87; histories **84–6**; and rate books 113; records of local

ACKNOWLEDGEMENTS

Grateful acknowledgement is made to the following sources for permission to reproduce material in this book:

CHAPTER 1: *Figures:* Figure 1.1: from the West Yorkshire Archive Service, Calderdale. *Tables:* Table 1.2: Plummer K. (1990) *Documents of life: an introduction to the problems and literature of a humanistic method,* Unwin Hyman.

CHAPTER 3: *Figures:* Figure 3.1: specimen page from the 1871 census, reproduced with the permission of the Controller of Her Majesty's Stationery Office; Figures 3.3, 3.4, 3.5: Public Record Office, Crown Copyright; Figures 3.6, 3.7: reproduced by permission of the Director of the National Archives, Dublin/photo: Colour Processing Labs Ltd. *Tables:* Table 3.8: Armstrong W.A. (1972) 'The use of information', in Wrigley E.A. (ed.) *Nineteenth century society: essays on the use of quantitative methods for the study of social data,* Cambridge University Press.

CHAPTER 4: *Figures:* Figure 4.1: National Library of Wales; Figure 4.2: W.T.R. Pryce; Figure 4.3: Avon County Libraries/Bath Central Library; Figure 4.5: courtesy of Northamptonshire Record Office (references: ER 3 1860 and ER 139b 1980); Figure 4.6: courtesy of Buckinghamshire Record Office (reference PR 222/1/5); Figure 4.7: from the christening register of the South Parade Chapel (Wesleyan), Halifax, June 20th 1813. Public Record Office (reference RG4/3011); Figure 4.8: from the baptismal register of the Roman Catholic Chapel of Cheeseburn Grange, in the Parish of Stamfordham, 1837. Public Record Office (reference RG4/3191); Figure 4.9: Stony Stratford Baptist Church, Bucks; Figure 4.10: from the Burial Register of the South Parade Chapel (Wesleyan), Halifax, September 1st, 1817. Public Record Office (reference: RG4/3011); Figure 4.12: Borthwick Institute of Historical Research, University of York (reference: Rowntree Poverty Survey schedule 1044, Rowntree P/P 23). *Tables:* Table 4.1: Todd A.E. (1989) *Basic sources for family history,* Allen and Todd.

CHAPTER 5: Figure 5.1: Pelling G. (1990) *Beginning your family history,* Countryside Books, © George Pelling 1990.

CHAPTER 6: *Figures:* Figure 6.1: Trustees of the National Library of Scotland; Figure 6.2: Liverpool Record Office, the City of Liverpool; Figure 6.3: Bodleian Library/Shelfmark C. 17:70. Oxford (7); Figure 6.4: Royal Geographical Society, London; Figure 6.5a, b: National Library of Wales; Figures 6.5c, 6.10, 6.11: W.T.R. Pryce; Figure 6.6: British Library; Figure 6.7: Mrs M.H. Pryce; Figures 6.8, 6.9: Mrs E.M. Pryce; Figure 6.12: Claire Grey Archive; Figure 6.13: Sue Isherwood/ARTS INFORM; Figure 6.14: Derek Bishton.

CHAPTER 7: Table 7.1: British Library National Sound Archive.

CHAPTER 8: *Figures:* Figure 8.1: courtesy of Buckinghamshire Record Office. *Tables:* Tables 8.20, 8.21: Lewis C.R. (1975) 'The analysis of changes in urban status: a case study of mid-Wales and the middle Welsh borderland', *Transactions,* 64, pp.49–65.

CHAPTER 9: Figure 9.2: Schürer K. and Anderson S.J. (1992) *A guide to historical datafiles held in machine readable form,* Association for History and Computing.

CHAPTER 11: *Figures:* Figures 11.1, 11.2, 11.3, 11.4: courtesy of the Powysland Club. *Tables:* Table 11.1: courtesy of the Powysland Club.

CHAPTER 12: *Figures:* Figure 12.1 (top): Gibson J.S.W. and Peskett P. (1993) *Record offices: how to find them,* Federation of Family History Societies; Figure 12.1 (left): Cole J. and Church R. (1990) *In and around record repositories in Great Britain and Northern Ireland,* Family Tree Magazine, © Rosemary Church and Jean Cole; Figure 12.1 (right): Codlin E.M. and Reynard K.W. (eds) (1992) *The Aslib directory of information sources in the United Kingdom,* 7th edn, The Association for Information Management; Figure 12.2: courtesy of Gloucestershire County Council.

CHAPTER 13: Figure 13.1: extracts from three 'Gibson guides': Federation of Family History Societies.

PLATES SECTION: Plate 1: courtesy of A. Francombe, Newport Pagnell; Plates 2a, b: B. Vossburgh, London; Plates 3a, b: courtesy the Powysland Club; Plates 5a, b: Mrs E.M. Pryce; Plates 4a, b, 6a, b, 7, 8, 9, 10, 11, 12, 13a, b, 14: courtesy W.T.R. Pryce; Plate 15: courtesy John Hunt; Plate 16: Royal Geographical Society.

COVERS: *Front (clockwise from top left):* Postcard, *c.*1905: courtesy W.T.R. Pryce; Llanfair Caereinion County Intermediate School reunion, *c.*1909: courtesy the Powysland Club; Identification cartoon for reunion photograph: courtesy the Powysland Club; Extract from 1861 *Census enumerator's book for Preston:* © Crown Copyright, reproduced with the permission of the Controller of Her Majesty's Stationery Office; Detail from map in Russell, C. and Lewis, H.S. (1901) *The Jew in London,* London, T. Fisher Unwin; Detail from Ordnance Survey first edition one-inch map, Plate XLVI, 1834: courtesy John Hunt; Family group, 1911: Sue Isherwood/ARTS FORUM. *Back (clockwise from top left):* W.T.R. Pryce (left) with father and brother, 1939: courtesy Mrs E.M. Pryce; Llanfair Caereinion parish church choir, *c.*1936: courtesy the Powysland Club; Detail from first edition Ordnance Survey 1:2500 plan, 1886: National Library of Wales; Photographer's advertisement on back of cabinet card print, *c.*1904: courtesy Mrs E.M. Pryce; Detail from map in Russell, C. and Lewis, H.S. (1901) *The Jew in London,* London, T. Fisher Unwin; Nineteenth-century print of New Lanark, Scotland: Trustees of the National Library of Scotland; Extract from householder's return, Census of Ireland, 1911: reproduced by permission of the Director of the National Archives, Dublin.

PERSONAL ACKNOWLEDGEMENT: Special thanks to Eleanor Nannestad of Lincoln Central Library and Professor Richard Lawton for comments on section 1 of Chapter 3 in this volume.